Tom Doak

# —The— Confidential Guide to Golf Courses

— *by* —

*Tom Doak*

PHOTOGRAPHIC CREDITS

Unless otherwise noted, all photographs in this book are by the author, Tom Doak. Shadow Creek Golf Club, pages 7 and 67, courtesy of Steve Wynn and the club; Prairie Dunes, pages 46 and 47, courtesy of P. Stan George; St. George's Golf & Country Club, pages 58 and 59, courtesy of Michael French; and Kapalua Golf Club, page 220, courtesy of Mike Klemme, Golfoto.



Sleeping Bear Press
121 South Main St.
P.O. Box 20
Chelsea, MI 48118

Sleeping Bear Ltd.
12 Chauntry Road
Bray, Maidenhead
Berkshire, England

*Printed in Canada*

*10 9 8 7 6 5 4 3 2 1*

*Library of Congress CIP Data on File*

# — ACKNOWLEDGMENTS —

*Sandpiper Golf Links, California.*

he highlight of writing this book has been the friendships I've fostered while compiling it. Though I've actually visited every course reviewed, I wouldn't have found some of the best of them without the recommendations of friends and colleagues throughout the world of golf as to which courses I should study as a budding architect. Along the way, I became something of a clearinghouse for information on what courses were worth seeing, because I was the one to check out every far-flung rumor.

Certainly, I had some support along the way, too: from my parents, who were as supportive of my golf education as of my college tuition; from Cornell University, which gave me the then-unprecedented opportunity to spend a year overseas studying the great courses of the British Isles; from Pete Dye and family, who allowed me to continue seeking out great courses during lulls in business; and from George Peper at *GOLF Magazine*, who gave me some official status when he put me in charge of the magazine's rankings of the best courses in the world, at the age of 23.

In this edition, I must also thank the handful of devoted "golf course nuts" who have been the main source of leads on new courses I should see through the years—fellow writers Ron Whitten and Jim Finegan, photographer Brian Morgan, Bill Shean, *GOLF Magazine* panelists Bob McCoy and Norman Klaparda, my colleagues Jim Urbina and Bruce Hepner, and golf professionals Ben Crenshaw, Bill Kittleman, Ken Macpherson, and Fred Muller. In recent years, I've been able to get around a bit more in foreign lands; special thanks are due to Lorne Rubenstein for showing me around Toronto, Tom Ramsey and Richie Benaud in Australia, Ian Beauchamp and Barry King in South Africa, and especially Masa Nishijima in Japan, where I simply could not have traveled without his help. Thanks, too, to Peter Dunn of Lucky Dog Productions, who funded my latest trips to Australia, South Africa, and Japan as an advisor to his "Fairways to Heaven" video of great holes around the world.

This time, too, I must thank a few devout readers of the underground edition of *The Confidential Guide* who have written or phoned me to make suggestions for the gossip section: Hal Phillips and Bob

*The Valley course at Royal Portrush, Northern Ireland.*

Labbance in New England, Mark Kessenich and Michael Fay in the Northeast, Robert Sidorsky in New York, Cal Waisanen in Upper Michigan, and Ran Morrissett in Australia.

Most of all, though, I must thank my wife Dianna and my little boy, Michael, for understanding my passion for golf and for travel, even though it takes me away from them more than any of us would like. Now that I have a home, though, and the opportunity to apply what I've learned on courses of my own design, someone else is going to have to explore the courses I've missed.

# Table of Contents

elcome to my book. Ten years ago, I put a private edition of this tome together for forty friends who were always asking me where they ought to go to play golf. At the time, there wasn't anything else like it; no golf writer or magazine would have the "bad taste" to print something negative about a course that gave them a freebie—or better still, a potential advertiser. So every golf course was "great."

My book was different. My interest was to learn about golf architecture by studying the best courses and attempting to discriminate between the bad, the good, and the best. So I scoured every available source to find new golf courses worth seeing, and checked them out for myself, sometimes three or four in a single day. My reviews assumed some familiarity with the famous championship courses, so I'd be free to wax lyrical about hidden gems, or play devil's advocate on well-publicized and highly regarded layouts. I also rated every course I'd seen on a 1–10 scale, as a frame of reference to balance what I wrote. Most of my readers encouraged me to publish it for a wider market, but I resisted for years because I didn't want to make my name as a critic first and a designer second.

Apparently, though, the idea of rating golf courses was a worthwhile one, because pirate copies of my book began circulating, and there have been several subsequent guides to golf courses. And still, this book is unique, because it is written from an entirely personal viewpoint, by a critic of the art of golf course design who has studied more than 900 courses around the globe. None of those other sources are familiar enough with great courses to know how badly their own favorites compare. My standards are higher—so much so that I may be criticized as an ogre by those who feel that there's no such thing as a bad day on the golf course.

For those of you who have skipped ahead to some of my reviews and already decided that I am an ogre (or worse), please read the "Doak Scale" before you demand a refund. My ratings are designed to quantify how highly I'd recommend traveling to see any course listed, and my scale is skewed to the left because the great majority of courses I've seen are well above average in quality. Everything rated "5" or higher has my seal of approval; but if I've given one of your favorite courses a "3," it may well be that you'd enjoy every course in this book with a rating of "3" or better.

Remember, too, that like any fine art, all golf architecture is a matter of opinion, as in fact is everything in the game of golf. There's no right way to swing a club, no right way to grow grass, and no right way to design a hole; there are only ideas that have proven more successful or more popular over time. You will undoubtedly disagree with some of my opinions. But I have spent a lot of time thinking about why I like or don't like a course: how well I played there has less to do with my opinion of a course than it does with most golfers.

***"Please read the 'Doak Scale' . . . everything rated '5' or higher has my seal of approval."***

Much of the controversy that surrounds this book owes to the fact that I am not only a critic, but a budding architect as well, and charges of conflict-of-interest will inevitably follow. I cannot deny my dual role; I can only assure you that I have always given my honest critique of the courses reviewed, and I have not been intentionally negative about the work of any designer simply to demean their work or to promote myself.

In fact, I do not mean to offend architects at all. As a designer, I understand that many of the perceived weaknesses of courses are caused by things outside the architect's control—insufficient acreage, budget constraints, or input from the client. Weak holes are often the result of necessary trade-offs: to get to the holes you savor, you have to play over inferior ground. When a hole disappoints, it's more often due to a lack of attention during construction (by architect and/or contractor) than to downright poor design. But you, the golfer/reader, don't care about excuses, only results; if you're paying $50 or $100 to play a course, or $1000 to get there, you have a right to know whether the negatives outweigh the positives.

At the same time, I insist on reserving the right to publicly disagree with an architect's design and to say why. Some others in the business consider it "unprofessional," or even unethical, for one architect to criticize another's work, but I respectfully disagree with their reasoning, and I've never been one to shy away from a good debate. Many architects have been so coddled by golf writers and public relations outfits, who print an endless stream of superlatives about their work, that they're starting to believe they're infallible. These architects want to achieve unimpeachable status, like doctors, whose methods are not open to question by the public at large; they would naturally prefer not to have to defend their designs in the light of intelligent criticism from any source, least of all a potential competitor. In the private edition of this book I made some throwaway funny/insulting comments about other architects, and I apologize if any of them were taken in the wrong light—I really did intend it only for 40 friends who understood my sense of humor. This time I've been more careful to confine my criticism to the courses themselves.

***"I believe that real golf is about interesting and exciting golf holes."***

Golf architecture is an artistic pursuit rather than an exact science, and as such it invites criticism. Indeed, I believe that any art must generate intelligent criticism if it is to flourish. I hope that this book will open the door to more discussion of the form. If any of you (architects included) wish to disagree with my criticism of a particular course, and take the time to detail your reasoning, you are welcome to do so; design is a constant learning process, and maybe I'll include your views in a future edition. However, I ask you to remember that it is inevitable that we won't agree on everything; if you find yourself in agreement with 85–90% of my assessments, please chalk up the rest as unavoidable.

So what are my personal preferences and prejudices? First and foremost, I believe that real golf is about interesting and exciting golf holes, not lavish clubhouses or expensive maintenance budgets. My highest standard for a golf hole is not that it play "tough but fair," as many low-handicappers demand, but that it offer a combination of strategic interest and golf shots that you relish hitting. On some courses, I could walk out to any fairway and stay there until dusk, trying to pull off the perfect shot. If a course has even one or two holes of that caliber, it's enough to excite me.

I love the variety of golf courses and holes that exists in the world; they're what makes traveling to play the game worthwhile. Today much of the business is driven by designer names, but the best designs are those that assume a unique character for themselves—a hint of local flavor that derives from the land itself. One of the reasons I'm so hard on modern creations is that the power of modern construction makes it much too easy for an architect to bulldoze away all the idiosyncrasies of a property and make all his courses look too much alike. If you live in southern California and never travel to Florida, you may not care that the Stadium Course at PGA West is largely a regurgitation of the TPC at Sawgrass. But if you've played one of them, there's not much reason to see the other.

My ratings also reward variety within each given course. On the best courses, no two holes are alike—each contributes something to the course as a whole, whether it's making us play a different club or a different shot, or adding to the emotion of the round. I'm particularly inclined to take note of a good set of par-3 holes and good short par-4's, since these are the holes that are within every golfer's grasp.

In 22 years of playing the game, I've run the full gamut of aptitude, from hitting it short and straight as a kid to longer and more erratic today;

from fading to hitting a hard draw. I've broken par a handful of times in my life, but haven't broken 90 considerably more often. Since I was a kid, I've relied on my short game for my ability to post a decent score, and so I'm especially fond of courses with interestingly contoured greens, greens complexes, and bunkers. These are the sculptural elements of golf course design, and they have a lot of impact on my overall appreciation. Many good players consider heavily contoured greens "unfair," but the point of the game is to hole out, and contoured greens add immeasurable interest in doing so; greens contouring is also the most effective and economical way to create interest in a golf hole.

***"If you're paying $50 or $100 to play a course, or $1000 to get there, you have the right to know whether the negatives outweigh the positives. This book does that for you."***

Aside from the attributes of the golf holes themselves, even I cannot help but be influenced by the ambiance of a course; indeed, I'd be foolish to try and ignore it, since it's one of the keys to the average visitor's enjoyment of the game. The beauty of the course, the atmosphere of the club, and the members' attitude toward the game all play their part in the total golf experience; but of these factors, I'm much more interested personally in the scenery than the service.

I also don't put much weight on the conditioning of the courses I've reviewed. For one thing, I've only gotten to see the majority of courses once or twice, and the conditions I encountered on the day in question may well not be indicative of the usual quality of maintenance. Nearly half the courses in this book are outside the United States, where they don't place the same emphasis on conditioning as the members of American country clubs. In the end, though, one of my tests of a good golf hole is that it remain interesting and playable under any conditions; it has to be so in order for the average player to enjoy it.

I do recognize that people have different tastes, and that few courses are universally admired, so I have tried to qualify my own personal feelings with some indication of whether a scratch player or a 25-handicapper might share them. Personally, though, I'm not a big fan of 7,000-yard courses, for the simple reason that to reach that total they must eschew the shorter holes, which provide the shorter hitter competitive chances and the architect license to create something unusual. Modern designers try to compensate for everything with multiple tees, but I play a lot of my golf with players better than myself, and I want to play from the same tees they do; so I think it's important that a 5- or even a 10-handicapper can find the back tees playable, though he may pile up a big score in doing so. Nearly all my absolute favorite courses include a good selection of short par-4 holes, and that keeps most of them below the 7,000-yard threshold. But I also appreciate courses that reward solid driving and long-iron play, so I'm not going to recommend 6,100-yard courses either, unless they're on exceptional terrain.

So, turn the pages, and enjoy. Feel free to write me and argue with my opinions of a particular course, or suggest other courses I ought to seek out so I can share them in future editions, or perhaps a newsletter for devoted readers. I don't have the free time to get around as much as I used to, but there's still nothing I enjoy more than discovering another good golf course—except making one, that is.

## —The Doak 0–10 Scale—

**0** - A course so contrived and unnatural that it may poison your mind, which I cannot recommend under any circumstances. Reserved for courses that wasted ridiculous sums of money in their construction, and probably shouldn't have been built in the first place.

**1** - A very basic golf course, with clear architectural malpractice and/or poor maintenance. Avoid even if you're desperate for a game.

**2** - A mediocre golf course with little or no architectural interest, but nothing really horrible. As my friend Dave Richards summed one up: "Play it in a scramble, and drink a lot of beer."

**3** - About the level of the average golf course in the world. (Since I don't go out of my way to see average courses, my scale is deliberately skewed to split hairs among the good, the better, and the best.)

**4** - A modestly interesting course, with a couple of distinctive holes among the 18, or at least some scenic interest and decent golf. Also reserved for some very good courses that are much too short and narrow to provide sufficient challenge for accomplished golfers.

**5** - Well above the average golf course, but the middle of my scale. A good course to choose if you're in the vicinity and looking for a game, but don't spend another day away from home just to see it, unless your home is in Alaska.

**6** - A very good course, definitely worth a game if you're in town, but not necessarily worth a special trip to see. It shouldn't disappoint you.

**7** - An excellent course, worth checking out if you get anywhere within 100 miles. You can expect to find soundly designed, interesting holes, good course conditioning, and a pretty setting, if not necessarily anything unique to the world of golf.

**8** - One of the very best courses in its region (although there are more 8's in some places, and none in others), and worth a special trip to see. Could have some drawbacks, but these will clearly be spelled out, and it will make up for them with something really special in addition to the generally excellent layout.

**9** - An outstanding course—certainly one of the best in the world—with no weaknesses in regard to condition, length, or poor holes. You should see this course sometime in your life.

**10** - Nearly perfect; if you skipped even one hole, you would miss something worth seeing. If you haven't seen all the courses in this category, you don't know how good golf architecture can get. Drop the book and call your travel agent—immediately.

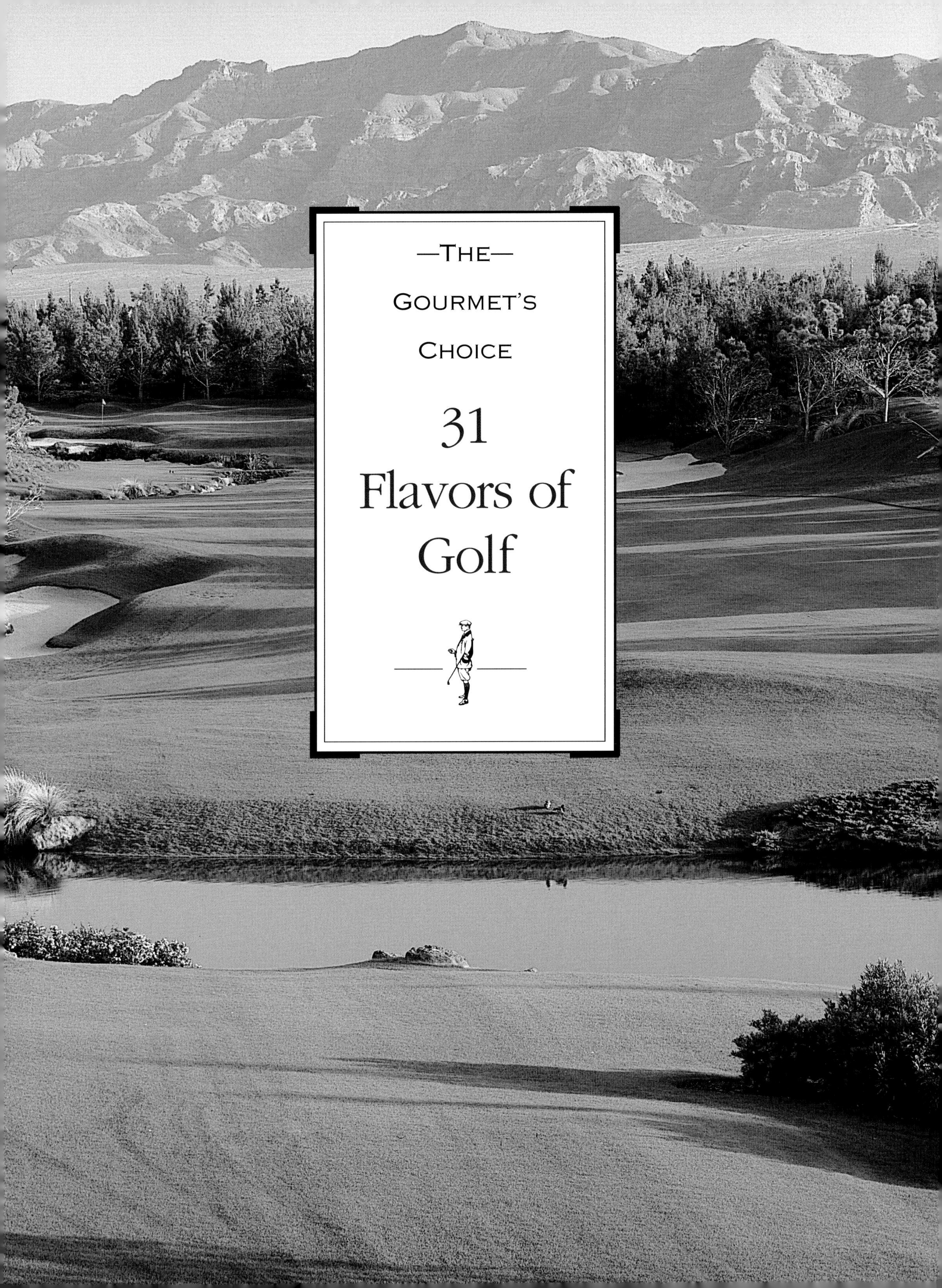

—THE—

GOURMET'S

CHOICE

# 31 Flavors of Golf

*The 20th hole at St. George's Hill.*

Although I envision this book being used mostly as a quick reference check for courses you're planning to see in your travels, I cannot resist the temptation to break out a few of my favorites in order to draw extra attention to them.

The hard part has been figuring out where to stop myself. My first thought was to do 18 courses, like Patric Dickinson's little book *A Round of Golf Courses,* which I have always admired; but with all the world to cover, I just couldn't pare down my list of favorites to so few. On the other hand, I didn't dare choose a big, round number like 50 or 100, for two reasons: first, because I would never have finished the book that way, and second, because I didn't want anybody to mistake this list for my selection of the world's "best" courses. I do that list for *GOLF Magazine,* and while I don't agree 100 percent (or even 85 percent) with the consensus list that is published, you'd better believe that Cypress Point, Royal Melbourne, and Shinnecock Hills would be on my list of "greatest" courses. But they're not in this chapter, primarily because I don't have much of anything to say about them which you haven't already heard.

Finally, I settled on the same number as those two great philosophers of our age, Baskin and Robbins, who decreed that 31 flavors was just enough variety for the true gourmet in the world of ice cream—next to golf, one of my favorite pastimes. Then, just to make things more difficult on myself, I decided for the sake of variety to limit myself to only one selection per architect. This rule has caused some great agonizing on my part—having to decide between Tom Simpson's Ballybunion and Cruden Bay, between Harry Colt's Muirfield, Portrush, and St. George's Hill, and worst of all between Dr. MacKenzie's Crystal Downs, Cypress Point, and Royal Melbourne—but it was heartening to discover that I really could find something to love in the work of so many different golf architects, plus the natural links of St. Andrews and North Berwick. Inevitably, not every course on my list will appeal to every reader, but the golfer who appreciates the natural variety of courses will find each of these a rich and unique experience to be savored.

Here, then, are the 31 flavors I've selected—not the 31 best golf courses in the world, but among the first I would take a good friend to see:

## The Gourmet's Choice

1. The Addington
2. Ballybunion
3. Casa de Campo
4. Commonwealth
5. The Creek
6. Crystal Downs
7. Desert Highlands
8. Durban Country Club
9. Forest Highlands
10. Garden City
11. High Pointe
12. Kawana
13. Lancaster
14. Merion
15. The National Golf Links of America
16. North Berwick
17. Pinehurst No. 2
18. Pine Valley
19. Prairie Dunes
20. Riviera
21. Royal Dornoch
22. Rye, England
23. St. Andrews
24. St. Enodoc
25. St. George's
26. St. George's Hill
27. Sand Hills Club
28. San Francisco Golf Club
29. Shadow Creek
30. Westward Ho! (Royal North Devon)
31. Woodhall Spa

# The Addington

CROYDON, SURREY, ENGLAND

The Addington was the private domain of the late J.F. Abercromby, a supremely talented golf architect who left too few courses for us to enjoy. He designed his two best courses here, close into London, in the years around the first World War, and stayed on to run them in the greatest traditions of autocracy until his death in 1935. It was "Aber" who coined the line, "I am the suggestion box," to a disgruntled visitor inquiring as to its location. Sadly, after the second World War, the New course and holes, such as the superb short par-4 8th (rated by Tom Simpson as the best of its length in Britain) were plowed under to make way for a housing development (one can only imagine the rage with which Abercromby might have greeted this plan had he still been alive), but thankfully his Old course has survived, and to this day it remains as a fitting legacy to its designer.

I think that without question The Addington was the most personal of Abercromby's creations, and most reflective of his own strong character. Many aspects of the design might be considered weaknesses by critics, but the course somehow stands above these, and makes apologies to no one. One might imagine Abercromby's own feelings about the 166-yard uphill 1st hole, which is certainly far from an ideal beginning to a golf course: "Well, damn it, that is the only way it all works out, so they will just have to accept it." There are no halfway measures at The Addington at all. Its shot values are just as starkly defined as the transition from the fairway cut to a fearsome primary rough: either a shot is good enough or it isn't, and the course is the sole arbiter of justice.

If I've given the impression that The Addington is a penal course, that's not entirely fair, although the heather and ravines do lend it some of the air of a Marine obstacle course. I'm not completely comfortable with the distinction most golf architects draw between "penal" and "strategic" architecture in the first place, since as long as a course gives you a chance to follow an errant shot with a great recovery, it can't really be considered unfair: courses that prominently feature out-of-bounds and water hazards are much more penal to my way of thinking. The saving grace of The Addington is that it's short enough to offer a decent chance to make some birdies and return a good score, as long as you temper your aggressiveness enough to keep the ball in play. Along the way it provides some one-of-a-kind thrills, such as the tee shot at the 10th, where you're asked to slam a drive over the top of a substantial lime tree growing up out of one of the ever-present ravines (with the trunk hidden from view, it looks like a giant gumdrop); or the second shot to the 12th, where you hopefully found one of the shelves of fairway at the corner of the dogleg so as to shorten the full-blooded approach across a deep valley; or the approach to the narrow shelf of green at the 225-yard 13th, where not having the strength to reach the green might be a blessing in disguise. Finally, there is the par-5 16th, where one must "run the gauntlet" on the second shot if trying for the green. All these are

*The 12th at Addington—a daunting prospect after a perfect tee shot.*

do-or-die shots if the challenge is accepted, but there is also a safer way to approach them if one has more modest aspirations.

I must qualify my recommendation of The Addington with the warning that its conditioning is unpredictable, even by overseas standards: you're likely to encounter greens that haven't been mowed in ten days on one trip, and return the next afternoon to find they've all been scalped. But if you can put these matters out of your mind long enough to enjoy a wild little layout, I urge you to go out of your way to visit The Addington Golf Club—it's one of a kind, and it will make you wish old Aber had built a few more.

| — SCORECARD — | | |
|---|---|---|
| | **Par 68/Bogey 71** | **6,216 Yards** |
| 1. 166 ? | 7. 150 | 13. 230 !! |
| 2. 555 ! | 8. 410 | 14. 365 |
| 3. 215 | 9. 355 | 15. 441 ! |
| 4. 435 ! | 10. 356 ! | 16. 494 ! |
| 5. 440 | 11. 135 | 17. 180 |
| 6. 390 | 12. 470 ?! | 18. 429 |
| Course architect: J.F. Abercromby, 1912 | | |

# Ballybunion

BALLYBUNION, COUNTY KERRY, IRELAND

You may have heard some outlandish statements about the quality of the Old course at Ballybunion, such as Tom Watson's endorsement of it as one of the top six courses in the world, or Herbert Warren Wind's pronouncement that it is "nothing less than the finest seaside course I have ever seen." Personally, I don't put much stock in other people's assessments of golf courses, but when they're right, they're right.

Ballybunion has changed tremendously in the ten years since I first set eyes on it—the addition of the New course, the surge in visitors, and most recently, a mammoth new clubhouse that takes the club facilities from the iron age to the plastic age (unfortunately, it looks a little like a Kroger's). But the featured attraction—the Old course—remains well preserved. Tom Simpson made a few changes to the course in the mid-1930s, but many of the best holes were already in place when he arrived, so we don't really know who to thank (other than the keen hand of Mother Nature) for one of the most brilliant routing plans ever conceived, which cuts back and forth between the coastline and the dunes so that not all the most spectacular holes on the course are encountered in a line. One can easily imagine a present-day architect saving the stretch of coast for just the last three or four holes (for an example, you need look no further than the new Tralee course just down the road), but on Ballybunion's Old course it is the 7th, the 11th, half the 16th, and half the 17th holes that occupy the prime real estate, and on your first round every moment from the 7th tee onward will be filled with anticipation over when your next encounter with the ocean may come.

As for the holes individually, I think the only really weak links in the chain are the back-to-back par-5's at the 4th and 5th, which are saddled with dull ground (perhaps, though, it was a wise decision to eat it up with long holes), and the short 14th up into a cleft in the dunes, which is a difficult shot with the wind over your right shoulder, but which stands out as artificial to the eye. But the rest of the holes are all-world in caliber, from the thread-needle approaches of the short 8th and long 9th to the spectacular clifftop 11th, and (a key for me) the contouring of the greens is subtle but excellently conceived, adding a dimension to the test that a lot of the British and Irish links are lacking. In the end, Ballybunion Old is one of the handful of courses to get the perfect "10" rating on the Doak scale, and I can't say more than that.

As most of you are aware, there is also a New course at Ballybunion, a Robert Trent Jones layout that has generated much comment since it opened for play in 1984. Like many new courses, it is one of those you are bound to either love or hate—because that's exactly how it treats your golf shots. If you're not hitting your irons within 25 feet of the hole, through a stiff breeze at that, you'll need strong legs just to finish the round. I don't see how any sane man can rank it superior to its older sister.

In the end, though, it must be admitted that the New course is one that gets the pulse

*The short 8th at Ballybunion was one of Tom Watson's choices for his "dream 18."*

going quicker, and the pioneer spirit in me says that is a mark of greatness; it's too bad the recent "softening" has taken some of that grandeur away, since it may have been the only thing the original design got right. But why waste our time arguing a point akin to whether Tommie Aaron was a good ballplayer? It's another member of the Ballybunion family, which is the reason you must go there.

| — SCORECARD — | | |
|---|---|---|
| **OLD COURSE** | **PAR 71** | **6,542 YARDS** |
| 1. 392 ! | 7. 423 | 13. 484 ! |
| 2. 445 ! | 8. 153 !! | 14. 131 |
| 3. 220 | 9. 454 ! | 15. 216 ! |
| 4. 498 | 10. 359 ! | 16. 490 ! |
| 5. 508 | 11. 449 !! | 17. 385 ! |
| 6. 364 ! | 12. 192 !? | 18. 379 |
| COURSE ARCHITECTS: TOM SIMPSON & MOLLY GOURLAY, REVISION, 1936 | | |

# Casa de Campo

LA ROMANA, DOMINICAN REPUBLIC

The crown jewel of the Caribbean, Casa de Campo has been identified by so many different names in its short lifetime (one publication I know of lists Casa de Campo, Cajuiles, and Teeth of the Dog as three distinct places) that it still hasn't established itself as a household word in the golf business, such as, say, Dorado Beach. Even with all the confusion, it's hard for me to believe that one of the twenty or thirty best courses in the world—located in an idyllic resort and complete with a Pete Dye label on it—can remain largely unrecognized while so many inferior courses achieve fame.

I'm not sure that I would pick Casa de Campo as my personal favorite of Pete Dye's courses, but I know that deep down it's Pete's own favorite, and I can understand why. For Pete this had to be the ideal job description—he was given total artistic control, including choice of site (a long stretch of coral-studded Caribbean coast), an army of Dominican laborers that allowed him to shape every contour by hand like the craftsman he is, and above all the time to experiment with the grasses and make subtle refinements in the design as he analyzed the strengths and weaknesses of the original layout. He's even had a couple of hurricanes to tear things up a bit, and nothing keeps Pete Dye happier than having some work to do on the golf course.

The final product is the prototype Pete Dye golf course: chock-full of outstanding holes with a spectacular bent to them, a tremendous selection of tees to temper the difficulties of the course for any level of player, a routing with a near-mathematical symmetry to the angles of the doglegs and location of the principal hazards, and a picture-postcard set of par-3 holes—three of the four consisting of more surf than turf. (Brian Morgan likes to say that Pebble Beach has seven holes along the sea, but only Casa de Campo has seven holes *in* the sea.) At the same time, Teeth of the Dog conspicuously

*A bird's-eye view of the 5th.*

*"Where Pebble Beach has 7 holes along the sea, Casa de Campo has 7 holes in the sea."*

avoids the public stereotype of Pete's work, relying mostly on native coral rather than railroad ties (there are only a few) to shore up the edges of hazards.

Again, there is a second course at Casa de Campo—the Links course, which is a misnomer if there ever was one—but its only outstanding characteristic is the impenetrable guinea grass that surrounds many of the holes. Guinea grass looks like something out of the Amazon jungle, or perhaps a mad scientist's plant-breeding experiment; it's so thick you could lose your golf *cart* in it.

When you combine all this with a quiet private resort and the climate-controlled semi-tropical environment of the Dominican Republic (the temperature hardly ever varies beyond 75° F. at one end of the scale and 87° F. at the other, regardless of season), you've got one of the best golf resorts in the world. If you're headed for the Caribbean and golf is part of the program, don't even think about going anywhere else.

— SCORECARD —

| TEETH OF THE DOG | PAR 72 | 6,820 YARDS |
|---|---|---|
| 1. 382 | 7. 231 ! | 13. 175 |
| 2. 378 | 8. 378 ! | 14. 505 |
| 3. 545 ! | 9. 505 | 15. 384 !! |
| 4. 327 | 10. 377 ! | 16. 185 ! |
| 5. 155 ! | 11. 540 | 17. 435 |
| 6. 449 ! | 12. 429 | 18. 440 |

COURSE ARCHITECT: PETE DYE, 1971

# Commonwealth

SOUTH OAKLEIGH, MELBOURNE, VICTORIA, AUSTRALIA

You know the old saying: a camel is a horse designed by a committee. The same goes for golf courses. It's overstretching the point to say that courses like Pine Valley and Merion are entirely the work of one man—indeed, if there's anything I have learned about the business in the past ten years, it's that surrounding yourself with talented people is the most important step in building a quality course. But, in both cases, it was the dedication of the principals that led them to new heights of architecture.

Commonwealth Golf Club, in the midst of the famed Sand Belt of suburban Melbourne, Australia, is the rare exception to this principle. While nearly all of its famous neighbors were designed or redesigned by Alister MacKenzie during his whirlwind tour of Australia in 1926, Commonwealth was extended to 18 holes in the same year by a committee of members led by Charles Lane and the secretary/manager, Sloan Morpeth. There is no record of whether one personality dominated the redesign; all we know is that they kept their priorities clearly in view, and produced one of the most pleasant and strategically pure golf courses one could hope to find.

The genius of Commonwealth is its adherence to one simple rule—that each green should be oriented or tilted in such a way that it cradles an approach from one side of the fairway, but shoulders away shots from the incorrect line of attack. For example, take Commonwealth's one water hole, the par-4 16th. It is only of medium length, and the green is safely removed from the water, so there is no sink-or-swim peril; but the curve of the dogleg to the left and the sprawling bunker defending the whole right side of the green, with another bunker at back left, clearly reward the golfer who can play confidently near the pond from the tee. The next hole is a very short par-4—almost driveable for the strong—but its green drains out sharply at the right middle, and those who have driven greedily through the corner of the dogleg to the left will have trouble holding their approaches on the green.

Almost every one of the two-shot holes at Commonwealth fulfills this strategic ideal, a testament to the work of the design committee; but, sad to report, the club's present green committee is not doing as well in its role of stewards. On my return visit in 1993 I was appalled to find they had decided to "strengthen" the wonderful 260-yard opening hole, which set the tone for the course by tempting one to drive to the apron of the green, but punished wayward drives severely because its long, narrow green was so difficult to hold with a half-wedge shot from a wide angle of attack. The new hole, doglegged to the right, sacrifices charm and strategy for a few measly yards of length: the hole is still a driver-wedge, but the design of the new green gives little imperative to place the tee shot.

Despite the background of its designers, the other secret of Commonwealth's success is that the construction of the course was left to a professional in that field—Vern Morcom, the

*The 11th green at Commonwealth, with more of Melbourne's beautiful bunkers.*

original Royal Melbourne superintendent, who mastered the secrets of natural-looking construction as taught him by Dr. MacKenzie. Commonwealth's marvelous greens and bunkers are testimony to his skill. It may not be the best golf course in Melbourne, but this is assuredly a course worth playing while you are there.

| — SCORECARD — | | |
|---|---|---|
| | **PAR 73** | **6,773 YARDS** |
| 1. 322 | 7. 179 ! | 13. 473 |
| 2. 508 ! | 8. 398 | 14. 349 |
| 3. 415 ! | 9. 133 ! | 15. 153 ! |
| 4. 350 | 10. 571 | 16. 388 ! |
| 5. 392 | 11. 401 ! | 17. 334 ! |
| 6. 549 | 12. 425 | 18. 432 ! |
| COURSE ARCHITECTS: CHARLES LANE & SLOAN MORPETH, 1926 | | |

# The Creek

LOCUST VALLEY, NEW YORK, USA

'm not quite sure why it is that I find Seth Raynor's designs so endearing. A surveyor by trade, he became Charles Blair Macdonald's right-hand man while assisting the creator of the National Golf Links, and later used Macdonald's notes and social connections to design golf courses from Bermuda to Hawaii. Raynor wasn't much of a golfer himself, so he put complete faith in his mentor's theories, and simply built new versions of the same tried-and-true golf holes on every course he designed. When modern designers do this—and they do—I find it boring and reprehensible, but for some reason I've always enjoyed seeing another Raynor course. His holes are like old friends, and it's been instructive to analyze and compare them to determine what are the key features that make one version of, say, the Redan work better than another, even if Raynor himself may not have known.

I've set foot on about 20 Raynor designs, and had the privilege of working on long-range plans for three—Camargo, Shoreacres, and The Creek. Each of these is blessed with very good natural terrain for golf, and it's very difficult to single one out as a favorite, but I've picked The Creek because it's the least well-known of the three, and because it has made such a stirring comeback.

It's easiest to identify a Raynor layout from the short holes, which are almost always a matched set. Ironically, in the case of The Creek, the par-3's are a bit weak. The famous "Redan," The Creek's 8th, is a mirror-image version, with the green angling off to the right and only a minimal tilt out to the back. The "Short" 17th is ringed by bunkers, but it's a fairly big target, and the contouring of its green is nowhere near as pronounced as on the 6th at National or some other Raynor adaptations. The "Island" 11th is more interesting, a full-blooded long iron or wood shot to a large island green wrapped in the bend of the creek, with a shallow version of the Biarritz swale through its center; but the "Eden" 4th, despite our best efforts at resuscitating it by deepening the bunkers and accentuating the pin placements, is still kind of dull.

Indeed, the first five holes at The Creek, all south of the clubhouse and parallel with the entrance drive, give the impression that the golf will be a rather dull affair. Then, as you cross the club's drive to the 6th tee, the course unfolds, as the holes stretch out before you down more than 100 feet to the shore of Long Island Sound, with my hometown of Stamford, Connecticut across the water in the distance. Here, too, the golf takes a sudden turn for the dramatic. The 465-yard 6th is one of the wildest holes in my acquaintance, sharply downhill with its punchbowl green tucked away to the left, a deep bunker at the front right, and a narrow berm surrounding all but the front left entrance. The straight approach over the bunker is daunting, but a perfectly judged shot to the left will be carried into the middle of the green by its pronounced tilt. From here in, it's great golf, with several dramatic two-shotters, including the short "Cape" 10th by the beach club, the

*The 16th hole at The Creek Club—a Seth Raynor masterpiece.*

14th with its alarming drive over the creek and the cattails, and the beautiful valley of the 16th leading up to the clubhouse.

All in all, the course is a bit short in length, but long on character, and it amazes me that it had been going through such pains in the several years before we were asked to restore it—Joe Dey, the former USGA director and the club's autocrat for many years, had been systematically filling in Raynor's bunkers in an effort to make it "more playable," à la the Augusta National. Where once there were more than 100 bunkers, Mr. Dey's ultimate plan was to reduce the total to four—proof, beyond a shadow of a doubt, that knowledge of golf does not necessarily translate into an understanding of golf architecture.

| — SCORECARD — | | | |
|---|---|---|---|
| | **PAR 70** | | **6,429 YARDS** |
| 1. ORCHARD | 376 ! | 10. SHORE | 308 ! |
| 2. VINES | 375 | 11. ISLAND | 220 ! |
| 3. FAIRVIEW | 382 | 12. SQUIRREL RUN | 357 |
| 4. EDEN | 176 | 13. CREEK | 439 ! |
| 5. LINDENS | 396 | 14. WATER GATE | 425 ! |
| 6. SOUND VIEW | 453 !! | 15. HUNCHBACK | 357 ! |
| 7. LONG | 521 | 16. OAK | 440 !! |
| 8. REDAN | 187 | 17. SHORT | 143 |
| 9. INFERNO | 420 ! | 18. HOME | 455 |
| COURSE ARCHITECTS: C.B. MACDONALD & SETH RAYNOR, 1923 | | | |

# Crystal Downs

FRANKFORT, MICHIGAN, USA

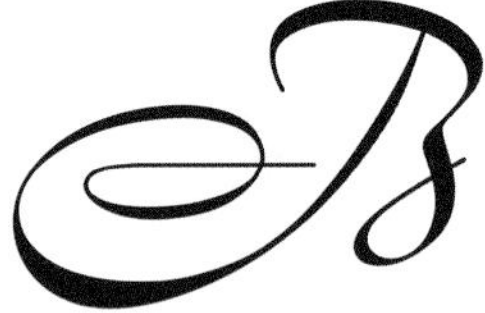

y now almost everyone who knows me has heard of Crystal Downs, Dr. MacKenzie's masterpiece that lured me to northern Michigan. I must accept some responsibility for its renown, since before I first saw it in 1982 it was almost unknown; and now that I'm a member there are times when I wish I'd kept my mouth shut. Its recent notoriety has caused the members to take the place more seriously, to the benefit of the maintenance and landscaping of the course; but the low-key atmosphere that helped make it a special place has been jeopardized by its new-found fame.

I've played the course maybe 60 times now, and every time is still a thrill. Like all of MacKenzie's work, it makes the absolute most of the given landscape, with bunkers placed to dramatize the terrain and the shots required.

The Downs is also one of the toughest courses I've ever played on which to post a good score. Par is 70 and the rating 74; but more important, there's only ever been one score better than 67, and with my six handicap I've only broken 80 about one out of every ten tries. Four factors conspire to defeat you:

- The wind, which can blow equally hard from north or south at any time of year.
- The greens—some of the fiercest ever contoured by the team of MacKenzie and Maxwell.
- The thick native roughs, which add so much to the character of the landscape, but threaten to turn any wild drive into a double bogey.
- MacKenzie's penchant for designing holes on the borderline of par, where strokes can slip away so easily or be regained so dramatically. In particular I note the four par-4's under 353 yards—each of them a unique use of terrain, and all birdieable for the 20-handicapper but bogeyable by the Tour pro—and the three long par-4's, which replace short par-5's in the course's makeup, where threes feel like eagles and fives are humbly accepted.

*"The Scabs" flanking the par-4 6th.*

*MacKenzie's genius shines through at Crystal Downs, virtually unknown until recent years.*

But singling out these holes does injustice to the rest—there's also a great set of short holes with tremendous variety, and two exemplary but very different true three-shotters. And I might add that Dr. MacKenzie managed to include all this variety in a course that measures just over 6,500 yards from the back tees, and it has no need of more length than that. Simply put, if you haven't seen Crystal Downs, your education in golf architecture is incomplete.

| — SCORECARD — | | |
|---|---|---|
| | **Par 70** | **6,518 Yards** |
| 1. 460 ! | 7. 335 ! | 13. 442 ! |
| 2. 425 ! | 8. 550 !! | 14. 147 |
| 3. 191 | 9. 175 !! | 15. 327 |
| 4. 409 ! | 10. 395 | 16. 588 ! |
| 5. 353 !! | 11. 196 ! | 17. 311 !? |
| 6. 384 !! | 12. 430 ! | 18. 400 |
| Course architects: Alister MacKenzie & Perry Maxwell, 1929 | | |

# Desert Highlands

SCOTTSDALE, ARIZONA, USA

hose of you who know me well will know that I love to play devil's advocate when it comes to critiquing golf courses. When Desert Highlands was being hyped for The Skins Game, I was arguing that it wasn't worth a crap; but now that a lot of people are down on Nicklaus' work, and Desert Highlands missed out on *GOLF Magazine's* Top 100 list, I feel compelled to defend this place. I'm not a big fan of Jack Nicklaus the designer: I think a lot of his designs would have been much more harshly criticized if his name didn't carry so much clout, and I think that he is almost single-handedly responsible for the inflation of golf course construction and maintenance budgets during the 1980s, because of his attitude that if his name was going on the finished product, cost could be no object in the construction. But Jack has never been afraid to take chances in his design work, and Desert Highlands is the classic example of making those chances pay off.

To critique Desert Highlands, one must speak in terms of desert golf, and those of you who have not been indoctrinated in modern Arizona golf must understand that desert golf is very different from the real game. As opposed to most pieces of land, where I believe that one of the highest goals of the architect is to integrate the course into the natural landscape, on a desert site it is theoretically impossible to integrate the two, because grass simply doesn't look natural growing among the cacti. To make matters worse, the modern water restrictions—which limit new Arizona courses to 90 acres of turf—absolutely ensure that the average golfer can't play the "hit it as you find it" game which the Scots invented. The desert course architect is forced to choose between making the course too narrow or making the carries from the tees too long. Either choice makes life prickly for the golfer having an off day with the driver, as all average golfers are wont to do regularly.

Desert Highlands stands apart in my mind, not only because it was the first desert course that I saw, but because it really was *the* first to carry out the concept to completion. The setting at the base of Pinnacle Peak is head and shoulders above all the other desert courses to date, and the unique design of the fairways and transition bunkers is a double plus—the width of the transition bunkers minimizes the severe penalty for straying off the 90 acres of grass, while the gull-wing design gives the course an artistically satisfying look that most of the other desert layouts don't have. The Weiskopf/Morrish layout at Troon may be more traditional, their Troon North more playable, Nicklaus' Desert Mountain complex more lavish, and the old Desert Forest club more pleasant and low-key, but only Desert Highlands has a touch of genius and a sense of originality. It also deserves applause for being the only development able to resist the temptation to build a water hole in the desert. Desert courses may never look natural, but a pond in the desert is wasteful as well.

From a golfing standpoint, most of the criticisms leveled at the Highlands are completely correct: principally, that the contours of the greens are overdone. They never would

*Desert Highlands' greens have multiple levels of intrigue.*

have looked "natural" in the desert anyway, but these greens are so modular that they look obviously contrived, which is even worse. If you're having a bad day with the iron clubs, putting can start to feel like playing Mr. Spock at that three-level chess game featured on *Star Trek*, because nearly every green is divided into several sections at different levels, and it's nearly impossible for the average player to hit and hold the correct section of the green unless he's hitting short irons.

I am also bothered by how Nicklaus designed Desert Highlands around his own game. From the back tees at the Highlands all the two-shot holes are in the medium-long range, with none but the opening hole to test finesse play, and none so long that Jack has to hit a really long club into them. And all but one of the three-shot holes make it as easy to get up and down from the sides of the greens as in front, which allows longer hitters to go for every par-5 in two with no fear of losing the advantage to a shorter hitter if they should misfire.

Nevertheless, to sit outside on a crisp desert evening and watch the sunset over Phoenix, and then the lights of Scottsdale coming on as the sky darkens, is absolutely breathtaking. The aura of greatness is here.

— SCORECARD —

| | PAR 72 | 7,099 YARDS |
|---|---|---|
| 1. 356 ! | 7. 190 | 13. 396 |
| 2. 584 !? | 8. 438 | 14. 417 ! |
| 3. 452 | 9. 567 ! | 15. 145 |
| 4. 211 ? | 10. 408 | 16. 244 ! |
| 5. 425 | 11. 564 ! | 17. 570 ! |
| 6. 431 ! | 12. 177 | 18. 524 |

COURSE ARCHITECT: JACK NICKLAUS, 1983

# Durban

DURBAN, NATAL, SOUTH AFRICA

For practical purposes, Durban Country Club is the most isolated great golf course in the world, even though it's two miles from the downtown of one of the busiest cities in South Africa. We no longer have to worry about landing on someone's political blacklist for going there, but for those who seek out the best courses, Country Club is a needle in the haystack of Africa, making the decision to go there most difficult for a course we know so little about. In fact, I might never have gone there myself had not my new friend Peter Dunn asked me to help him put together a video on the 18 greatest golf holes in the world. When the third at Durban came up a winner, so did I, for it provided me the excuse and the expenses to make this trip.

Does the golf course live up to its billing? Well, almost. The unevenness of the golf course is disappointing: several of the holes at the north end of the course (6–7, 10–11, 14–16) are saddled with extremely flat, dull property, and on these holes the lack of outstanding bunkering or greens contouring is felt strongly. But we were received so warmly (just short of the second coming of Charles Lindbergh) that it is downright rude of me to point this out.

On the positive side of the ledger, the famous "first five" holes, the par-5 8th, and the two finishing holes are absolutely outstanding and, in some cases, unique holes which everyone should see in their lifetime. These are the holes laid out among the dunes, separated from the Indian Ocean shore by a freeway and the dense bush vegetation along the dunes that hide it; but unlike any links course you've seen, Durban's best holes are set across the very tops of the dunes, as well as through the valleys between them. The dramatic par-3 2nd plays across the highest part of the property, with tee and green along a dune ridge; there's a bit of a valley in front of the green for safety, but a wild shot to the right is in the bush, and to the left it's a long way down to the valley below. The tee of the famous par-5 3rd is atop another dune, affording a great view down into the narrow, undulating fairway in the valley ahead—it's like looking down the barrel of a gun, and it puts the tee shot at the full mercy of the wind. In truth, while this is a great par-5 hole, it's not one of the four best par-5's in the world; it just happens to fall in the perfect place for those eclectic 18's, because there's not much 3rd hole competition. In fact, I liked Durban's par-5 8th with its overlapping dunes in the second-shot landing area as much as I did the famous 3rd—but not as much as I like the 8th at Pebble Beach, Crystal Downs, or Royal Troon.

The two finishing holes are also unique. At the 17th, one drives uphill onto a ridge coming from the right; a hook careens off the ridge down into a deep bowl of fairway, leaving a pretty much blind shot to the green, which is set behind another undulating punchbowl on the approach. The 18th is one of the neatest driveable par-4 holes I've ever seen, with the fairway along a high ridge at a slight left-to-right angle from the tee, a steep drop to the right, and a funky little dip like St. Andrews' Valley of Sin just in front

*The undulating 17th at Durban Country Club.*

of the green, which sits smack in front of the clubhouse. For the professionals it's a definite chance for a two, and they really need to make birdie to keep pace with the field; but if you don't drive the green it can be a very awkward pitch. For amateurs, the distance is just short enough to tempt everyone to overswing, which can bring a five into the picture, while the difficult pitch makes for fewer threes than you would think. It makes for a very exciting finish to any tournament, match, or even a casual round.

As for how it fits among the best courses in the world, it's hard to call. There are enough great holes that it must definitely be in there somewhere, and it's not a "cult" course like Cruden Bay or St. Enodoc, where there are some wild and weird holes you have to overlook. But when you average in the several dullish holes, I can't quite give it the same recommendation as some of my other favorites.

| — SCORECARD — | | |
|---|---|---|
| | PAR 72 | 6,639 YARDS |
| 1. 385 | 7. 375 | 13. 334 |
| 2. 188 ! | 8. 502 !! | 14. 516 |
| 3. 513 !! | 9. 424 | 15. 187 |
| 4. 173 | 10. 550 | 16. 416 |
| 5. 460 ! | 11. 456 | 17. 387 ! |
| 6. 352 | 12. 149 ! | 18. 273 ! |
| COURSE ARCHITECTS: LAURIE WATERS & GEORGE WATERMAN, 1922 | | |

# Forest Highlands

FLAGSTAFF, ARIZONA, USA

People from the East Coast always speak of the Midwest as being a desert in terms of golf, but for me the most disappointing region of the country has always been the West, excluding California. Despite all the great scenery and all the spectacular national parks, the best golf courses are mostly genteel parkland with distant views. The exception to the above sentiment is Forest Highlands, the first golf course I've seen that Ansel Adams would want to take a picture of, and which is at the same time worth playing for the golf. A development course set at 7,000 feet near the town of Flagstaff, it wanders among the ponderosa pines with dramatic elevation changes, natural creeks, and views of the San Francisco Peaks at the southwestern end of the Rocky Mountains, and it definitely feels as though it belongs in the same region as the Grand Canyon (two hours to the north) and the town of Sedona (an hour south on the way to/from Phoenix).

The 7,000 foot elevation led architects Weiskopf and Morrish to put together an odd mix of holes. At this altitude golfers hit the ball as much as ten to twelve percent farther, rendering it almost impossible to build a par-4 hole of strong character: even the longest par-4 of 470 yards is a driver-wedge for the pros here. So, the architects defended par by building six short holes, each of them a different length and three of them over 200 yards, to require some long-iron approaches; two short par-5's, which for the professionals are easily reachable at this altitude but test their long irons; three par-5's of over 600 yards, which isn't nearly as much as it sounds here (even I reached the 18th hole, downhill through a valley, in two from the 585-yard marker); and only seven par-4 holes, two of them of the driveable genre that Morrish and Weiskopf try to include somewhere on every course they design. This arrangement does, in fact, make the course play much more evenly in relation to par than a more conventional array of holes; but it does have an unsettling side effect—that you never get into a rhythm of hitting the driver, because there's a par-3 every other hole from the 4th through the 14th. (Indeed, if you elect to play safely on the short par-4's, you might never hit the driver on consecutive holes at Forest Highlands.)

Apart from this one quibble, I think that Forest Highlands is a wonderful course. The fairway clearings are ample, giving the course a scale to complement the scenery around it; the little waterfall at the 4th green is the only feature that doesn't look like it's been there forever. Despite their unusually small number, the two-shot holes are the class of the course, particularly the long 7th, with a large pine looming over the left side on the second shot, and the dramatic 9th, from its high tee into the valley below; meanwhile the short and long holes complement each other well. Many of the holes are well secluded by the topography, so I don't think that the course will suffer a loss of character once the development is sold out. I look forward to checking back on it in a couple of years, just to make certain.

*Forest Highlands' 17th tempts you to drive the green, a favorite ploy of architects Weiskopf and Morrish.*

| — SCORECARD — | | | |
|---|---|---|---|
| | **PAR 71** | **7,051 YARDS** | |
| 1. North by Northwest | 377 ! | 10. Fatwood | 205 ! |
| 2. Road | 336 | 11. Gambel Oak | 468 |
| 3. Ponderosa | 601 | 12. Indian Paintbrush | 229 |
| 4. Waterfall | 177 ! | 13. Springs | 536 ! |
| 5. Meadow | 528 | 14. Covered Bridge | 163 |
| 6. Three Pines | 218 | 15. Wagon Trail | 638 ! |
| 7. Clubhouse | 478 ! | 16. San Francisco | 430 |
| 8. Ridge | 190 | 17. Aspen | 390 !! |
| 9. Valley | 478 !! | 18. Elk Crossing | 609 |

**Course architects: Tom Weiskopf & Jay Morrish, 1988**

# Garden City

GARDEN CITY, NEW YORK, USA

y wife is rather offended by the fact that I've taken the job of consulting architect to Garden City Golf Club, one of those last bastions of prejudice, the all-male golf club. But how could I refuse? It's the easiest job in the world, because they really don't need to do much of anything to the course—the only thing we've done of note is to cut down some of the trees to open up vistas across the course, and even I am surprised at the esthetic difference it's made. Best of all, the job comes with the fringe benefit of getting to play there a couple of times a year, and I've actually learned something about design from my study of the course, which doesn't happen often at the "latest wonder" courses I go to see.

The credit for the outstanding character of the golf course must be divided three ways. Mother Nature gets top billing, because I'm sure what most golfers remember most about Garden City is the grass—tight fairways and greens that roll fast and true, and waist-high fescue roughs that remind one of Muirfield. (Only the roughs at Shinnecock Hills and Indianwood (Old) can rival Garden City's among American layouts.) This speaks well of the soil itself, for although the contours of the ground at Garden City are fairly sedate, the sandy base provides the perfect drainage that makes such turf conditions possible on a day-to-day basis.

After the rough, what golfers tend to remember most about Garden City is probably the bunkers—particularly the fairway bunkers, small deep pits seldom seen in the American golf landscape, but which don't appear at all out of place on the open plain of Garden City. Most of these bunkers were placed around the course by Walter Travis, who adopted the club as his second home fresh on the heels of his victory in the 1904 British Amateur Championship. Many of Travis' bunkers are inescapable with any club but a wedge (in his days, a niblick), but Travis understood well that such hazards aren't as unfair or boring as some American golfers complain—they normally extract a 3/4 shot penalty, requiring a good pitch to the green in order to save a par, but their value increases dramatically on holes of certain lengths. For example, where the golfer is tempted to take a slightly longer club on a par-5 to get himself within easy reach of the green with his third, or to play for the green on one of the shortish par-4 holes for which Garden City is renowned, the daring shot not cleanly struck from the sand may leave the ball in the bunker. Garden City bristles with holes of such length, making it a superb match play course. Meanwhile, to balance the severity of rough and bunkering, the fairways of the course are fairly generous for the club golfer's enjoyment.

But what's really allowed Garden City to stand the test of time is the equitable simplicity of Devereux Emmet's green complexes. They're basically just a ground-level extension of the fairway as on many Scottish courses—but most of Garden City's greens tilt slightly to the back as well as to one side. This combination of speed and tilt has ensured that it remains diffi-

*Garden City's rare par-3 finishing hole requires a decisive finishing stroke.*

cult to get the ball close to the hole on an approach shot, even though modern golfers are approaching these greens with much more lofted clubs than the architect must have envisioned. At the same time, the older club member always has his chance to get the ball close with a 3-wood approach, if only it is straight enough and the strength perfectly judged, so the club has never felt the need to make the concession of forward tees for the weaker players. There's basically only one tee per hole, and if the wind's blowing in your face on a long par-4 on a given day, you just have to accept that the hole is going to be especially hard. *That's* Scottish golf.

Too many modern architects provide all sorts of tee and pin placement options, and then blame the superintendent (for setting up the course wrong) or the golfers themselves (for playing the course from too far back) if a hole gets to be unplayable. But the lesson of Garden City is that giving the golfers some leeway—not making it harder—is what's enabled the course to stand the test of time.

— SCORECARD —

| | PAR 73 | 6,882 YARDS |
|---|---|---|
| 1. 302 ! | 7. 550 ! | 13. 538 |
| 2. 137 ! | 8. 418 | 14. 343 |
| 3. 388 ! | 9. 323 | 15. 447 !! |
| 4. 523 | 10. 414 ! | 16. 405 ! |
| 5. 360 ! | 11. 416 ! | 17. 495 |
| 6. 440 | 12. 193 | 18. 190 ! |

COURSE ARCHITECTS: DEVEREUX EMMET, 1898, & WALTER TRAVIS, 1902

# High Pointe

WILLIAMSBURG, MICHIGAN, USA

must admit to a bit of hesitation in placing one of my own courses among this elite selection, because I'm the first to scoff when other modern architects have the audacity to vote for their own courses among the top ten in the world. I have a lot more respect for the great courses of the world than that. However, the criteria for qualifying for this particular chapter is only that the course would be among the first I would take you to see, and whether or not it eventually makes others' lists of great courses, you'd better believe I'm determined to hear what you all have to think about High Pointe.

The property was so special here—way better than anything I'd seen while working for Pete Dye—that my first goal was to make the course more a product of the land than of myself. Every architect nowadays professes to "work with the land," but somehow almost all courses wind up reflecting the architect's style. Indeed, in today's "signature course" era, many developers actively seek the stereotyped trademarks of their chosen architect's style. My goal was much easier to achieve because I wasn't yet aware how my own "style" would be defined by others, but I still went way out on a limb by opting for the least possible disturbance, even in building greens. Some of the features I left, such as the small crowned greens at the 3rd and 14th holes, or the rolling fairways of the 10th and 14th, have been controversial because they require unconventional tactics—for example, on the 10th, which is most safely approached by laying up slightly on the tee shot to the crest of the landing area and then hitting a full 200-yard shot up to the semi-blind punchbowl green. Even my wife thinks I should have moved more dirt here, but it would have blown the whole concept; besides, the receptiveness of the green site makes it an easy "bogey 5."

My second goal was to design holes that give maximum advantage to imaginative shot-making—the principal difference I found between the British courses I grew to love and the current era of American design. Accomplishing this required two things—a firm playing surface (see goal #3), and a design that utilized steeper undulations for the fairway landing areas and green sites, so that the golfer would be forced to consider the slopes in playing the hole. Again, modern designers tend to flatten out all borderline slopes in the interest of "fairness," but in doing so they allow the well-equipped modern golfer to approach every hole the same, instead of playing shots in an attempt to counteract and minimize the bounce of the ball. I guess I sort of expected that some golfers wouldn't understand the strategies of holes such as the 8th, where the top tier of the green is designed shallow so that the best approach is to land the ball in front with enough momentum to climb up the terrace in the green, rather than fly it to the back and pray. Unfortunately, since it's a resort-area course, few golfers become familiar enough to understand the shots it's built for.

My third and most idealistic goal was to bring the Scottish approach to maintenance and

*One of the few modern day courses which rewards old-fashioned shotmaking.*

fescue grasses to the USA, by designing the course so that it would be playable under less-than-perfect fairway conditions—so that the budget could be kept austere and the green fees affordable. Most modern designers preach perfect conditions regardless of cost; but they've become so used to lavish budgets that now they design courses featuring forced carries into small greens, without even thinking that those shots will be unplayable if the management can't afford to keep up that standard. To date, the experiment has been a very mixed success. We've found, to others' surprise, that in the sandiest soils the fescue can produce superb fairway turf with significant reductions in fertilizer, pesticide, and water use. But it's difficult to maintain a uniform stand, and paying customers expect perfection at any price.

Nevertheless, High Pointe works. The holes still reward thoughtful play and the beauty of the land is still intact, and although conditions are spotty at times, the course remains eminently playable. Best of all, we kept the costs in line—the green fee for walkers ranges from $35 down to $15 for twilight play. Those are the parts of golf I value most.

| — SCORECARD — | | | |
|---|---|---|---|
| | PAR 71 | | 6,844 YARDS |
| 1. FIRST | 386 | 10. HIMALAYAS | 425 !? |
| 2. BRAID'S | 360 ! | 11. SUMMIT | 168 ! |
| 3. BARN | 458 ! | 12. HOLE O'CROSS | 412 ! |
| 4. REDAN | 199 ! | 13. SADDLE | 434 !! |
| 5. ORCHARD | 377 | 14. HOG'S BACK | 396 !! |
| 6. FIELD | 516 ! | 15. LOOKOUT BELOW | 182 |
| 7. TART | 347 ! | 16. DOGLEG | 447 |
| 8. KALKASKA ROAD | 451 ! | 17. THE NATURAL | 217 ! |
| 9. LONG | 557 | 18. POND | 512 ? |
| COURSE ARCHITECT: TOM DOAK, 1989 | | | |

# Kawana

KAWANA, ITO, SHIZUOKA, JAPAN

A golf trip to Japan is, practically speaking, beyond the reach of most of the dedicated golfers who will read this book. Between their booming economy and the unfavorable (from our end) exchange rate, you simply can't afford to make the trip, and even if you wanted to, it would be next to impossible to make the arrangements to visit the older courses, which would be the only good reason to go. The one exception to this problem is the famed seaside resort of Kawana, which is good enough to merit a trip if you get as far as Tokyo.

The Kawana Hotel lies 2-3 hours by train (to Atami station) and taxi south of Tokyo on the Izu Peninsula, a dramatic landform very reminiscent of the Monterey Peninsula, except with steeper sides. (It's no wonder the Japanese feel so at home at Pebble Beach.) Kawana's Fuji course is no Pebble—it doesn't command as great a length of shoreline, and the natural contour of the land is hillier, more like Mid Ocean than Pebble Beach. But it is a great course, thanks to the routing and the dramatic bunkering prescribed by the British architect C.H. Alison, who on one brief tour of the country designed or consulted on virtually all of the worthwhile golf courses there today, including Kasumigaseki, Tokyo Golf Club, Nagoya Golf Club, Hirono, and Naruo, the hidden gem of Japan. If not the best, Kawana is easily the most dramatic of the bunch—more dramatic than any but the ridiculous modern Japanese courses, which border on parody.

I was frankly shocked by the spectacular beauty of the property, since I had never seen any good pictures of it printed anywhere before, but it is possible to point a camera in almost any direction and come up with something worthwhile—even if Oshima Island is shrouded in fog and the distant view of Mount Fuji from the far end of the course is obscured by clouds. For example, the first tee shot drops 80-100 feet to the valley below, and then the approach is uphill to a green with the Pacific Ocean behind—a dramatic start. The second hole, like the 11th, 12th, and 15th to follow, runs high above the rocky shoreline, with the first of Alison's deep fairway bunkers waiting at the crest of a valley to swallow up a short drive, and another frightening pit at the left front of the green. Similar critically placed bunkers lie in wait on nearly all of the driving holes, perfectly placed for today's good player, although the longest hitters might clear many of them without a care. Still, don't waste much time perusing the scorecard below, for the playing lengths of holes are dramatically altered by the terrain—the 3rd, 6th, 12th, and 17th are dramatically uphill and all very difficult to reach in two from the championship tees, while the 4th, 11th, and 15th all play much shorter than the card might indicate.

There is also a second course at Kawana—the Oshima—which I didn't even get to see in my one-day whirlwind tour of the property; I was so excited to see and photograph the Fuji course that I didn't even ride around its sister. The second course is only 5,600 yards, but there are supposed to be a couple of holes along

*Looking back from the 14th at Kawana, graced by the spectacular beauty of Mt. Fuji.*

the shore that are worth the price of admission—at least, when you aren't held accountable for the $250 green fee.

Despite the undeniable beauty of Kawana, some will be turned off by the greens, which are covered in korai, a coarser and slower-putting grass than even our Bermuda grass. Most of the holes operate on the two-green system (still commonplace in Japan—to spread out the wear during the hot and humid summers), and the sub-greens at Kawana, though not often used, are vastly inferior in interest to the main greens—tantamount to playing Pebble Beach with 15 temporary greens. The resort badly needs to rebuild its greens to modern specifications, but they don't want to close the most popular course in the country to do the work—and we don't want them to bungle the job in the process by changing the size of the greens significantly. Until this problem is resolved, the Fuji course is the one selection in my Gourmet's Choice that must be preceded with an asterisk. But it's still a major league accomplishment, just like Roger Maris' 61 homers.

— SCORECARD —

| FUJI COURSE | PAR 72 | 6,691 YARDS |
|---|---|---|
| 1. 415 ! | 7. 393 ! | 13. 395 !! |
| 2. 411 ! | 8. 150 | 14. 416 ! |
| 3. 450 ! | 9. 367 | 15. 470 !! |
| 4. 482 | 10. 143 | 16. 185 |
| 5. 181 | 11. 619 ! | 17. 410 ! |
| 6. 434 ! | 12. 404 ! | 18. 366 |

COURSE ARCHITECT: CHARLES ALISON, 1936

# Lancaster

LANCASTER, PENNSYLVANIA, USA

It's just a bit of a stretch for me to include Lancaster in this Gourmet's Choice; I have to admit that it doesn't inspire the passion in me that many of the other 30 courses here do. On the other hand, during my summer in Philadelphia in 1992, I was mightily impressed with the portfolio of classic parkland layouts there designed by William Flynn, including Philadelphia Country Club, Rolling Green, Manufacturers, and Huntingdon Valley; and on reflection, Lancaster left the impression of being (by a nose) the best of the bunch.

While Lancaster's terrain may not be unique, the course does possess many of the things that I admire in golf courses. The property has a good mixture of hills, some gentle and some very steep, as well as the river and a narrow creek, which come into play on several holes on the front side. There are some wonderful putting greens—like the 5th, 6th, and 11th—full of contours subtle and severe. And there is a great mix of golf holes. There are two terrific par threes—the downhill 6th, with a gently rippling green next to a stream, and the strong Redan-like 8th, 200 yards uphill across a deep valley with a left-to-right falling green full of smaller undulations. (Still, these are no match for the four or five great short holes at Flynn's other Philadelphia-area courses, in fact, it occurs to me that Philadelphia probably has more great short holes than any other city, though Melbourne and London might contend.) But it's Lancaster's collection of two-shot holes which set it apart from the others.

I had only walked the golf course on my first visit, and when I came back with my clubs, my perception of the design changed dramatically. From a scorecard analysis, the weakness of Lancaster appears to be the run of short par-4's on the front side, which throws off the balance of the course; and when you walk the 4th and 5th, both laid out around a beautiful brook, you say to yourself, "Gee, it's too bad these holes aren't 40 yards longer." Playing them, however, you realize that they're good (not pushover) short par-4's for the low-handicapper, but for the 15-handicapper or senior they are scaled-down *great* holes—the fifth is about as good a green complex as you could find for a 160-yard 4-iron approach. The point being: why do the shot values of every hole have to be tailored to the scratch player? A modern architect would have designed the 5th green for an 8-iron approach and eliminated the approach at front left, but then the vagaries of the topography would have made it much too difficult for the members. Flynn's decision was to make these early holes for the middle-handicap members, and balance his design with stronger par-4's like the 9th through 11th to test the scratch player.

Like every parkland course I saw in the Philadelphia area—with the sole exception of Merion—Lancaster would get even better if you gave me two days with a chain saw to clean up the mess of years of overzealous landscape committee tree-planting. Actually, though, some of the worst trees here are natives, such as the sycamore which overhangs the creek at the 6th,

*Lancaster is among the best in an area rich in golf courses.*

and has now grown to block off the direct line between tee and green. But let's not nitpick; unless an unfortunate encounter with the bark ruins your day, Lancaster is one of the most pleasant rounds of golf you'll find.

| — SCORECARD — | | |
|---|---|---|
| | **PAR 70** | **6,604 YARDS** |
| 1. 419 | 7. 514 ! | 13. 521 |
| 2. 374 ! | 8. 199 ! | 14. 383 |
| 3. 392 | 9. 426 | 15. 439 |
| 4. 345 ! | 10. 454 ! | 16. 353 ! |
| 5. 357 !! | 11. 447 ! | 17. 174 |
| 6. 180 ! | 12. 180 | 18. 447 ! |
| COURSE ARCHITECT: WILLIAM FLYNN, 1920 | | |

# Merion

ARDMORE, PENNSYLVANIA, USA

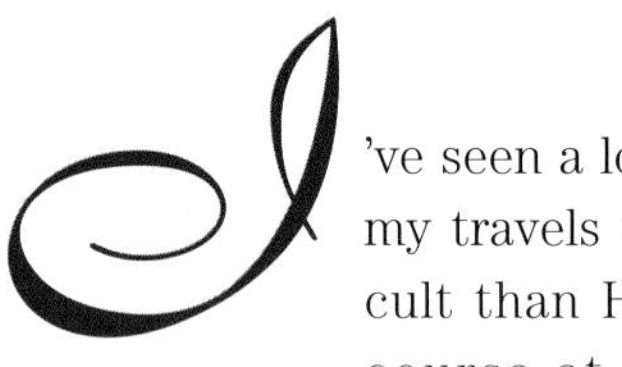've seen a lot of golf courses in my travels that are more difficult than Hugh Wilson's East course at Merion, and that were more spectacular also. But somehow Merion has an aura of perfection to it that all the other courses lack—every nook and cranny of the property is so well utilized, it is about the only course I know of where a self-professed golf architect would be hard pressed to suggest any concrete changes that might improve the layout. For that reason, I believe it's one of the first courses any young golf architect should study, and I am in awe of Hugh Wilson, the man who designed both Merion courses but practically nothing else in his brief career.

More than any other architect, Hugh Wilson seemed to have the knack for making 375 yards of real estate into a strategic golf hole simply by using the natural contour of the land, placing a half dozen bunkers, and contouring a putting green. No doubt he learned this skill from his six-month study of the great British links; but unlike Charles Blair Macdonald, who profited from a similar study, Wilson avoided direct imitation of the most famous British holes. Only the 3rd at Merion East, a Redan hole, is immediately reminiscent of a British model. The other 17 holes simply employ the best features of the property at hand—the road to the right of the 2nd, the tilt of ground at the 5th, the creek at the 11th, and the quarry at the last three holes—with brilliantly placed bunkers to highlight the difficulties of each hole.

On such a cramped piece of ground (the East course and clubhouse take up only 126 acres), it is tempting to credit much of the routing's success to the luck of the draw, but remember that Wilson didn't come up with this layout at first crack. Until 1924, several holes involved crossing Ardmore Avenue, and it was only when traffic started to become a concern that Wilson suggested purchasing the ground for the present 11th green and 12th tee, and rerouted the course to create the present 1st, 2nd, 10th, 11th, 12th, and 13th holes. Consider also that one small change made possible six of the best holes in America—perhaps there is something to the notion of redesign after all. In your examination of the course, do not fail to notice that to get the most out of his piece of ground Wilson included only two par-5 holes (probably since British links seldom included more than two long holes in the old days), and that the routing is "unbalanced" since these holes aligned themselves as the 2nd and 4th.

I know that there are some detractors of Merion out there, who point out its lack of total length and lack of emphasis on driving play as weaknesses. My own concern is over narrowing fairways to the point that the only strategy involved is in clubbing down off the tees in order to be sure of staying out of the rough. In the last Opens at Merion and Oakmont, the fairways were so narrow that not even Calvin Peete could be confident enough to aim for a particular side. But the real problem is that modern golf-equipment technology has outstripped Merion and some of its sisters, and the real so-

*The wicker basket atop the flagstick gives no hint of the wind for the approach to Merion's 12th hole.*

lution is simply to make the professionals play them (and everywhere else) with a ball that doesn't fly quite so far or spin quite so fast.

I still don't know Merion as well as I would like to, but I know it well enough to recommend it to all of you as a course that will reward careful study.

| — SCORECARD — | | |
|---|---|---|
| EAST COURSE | PAR 70 | 6,482 YARDS |
| 1. 362 ! | 7. 350 | 13. 127 ! |
| 2. 536 ! | 8. 360 ! | 14. 408 |
| 3. 181 ! | 9. 193 ! | 15. 366 |
| 4. 600 ! | 10. 310 | 16. 428 ! |
| 5. 418 !! | 11. 369 ! | 17. 220 ! |
| 6. 420 | 12. 371 ! | 18. 463 ! |
| COURSE ARCHITECT: HUGH WILSON, 1911–1924 | | |

# The National

SOUTHAMPTON, NEW YORK, USA

When I found my own golf club, I hope that it can somehow exude the same spirit as the National Golf Links of America. Other golfers get nostalgic over the home green at St. Andrews or Magnolia Lane, but for me no place can match the overpowering golf atmosphere that hits you when you pass through the gate at The National. Instead of avoiding the course, the entrance comes right in beside the 18th tee, so that from the moment you enter the club grounds you are confronted with great golf holes: the 18th climbing past the clubhouse alongside Peconic Bay straight ahead, and the 17th leading down from the famed windmill on the hill to the left. Since the public roads leading into the golf course cut across the 8th and 11th holes and also pass close by the 14th green, it is almost impossible not to become psyched up for the game ahead before one has even parked the car.

The National, of course, is the masterwork of Charles Blair Macdonald, who conceived it as a treasury of the best of British golf architecture that would elevate the appreciation of the game in America. Some of the holes are fairly closely modeled after famous British links holes—the Redan, the Road hole, the original Sahara at Sandwich—which makes for interesting comparison, particularly since Macdonald intended to improve on the originals. But whether original designs or borrowed concepts, all of Macdonald's holes follow the natural terrain beautifully, so that there isn't a weak or out-of-place hole on the course.

Many dismiss the layout of The National as "old-fashioned," but in truth the greatest weakness of the course today is the "improvement" of the newfangled irrigation system, which has made the fairways too lush and put the natural contours of the fairways and Macdonald's bunkering in a false light. In C.B.'s day, and in fact right up until the early 1970s, the golf course was essentially a links in the firmness of the ground and the degree to which the bounce and roll of the ball affected the outcome of the drive, so that the severe contours of the fairways (such as the hog's back of the 5th) carried the ball far away to Macdonald's bunkers; but today the ball barely rolls at all after landing, and the goat-hill fairway lies that result are a poor substitute for the bunkering. If there is one course in America that would benefit most from a severe drought or Depression, The National is it.

As for the individual holes, the important thing is not to argue about which is best of all (I am partial to the 17th myself, though many other holes would be good enough on another course), but to notice that there is not a single bad or even commonplace hole in the bunch. This was Macdonald's great achievement—not even the great links of Britain at the time could claim to have 18 good holes, and sadly all too few courses since the National have lived up to its legacy.

One other aspect worth noting is this: Macdonald, like many other architects, seems to

*National Golf Links reeks of all the fine qualities of classic architecture—playability and challenge.*

have built his masterpiece right at the start (rather than the culmination) of his career. Consider also Tillinghast's San Francisco G.C., Dye's Crooked Stick, Nicklaus' Muirfield Village, and such individual efforts as Oakmont, Pebble Beach, Merion, and Pine Valley—all the first large-scale projects attempted by their designers, and arguably as good as any they built in their careers. Is it possible that architects use up all their original ideas early on, and live off that success forever after? Donald Ross and Alister MacKenzie provide notable exceptions to the theory, but maybe that is just more evidence in the case to make them the best of the bunch.

**— SCORECARD —**

| | Par 73 | | 6,745 Yards |
|---|---|---|---|
| 1. Valley | 320 ! | 10. Shinnecock | 457 ! |
| 2. Sahara | 271 !? | 11. Plateau | 431 |
| 3. Alps | 426 ! | 12. Sebonac | 437 |
| 4. Redan | 196 !! | 13. Eden | 170 |
| 5. Hog's Back | 476 | 14. Cape | 359 ! |
| 6. Short | 130 ! | 15. Narrows | 392 ! |
| 7. St. Andrews | 478 ! | 16. Punchbowl | 401 |
| 8. Bottle | 390 !! | 17. Peconic | 368 !! |
| 9. Long | 540 ! | 18. Home | 503 ! |

Course architect: C.B. Macdonald, 1909

# North Berwick

NORTH BERWICK, EAST LOTHIAN, SCOTLAND

ew people would argue with the selection of St. Andrews as Scotland's most devoted golfing town, but did you ever stop to think about which town would be number two?

In earlier times, North Berwick's West links were *the* mecca for Englishmen on golfing holidays, and produced their own school and style of golf—the local players naturally developed short swings and masterful short games to overcome the tricky short approaches the course demanded. (Bernard Darwin wrote a fascinating essay on this very subject in *The Book of The Links,* sort of an adaptation of his grandfather's theory of natural selection as it pertained to the era of golf when the majority of players developed their games entirely over a single course.) On more wide-open courses the North Berwick men were of little concern in championship play, but in matches at home they were almost invincible.

It is still a course that calls for more clever approaching than any I have seen, and all the famous holes remain basically unaltered since David Strath formalized the course in 1878. His layout included the most imitated hole in all of golf: the Redan 15th. It is a short hole of about 190 yards with its green set at a 45° angle away to the left behind a deep bunker, and falling gradually away to the left and rear. One's first view of the hole can be disappointing, because many of its terrors are obscured from the tee by a ridge some 40 yards short of the green; but depending on the prevailing conditions of wind and speed of ground, the tee shot may call for a draw, fade, or half-running approach to achieve optimal results, unaffected by modern improvements in equipment.

Unfortunately, the incomparable quality of the Redan has led many to draw the conclusion that it is the only hole at North Berwick worth playing, which is most emphatically not true. In fact, progressing backward from the Redan there is a long line of good holes, including two others which provide as good a class in architecture. "The Pit" is the 13th, a 347-yarder that is one of a kind: the green lies in a small hollow just beyond a low, free-standing stone wall left over from an earlier time, and one has the option of hugging the left side off the tee in order to pitch more or less along the line of the wall, or playing well out to the right so as to pitch across its line. The beauty is that it is not a hard hole, but the one error that will prove fatal is so conspicuous that it is hard to put the fear of foozling the pitch out of mind. The 374-yard 12th is one of the world's best examples of just how simple golf design can be: a generic dogleg left with a critically placed pot bunker in the nook of the dogleg and another just to the right of the green, which falls away to the left, giving every advantage to the player who hugs the corner closest. It would be very interesting to watch players attack this hole on several consecutive days, steering away from the bunker at first and then gradually starting to hug the corner more and more closely, until one day they make a fatal pull into the bunker itself and begin the process all over again.

*An ancient stone wall defines the strategy of the 13th at North Berwick.*

There are also some holes that only a mother could love, like the 1st, which one contemptuous golfer of a previous generation played with a putter from the tee followed by a mashie approach, or the 270-yard 18th, where the principal hazard preventing one from taking a full-blooded rip at the green is psychological—the fear of smashing the windscreen of one's own car, parked along the road just to the right of the fairway. And then there is the 16th green, where it is quite possible to putt off the green entirely, playing from one shelf to the other. Just *don't ask* how I know.

— SCORECARD —

| West Links | Par 71 | | 6,317 Yards |
|---|---|---|---|
| 1. Point Garry out | 328 ? | 10. Eastward Ho! | 161 |
| 2. Sea | 435 ! | 11. Bos'n's Locker | 495 ! |
| 3. Trap | 459 | 12. Bass | 373 ! |
| 4. Carl Kemp | 184 ! | 13. Pit | 347 !! |
| 5. Bunker's Hill | 379 | 14. Perfection | 382 ! |
| 6. Quarry | 162 ! | 15. Redan | 192 !!! |
| 7. Eli Burn | 353 | 16. Gate | 403 |
| 8. Linkhouse | 476! | 17. Point Garry in | 422 ? |
| 9. Mizzentop | 496 | 18. Home | 270 |

Course architect: David Strath, revision, 1878

# Pinehurst

PINEHURST, NORTH CAROLINA, USA

I may get thrown out of the Donald Ross Society for saying this, but the truth is, I'm not as big of a Donald Ross fan as many other architectural buffs are. Don't get me wrong; I have enormous respect for his ability as a designer, and could easily count a dozen Ross layouts—from the famous Seminole and Inverness, to obscure gems like Holston Hills (Tennessee), Linville, Highlands, and Roaring Gap (North Carolina), and Whitinsville (Massachusetts)—among my personal favorites. But he took on so many projects that he couldn't devote very much of his own time to most of them, so you can't depend on every Ross course being worth the trip.

The only Ross course that you can be sure got 100% of Donald's attention is Pinehurst No. 2—unquestionably his masterpiece, and a certifiable work of genius—which he had the luxury of evolving on the ground over a period of more than 30 years. The intricately contoured greens and approaches that are the makings of the course weren't there originally, you see, because the original Pinehurst No. 2 had sand greens, no one yet having figured out how to make Bermuda into a good putting surface. It wasn't until the late twenties that Ross could be confident of establishing putting greens, and by then he knew the holes of No. 2 so well that his strategies in contouring and bunkering the greens were intricately developed in his mind.

The makings of Pinehurst No. 2 are the green complexes, which are quite simply the best I've seen on any course. The slightly raised, intricately contoured greens and the fairway-height bumps and hollows that surround them are identified by many amateur architecture buffs as the epitome of the Ross style, but in fact they are unlike almost all other Ross courses I've seen. Some aficionados have also compared the greens at No. 2 to those of Ross' home, Royal Dornoch, but although both courses require a deft touch around the greens, Dornoch's plateau greens are generally bigger, more elevated, and more well-defined than those of No. 2. It amazes me that a style so brilliant has never been copied or emulated by another designer, and one of these days I'm going to try and imitate Pinehurst No. 2 myself, just to see if it can be done.

The unbelievable part about Pinehurst No. 2 is that a lot of people think the course is dull, because it's so wide open off the tees, and because there's no obviously penal rough around the greens. They don't understand that unless they drive the ball well, and to the right spot in the fairway, they're going to leave themselves a lot of very tricky chips and pitches as a product of their misplays through the green. Still, I'd have to agree with Pete Dye that it's wrong for anyone to describe the greens of No. 2 as "subtle." As Pete says, "On the first hole, you've got a five-foot-deep bunker with an almost vertical face to the left of the green, and a humpback green with a bunch of severe dips in the ground to the right of it. What's so subtle about that?"

I have heard it said that No. 2 lacks outstanding holes, but that's hogwash: in fact,

*Ross' genius culminates at Pinehurst, his ultimate creation. All golfers should experience it.*

every one of the first five holes is worth considering in a list of America's best, and they certainly aren't the five best holes on the course. There are just so many very good holes that it's impossible to single one out. Of course, there are no heroic tee shots to be played across the ocean's edge or anything like that, but there aren't any holes like that on the great British links, either. And that's the final great appeal of No. 2—that you can play it all day without mastering it, but without fear of ever losing a ball. (As Don Padgett, the director of golf, said to me, "With all the pine-needle roughs, if you lose a ball on No. 2, your game is in serious trouble.")

As far as the other six Pinehurst courses are concerned, there is a lot of good golf. Still, I would have to agree with Charles Price, who wrote that comparing another of Pinehurst's courses favorably to No. 2 would "draw a laugh even from their architects." It's that good. Just give yourself a little time to figure it out.

| —SCORECARD— | | |
|---|---|---|
| **No. 2 Course** | **Par 72** | **7,020 Yards** |
| 1. 396 ! | 7. 401 | 13. 374 ! |
| 2. 441 ! | 8. 487 ! | 14. 436 ! |
| 3. 335 ! | 9. 166 ! | 15. 201 ! |
| 4. 547 | 10. 578 ! | 16. 531 ! |
| 5. 445 ! | 11. 433 ! | 17. 190 ! |
| 6. 212 ! | 12. 415 ! | 18. 432 ! |
| Course Architect: Donald Ross, 1903–1935 | | |

# Pine Valley

PINE VALLEY, CLEMENTON, NEW JERSEY, USA

f there is one thing I can be proud of by changing the journalistic rankings of golf courses to numerical order, it is that I've changed the reputation of Pine Valley from that of the "toughest" golf course in America to simply the "best"; too much of Pine Valley's aura always centered around difficulty.

Yes, Pine Valley is difficult. George Crump wanted it that way, and the club's "local convention," which overrides Rule 28 and eliminates the option of taking relief from an unplayable lie in the jungle, has assured that the standing bet against any player breaking 80 on his first visit will withstand the majority of challengers. But while that may be part of the legacy of Pine Valley, it has obscured for many the fact that the course possesses more truly outstanding holes than any other I've seen (if we hadn't limited the selection of America's top 100 golf holes to two per course, seven Pine Valley holes would have made the list), and that it all blends together superbly in spite of the fact that several architects had some hand in the design, and that the course is a pure golf experience, with no distractions, from first tee to last green.

Actually, with all the improvements in modern playing equipment, I don't think the course is nearly the demon it used to be. There are six par-4 holes under 400 yards and just one of more than 446, and 446 yards just isn't as long as it used to be—Scott Verplank described that hole (the great 13th) to me like this: "It's only a short iron approach shot, and the green is so huge you can hardly miss it, but it's still hard to get the ball close." Which I found amusing, because that's how some of us mortals used to think about the *third* shot if we had successfully laid up out to the right with a 3-iron second. It's not nearly as terrifying as it once was—the sandy wastes that set off the island target areas aren't nearly as conspicuous as they once

*The terrifying 2nd.*

*The greatness of Pine Valley is in all of the great minds that Crump consulted in building it—Colt, Flynn, Thomas, and Tillinghast.*

were, and the management has deliberately grown a bit more grass in places and cleaned out the trees in lots of others, to help get people around. For a while there they were also making the greens super-fast to try and preserve the difficulty level for top players, but thankfully they've cut back on that—the bold contours are worry enough at average speeds. But it's still probably the most intimidating course in the world for the 25-handicapper (who the members are strongly discouraged from inviting in the first place), which is why I worry about it being held up as the *ideal* course in the world. For the true test—most interesting to all levels of players—St. Andrews wins hands down.

But don't let all these disparaging remarks about the course fool you: deep down, it's still golf's most awesome experience, a shining example of golf architecture in the raw so that even the color-blind can understand it.

| — SCORECARD — | | |
|---|---|---|
| | PAR 70 | 6,765 YARDS |
| 1. 427 !! | 7. 585 ! | 13. 446 !! |
| 2. 367 ! | 8. 372 !! | 14. 185 |
| 3. 185 ! | 9. 432 ! | 15. 603 ! |
| 4. 461 ! | 10. 145 ! | 16. 436 ! |
| 5. 226 ! | 11. 399 ! | 17. 344 ! |
| 6. 391 ! | 12. 382 | 18. 424 ! |
| COURSE ARCHITECTS: GEORGE CRUMP & H.S. COLT, 1912–1918 | | |

# Prairie Dunes

HUTCHINSON, KANSAS, USA

ere I to set out looking for classic terrain on which to build a great golf course, the Great Plains of America are certainly not the first region of the country I would think to explore, but even I can be wrong sometimes. For one thing, it is the windiest region of the USA, an important element if we wish to pose the classical problems of the great British links; there are wide-open vistas, as on the great seaside courses; and in isolated pockets there exists some great terrain. Prairie Dunes is the cream of the crop.

Prairie Dunes' fame in the USA rests largely upon comparisons to the great Scottish links, but the link is a tenuous one. Yes, there are dunes and mostly sandy soil, and the plum thickets and yucca plants do pose some of the same thorny problems as the heather and gorse native to British links. But the turf at this latitude will never achieve the firmness of a true links, nor do the cottonwoods at one end of the dunes have any counterparts in links golf. Most of all, God never created contours as severe as Perry Maxwell's savage rolls in the putting greens of Prairie Dunes.

That doesn't mean Prairie Dunes isn't a superb course, and all the better for being unique in the golf world. For twenty years after its foundation in 1937 the course consisted of only nine holes, and the course gained the reputation of being the best nine-holer in America before Press Maxwell (Perry's son) extended the course to 18 holes in 1956. Maxwell, Sr.'s original nine holes (presently nos. 1-2-6-7-8-9-10-17-18) are probably still the nine best holes, but there are also some good ones among the newer nine, and the course does benefit from getting back into a corner of the property with a somewhat different look at the 14th and 15th. Like the best links, the formation of the dunes is quite differ-

*The heroic 8th.*

*P.J. Boatwright's favorite par-5—the 17th at Prairie Dunes.*

ent from one section of the course to the next, which makes for an interesting variety of holes all brought together by one constant—the difficult greens, many of them whale-backed slightly at the back so that putting from one side of the green to a hole cut in the other is always an adventure.

There is a large additional acreage of dunes adjacent to the present golf course that has yet to be developed, and the club itself owns enough to have plans for a third nine if demand ever warrants it: an idle daydream any golf architect must consider.

| — SCORECARD — | | |
|---|---|---|
| | **PAR 70** | **6,542 YARDS** |
| 1. 424 | 7. 507 | 13. 377 |
| 2. 156 ! | 8. 420 !! | 14. 363 |
| 3. 365 | 9. 419 ! | 15. 206 ! |
| 4. 164 | 10. 181 !! | 16. 420 |
| 5. 439 | 11. 450 | 17. 497 ! |
| 6. 382 ! | 12. 387 ! | 18. 385 ! |
| COURSE ARCHITECTS: PERRY MAXWELL, 1937, & PRESS MAXWELL, 1956 | | |

# Riviera

PACIFIC PALISADES, CALIFORNIA, USA

Before I had played Riviera, I must admit that I wouldn't have ranked it any higher than 50 other American courses. From outside the ropes, Riviera isn't a very spectacular test at all, located down in the bottom of a large canyon below the famed clubhouse with not a lot of elevation change to it, and very little in the way of color contrasts because the fairways and roughs are all the same peculiar adapted species of grass known as kikuyu, which Gary McCord likens to velcro. But appearances can be deceiving, and in this case they do not do the golf course justice.

From inside the ropes, where I try to confine my play, Riviera is about as good a strategic golf course as you'll ever find. I should have expected as much of George Thomas, since his book, *Golf Architecture in America,* is probably the clearest perspective ever written on the art of course design, including graphed-out drawings of ideal holes with incredibly complex multiple fairways. But until Riviera I must admit I was less impressed with Thomas' actual courses than with his book: the North course of the L.A. Country Club is an excellent parkland test but not in the 9-10 range on my scale, while Bel Air and Ojai both show flashes of greatness but have been altered to a considerable degree. Riviera has resisted change—the surest test of a great course.

Individually the holes are almost unanimously solid, brilliantly set off by eucalyptus trees and a smattering of Thomas' superb bunkers—in the contouring of sand hazards, not even MacKenzie was a greater craftsman. But the key to the golf course is the precision of its bunkering placement—they cover the greens like an all-pro defensive back, forcing you to place the tee shot and threatening to intercept any indifferent approach. The course is also well-balanced, with trouble to the left of one hole and to the right of the next, so that a player who can fade the ball has an advantage on certain holes and one who favors the draw has the upper hand on others. And yet, while the eucalyptus are certainly present, there are very few holes where they come into play for anything but a bad miss, and the greens, while well conceived, are not frightening in their contours. The course gives you opportunity to score, but only if you maneuver the ball where your ability allows it and show patience where your game is weak. Perhaps that is why Hogan enjoyed such success here.

The long finishing hole is renowned for the impact it has had on tournaments, and it is indeed a great gallery hole for the finish, but to me there are several other holes of more interesting design. The back-to-back long holes to start are a favorite Thomas opening gambit (although I'm told the 2nd was originally played from the white tee, which they still use for tournaments), but you'll notice right away that the pitch to the 1st calls for accurate depth judgement and the major trouble is a bunker at front right, while at the 2nd the long approach is to a narrow target, with most of the trouble at the left. The long approach to the 3rd is defended

*Riviera was created from uninspired property. George Thomas thought it was such an impossibility, he waved his design fee. But his creation continues to challenge all levels of golfers.*

by an angled bunker to the right of the green; the adapted Redan at the 4th has a huge sentinel bunker on the left. So it goes throughout the course. For many, the best hole of all is the 10th, a short par-4 to a tilted green which does not take kindly to impatient tactics, while the long two-shot 15th with its gull-winged green is probably the strongest hole of all.

Riviera is also the club at which you're most likely to encounter Peter Falk on the practice green, but it's much more than a hangout for celebrities—the celebrities are here for the golf.

| — SCORECARD — | | |
|---|---|---|
| | PAR 71 | 6,946 YARDS |
| 1. 501 ! | 7. 406 | 13. 420 |
| 2. 460 | 8. 368 ! | 14. 180 |
| 3. 434 ! | 9. 418 ! | 15. 447 ! |
| 4. 238 ! | 10. 311 !! | 16. 168 ! |
| 5. 426 | 11. 561 | 17. 578 |
| 6. 170 !? | 12. 413 | 18. 447 ! |
| COURSE ARCHITECT: GEORGE THOMAS, 1926 | | |

# Royal Dornoch

DORNOCH, SUTHERLAND, SCOTLAND

For some people, a trip to Dornoch is a pilgrimage to see the little town and the links where Donald Ross nurtured his love for the game; for others, it is an escape to the one great Scottish links that has yet to be completely overrun by tourists from the United States and Japan. You can ignore all these puny rationalizations: go and see Royal Dornoch because it's a perfect 10 on the Doak scale, and no one should miss it.

The most significant feature of Dornoch's design is its greens. Most of them are sited atop good-sized natural plateaux, and all are open at the front to allow a carefully judged approach to bounce on, yet carefully conceived to receive that shot only from a particular spot in the fairway. Most of the strategic arrangement of the course was accomplished by the club secretary near the turn of the century, John Sutherland, with some input from a young protégé named Donald Ross. Thus arranged, Royal Dornoch can provide a good test for the best players, while remaining a fairly wide-open driving course for the average player.

There are also the added advantages of remoteness, beauty, routing, and superb individual holes. Dornoch, at the same latitude with Hudson Bay in North America, is so isolated from the concentration of other good Scottish courses that when I lived over there in 1982–83, even a lot of the Scots had written it off as too far to go, even though it was only a five- or six-hour drive from St. Andrews. Word has it that new roads have dramatically reduced the drive time, but the course's panoramic views of the Dornoch Firth and the Highlands remain, for now, largely unsung. The routing—eight holes out along the line of a great gorse-covered bluff, eight holes back along the gentle curve of the beach, and the last two holes into the middle and back—is elegantly simple, and yet the outward holes' use of the bluff is brilliant, with three holes atop its height, the great stretch of par-4's from the 3rd through 5th holes sheltered

*The 5th and 12th at Dornoch.*

*The trip to Dornoch is long, but the trip home is much longer.*

on the linksland underneath (two of these with elevated tees), the short 6th hole shelved into the side of the bluff with a steep fall at the right shoulder of the green (slice your tee shot and you'd settle for a 4), and finally the 8th, whose fairway falls mysteriously away over the edge of the bluff toward the village of Embo in the distance. There are great holes coming in as well, the most celebrated of which, the 459-yard 14th, or "Foxy," with its beautiful natural plateau green, is only appreciated after you have mastered the tricky approach—and you won't do it in the first couple of tries.

As for other pursuits, Dornoch is about the sleepiest town you will ever find in the golf world—there isn't much else to do except drive out into the country to see the sights (up to the north toward John O'Groats or toward Loch Shin in the interior), and there isn't even much choice for dining out other than the few major hotels (the Burghfield House is the "in" place to stay). But there are 18 hours of sunlight a day here in high summer, and the golf is so good that it's difficult even to enjoy the hospitality of the upstairs club bar for very long before going back out for another crack. If you want more than that, you're reading the wrong book.

— SCORECARD —

| | Par 70 | | 6,577 Yards |
|---|---|---|---|
| 1. First | 336 | 10. Fuaran | 148 ! |
| 2. Ord | 179 ! | 11. A'chlach | 445 |
| 3. Earl's Cross | 414 ! | 12. Sutherland | 504 ! |
| 4. Achinchanter | 418 ! | 13. Bents | 168 |
| 5. Hilton | 361 ! | 14. Foxy | 459 !! |
| 6. Whinny Brae | 165 !! | 15. Stulaig | 322 |
| 7. Pier | 465 | 16. High Hole | 405 |
| 8. Dunrobin | 437 ! | 17. Valley | 406 ! |
| 9. Craiglaith | 499 | 18. Home | 457 |

Course Architect: Old Tom Morris

# Rye

CAMBER, RYE, EAST SUSSEX, ENGLAND

I am the first to admit that not every course I've selected for the "Gourmet's Choice" will provide a difficult test for scratch players: fun, as opposed to difficulty, is the most critical qualification for this particular list. But Rye's lack of support as one of the best courses in Britain has always puzzled me, because in addition to its esthetic merits I believe it is certainly one of the most difficult courses in the world to play in par figures.

Of course, one of the reasons the medal play record is so high is that hardly anyone at Rye ever plays for a score; match play is the name of the game here, including the one major competition of the year held over the links—the President's Putter competition against the elements each January. Then again, one of the main reasons for the club members' choice of formats is the trying nature of the test, summed up by Bernard Darwin 70 years ago:

> "For the few who are artists in using the wind Rye is a paradise; for the majority who are not, it is a place of trial and disillusionment. Disillusioned, too, will be they who imagine that they know all that there is to be known about wooden clubs . . . At Rye they must be prepared to hit brassey shots—long, straight brassey shots too—with one foot on a hummock and the other in a pit. If they cannot do it, they must be content to take five far more often than they like."

The layout has been changed since the original H.S. Colt routing of 1894, and now lies entirely south of the road to Camber, but it still must basically follow the lines of the long sandhill ridges, which run parallel to the shore, and since the prevailing wind lies perpendicular to the lines of the ridges, most of the holes must frequently be tackled in a violent crosswind. Its routing is ingenious, attacking the ridges in almost every possible configuration: there are holes along the valleys, holes from ridgetop to ridgetop, holes crossing the ridges laterally, holes set into the sides of the sandhills, and one hole—the 430-yard 4th—that amounts to a high-wire act along the crest of the highest ridge. There are basically just three lengths of holes in the mix at Rye: five spectacular short holes that will make or break any chance of a decent score, a couple of short par-4's that offer some birdie chance, and the rest long two-shotters (although the 1st hole has now been extended slightly so it can be called a par-5) that will wear down even the strongest of hitters. It is widely said that the second shots at the short holes are the key to scoring at Rye (because it is almost assured that one or two of these tiny targets will be missed, and the penalties around them are most severe), but I would like to meet the man who could hit the greens of all the two-shotters in regulation.

Most amazing to me is the fact that the present course was pieced together over the generations, to include the best ideas of several different designers. Of the best holes, only the

*The 7th at Rye, one of five reasons "the toughest shots at Rye are the 2nd shots on the par 3's."*

present 5th and 16th were the same in Colt's original plan. The short par-4 9th was part of Tom Simpson's 1932 plan to make the course safe from the Camber road; the difficult 4th and 8th, the ideas of Sir Guy Campbell in 1938; and the short 2nd and 7th holes were built by the secretary and the greenkeeper after the Second World War.

Rye is a somewhat exclusive club (as befits the unofficial home of the Oxford and Cambridge Golfing Society) and may require advance introduction to play, but if you approach the club on the same terms as Muirfield I think you'll be welcomed. If you entertain thoughts of matching par, I'll be happy to book your wager.

| — SCORECARD — | | |
|---|---|---|
| | **PAR 68 /BOGEY 72** | **6,505 YARDS** |
| 1. 483 | 7. 163 !! | 13. 436 !? |
| 2. 185 ! | 8. 430 | 14. 185 |
| 3. 455 | 9. 320 ! | 15. 440 ! |
| 4. 430 !! | 10. 435 | 16. 430 ! |
| 5. 175 ! | 11. 350 | 17. 235 |
| 6. 485 ! | 12. 430 | 18. 438 ! |
| COURSE ARCHITECT: SIR GUY CAMPBELL, REVISION, 1938 | | |

# St. Andrews

ST. ANDREWS, KINGDOM OF FIFE, SCOTLAND

A lot of tourists make one trip in their lives to St. Andrews, spend four hours on the Old Course without much of a clue as to what they're looking at, and come away convinced that the reputation of the golf course is built on its history and tradition. So I want to state this emphatically: I'm including St. Andrews in this section because I really do think that the Old Course is one of the very best golf courses in the world, laying history, tradition, and atmosphere totally aside. If we disagree on that point, I'll bet it's because I had the opportunity to live in St. Andrews just long enough to understand the true nature of the golf course, and I doubt that you have.

The Old Course is appealing at first glance because of the charm of starting and finishing in town, but it is by no means a spectacular landscape: I wish I had a dollar for every time I heard a first-time visitor jump off the tour bus near the first tee and wonder, "Is this what all the fuss is about?" Then the guy dumps his second shot into the burn in front of the first green, either because he was trying to get too fine with it or because he was lulled to sleep by the wide-open fairway and didn't concentrate enough to make a solid tee shot, and he doesn't even understand he's been had. That's the way the Old Course plays. On nearly every shot in the round there's plenty of room to miss the shot and get away with it, but you'll have to do a lot of work with a mallet putter from 60 and 70 feet away if you're going to post a decent score that way; and it's just as true that on every shot there is a particular stroke to a particular spot that will yield great results, but it is beyond the abilities of most players to determine and produce the correct stroke at the given moment.

The unique challenge of the Old Course is that tactics play just as big a part as execution, because the holes were laid out without any architect's imposition of "correct" strategy to them at all. It is entirely up to you to figure out the optimal line of attack given the conditions of wind, ground, and pin position, and weigh the risks accordingly. There are so many hazards that every time you (or your opponent) hit a shot, unless it finishes within ten yards of where you aimed it, you ought to reevaluate what you want to try to do with the next shot. Of course, if you aren't familiar with the positions of all the hazards and consequences of a particular pin position, and have to rely on your caddy to supply the tactics, you're missing half the challenge, which is why most one- or two-time visitors never really appreciate the course, though most would never dare reveal their secret in public.

Another consequence of its evolution is that many of the individual holes are unique to the world of golf, because there was no architect to decide they were unfair: thus one can encounter a mound right in front of the 4th green that deflects a dead-straight approach well off to one side, or a nest of blind bunkers in the middle of the 12th fairway just at the range of a normal drive, or finally a green that requires a long-iron approach threaded between a nasty pot bunker on the left and a metalled road flanking the right

*The Old Course at St. Andrews cannot be deciphered at first glance.*

rear of the green. If you can accept them as they are and determine the best way to attack, you'll discover that golf is a fascinating game.

That's why the Old Course is one of the world's best, but it is by no means all there is to St. Andrews. For starters, there are other golf courses to be enjoyed: the New course, which has not the strategic merits of the Old but is a good test with fewer arresting holes, and the Eden, which is short at 5,900 yards but features a superb set of H.S. Colt par-3 holes. No trip to St. Andrews is complete without a round on the Ladies' Putting Course, a series of moguls over which one can play a putting clock, something akin to miniature golf without the rails. You can also take a walk along the beach where they ran in "Chariots of Fire," see the ruins of St. Andrews castle or cathedral (including the graves of Tom Morris and Allan Robertson), visit the university, or just enjoy the atmosphere of a town where nearly everyone—tourist or citizen—loves the game of golf and is happy to meet another member of the fraternity. St. Andrews is every golfer's second hometown.

—SCORECARD—

| The Old Course | Par 72 | | 6,933 Yards |
|---|---|---|---|
| 1. Burn | 370 ! | 10. Bobby Jones | 342 |
| 2. Dyke | 411 ! | 11. High (in) | 172 !! |
| 3. Cartgate (out) | 371 | 12. Heathery (in) | 316 !? |
| 4. Ginger Beer | 463 ! | 13. Hole o'Cross (in) | 425 ! |
| 5. Hole o'Cross (out) | 564 ! | 14. Long | 567 !! |
| 6. Heathery (out) | 416 | 15. Cartgate (in) | 413 |
| 7. High (out) | 372 | 16. Corner of the Dyke | 382 !! |
| 8. Short | 178! | 17. Road | 461 !!! |
| 9. End | 356 | 18. Home | 354 ! |

Course architect: Nature

# St. Enodoc

ROCK, WADEBRIDGE, CORNWALL, ENGLAND

I must begin with a confession: I shot probably the best round of my golfing career at St. Enodoc, a one-under-par 68 that included six birdies, and most of you will understand that it is hard to set aside that sort of experience in one's objective evaluation of a golf course. But for golf course architecture buffs, the tie between success in play and a favorable opinion of the architecture works both ways; in fact, I feel sure that some of the better players on the Tour would have had many more successes if they had postponed any interest in architecture until after their playing careers were over, because there are clearly some holes where they allow their dislike for the design to affect their concentration on scoring.

Anyway, I fell in love with the St. Enodoc four days before my great round, when I walked the golf course for the first time, and the anticipation of playing it is what led to my roller-coaster round. That round, in fact, was very much in line with the nature of the golf course: there are very hard holes and easy holes, good holes and bad holes, and for a true fan of architecture the changing moods of the course can really get under the skin. Whatever the result, the beautiful views of Daymer Bay, the magnificent dunes, and the remote Cornwall landscape are sure compensation for one's errors of execution, which is why St. Enodoc is a popular "holiday" course for Britons on summer vacation.

But I must assure you that the golf course has more to offer than scenery. There are some truly outstanding holes at St. Enodoc, some of which might benefit from a bit of added length but nevertheless have the unmistakable raw stuff of greatness about them. The 1st hole is a good introduction to the course, with plenty of room for the opening tee shot but a bit more trouble nearer the green, with the first of the course's many distracting views adding to its difficulties when one passes through the saddle of fairway some 60 yards before the green. The 2nd is a strong two-shotter to a high green and the 3rd equally long but downhill, with a rickety stone wall to be hurdled 50 yards before the green. The 4th may be the best hole in the world of its particular length, 278 yards, with an out-of-bounds field encroaching into play from the right, and a narrow plateau green angled off to the left providing an awkward target for a pitch from the left of the fairway.

There are other good holes, and one more great one at the finish, but without question the two holes at St. Enodoc that live in memory are the 6th and 10th. The former is really not a difficult par-4, but the drive has to be laid up a bit and the approach must carry blindly over the corner of the most mountainous bunker in the golfing world, which is actually no more than the eroded face of a massive sandhill (see page 349). If one had to clear its height with a 4-iron instead of a number 9, it would feature prominently in a Stephen King movie about golf. Later, at the 10th, comes one of the rare holes in the world that has been made more frustrating by the improvements in modern golfing equipment. Originally its long curve along a nar-

*St. Enodoc is a roller-coaster ride of golf you'll never forget.*

row stream valley toward the ancient stone church behind its green was clearly a three-shot affair, but since the distance is only 460 yards one is now expected to cover it in two, and the great knobby hill that cuts the fairway down to nothing at 220 yards from the tee effectively reduces the listed par of the hole to a cruel joke.

In a way, I'm afraid to go back to St. Enodoc for fear of spoiling one of my most pleasant golfing memories, but for the rest of you I can recommend it heartily, even if it has its weaknesses.

| — SCORECARD — | | |
|---|---|---|
| | **Par 69** | **6,188 Yards** |
| 1. 518 ! | 7. 394 | 13. 360 |
| 2. 438 | 8. 155 | 14. 355 ? |
| 3. 436 ! | 9. 393 | 15. 168 |
| 4. 278 ! | 10. 457 !? | 16. 482 |
| 5. 160 | 11. 178 | 17. 206 ! |
| 6. 378 !? | 12. 386 | 18. 446 !! |
| Course architect: James Braid, 1907–1936 | | |

# St. George's

ISLINGTON, ONTARIO, CANADA

I seem to have a thing for golf courses named in honor of dragon-slayers; I've seen three with the mantle of "St. George's," and each of them is among my favorites. (The only one of the three that isn't represented here is Royal St. George's, or Sandwich, which you've all seen in recent British Opens.) Funnily enough, each is a classic example of one of the three distinctive golf terrains. Sandwich is a links on a heroic scale; St. George's Hill, following, is an undiscovered heathland gem. Then there is Toronto's St. George's, which happens to occupy one of the best pieces of pure parkland terrain I've ever seen for golf; if Winged Foot or Oakland Hills had contour like this, they'd really be 10's on the Doak scale.

I'm not sure if St. George's is really the Canadian master Stanley Thompson's *best* course, because I still haven't been to Banff and Jasper Park. But I think his routing for St. George's makes more of the contours than I could have done. Instead of routing holes across the sideslopes, like I am inclined to do, Thompson directed a lot of his holes here alongside or through terrific natural valleys maybe 15 to 20 feet deep, with stunning results. The par-4 holes on the front side make the best use of this technique, forcing you to drive perilously close to the brink of the valleys if you want the best angle into the greens.

After a wonderful front nine, the second half of the course is not quite as interesting in its undulations, but turns up the difficulty a notch or two to make for a very tough finish. The strongest hole may be the par-4 14th, where the second shot should carry a diagonal creek that crosses in front of the green and continues along its left flank; but the long 15th, with its green site atop a hill added by architect Robbie Robinson prior to the 1968 Canadian Open, is the most memorable and intimidating of the entire 18. The greens are not quite as diabolical here as in Thompson's design for Cape Breton Highlands, but there is always a tilt to

*Thompson's pure parkland terrain at St. George's.*

*The par-4 14th crosses a creek on the drive and approach.*

them and undulation in some, too—I found myself putting past the hole more often than I'm accustomed to.

St. George's has lost a bit of its prestige in Canada to snazzy, expensive newcomers in the Toronto suburbs like Glen Abbey, The National, and now Devil's Pulpit; but I would prefer to play here any day, or especially if confined to one of the four on an everyday basis. It's the kind of course a member would never tire of.

| — SCORECARD — | | |
|---|---|---|
| | **PAR 71** | **6,790 YARDS** |
| 1. 370 | 7. 440 ! | 13. 213 |
| 2. 433 !! | 8. 223 ! | 14. 446 ! |
| 3. 198 ! | 9. 538 | 15. 570 !! |
| 4. 474 | 10. 377 ! | 16. 203 |
| 5. 410 ! | 11. 520 | 17. 446 |
| 6. 146 | 12. 380 | 18. 403 |
| **COURSE ARCHITECT: STANLEY THOMPSON, 1929** | | |

# St. George's Hill

WEYBRIDGE, SURREY, ENGLAND

In previous editions of this "Gourmet's Choice" I have sung the praises of such heathland gems as Sunningdale and Swinley Forest, both in the heart of the Sand Belt region southwest of London. Now, I am ready to confess the truth: my lasting impression was that St. George's Hill was the best of the bunch.

I'm coming clean now because I checked up on the course on my most recent trip overseas, and I'm still just as convinced of its quality. They've recently upgraded the third nine holes, left over from an original 36-hole plan, to spread out the play over 27 holes, but it's still quite narrow, so except for one must-see short hole—the new 20th—you'll want to stick to the original eighteen. Like its neighbors Coombe Hill, Camberley Heath, Swinley Forest, or the New course at Sunningdale, St. George's Hill is a Harry Colt design, and it is also one of the first successfully integrated housing development–golf courses in history—successful because the housing stays in the background, and never really intrudes on the golf experience. Today it is an elite neighborhood populated by doctors and professionals; I wouldn't mind living there myself, if I had about a million quid to spare.

The opening hole might be considered forbidding by some, but I enjoyed its straightforwardness—a smash across a valley and the entrance road to a rising fairway, with a saddled green at the top of the opposite ridge. The next four holes really get things going: a tough downhill par-4 requiring a second shot across a stream valley, a Redan-type short hole, a very short drive-and-pitch hole that tempts one to unleash the driver, and a medium-long uphill par-4 with a cross-bunker to hurdle for the second shot.

There is even sterner golf to come on the back nine, but the two holes that really stand out in my mind today are the 8th and 10th. The former is not really an outstanding par-3 from a

*The 20th hole.*

*H.S. Colt's masterpiece of architecture shines in the 8th at St. George's Hill.*

strategic point of view—it's a dropping shot across a valley to an ample target—but the yawning bunker in front of the green was one of the most memorable hazards I've encountered in the game, although a recent reconstruction has stripped it of some of its raw power. The par-4 10th is one of the best Alps-type blind par-4 holes I've ever seen, with a diagonal ridge running across the fairway from left to right, so that the drive down the right-hand edge may get a glimpse of the green and a favorable kick off the slope to the left of the green, while the drive to the left makes the second shot inclined to kick into a bunker short right of the green.

Some of my friends in England think I'm nuts to put this course in this category, but I'll happily go out on a limb here. If you don't like this course, I'll take the blame; but don't forget to thank me if you like it half as much as I do.

| — SCORECARD — | | |
|---|---|---|
| | PAR 70 | 6,492 YARDS |
| 1. 380 ! | 7. 480 | 13. 424 ! |
| 2. 465 ! | 8. 175 !! | 14. 210 ! |
| 3. 197 ! | 9. 370 | 15. 537 ! |
| 4. 269 ! | 10. 431 !! | 16. 436 |
| 5. 385 ! | 11. 117 | 17. 414 ! |
| 6. 466 | 12. 348 | 18. 388 ! |
| COURSE ARCHITECT: H.S. COLT, 1913 | | |

# Sand Hills

MULLEN, NEBRASKA, USA

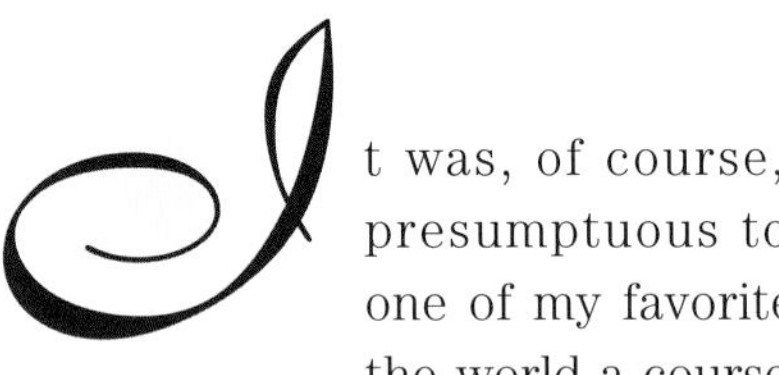

t was, of course, somewhat presumptuous to choose as one of my favorite courses in the world a course that wasn't even finished; I first wrote it up for the Gourmet's Choice a year before the course was in play. Now that I've actually played the finished product, it's much less of a stretch to keep it here.

The Sand Hills are no less than one of the great wonders of the golf world—a region of sand dunes fully 60 miles in latitude and I don't know how far from east to west, with endlessly rolling contours. Until a couple of years ago, though, no golfer knew much about them, because the Sand Hills are located in northwestern Nebraska, an hour's drive from the nearest town of any size (North Platte), and four hours from metropolitan Denver or Lincoln. It is, then, highly speculative to be building a golf club there, and I must give all the credit in the world to the few visionaries, led by founder Dick Youngscap, for putting their money on the line to try it.

Then again, I don't really see that there's a lot of risk involved here, because the principals spent days of reconnaissance via helicopter to choose a perfect site for their course—so perfect that they moved dirt in spoonfuls to create greens and tees, and in fact so perfect that they didn't even have to contour half the greens. Forget the sales pitch—this course was, literally, already there. The first time I saw it, in the spring of 1993, the only thing that had been done was to flag out the margins of the fairways on the ground and mow down the prairie grasses, yet when we reached the turn we got out our golf clubs and hit it around the back nine, and had a real sense of playing every hole. It took some money to put in the irrigation system and grass the place, but it cost practically nothing to physically build it.

This is not to discount the work of the designers, who must have gone through endless permutations of potential routings, because in some parts of the course you could literally place a tee and build a good hole in any of three or four different directions. Sooner or later, though, there comes the time to "put up or shut up," and although I'll always wonder what hole they might have sacrificed to return the 9th hole to the clubhouse, I cannot honestly imagine that anyone else could have done better. By my count, there were a dozen excellent holes out of 18 before they moved a blade of dirt here, and I'm mightily impressed by what they did with the 4th, 8th, and 13th holes, where Coore and Crenshaw had to create more than they let on.

How good is this course? I can't give it a 10 on the Doak scale, because that's not a judgment that can be made in a single visit, but it's the only course built in a long time that even had a chance to get to that level. I look forward to reserving final judgment for several more trips to come.

*Architects Coore & Crenshaw didn't build Sand Hills; they discovered their golf holes among the dunes.*

*Photo to the right shows the property prior to construction and the photo above shows a hole cleverly crafted into the sandy terrain.*

| —SCORECARD— | | |
|---|---|---|
| | PAR 71 | 6,980 YARDS |
| 1. 549 ! | 7. 283 ! | 13. 221 ! |
| 2. 418 | 8. 367 | 14. 508 ! |
| 3. 216 !! | 9. 371 ! | 15. 469 ! |
| 4. 449 ! | 10. 472 ! | 16. 612 ! |
| 5. 387 | 11. 408 ! | 17. 168 ! |
| 6. 198 !! | 12. 417 ! | 18. 467 ! |
| COURSE ARCHITECT: BILL COORE & BEN CRENSHAW, 1995 | | |

# San Francisco

INGLESIDE, SAN FRANCISCO, CALIFORNIA, USA

In all the lists of the best golf courses in America, San Francisco Golf Club comes out second to its neighbor, the Lakeside course at Olympic. I cannot help thinking that if the U.S. Opens of 1955 and 1966 had been held somewhere else, modern opinion would be more in line with my own.

To compare the two courses, all you need to do is go stand on any tee. Olympic is one of the most claustrophobic driving tests in the world—the pines and eucalyptus planted to strengthen the course after it was laid out on a basically bare hillside are so thick today that if you stand on a tee for too long you'll start to feel the trees growing inwards. There's only one fairway bunker on the golf course, because that's about all they had room for. I'm not arguing that Olympic is a bad course, but I certainly don't understand why anybody would prefer it to a more open, prettier layout with magnificent sprawls of fairway sand and clever contours to the greens, which is Tillinghast's San Francisco Golf Club in a nutshell. From my standpoint, even Olympic's record as host to major championships is indicative of its weaknesses. Disagree? Okay, you take Fleck, Casper, and Scott Simpson; I'll take Hogan, Palmer, and Tom Watson.

But San Francisco Golf Club is the topic here, and it is a course that deserves our undivided attention. It is Tillinghast's first masterpiece, coming after Shawnee-on-the-Delaware but years before any of his great Eastern parkland courses, and represents an altogether unique example of his early style. It rewards long and straight hitting as all good courses should, but is for the most part far less fearsome in its extractions for poor approaches than Baltusrol or Winged Foot; on the other hand, the sprawling fairway bunkers set at all sorts of odd distances from the tees require great judgement in selecting the line of play for the moment, and make the course a much different proposition in various winds than Olympic, which faces east on a sheltered slope. As far as providing "room to play" and the corresponding strategic element, there is no doubt that San Francisco Golf Club is a superior course.

While there are many fine holes to choose from, one deserves special mention because it was Tillinghast's own personal favorite of his very productive career, and is a favorite of mine also. The par-3 7th is known as the "Duel hole" because the canyon in which its green lies was the scene of the last duel in American history, near the turn of the century; the short hole that resides there now is perhaps the best "drop-shot" par-3 in all of golf. The long, kidney-shaped green is divided in two by a hump-backed ridge that plays a great part in the strategy, because a shot lighting on its reverse slope can be sent careening into one of the nasty bunkers that guard the back of the green; when the pin is set not far behind the ridge, one must carefully weigh the risk of playing to the back half versus laying up safely on the front

*Tillinghast's personal favorite, the Duel Hole at San Francisco Golf Club.*

projection of the green and putting over the ridge.

I wish that the members of this club were not so overly concerned with their privacy (they're one of the few clubs I know that goes to great lengths to avoid publicity for the merits of their course), because their golf course should be studied and emulated elsewhere; but I suppose I can forgive them for wanting to keep the course to themselves, just as long as they allow me to return and enjoy it now and then.

| — SCORECARD — | | |
|---|---|---|
| | **PAR 71** | **6,623 YARDS** |
| 1. 518 | 7. 184 !!! | 13. 375 |
| 2. 427 ! | 8. 388 | 14. 337 |
| 3. 381 ! | 9. 570 ! | 15. 161 |
| 4. 218 | 10. 410 ! | 16. 365 ! |
| 5. 382 ! | 11. 159 | 17. 423 ! |
| 6. 414 ! | 12. 405 ! | 18. 510 ! |
| COURSE ARCHITECT: A.W. TILLINGHAST, 1915 | | |

# Shadow Creek

NORTH LAS VEGAS, NEVADA, USA

n complete contrast to the Sand Hills, let us move abruptly to Shadow Creek, one of the great man-made wonders of the golfing world. Until I saw it, I never believed that money and genius alone were enough to create a course that would rival the greatest spectacles of Nature. Now, I do.

Shadow Creek allows this leap of faith almost instantaneously, because we had already accepted that Tom Fazio was in the rarefied atmosphere of architects capable of building classic courses—yet there is no question that Shadow Creek is his masterpiece. The variety of holes is outstanding by any standard, but it stretches the imagination to remember that the course began life as a barren, tilted desert plain, because the landscaping job is so thoroughly complete.

Fazio modestly gives credit to his client, Steve Wynn, for many of the innovations that set Shadow Creek apart from the rest of modern golf architecture. His insistence on involving the best people in all fields certainly had an impact on the landscaping of the golf course; somewhere among the 21,000 trees, and the very realistic three-quarter-mile stretch of artificial creek, this course graduated from the realm of a golf architect's imagination to an even bigger production. I am also quite sure that Wynn's understanding of the nature of showmanship helped Fazio to show an all-important measure of restraint through his design, so that the course has a flow of highs and lulls before building to a brilliant climax. Most modern architects would have started the high drama on the first or second hole, and by the time the 18th rolled around you'd be dead; but that's not at all the case at Shadow Creek. (Indeed, the short par-3 17th and the short par-5 18th are highly dramatic, but offer enough hope of birdies at the finish that the customers often leave with a good taste in their mouths.)

The variety of landscapes Fazio managed to create for his short holes is astonishing—it's difficult to imagine that the 5th hole was once virtually flat ground—but I do think that the longer holes suffer a bit because they're almost all enclosed in artificial valleys you cannot see out of. Lots of people, including Steve Wynn, like a golf course where you can't see any but the hole you are playing (Pine Valley is often cited for this feature), but I personally prefer the occasional open vista, and I think that more variety could have been obtained if a couple of holes had been shaped in tandem—say, short par-4's with some excessive contour, like the 5th and 6th at Crystal Downs. Indeed, they might have orchestrated some dramatic longer views and visual effects, secure in the knowledge that there would be no unwanted guests to spoil the picture.

It's a shame, I think, that Shadow Creek's recent ranking as the eighth best golf course in America was the focus of controversy over *Golf Digest's* last rankings, because there are much worse mistakes on their list. The red-carpet treatment afforded the few V.I.P.'s who get to play here certainly must sway their judgement

*Fazio's masterpiece, Shadow Creek—*
*a stark contrast to the surrounding desert.*

slightly in its favor, but not much more than it does at Augusta National or Seminole.

In the end, that's the difference between Shadow Creek and the Sand Hills (or Merion or Cypress Point). I would never claim I could have built a better golf course on the given property than any of the latter, but I'll never admit to myself that I could not do better than Shadow Creek given a blank slate and an unlimited budget. There isn't any objective way to evaluate the perfection of a work of art that's entirely manufactured, but Shadow Creek is now the standard by which all other works of this type will be judged. I just hope that someday I have the opportunity to surpass it.

— SCORECARD —

| | PAR 72 | 7,175 YARDS |
|---|---|---|
| 1. 404 ! | 7. 567 | 13. 232 ! |
| 2. 401 | 8. 166 | 14. 460 ! |
| 3. 443 ! | 9. 409 ! | 15. 438 !! |
| 4. 553 ! | 10. 426 | 16. 581 |
| 5. 206 ! | 11. 327 | 17. 164 !! |
| 6. 476 | 12. 395 ! | 18. 527 !! |

COURSE ARCHITECTS: TOM FAZIO & STEVE WYNN, 1989

# Westward Ho!

WESTWARD HO!, DEVON, ENGLAND

It is clear to me, as I present this course among my favorites, that most American golfers are not prepared to see Westward Ho! (The exclamation point is an integral part of the town's name.) It's a storied club, and there is interesting golf out on the links, but the term that leaps to mind here is culture shock.

The Royal North Devon Golf Club was founded in 1864, which, I was surprised to learn, makes it the oldest continuously active golf club in England (it really is a Scottish game after all, you see). It is also a club of major import in the history of championship golf, for it was the neighboring town of Northam which produced the great English champions, Horace Hutchinson and J.H. Taylor, and it was amid the dunes and the Great Sea Rushes of Westward Ho! that they developed their attacking style of play.

From initial appearances things may not have changed much from the days of Hutchinson's youth, when the first players out in the morning cut the holes for the day with a pocketknife and marked them with feathers. The course occupies common land, and many of the citizenry's sheep and horses can typically be found grazing over the links. The first impression of the opening drive is that it will be impossible *not* to hit one of the unsuspecting beasts, but after a couple of holes one gets used to the four-legged gallery.

After two holes across flat, almost swampy ground, we reach the dunes. At the 4th, one must drive over the vast sleepered cross-bunker known as the "Cape," no longer a formidable carry unless there is a strong headwind, but the ancient perils of which are readily apparent. The 5th is a fine short hole, and when the weather is stirred up offshore there are few more beautiful prospects in golf than that from the 6th tee, with the fairway ahead as restless as the Atlantic surf pounding onto the beach close beside on the left. But *the* hole on the way out is the 9th, one of the world's most ingenious par-5's. It commonly plays downwind and is therefore physically reachable in two shots, but the small plateau green is too shallow to hold with a long approach that carries the bunker in front; to be putting for eagle, one has to use some mounds to the right of the approach to steer the ball up onto the green, so there is covert advantage in driving to the right of the fairway instead of just bombing away aimlessly.

At the 10th we suddenly move into the domain of the Great Sea Rushes, a unique vegetative hazard that is something akin to a low, spiky form of pampas grass: at any rate, a ball hit into the Rushes is essentially a lost ball, and that is a sufficiently frightening prospect from the tees of each of the three two-shotters that begin the back nine. The escape from the Rushes offered by the 13th is likely to be tempered by a stiff headwind, which puts the green virtually out of range in two shots, and makes the succeeding short hole a difficult three. But perhaps the most difficult hole of all on this incoming nine is the 16th, a plain, short one-shot-

*The Royal North Devon Club's golf course is as unassuming as its co-tenants, who help maintain the fairways.*

ter with a nastily crowned green. (It is interesting to observe that because of the greater effects of the wind on a higher shot, the shortest one-shot holes in Britain are often the most deadly, particularly for overseas visitors who have not mastered the three-quarters punch shot.) Two dullish long holes back across the marshy ground to the clubhouse complete the round, but one's scorecard is not complete until the cross-bunker in the 17th fairway and the burn at the last hole are safely hurdled.

You'll have to put up with a lot of unique obstacles to enjoy Westward Ho!, but that's a great part of what makes it worth playing in the first place.

| — SCORECARD — | | | |
|---|---|---|---|
| | Par 71 | | 6,644 Yards |
| 1. Burn | 478 ? | 10. Shinnecock | 376 ! |
| 2. Baggy | 410 | 11. Plateau | 368 |
| 3. Sandymere | 425 | 12. Sebonac | 425 ! |
| 4. Cape | 354 !? | 13. Eden | 440 |
| 5. Table | 137 ! | 14. Cape | 201 |
| 6. Crest | 410 ! | 15. Narrows | 434 |
| 7. Bar | 395 ! | 16. Punch Bowl | 145 ! |
| 8. Estuary | 197 | 17. Road | 554 |
| 9. Westward Ho! | 479 !!! | 18. Home | 416 |
| Course architect: Herbert Fowler, revision, 1908 | | | |

# Woodhall Spa

WOODHALL SPA, LINCOLNSHIRE, ENGLAND

When I began assembling the rankings of the best golf courses in the world for *GOLF Magazine,* the name of Woodhall Spa was vaguely familiar within England as the home of an open mixed foursomes tournament in the autumn, but certainly not well known outside the country. Lately I have grown accustomed to seeing it acclaimed as "the finest inland course in Britain," and it now ranks 27th in the world on the *GOLF Magazine* list, with little chance of slipping far. Talk about people jumping on your bandwagon!

One of the great charms of Woodhall Spa (aside from the lilting name) is the unexpectedness of its location: in a country which fairly abounds with fine golfing terrain, the fens of Lincolnshire are the last place one might expect to find good golf. But there it is, an oasis of sandy heath in a small town off the beaten track, with enough length to it for any championship and undoubtedly the deepest bunkers of any British inland course (Ganton's are a solid but distant second) guarding its greens.

Some visitors have compared the course to Pinehurst in terms of its terrain, but in fact the comparison is a poor one: Pinehurst, or at least Pinehurst No. 2, is made by the brilliant contouring of its greens, and that is the one aspect of design in which Woodhall Spa can be found wanting. Certainly, however, the small resort communities resemble one another in the way they revolve around their golf courses, and between the two there are so many fine golf holes that it is very hard to select favorites. In trying to fill out eclectic 18's, many writers have been inclined to choose from Woodhall Spa's shorter two-shot holes (the 17th is most often cited) because good holes of that length are so scarce on other courses, but in going around the golf course those holes don't particularly stand out to me—they are simply one category singled out from a collection of 18 superb holes of varying lengths. The longer two-shot holes and the three-shotters also have much to recommend them; but for me it is the

*Woodhall Spa is renowned for having the deepest bunkers of any course in Britian.*

*The 155-yard par-3 5th hole.*

three short holes that leave the most lasting impression, thanks to the ferocious bunkers that surround their greens. At the 5th, and again at the 12th, just climbing down to a ball in one of the flanking bunkers is like hopping into a foxhole, and once inside you will certainly have no view of your target and possibly no room to swing at the ball on the correct line to the hole.

Another unique feature of Woodhall Spa is that if one moves up to the forward tees (a savings of only a couple hundred yards overall), three of the four long holes—including the 18th, where a huge oak intervenes from the right of the fairway—are reduced below the arbitrary 475-yard limit of par-4 holes, and therefore the listed par goes down by three shots, making Woodhall Spa the only course I know on which those trying to match par would be better advised to play from all the way back.

— SCORECARD —

| MEDAL TEES | PAR 73 | 6,866 YARDS |
|---|---|---|
| 1. 363 | 7. 435 | 13. 437 ! |
| 2. 408 | 8. 193 | 14. 489 ! |
| 3. 417 ! | 9. 560 ! | 15. 325 |
| 4. 415 ! | 10. 333 ! | 16. 398 |
| 5. 155 | 11. 442 ! | 17. 322 ! |
| 6. 506 | 12. 152 ! | 18. 516 ! |

COURSE ARCHITECT: S.V. HOTCHKIN, 1926

DIRECTORY

— OF —

# American Golf Courses

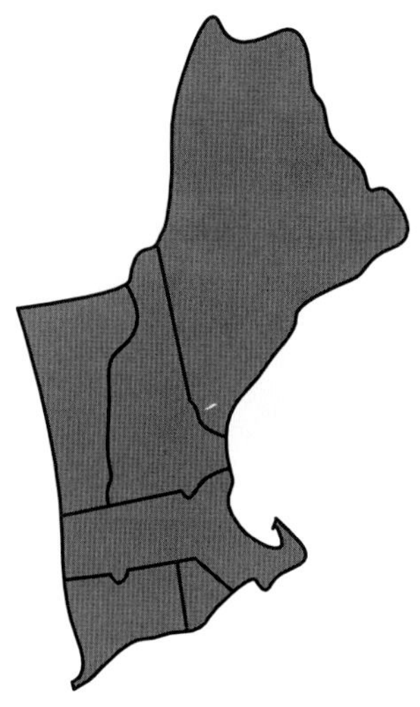

## NEW ENGLAND

The birthplace of American civilization is also, primarily, the birthplace of American golf, as the majority of the country's turn-of-the-century layouts were located here, and the immigration of Donald Ross to Oakley CC in 1899 was a watershed moment in American golf development. In the early years the other prominent architects active in the region were partners Wayne Stiles and John Van Kleek, while in more modern times the market has been dominated by the historian Geoffrey Cornish and his more recent partner, Brian Silva.

New England terrain is typically hilly and rocky, and property in the Boston–New York corridor vastly expensive, so it's quite common for vintage courses to be shortish and rugged, with no room to expand. For me, that's great character, although it's not everyone's cup of tea. The quintessential New England experience: Yale, The Country Club, or Ekwanok.

## MAINE

***Kebo Valley Club,*** *Bar Harbor. Herbert Leeds, 1897, with nine holes added by Andrew Liscombe.*

A nice, natural layout at the upper end of Bar Harbor near the entrance to Acadia National Park, with some really nice views of Cadillac Mountain. The first few holes are in a valley below the small modern clubhouse; then the course runs straight away down a stream valley, and crawls back uphill for the finish. Where the holes fall just in the right place along the contours (in particular at the par-4 8th), there is some good golf; but too many of the holes roll along awkwardly, with the problems of semi-blindness. One other feature worth seeing is the cross-bunkers (more like a hillside covered in sand, with a green set atop the hill) at the par-4 17th, where President Taft once took a great many strokes. However, be warned: rocky subsoil means the drainage (and therefore conditioning) is below standard. 4. [5/89]

*—Gossip—*

My two main sources for New England, Hal Phillips of the *GOLF COURSE NEWS* and Bob Labbance, author of *The Maine Golf Guide,* have both scolded me for not seeking out Northeast Harbor GC, just a few miles further out past Bar Harbor. Until recently it was 15 holes by Stiles and Van Kleek, but Geoff Cornish has completed the other three holes, which were laid out in the 1930s; it's rumored to have an outstanding collection of short par-4's. The other most celebrated course is Robert Trent Jones Jr.'s Sugarloaf, on a mountainside deep in the north woods, which is a very difficult, love-it-or-leave-it track. Other possibilities include Donald Ross' Portland Country Club; Walter Travis' Cape Arundel, near George Bush's summer place; Brian Silva's Sable Oaks, a difficult daily-fee south of Portland; and the vintage nine-hole North Haven Island GC, by Stiles and Van Kleek.

## NEW HAMPSHIRE

***Wentworth-by-the-Sea GC,*** *Portsmouth. Original nine by Donald Ross, 1910; expanded to 18 holes by Cornish and Robinson, 1965.*

A pretty setting for a golf course, but there really wasn't enough land or enough dirt to make 18 holes here. What's left of the original nine is modestly interesting (especially the par-5 8th, which curves around an ocean cove), but much of the expansion is characterized by severe contours and rock outcroppings in the fairways, and swampy roughs. The par-4 14th is absurd—a Cape hole with a large, domed green patrolled by a single pine tree directly in front. 3. [5/86]

*—Gossip—*

My last edition held out high hopes for Hanover CC near the Dartmouth campus, but a member wrote in to tell me how badly they'd screwed it up over the years. Bob Labbance's descriptions of the nine-hole Stiles & Van Kleek–designed Hooper GC in Walpole and the very private Bald Peak Colony Club, by Donald Ross, are enough to arouse my interest if I had a spare day here. The top-rated course in the state is Shattuck GC, a new Brian Silva layout, in Jaffrey, a reasonable drive from the northwestern suburbs of Boston, but, rumor has it, an unreasonably difficult test of driving.

## VERMONT

***Ekwanok CC,*** *Manchester. John Duncan Dunn and Walter Travis, 1899, with revisions by Geoffrey Cornish, 1957–65.*

A marvelous place to go play golf for a few days and get away from sticky New England summers; after that it would likely grow dull. The midsection of the course (from the 7th tee to the 14th green) is an exhilarating stretch of holes over hilly terrain, but the holes around the clubhouse are much less interesting topographically. The 585-yard 7th, with its elevated tee and blind second shot from a bowl of fairway up through a gap between two huge knobs, is worth a point and a half on its own. 6. [7/85]

*—Gossip—*

I wish I had stopped long enough in Manchester to see the town's two other courses, Equinox, the Walter Travis design that has just been extensively remodeled by Rees Jones, and Manchester CC, reputedly one of Geoffrey Cornish's finest design efforts. The Lake course at the Queechee Club is another of Cornish's personal favorites. Rutland Country Club is the only other course I've heard about.

## MASSACHUSETTS

***Blue Rock Par-3 GC,*** *South Yarmouth. Geoffrey Cornish, 1961.*

A very enjoyable little course, with the full range of lengths from 110 to 240 yards represented and two or three first-class water holes, ideal perhaps for a family outing on a summer evening on the Cape. Its quality makes me think that on a really good piece of ground studded with ravines and severe undulations—which would make a full-scale course impractical—you could build a par-3 course that would be out of this world. 3. [10/73]

***The Country Club,*** *Brookline. Willie Campbell, 1894, with Primrose nine added by William Flynn, 1927, and modifications to composite course by Geoff Cornish and Rees Jones.*

A lot of people talk down The Country Club, asserting that its fame as venue for the historic triumph of Ouimet over Vardon and Ray in the 1913 U.S. Open outweighs the merits of the golf course. In truth, there are a very good 27 holes here, although the insistence of the USGA on screwing around with a composite 18 makes it harder to rate. The character of the course is dominated by the tiny, canted greens and occasional outcroppings of rock, which serve as driving hazards on the brilliant par-4 3rd and par-5 11th (or 9th, on the composite course). The 18th, with its green protected by a long cross-bunker across the front and an overhanging oak in back, makes a good old-fashioned finish.

I have yet to see the changes Rees Jones made to the layout prior to the last U.S. Open, but on TV only a couple of the holes looked significantly different. He is to be credited for sprucing the course up without screwing it up, but perhaps he also reaped some of the credit for the parts he left alone, simply because no one remembered it from before; 95% of the character dates to the original layout. 8. [6/82]

***Crumpin-Fox Club,*** *Bernardston. Robert Trent Jones and Roger Rulewich, 1978–1990.*

An upscale public course ahead of its time, it's packed on weekends even though it's up in the boondocks—a solid hour north of Springfield, and two from Hartford. The original (back) nine was widely acclaimed as one of the best nine-holers in New England; Rulewich has always been especially fond of it, because he spent a lot of time amid the trees and the ledge rock when business was slow elsewhere. The new nine isn't as good, naturally, thanks to a couple of awkwardly sharp doglegs, but it's not so poor that they should have stopped at nine. Three of the par-3 holes are excellent—especially the short 11th, to a pocket green set into the side of a rough hill—but the 15th is very awkward, across water to a green that falls away to the right rear, off the back of the dam. Overall, though, the course is a winner: tight enough to make a strong player think twice, but short enough for the average golfer to handle. 6. [10/91]

***Essex Country Club,*** *Manchester. Donald Ross, 1910, with revisions by architect/superintendent Skip Wogan.*

I liked this course better than some of the more famous layouts in the north Boston suburbs, probably because Ross was the professional here for several summers, and had time to tinker with the course. There is an excellent set of short holes, and the architect used all the advantages of a good piece of ground. 6. [5/86]

***Fresh Pond Municipal GC,*** *Cambridge. Walter Johnson, 1932.*

This wasn't the same Walter Johnson who pitched for the Senators, but he struck out here. It's right off a bus route from Harvard Square, but not worth the fare. Nine holes. 1. [10/78]

***Kernwood CC,*** *Salem. Donald Ross, 1914, with modifications by Bill Mitchell, 1950, and Geoffrey Cornish, 1968–91.*

I went to see this one on the basis of a 1928 *Golf Illustrated* piece that included the par-3 9th at Kernwood in the makeup of "The Ideal Course"; but don't ask me why they picked such a mundane hole. There

was one hole worth seeing: the short par-4 7th, with its tee shot across a finger of Boston Harbor. Too bad the rest of the course does not live up to it. 3. [5/86]

***The Kittansett Club,*** *Marion. Fred Hood, 1923, with some advice from William Flynn and Hugh Wilson (not a bad review board).*

The only course Hood ever designed, in one sense it is a one-hole course, because the famous par-3 3rd across a seaweed-strewn beach to a built-up island of green is in a class by itself. The supporting cast of holes is solid, but in my opinion not all they're cracked up to be; only the excellent balance of the overall layout, combined with the windy location, make it a solid test of golf. 6. [6/82]

***Myopia Hunt Club,*** *South Hamilton. Herbert C. Leeds, 1896–1901.*

A really wonderful, old-fashioned layout imbued with a great sense of history, as you might expect from a club that hosted four U.S. Open championships around the turn of the century. The ground is on the hilly side, and not every hole is a wonder—there are a couple of 270-yard par-4's—but no true golfer could fail to be inspired by the prospect from the 2nd or 12th tees, or scared by the array of bunkers at the short 9th, and the 392-yard dogleg 4th might very well be the best hole of its length in the free world. The club maintains a very low profile these days, but do not overlook it in your travels. 7. [5/86]

***Oak Hill Country Club,*** *Fitchburg. Original nine by Stiles and Van Kleek, revised and expanded to 18 holes by Donald Ross, 1921; restoration by Bruce Hepner, 1995.*

A minor hidden gem with a fine reputation in New England, thanks largely to the strength of the six two-shotters on the back nine, which make it a tough tournament venue. The original (front) nine is the weaker half and has seen the majority of the revisions over the years, but there's nothing weak about the finish in general or the uphill par-4 18th in particular. 5. [10/94]

***The Orchards GC,*** *South Hadley. Donald Ross and Walter Hatch, 1922–31.*

Friends of mine, particularly Brad Klein and Ben Crenshaw, have raved about this course, but I think it is best kept in the perspective of a "hidden gem." If you went out of your way to see it you might well be disappointed, because there are no terrific holes; but if you just stumbled across it you'd think it was super. It's actually somewhere in between: a pleasant, somewhat hilly course with a nice set of greens, particularly memorable for the fescue faces of its bunkers, which have been allowed to grow wild. 6. [7/85]

***Salem CC,*** *Peabody. Donald Ross with Walter Hatch, 1925.*

This has always been the flagship of the Donald Ross layouts in the area, and one thing in its favor is that it hasn't been tampered with much since it was built, but I guess that led me to expect too much of it. There are a few really good holes, among them the first and last and especially the short par-4 13th; but I did not find it head and shoulders above Winchester and Essex. 6. [5/86]

***Whitinsville GC,*** *Whitinsville. Donald Ross with Walter Hatch, 1923.*

A peculiarly quiet spot in the teeming New York–Boston corridor, Whitinsville is hands-down the best nine-hole course in America—especially now that Brian Silva (a Whitinsville member) is adding nine to Ross' Rolling Rock in western Pennsylvania. Since the course enjoys heavy play from the membership, opportunities for visitors to play are limited—but eminently worth making the arrangements. Six of the nine holes are truly outstanding, most of all the finishing par-4—

which Ross diagrammed for George Thomas' book—an excellent driving hole skirting a pond to a high plateau fairway. The only weakness in the course is its lack of other complementary strong par-4 holes; the 3rd and 4th, across Fletcher Street, would especially benefit from a bit of length. They may have to tackle you to stop you from going around a second or third time. 8. [10/94]

***Winchester CC,*** *Winchester. Donald Ross, 1903–28.*

A wonderful parkland layout on sloping land in Boston's northwest suburbs. The green complexes are not full of the intricacies that come to mind at the mention of Ross' name, but a superb routing plan yields a wonderful variety of holes. The first four or five holes, working up the hill from the clubhouse, may cause you to doubt my recommendation; but from then on you won't see anything less than a first-class golf hole, with the possible exception of the short 14th. There is even a bit of flair from the old master at the par-5 13th, with a split fairway landing area, but it fits in very naturally, as the upper "A" landing area is a natural shelf surely underlain by rock, surrounded by deep fairway bunkers but offering a much better line for the second. Every bit the equal of Salem, for me. 6. [6/89]

***Worcester CC,*** *Worcester. Donald Ross, 1914, with some modifications by Geoff Cornish.*

Quick quiz: what course was venue for the 1925 U.S. Open, 1960 U.S. Women's Open, and the inaugural Ryder Cup matches of 1927? If you knew it was Worcester Country Club, you're one up on me.

Worcester isn't a course that would still rank as a venue for that kind of major tournament (though, come to think of it, it's a lot better than The Belfry or PGA National), but it still ranks as a really good test for most of us. It's on the hilly side and a fairly tight piece of ground, so there are some weak places in the routing, but there are also a few top-notch holes, including the difficult par-3 13th. 5. [5/86]

### —*Gossip*—

There are still a lot of courses in Massachusetts I'd like to see sometime, many of which may be in the 5–6 range, and a couple possibly higher than that. The top two, according to my readers, are Taconic Golf Club in Williamstown, a beautiful layout in the Berkshires which as home to Williams College is one of the best college courses in America, and Oyster Harbor, a Ross gem on a private peninsula on the south side of Cape Cod, which turned my mom and me away at the gate many years ago. Also on the Cape there's Eastward Ho!, Herbert Fowler's only U.S. design, and Hyannisport Club, adjacent to the Kennedy compound; third-hand info has Woods Hole GC a potential sleeper. Off the mainland, Sankaty Head on Nantucket, which was high on my gossip list last time, has gotten wildly mixed reviews from readers—a great spot, but maybe not a great design—while Bill Clinton has been doing his best to make Farm Neck on Martha's Vineyard famous. Around Boston, a new Brian Silva course named Shaker Hills in the Boston suburbs has gotten good reviews; also Ross' Charles River Country Club, the 36-hole Stow Acres public facility, and the very exclusive Dedham Golf and Polo Club. To the west, the nine-hole layout at Longmeadow CC may be a sleeper.

## RHODE ISLAND

***Agawam Hunt Club,*** *East Providence. Willie Park, Jr., with modifications by Donald Ross, 1911.*

One of several little-known Ross layouts in the state. The property is very tight, to the disadvantage of some of the holes, but the good par-3 holes are indicative of the quality of design. A fairly exclusive club for its modest trappings. 4. [6/82]

***Metacomet CC,*** *East Providence. Donald Ross, 1921, with restoration work by Ron Prichard.*

Seldom mentioned in the same breath as its neighbor Wannamoisett, but what it lacks in difficulty and severity of greens is largely offset by a property rich in undulation and character. The strong par-4 14th might be the best hole in the Ocean State, but they could stand to lose the tree that obscures the left half of the first green, and I can't believe that Ross planned the all-carry par-3 10th at today's 230-yard length. 6. [10/94]

***Misquamicut Club,*** *Watch Hill. Club founded 1899, designer unknown; modifications by Donald Ross, 1923.*

For those of you searching Rhode Island for hidden Ross gems, this is not the place: most of the character of the course derives from the original layout, which is vaguely in the Macdonald style with built-up platform greens and deep grass-faced bunkers. There are some excellent-looking holes, including the par-4 1st, 9th, and "Alps" 10th, but today these all weigh in as light-heavyweights or even middleweights, instead of the bruising holes they were meant to be. After the 11th, a neat short par-4, play descends to flat ground near the beachfront, where Ross' influence is more in evidence, but these holes are of a different character than the first ten and are perhaps sounder but less inspiring. The long par-3 18th, over a deep grassy chasm back uphill to the clubhouse, is a memorable if not a classic finish. 5. [10/89]

***Newport CC,*** *Newport. Original holes by William F. Davis, 1894, with revisions by A.W. Tillinghast, Donald Ross, and Orrin Smith.*

A course with definite seaside flavor, its exposure to the wind and lack of fairway irrigation can make for some interesting shots after a long summer, as we saw during the 1995 Amateur. Its great history and unusual bunkering (dramatic flashes of sand divided by narrow grass fingers, retrofitted onto the faces of what were originally large oval caverns) also certainly give it charm. But there is just enough featureless ground, especially the low-lying holes at the finish, to keep it off my short list. 6. [10/94]

*The 3rd green at Ross' Wannamoisett.*

***Wannamoisett GC,*** *Rumford. Donald Ross, 1914–1926.*

A great study in getting a difficult course out of a small acreage. Most clubs or architects would surely have made one of the two opening holes a par-5, but even at 449 and 473 yards they're both fours at Wannamoisett, so the par of 69 is hardly ever in jeopardy. Then there are the greens, which feature a tremendous variety of tilt and undulation, and which ring the alarm bell on the Stimpmeter throughout the cool Rhode Island summers. My favorite holes were mostly in the first half—the long 2nd with its approach over a stream, the short 3rd whose distinctive plateau green was the model for the Donald Ross Society's logo, the hog-backed short par-4 7th, and the par-3 8th. But the fairly flat topography and narrow hole corridors didn't inspire true love in my heart. 7. [10/94]

*—Gossip—*

Clearly, I haven't done Rhode Island any justice in my travels. Donald Ross maintained a summer office in Little Compton, Rhode Island, a fact which makes Point Judith, the Warwick CC, and the Rhode Island CC course in West Barrington all worth investigating. There are probably more good courses here than in all of Connecticut.

## CONNECTICUT

***Brooklawn CC,*** *Fairfield. A.W. Tillinghast, 1928.*

Unfortunately, Tillinghast didn't get to go at this project from scratch; he inherited a routing plan from a previous course on the same site that included several parallel fairways along a fairly steep grade—holes one remembers only by sorting out the ups from the downs. Still, a good set of greens and an occasional notable hole (such as the par-5 7th) are enough to make it a suitable venue for smaller championships, such as the U.S. Women's Open of 1978. 5. [6/80]

***The Connecticut Golf Club,*** *Easton. Geoffrey Cornish, 1966.*

A limited-membership, all-male club founded by Lawrence Wein, the Donald Trump of the sixties; few people stumble across it while driving by, as I did. It's the only Cornish layout I've seen that aspires to be more than a functional golf course for all ranges of handicaps: he was instructed to build a course in the style of the Augusta National, and succeeded at least as far as scale is concerned. However, Cornish-style bunkers and green contours pose no threat to MacKenzie's for artistry. 5. [7/80]

***CC of Darien,*** *Darien. Alfred Tull, 1958, with modifications by Hal Purdy.*

Whichever of these two architects designed the "untouchable" 620-yard 13th hole should be put to sleep: the only thing it's good for is as an emergency landing strip for small aircraft. The rest of the course is better, but nothing special. 3. [4/81]

***CC of Fairfield,*** *Fairfield. Seth Raynor, 1915.*

The clubhouse setting, on a slope overlooking Long Island Sound, is very impressive, but most of the course occupies low-lying ground and suffers from poor definition—unusual for a Raynor design. Best hole is the par-5 8th along the foreshore. 4. [6/86]

***CC of New Canaan,*** *New Canaan. Original nine holes by Willie Park Jr., extended to 18 by Alfred Tull, 1947, with subsequent revisions by Robert Trent Jones.*

A wooded, rolling parkland course that is notable for three topographically excellent par-5 holes (the 6th, 13th, and 16th), a rare feat in the course design business. Most of the rest of the course is rather forgettable, and I'm curious which holes each architect is responsible for, although I have a hunch. For an affluent club, the course was in pretty crummy shape the one time I saw it. 4. [7/83]

***D. Fairchild Wheeler Municipal GC,*** *Fairfield. Red Course by Robert White, 1933.*

I'm told the No. 1 course isn't so awful but I've only played the No. 2, which should be barred from displaying the same number as Pinehurst No. 2. A terrible mix of severe sidehills, dull flat holes, and intrusions such as power lines. 1. [6/80]

***E. Gaynor Brennan Municipal GC,*** *Stamford. Maurice McCarthy, 1925.*

The other public course in my hometown (there are only two for a city of 110,000), and the main reason Sterling Farms is so popular. They tried to remove the stigma a few years ago by changing its name (it is still known locally as Hubbard Heights), but no name change can make up for a banal routing plan, poor upkeep, and a cramped site. My cousin Ken likes to point out that, owing to a steep sidehill section and one particularly elevated tee, it is not unheard of to see four golfers in the 6th fairway, each of them playing a different hole. 1. [5/78]

***Fairview CC,*** *Greenwich. Robert Trent Jones, 1970.*

A typecast Trent Jones layout, but the steeply sloping site makes it one of his weaker efforts. Tee and green sites required massive cut and fill work, detracting from the natural feeling of being out in the woods, while several uphill holes are less than stimulating. It's also a bitch to walk. 4. [10/89]

***Hartford GC,*** *West Hartford. Donald Ross, 1925, with revisions by Orrin Smith and Bill Mitchell, 1946, William and David Gordon, 1965, Robert Trent Jones, 1966, and Geoffrey Cornish, 1972.*

Think enough people have tinkered with this course? Well, they've just now hired Stephen Kay to "restore" it. There isn't much old-time character left, although there are a couple of outstanding holes—the par-4 7th, with a diagonal drive across a creek, and the long par-3 8th, both with tiny greens. Otherwise, its reputation is more as a well-heeled club than an outstanding course. 5. [10/91]

***Millbrook Club,*** *Greenwich. Geoffrey Cornish, 1963, with revisions by Frank Duane and Stephen Kay.*

An affluent housing community club with nine holes tightly but pleasantly packed into the wooded, rocky terrain. Several of its golf holes are pretty good, but any recommendation must be tempered with a severe thunderstorm warning: when it rains, Millbrook's 8th fairway is the low point of Fairfield County. 4. [10/88].

***New Haven CC,*** *Hamden. Willie Park, Jr., 1920.*

A conservative club and a fairly sedate, well-groomed course, little changed since 1920. The front nine ascends a ridge overlooking the clubhouse, with the back nine below. There are a couple of wonderful greens, including the par-4 1st; but the relatively large greens and preponderance of 390-yard par-4's fail to give it much bite, and there's no room to expand significantly. 5. [10/94]

***Patterson Club,*** *Fairfield. Robert Trent Jones, 1947.*

A classic example of Trent Jones' early period—a parkland layout featuring savagely rolling greens. Sadly, but also typical of Jones' style, there is a lack of memorable individual holes. 4. [6/86]

***Richter Park GC,*** *Danbury. Edward Ryder, 1964.*

Strictly in the context of a public course, this one is pretty good, but that's not saying much. The layout is just a bit better than "blah," helped considerably by the pleasant, rolling, wooded site, but the holes that have the most potential or visual interest are the worst architecturally. Just a few years ago this was rated one of the 50 best public courses in the United States, but the advent of new "upscale daily-fee" courses in other states has certainly passed it by. 4. [6/88]

***Round Hill Club,*** *Greenwich. Walter Travis, 1920, with modifications by Robert Trent Jones.*

A long-in-the-tooth club with an excellent little course, although it suffered greatly from the Dutch Elm blight. There are a couple of really excellent holes, the 2nd and the sidehill 16th, both of them classic short par-5 holes. 5. [8/80]

***The Stanwich Club,*** *Greenwich. William and David Gordon, 1960.*

A lot of people actually consider this to be the best course in Connecticut, which is a sad commentary on the competition. It's a difficult course—7,000 yards fraught with hazards, the ideal local qualifying site for U.S. Opens—but, like so many courses of its generation, it lacks any distinct character of its own, apart from its Z-shaped par-5's, which may be a Gordon trademark. The one mitigating factor is that it's among the most immaculately conditioned courses in America, with lightning-fast greens every day. 6. [7/80]

***Sterling Farms GC,*** *Stamford. Geoffrey Cornish and Bill Robinson, 1971.*

The prototypical Cornish layout, designed with modest intentions for a limited budget, and well suited to providing basic golf in an area starved for public courses, though they've grass-faced the bunkering so it no longer looks anything like Cornish's style. The layout is cramped and occasionally falls awkwardly on the hilly property, but there are a few interesting holes, and I hear it's in fabulous condition in recent years. It also has the unique distinction of being half a mile from where I grew up. All towns should have a municipal course this good, and a junior program like they had when I grew up ($1 per round). 3. [8/86]

***TPC of Connecticut,*** *Cromwell. Orrin Smith and Robert J. Ross, 1930; redesign by Pete Dye, 1983–84.*

This course has now been completely redesigned by my former boss Bobby Weed, in-house designer for the PGA Tour, and the latest layout has generated much praise. This is in vivid contrast to the previous version I knew, which was all too symptomatic of the Tournament Players Club chain—excellent from a spectator viewing standpoint, but not a course you would have picked to host a tournament based on the golf it provided. But the real story is complicated: Pete Dye made some band-aid level redesign efforts to a public golf course in order to get the tournament committed here, with the idea of making more extensive alterations later, but before step 2 the Tour bought the golf course and started selling corporate memberships, unwilling to close the course to complete Pete's redesign. The last three holes (which have been pretty much retained, except for new bunkering) are the best gallery holes in the world so far, but hopefully the new layout is less awkward than the old. [10/84]

***Wampanoag CC,*** *West Hartford. Donald Ross, 1924, with revisions by Brian Silva.*

It was several members of this club who started the Donald Ross Society, out of disdain for the changes that were made here a few years ago. The course never belonged on anyone's Top 100 list, but it was a very enjoyable members' course, with an excellent routing on a fairly hilly site: the downhill par-5 6th and the long par-4 15th are still outstanding holes. But the redesign work is incomprehensible: tiny pot bunkers do not belong in this parkland landscape. The club wasted an even larger sum on refurbishing the clubhouse, and at last report was trying to avoid bankruptcy. 4. [10/91]

***Wee Burn CC,*** *Darien. Devereux Emmet, 1923.*

One of the ritzier clubs socially in Fairfield County, and a pretty good golf course, too. The terrain is not as severe as at some of Emmet's early designs in upstate New York, so the architecture is less spectacular but somewhat more polished, and there are quite a number of good holes. 5. [8/80]

***Woodway CC,*** *Darien. Willie Park Jr., 1916, with revisions by Maurice McCarthy and Geoffrey Cornish.*

One of the better country clubs near my boyhood home, but for some reason I'd never even walked it until recently. A major rock-studded hill in the center of the property and a rushing stream in back that has been dammed up in two places to make par-3 holes over water are the principal natural features, and they have been utilized on quite a few holes; but the golf course is too tight in places and a bit too hilly in others. I might have liked it better had not Cornish pushed to include it in the ASGCA/*USA TODAY* ranking of the top courses in America as his token choice—when they're leaving out courses like Los Angeles Country Club for Woodway, it takes on a different light. 4. [10/90]

***Yale University GC,*** *New Haven. Charles Blair Macdonald and Seth Raynor, 1926.*

One of the landmark courses of Macdonald's career, and possibly the only course in my home state worth seeing. The ground was entirely wooded, rocky and extremely hilly, and the course reflects that character today in some of its more severe holes, such as the blind 3rd and roller-coaster 18th, as well as in its notoriously poor conditioning. The par-3 9th hole, with a deep gulley traversing its green, is justifiably world famous, but the long par-4 4th (cited by Ben Crenshaw for its "perfect use of water as a driving hazard") and the freestyle adaptation of the Redan at the 13th are even better. The lack of alternate tees makes it perhaps a little too strenuous for the short hitter and a little short for today's pros, and the lack of an adequate water supply means shabby conditions in droughty years. But the combination of severe bunkering and an alarming set of greens makes Yale a course to remember, and it's far and away the best course to check out if you've got a day to kill in Connecticut. 8. [8/93]

*The 8th green at Yale.*

*—Gossip—*

The only courses I'm even remotely interested in checking out are Shuttle Meadow CC (W. Park), Shenecossett GC (Ross), and the course at Hotchkiss School, designed by former schoolmaster Charles Banks. Also I should mention that while Fishers Island Club is actually part of New York State territory, it is reached via ferry from New London, Connecticut; that way we can claim two exciting courses in the state instead of just Yale.

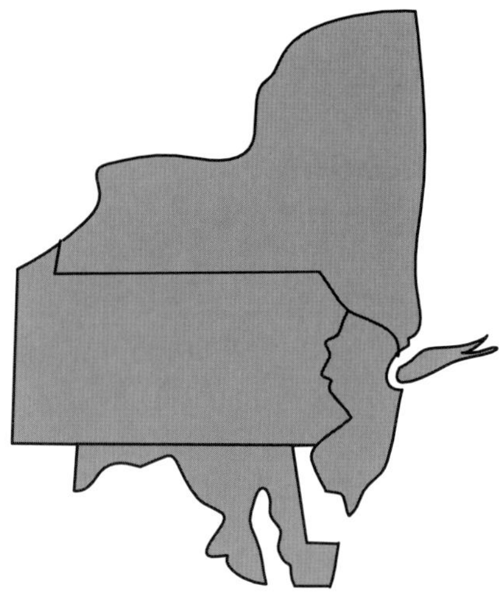

## MID ATLANTIC STATES

Unquestionably, the New York to Washington corridor comprises the greatest concentration of golf courses in the world. Having grown up in the New York area, I'm inclined to rate it alone at the top for the variety of courses between the Hamptons and northern New Jersey; but living in Philadelphia three years ago convinced me that it's not far behind, with a quintet of William Flynn gems backing up Merion and Pine Valley.

It isn't necessarily great land that has been responsible for this concentration of courses—it's great architects. Macdonald and Raynor both came from the New York area, and Robert Trent Jones and son Rees were both based in northern New Jersey; while the Philadelphia school of design began with Hugh Wilson and George Crump, continued through William Flynn and A.W. Tillinghast, who each did the majority of their work in the region (not to mention George Thomas, who took his practice to southern California), and continues to the present day through William and David Gordon and George and Tom Fazio. It's no accident that good courses beget more good courses—every course sets a new standard for others to compete with, while designers learn the secrets of their predecessors.

## NEW YORK

***The Apawamis Club,*** *Rye. E. Maturin Ballou, 1898, with modifications by Tom Winton, George Fazio, and David Postlethwait.*

A *very* conservative club, epitomized by the name given to the double row of cross-bunkers below the 4th green: "Eleanor's Teeth," in honor (?) of the former First Lady. The course hasn't changed much since hosting the U.S. Amateur of 1911, won by Harold Hilton of Hoylake in extra holes after a fortuitous rebound out of the woods at the 37th. I haven't seen the course since my friend David Postlethwait did some reconstruction work to the bunkers: he talked about making some major cuts to eliminate a couple of the half-blind shots that were a feature of the course, but I don't know if he took things that far or not. 4. [7/83]

***The Atlantic GC,*** *Bridgehampton. Rees Jones, 1991.*

I'm just not enamored with The Atlantic; it's the perfect example of the gap between my definition of a great course and *Golf Digest's.* It is indeed "tough but fair," and therefore appealing to low-handicap players; and it's almost perfectly groomed by Bobby Ranum, one of the best superintendents I know. But there's nothing particularly interesting or unique about its golf holes. Most of the long holes are fairly straight, and the mounding runs in ridges down the sides, with practically none of the contour working into the valleyed fairways, so that even with all its native grasses it's obviously unnatural. (The only British links it looks like are Birkdale and Hillside, and why would anyone copy them?) Bottom line: a pretty good course, but if you prefer it to The National, you take scoring way too seriously. 6. [9/93]

***Bedford G & Tennis Club,*** *Bedford. Devereux Emmet, with revisions by Geoffrey Cornish.*

A nice, quiet Westchester country club with a pleasant if not overtaxing parkland course. There are some fair holes, but nothing more. 3. [7/83]

*Bethpage Black, Tillinghast's masterpiece for the public.*

***Bethpage State Park GC's**, Farmingdale. Black course by A.W. Tillinghast, 1936.*

This five-course golf factory handles the brunt of public course traffic for Nassau County, making it horribly crowded and poorly maintained, but the flagship Black course survives as a layout of unmistakable quality throughout. Some of the bunkers are cavernous, and there is plenty of contour at hand to lend character to a number of outstanding holes, including the short par-5 4th, the short 17th, and my own favorite, the 438-yard 5th, with its slanting fairway and summit of green. You have to hit it on an off-peak day—no course in the world is worth a four-hour wait and a six-hour round, which is standard fare here on a summer Sunday—but at least their refusal to allow carts on the Black keeps the schlepps away. 7. [10/90]

***Blind Brook Club**, Rye. George Low, 1916, from a routing by Seth Raynor.*

A very subdued layout serving as home to an all-male club with an elderly membership. Only in one corner of the property (near the convergence of the 4th, 5th, and 12th holes) does the course stand out in my memory. 4. [7/85]

***Calverton Links,** Calverton. Cole Hayes, with advice from Karl Olson, 1994.*

A new little nine-holer for the mid-price market. The soil is perfect and the vegetation (pines, ferns, and an old sand pit) adds some character, but the property is quite narrow at one point and things could get dangerous. Best or worst hole will be the par-5 7th, with some neat natural features, but awfully narrow. [9/93]

***Cardinal Hills GC**, Randolph. Architect unknown.*

The original nine holes here date from the twenties, and though tightly compacted and basic in construction they have quite a bit of character,

thanks to a sidehill site crossed by a deep valley, and some lovely trees. The more recent holes, which comprise the middle of each nine, are very basic, laid out across an open hilltop with push-up greens and no bunkering. We've made some suggestions on revisions. 3. [5/94]

***Century CC,*** *Purchase. H.S. Colt and Charles Alison, 1926, with revisions by Robert Trent Jones.*

One of Westchester County's sleepers, an excellent parkland layout that makes up in strength for what it might lack in character. It is not an outstanding course by Colt's high standard, but it deserves to be better known. For you history buffs, I might add that Ben Hogan spent a lot of time on the practice tee while serving as an assistant pro here. 5. [7/85]

***Clearview GC,*** *Bayview, Queens. William Tucker, 1928.*

I walked this one briefly to see if it was related to Alister MacKenzie's lost Bayside Links, built just after 1930; but apparently most of that course was further down the hill—land that has since been consumed by the Cross Island Parkway and the approach to the Throgs Neck Bridge. Clearview, an American Golf Corp.–managed facility, is a New York City muni in all the usual ways. 2. [4/95]

***Cold Spring CC,*** *Cold Spring Harbor. Charles Blair Macdonald and Seth Raynor, 1923, with revisions by Robert Trent Jones.*

Originally designed as a private course for Otto Kahn's estate, the club was reorganized in 1935. The course is only marginally well preserved, as the hazards were laid out extra-wide on the fairways (one suspects Mr. Kahn was not a good golfer), and subsequent tree-planting has made many bunkers redundant. But there is some good property at holes like the par-4 5th and the 15th, and Kahn's castle home (viewed from beside the 14th or 16th greens) is one of the most impressive buildings in golf. 4. (7/95]

***The Concord Hotel GC,*** *Kiamesha Lake. Championship "Monster" course by Joe Finger, 1964.*

They should call this the "monstrosity" course. It's just a style I hate—too long, too wide open, the greens are way too big, there's too much water, and to make a long story short it's too bad they ever built it. Airmail it to Houston. 4. [5/86]

***Cornell University GC,*** *Ithaca. Robert Trent Jones, 1940.*

A good case study of Jones' architectural career: the course is no great wonder, but it's a good test of golf over a fairly pretty piece of ground, and its design grew on me during my school years, so maybe there is more to Jones' other work than I see on my whirlwind visits. The course was much different for me from the blue tees than the white, even though there's only about 350 yards difference between them. Its best feature is that it's close to campus and seldom crowded on the weekdays, so it was ideal for squeezing in a few holes before dark and getting one's mind off school—except there's not much golf weather in Ithaca during the school year. 4. [6/86]

***CC of Ithaca,*** *Ithaca. Geoffrey Cornish, 1958.*

A fairly dull parkland layout that replaced the old Ithaca Country Club, a Tillinghast layout that was plowed under to create Cornell's North Campus dorms. Wish I'd seen the old one. 3. [10/81]

***CC of Rochester,*** *Rochester. Donald Ross, 1914, with alterations by Robert Trent Jones.*

A pleasant, well-maintained parkland course on less rolling terrain than Oak Hill, but a much more typical country club course, without any of the memorable holes that set its neighbor apart. 4. [10/80]

***CC of Troy,*** *Troy. Walter Travis, 1927, with minor revisions by Geoffrey Cornish and Mark Mungeam, 1990.*

A very good layout that traverses some steep hills. The greens are still the Travis originals and full of character, and the combination of serious contouring with the general grade of the hill can make deciphering the correct line quite difficult. Unfortunately, the original bunkering has largely been lost (though the club is now taking pains to try and restore some of it), and the "Johnny Pine-Tree seeds" have destroyed the open character of the course, which must have been quite something, since few holes run directly parallel. Hopefully they will succeed in desanitizing the last thirty years of committee work. 6. [8/93]

***Crag Burn Club,*** *East Aurora. Robert Trent Jones, 1971.*

One of my favorite Jones courses, largely because I didn't expect much of it to begin with, I suppose. Laid out on the site of an old farm well out in the suburbs of Buffalo, it features many good holes without being over-stylized like many Jones layouts, and the maintenance decision to let long grasses grow between the holes gives it a very nice look. I don't think the par-5 2nd hole is as good as Scott Verplank thinks it is (he put it among the best holes in the country), but there are plenty of good reasons to check out Crag Burn. 6. [6/86]

***The Creek Club,*** *Locust Valley. Charles Blair Macdonald and Seth Raynor, 1923, with restoration by Tom Doak and Gil Hanse, 1992.*

See the "Gourmet's Choice." 7. [6/95]

***Deepdale Club,*** *Manhasset. Dick Wilson, 1956.*

Maybe the most reclusive club in America, a vestige of the USGA/Calcutta scandal of the early 1960s, Deepdale avoids notoriety to the extent that if you're on a course-rating panel, they'll ask the members not to bring you out. Too bad—it's one of Wilson's very best, an excellent layout in prime condition, as you might expect of a course that (outings aside) hosts maybe ten rounds per day. The layout has an overabundance of sharp doglegs, but there are a lot of good, strong par-4 holes here, and the greens are notorious for their combination of speed and tilt—in fact, the long par-4 15th must just be unplayable, with the greens above ten on the Stimpmeter. 7. [8/94]

***Engineers GC,*** *Roslyn. Herbert Strong, 1918, with revisions by Devereux Emmet, 1921, William Gordon, Frank Duane, and Gil Hanse.*

A sporty course with cult potential—you'll either love it or hate it. The hilly property gives plenty of opportunity for creative shotmaking, and hopefully the new long-range plan (under the auspices of my former assistant, Gil Hanse) will get them to mow out aprons so golfers can take advantage of the bounces above the greens, instead of simply being screwed by the bounces to the low side. There are several strong candidates for lists of the best, worst, and most unusual holes and greens, but the signature hole is certainly the 94-yard 14th, which is being restored to the routing after years laying fallow. With a narrow shelf of green falling slightly away from the tee, deep bunkers on both sides, and a steep fall to the right off the ridge, it earned the "Two or Twenty" moniker given to it in the twenties; but the fall-away green is large enough to stand up to traffic and still skinny enough to make you pucker up on the tee. 6. [6/95]

***En-Joie GC,*** *Endicott. Ernie Smith, 1927, with revisions by Bill Mitchell, and later by David Postlethwait, 1983–86.*

A tightly packed public course that takes great pride in its role as host to the annual B. C. Open, one of the few low-key Tour events left these days. The numerous parallel fairways have encouraged the club to spend tournament profits on tree-planting programs that ran wild until recently, when they decided to start tinkering with the architecture of the course instead. Some of the more recent changes have been done with "stadium golf" in mind, and the locals are giddy over being able to play on a course that is up to date with the latest trendy architecture, even if it doesn't really fit in with the rest of the course. A clear example of giving the public what it wants. 3. [10/84]

***Fishers Island Club,*** *Fishers Island. Seth Raynor, 1917.*

One of the great "hidden gems" of the world, it's located at the west tip of a summer resort island in the middle of Long Island Sound, populated by the Hobe Sound crowd. Esthetically, this is one of the world's most beautiful courses, thanks to the elevations of the property and the tremendous views from both the north and south shorelines out across the Sound; but it is one course where the "engineered" look of Raynor's greens and bunkers detracts from the natural beauties of the property. I personally think it's becoming a bit overrated in the *GOLF Magazine* rankings, but I cannot deny that on a breezy summer's day, Fishers Island is one of the most idyllic places possible for a round of golf. 7. [7/85]

*Fishers Island—secluded and spectacular.*

***Fresh Meadow CC,*** *Great Neck. H.S. Colt and Charles Alison, 1925, with revisions by Orrin Smith and Bill Mitchell, 1938.*

The original Fresh Meadow course, a Tillinghast layout that hosted the 1932 U.S. Open (won by Gene Sarazen), was plowed under for housing after W.W. II, and the club moved here, taking over the original Lakeville CC course. It's a somewhat hilly layout, but lacks the detail work around the greens and in the contouring of the bunkers that might have made it a success. 4. [4/86]

***Garden City Golf Club,*** *Garden City. Devereux Emmet, 1899, and Walter Travis, 1906, with some modifications by Tom Doak, 1991–94.*

See the "Gourmet's Choice." 8. [6/95]

***Garrison GC,*** *Garrison-on-Hudson. Dick Wilson, 1963.*

I did a double-take when I looked up who had built this one; it's notable for steep inclines of fairway and narrow holes through trees, which isn't the typical Wilson style at all. The architecture is less than classic, but it still might be a pleasant change of pace after one too many of the gussied-up park courses common to Westchester. The name is derived from the property's previous tour of duty as a Revolutionary War era fort. 4. [10/84]

***Hillandale GC,*** *Huntington. Hal Purdy, 1961.*

One of the most rinky-dink little courses I've seen, out to the west of Cayuga Lake where nobody would ever look. (Hardly a prime location for a public course.) Memorable only because it consisted of ten holes, with alternate tees to be used for the front and back nines and then separate 9th and 18th holes. 1. [5/80]

***Inwood CC,*** *Inwood. Original layout 1901, with modifications by Herbert Strong, 1911, Hal Purdy, and Frank Duane.*

Basically the same course as it was when Bobby Jones won his first major championship here, although silly tree-planting on the marshside holes and loss of form on the bunkering have detracted from it. Look for the plaque in the 18th rough that marks the spot from which Jones hit a 2-iron across the lagoon to six feet on the last hole of the Open—even though you may produce the same shot today with your Ping 5-iron. Just across the marsh from Kennedy Airport—look down next time you're flying in. 5. [9/95]

***Knollwood CC,*** *Elmsford. A.W. Tillinghast, c. 1921, with revisions by Charles Banks.*

Another good park layout with two memorable holes: the superb 18th, a long dogleg-right par-4 along the length of a narrow pond that must be crossed by both drive and approach (but also possessing the natural contour that most holes of this description lack), and the 90-yard 19th, which was constructed to settle ties on the walk from the 18th green back to the clubhouse. 5. [4/84]

***Leatherstocking GC,*** *Cooperstown. Devereux Emmet, 1909.*

An excellent diversion if you get tired of the stuffiness inside the Baseball Hall of Fame. The short, old-fashioned layout touches both the lake and the hills across the north road out of town, featuring well-shaped greens, a few leftover cross-bunkers from the early days, and a memorable par-5 18th hole along the lakeshore with its tee on an island 150 yards out in Otesaga Lake. 5. [6/80]

*Looking up the Hudson from the 9th green at Garrison.*

***Links at Hiawatha Landing,*** *Owego. Brian Silva, 1994.*

A new public layout totally shaped from a floodplain site adjacent to the Susquehanna River. There wasn't much here to work with; but I was mostly preoccupied with trying to figure out who in Owego was going to support a $3 million daily-fee layout. [5/94]

***The Links Golf Club,*** *North Hills. Charles Blair Macdonald, 1919; plowed under, 1985.*

In a eulogy, there is always the tendency to dismiss the weaknesses of the departed and canonize him for the most basic of human qualities. I suppose the same is true of golf courses, especially since their mortality is not preordained; no good golf course should ever face the fate of The Links, which ceased to exist under the combined pressures of rising real estate taxes and a membership so reclusive that its number dwindled to nothing. Others remember it as one of the easier courses on Long Island to put in a good score, but for me the usual Macdonald/Raynor holes were a perfect fit on the small property. At 225 yards, the left-to-right Redan 13th was certainly the most severe tribute to that famous North Berwick hole ever constructed—even if you played safely off the tee, the least error on the pitch to the green could spell disaster. And there were several good holes of its own, above all the par-4 5th, with its approach across a deep valley. My round of golf here with P.B. Dye, on a foggy, drizzly afternoon when both of us understood that the course was soon doomed to die, was one of my most memorable golf games. R.I.P. [4/84]

***The Maidstone Club,*** *East Hampton. Willie and John Park, 1899.*

One of the oldest clubs in America, and a social institution even in the socially elite precinct of the Hamptons. It is an odd course in that it has two distinct characters, with the holes closer to the clubhouse traversing inland lagoons, and the midsection of the course on true linksland protected by a narrow strip of dunes from the Atlantic itself. The par-4 9th is a classic British links type of hole, and the 14th with the ocean for a backdrop must rank among the country's great short holes. The course is just 6,332 yards in all, but there is usually plenty of wind about to liven things up. 7. [9/94]

***Mark Twain GC,*** *Elmira. Donald Ross, 1937.*

I must credit my brother Dave for this "find," a real hidden gem laid out on a hillside and operated by the town of Elmira. There are some wonderful holes and some wild greens, and it's in country-club shape, though in their reluctance to modify the course they have lost the shapes of the bunkers by failing to edge them. But no complaining—for $12, it's the best value in golf I've seen in years. P.S.—Why Mark Twain? After all his world travels, he died and was buried in Elmira. 5. [5/94]

***Meadow Brook Club,*** *Jericho. Dick Wilson, 1955.*

The Atlantic of the fifties, and one of the reasons I've never been able to understand Dick Wilson's popularity as an architect. It's a very tough "test of golf" from the back tees, with large bunkers flanking the elevated greens, and plenty of length, but I can barely remember one hole from another. I suppose there must be a certain subtlety to it, and I've never been back to reassess it after my one walk-through, but I just didn't see any character to the place. 5. [6/80]

***Metropolis CC,*** *Greenburgh. Herbert Strong, 1924.*

Just another of the many reasonably good parkland courses of Westchester, set on hillier ground than the majority, with one renowned hole, the narrow downhill dogleg par-4 6th. 4. [4/84]

***Nassau CC,*** *Glen Cove. Devereux Emmet, c. 1915, with revisions by Herbert Strong and Frank Duane.*

Another old-fashioned layout and sister club to the pair from Locust Valley, although it lacks the strength and condition of Piping Rock or the majesty of The Creek. The old photos I've seen show some wild bunkering, and at various times they've started to restore some of it, but every time they approach the old stuff the membership complains it's too difficult and they back off. 4. [8/92]

***National Golf Links of America,*** *Southampton. Charles Blair Macdonald, 1909.*

See the "Gourmet's Choice." 10. [8/95]

***Nissequogue CC,*** *St. James. Edgar Senne.*

The early holes head out to Long Island Sound, and the par-3 2nd, from a high tee along the beach, is spectacular; but it quickly turns back inland for some hilly holes as uneven in quality as the terrain itself. The only other memorable hole is the par-3 9th, with a hard-to-believe sidehill-shelved green. 4. [3/95]

***North Shore CC,*** *Glen Head. Charles Banks, I think.*

One of the strangest courses I've run across. Cornish and Whitten's research credits this course to A.W. Tillinghast, but they've got to be wrong, because all the most dramatic greens are dead ringers for Banks' Whippoorwill. The steeply hilly site makes for some severe holes, and a couple of the greens are as wild as I've ever seen: multi-tiered affairs with three or four feet of elevation between the tiers, as at the 14th, 15th, and 17th. The most memorable hole is the par-5 16th, about 550 yards, featuring a great approach over a deep undulating valley the last 225 yards to the green—but the tee is back in a chute of trees, so you have to snap-hook your drive if you want to get more than 210 yards without going through the fairway. That's the way the whole course goes: it has some great pieces, but never quite puts them all together. 4. [10/90]

***Oak Hill CC,*** *Rochester. East and West courses by Donald Ross, 1926; East course modified by Robert Trent Jones and George and Tom Fazio.*

Oak Hill East is consistently ranked among the 50 best courses in the world by my *GOLF Magazine* panel, and anyone who watched the 1995 Ryder Cup knows it can still keep good players at bay. But I wouldn't rank the course that highly, since a lot of the appeal of the course was its honest, singular character, and the Fazio holes are so different. It's hard to believe that anybody would tear up one of the best holes in the country (the old par-4 6th East) in order to make a redesign scheme work, but it was done here. And who really wants to watch Curtis Strange bogey home from 16? 7. [6/82]

Oak Hill West, in contrast, wasn't as good a layout and hasn't been landscaped quite as extensively as its big sister, but it is a more authentic Ross design, with relatively little tampering down through the years. It's not of U.S. Open length, but it's big enough for most of us, and some members insist the back nine is the best nine holes at the club today. 6. [6/82]

***Piping Rock Club,*** *Locust Valley. Charles Blair Macdonald, 1917, with revisions by Robert Trent Jones and restoration by Pete Dye (Tom Doak and Woody Millen), 1985.*

Not at the top of the list of Macdonald layouts, but certainly a fine golf course in its own right, laid out over open parkland on terrain reminiscent of Chicago Golf Club. It was a bit on the short and wide-open side for today's big hitters, but the revisions with which I assisted have supplied needed difficulty

without diverging from the Macdonald character. Too bad you missed the "Principal's Nose" hazard I added in the middle of the fairway at the uphill par-5 10th hole; it was the subject of some Woking-style debate before they removed it. 6. [6/95]

***Quaker Ridge GC,*** *Scarsdale. A.W. Tillinghast, 1926, with alterations by Robert Trent Jones.*

Perhaps a more honest layout than its illustrious neighbors at Winged Foot, the Quaker Ridge course relies more on natural undulations and less on wicked greens for its challenge; but the club has shunned tournaments as steadfastly as Winged Foot has embraced them, so that Quaker Ridge's reputation is largely a matter of hearsay. I personally believe it is an excellent parkland layout, especially in the stretch from the 4th through 7th holes, but a bit of a letdown on the back nine. All in all it is no more outstanding than Ridgewood in New Jersey, and not as unique as San Francisco Golf Club or Somerset Hills, within the context of Tillinghast's career. 8. [7/83]

***Rockaway Hunting Club,*** *Cedarhurst. Tom Bendelow, 1900, with revisions by A.W. Tillinghast.*

More of the Bendelow routing than of the Tillinghast polish is in evidence today; on a large-scale map, the bayside site looks promising, but the reality is a disappointment. The par-4 9th hole along the water made my *GOLF Magazine* list of the best holes in America, but I didn't find it any better than a hundred other long par-4 holes along the water. Some depth to the bunkering would help it, but deeper bunkers would be underwater at high tide. 4. [6/86]

***St. Andrews GC,*** *Hastings-on-Hudson. Club founded 1888; present course originally laid out by Harry Tallmadge and W.H. Tucker, 1896, and completely remodeled by Jack Nicklaus and Bob Cupp, 1985.*

Many of you may know the history of this club, and of Nicklaus' intervention to "save" it, but architecturally the result is a dismal failure. The original course was quite cramped, and had only one hole worth seeing, a short par-4 with a 150-foot drop from tee to fairway, encouraging big hitters to see how far (and, as a result, how far off line) they could hit it. The revision screws up this hole by lengthening it so that no one is tempted to take a rip at the green, spacing the original 18 holes out into 15 newfangled but not particularly great ones, and adding three new holes on ground atop the hill next to the new condos. Clearly, judging from the ridiculous new par-5 11th, the scheme was more about condos than golf. 3. [7/88]

***St. George's G & CC,*** *Stony Brook. Devereux Emmet, 1917.*

Emmet built this course from part of his own estate, which makes it worth seeing. The property is fairly cramped, and divided by a busy road; it has also been excessively planted over the years to try and protect one fairway from another, spoiling the views across pretty expanses of fescue waving on the hills. There are several holes of merit, mostly in the latter half: the long 12th and 13th are he-men holes, and the par-5 18th around a deep hollow would be gorgeous, if they could pull out the cedar trees inside the dogleg without getting someone on the 15th green killed by an over-ambitious pull-hook. 5. [5/95]

***Sands Point CC,*** *Sands Point. George E. Reynolds, c. 1900, expanded to 18 holes by A.W. Tillinghast; revisions by Robert Trent Jones, Frank Duane, Stephen Kay, and Ron Forse.*

A wealthy club that is now trying to restore features it destroyed years ago, in trying to keep up with the times. There are several good par-4 holes on the front side and one massive par-5 on the back. 5. [5/95]

***Shinnecock Hills GC,*** *Southampton. Club founded 1891; present course by William Flynn with Toomey and Dick Wilson, 1930.*

I'm impressed how simple and straightforward Shinnecock is—the greens and bunkering aren't all that different from Flynn's parkland designs, but the beautiful native roughs and the dramatic undulations of the property give it a character all its own. It's not really a links-style golf course, as you don't have much opportunity to play bump-and-run shots on the ryegrass fairways, and the changes of elevation play a role. (The middle holes at Maidstone are closer to a true British links.) But it is one of the game's greatest examinations in using the wind, as the two prevailing winds (which are 90 degrees opposed), combined with the frequent changes of direction in the routing, ensure that you'll have your fill of the wind from all quarters. A great course to play every day, as well as a proven championship venue; not many courses can claim both. 10. [9/95]

***Sleepy Hollow CC,*** *Scarborough-on-Hudson. Original layout by C.B. Macdonald, with major revisions by A.W. Tillinghast and Robert Trent Jones.*

This is probably Westchester's best kept secret, a wealthy club set high up on a ridge overlooking the Hudson River. It is beautifully maintained and possesses some marvelous holes, among them Tillinghast's long par-4 8th with a heaving fairway, the short par-3 10th across a pond at the upper end of the course, and Macdonald's short 16th across a ravine that commands a magnificent river view. 7. [5/88]

***Springville CC,*** *Springville. Architect unknown.*

Most of the course is relatively flat and dull, except for the odd interrupted fairway mowing patterns, which are interesting at first but quickly grow annoying. But the far end of the course descends by narrow tree-lined corridors into the Cattaraugus River gorge, with some wild and woolly results—the downhill par-3 12th and par-5 13th both deserving to be on a list of the "sportiest" holes in golf. They're now building some new holes on the flats, in order to eliminate or change some of the excesses of the gorge holes—a plan that will either vastly improve the course or strip it of all its character. 3. [6/95]

***Suffolk County GC at Timber Point****, Great River. Original 18 by Colt and Alison, c. 1925; expanded to 27 holes for the county by Bill Mitchell, 1972.*

In the dim past, this course was one of Pine Valley-type island fairways surrounded by beach sand, with a uniquely spectacular open look to it; but when the club went bankrupt and the county squeezed things together to expand the facility to 27 holes, most of the character went out the window. There is still one hole—the 5th on the present Blue course, a par-3 with a Gibraltar-like profile against the bay—where traces of the past can be appreciated. 3. [10/82]

***Tam O'Shanter Club****, Muttontown. Architect unknown, c. 1960.*

One of the most poorly constructed courses of all time, with green sites located atop sinkholes and dumping grounds or cut into the sides of hills where water seeps out during heavy rains. The superintendent asked me for advice on rebuilding his 9th green; I got out of there as fast as I could. You'd have to blow up the whole course to accomplish anything. 2. [10/85]

***Town of Hempstead GC at Lido**, Lido Beach. Robert Trent Jones and Frank Duane, 1965.*

Just your basic blah municipal layout today, giving no hint of its storied past, but consider that when the original *Golf Illustrated* ran a series on America's greatest courses in the mid-twenties, their first three issues were devoted to The National, Pine Valley, and *Lido Beach.* That gives you some idea of the prestige achieved by C.B. Macdonald's artificial links erected between the Atlantic and Reynolds Channel on the real estate now occupied by housing just to the west of the present course. Someday I'd like to try and recreate it on another site, or at least the famous alternate-route 4th hole and the finisher, which was an adaptation of Alister MacKenzie's 1914 *Country Life* contest-winner. Current layout: 2. [11/81]

***Village Club of Sands Point,** Sands Point. Original nine by Robert Trent Jones, 1954, with renovations by Frank Duane.*

A fairly dull nine holes developed from the Guggenheim estate by IBM as a corporate retreat, but recently bought out by the town for a private village club. We are studying expansion to 18 holes, which could have great potential if the town's non-golfers will allow us to use the best parts of the property. 3. [6/95]

***Village of Lake Success GC,** Lake Success. C.B. Macdonald and Seth Raynor, with modifications by Orrin Smith.*

The original Deepdale, this course was abandoned by the club in the 1950s and turned over to the village when the present Deepdale was built. It looks like a Macdonald course in the bunkering and green shapes, but falls far short in the design of the individual holes, whether due to revisions or an inferior routing. 3. [10/94]

***Westchester CC,** Rye. Walter Travis, 1922, with modifications by William Flynn, Tom Winton, Alfred Tull, Joe Finger, and Rees Jones.*

I've only seen the course as it's set up for the Westchester Classic, which I believe is the West course with its nines reversed. It occupies much hillier ground than all the other area courses, except for Metropolis and Garrison, but the contours are well employed in the routing so that vicious climbs are kept to a minimum. A good layout, and of course it has all the facilities now *de rigeur* for a tournament site: the clubhouse makes Riviera's look like a mud hut. 5. [6/86]

***Westhampton CC,** Westhampton. Seth Raynor, 1915, with revisions by Brian Silva.*

Raynor's first solo design, Westhampton is a short, tightly packed seaside/village course with some unusual holes and greens, clearly done before he had his ideas down pat. The first two holes are short and straightforward and the punchbowl par-3 3rd is strange, but from there through the 15th is a series of strong holes that continues to hold its own. 5. [9/95]

***Whippoorwill Club**, Armonk. Charles Banks, 1930.*

Bryant Gumbel is a member here, and he must like his golf on the "sporty" side, because Whippoorwill is a real roller-coaster ride. Some consider the course Banks' masterpiece, maybe because his steam-shovel approach to creating deep bunkers and elevated greens worked well on this extremely hilly site. Anyway, the course features some of the prototype Macdonald/Raynor holes (including a great "Biarritz" 8th, and a ridiculous "Redan" 11th over a pond), but it's the hilly par-5 6th with an unbelievable green and the split-fairway par-4 14th that are the most distinctive holes. Worth a look; I'm curious if it's really playable. 5. [3/90]

***Winged Foot GC**, Mamaroneck. East and West courses both designed by A.W. Tillinghast, 1923.*

Winged Foot West is unquestionably one of the country's most demanding tests, perfectly filling the club's prescription to their architect for "a man-sized course." The greens are small and steeply banked, and every one but the last is flanked by deep bunkers to both sides, making them especially small targets for the long-iron approaches all too often required. Still, there is nothing intrinsically unique about the course in contour or scenery; it seems like one ought to be able to build a course just like it on any piece of parkland, given enough land and the courage to build green complexes this severe. 9. [5/84]

Winged Foot East, on the other hand, is a bone of much greater contention. There are those who believe it's better than the West course, because it has more variety of terrain (including a lake and a stream in play) and relies less on length and steep greens for its challenge; but I think it is sorely lacking for great holes such as the 10th or 18th (or even the 11th) on the West course. Its closest approach used to be the East 10th, a good shortish par-4 with the great elm by the clubhouse for a backdrop; but without The Tree, even it is just another hole. 6. [5/84]

***Wolferts Roost CC**, Albany. A.W. Tillinghast, 1921, with seven new holes and other revisions by Leonard Ranier, 1931.*

A well-respected club for its close-in location to the capital, but the steadily sloping site and the small acreage handicap the layout, and the trees planted over the last thirty years to divide parallel holes have crowded out much attempt at strategy. The signature par-3 15th over a pond is right below the clubhouse. There's a USGA decision to confirm that the shot that carries the green and a small berm behind it, catches the driveway, and rolls down the hill out the front gate must indeed be treated as out of bounds. 4. [8/93]

*—Gossip—*

I believe I've covered the best of New York State, but so many fine architects have worked here that there's always something more to explore. On Long Island, I have yet to see Montauk Downs out near the tip. In the metropolitan area the big news is Hudson National, a Tom Fazio mega-project north of Sleepy Hollow that is set to open next year. Upstate, they tell me that the McGregor Links in Saratoga, a wild Devereux Emmet layout, has been bastardized but is still good fun, and there's also the restored Donald Ross layout at the Sagamore resort on Lake George, which gets outstanding reviews. For a real sleeper, try The Park Club near Buffalo, or Donald Ross' Teugega CC in Rome.

## NEW JERSEY

***Atlantic City CC**, Northfield. William Flynn, 1923, with modifications by Leo Fraser.*

I didn't really know what to expect from this course, and though I didn't fall in love with it, I liked what I saw. The majority of the layout is parkland with some undulations, but the back nine includes a few flattish seaside-type holes overlooking the marshes and Atlantic City in the distance, with combination waste area/cart paths and a bit of water in play. The greens are modestly interesting, although a couple have obviously been recently modified and have out-of-place modern edges. 6. [6/89]

***Baltusrol GC**, Springfield. Upper and Lower courses by A.W. Tillinghast, 1922, with major modifications to the Lower course by Robert Trent Jones, 1953.*

Baltusrol Lower is one of the few good examples of golf course redesign I've seen; originally the Upper course had far and away the more character of the two, but Jones' strengthening efforts brought the Lower course up to modern championship length without infringing upon the subtle character of the original Tillinghast design. There are several excellent holes, notably the back-to-back par-5's at the finish, the dogleg 13th, and the short 4th (though I think that hole is a bit overrated). On the other hand, the holes at the far end of the course are resigned to flat ground and some of them are still fairly ordinary, so I hesitate to rate the Lower course as high as 8. [6/82]

Baltusrol Upper, in contrast, is not quite up to championship length these days, but sits higher up on the hill than its big sister and remains an untinkered-with Tillinghast design full of character. The starting and finishing holes represent some of the best steep sidehill architecture I have seen. Stay aware of the fall of the mountain on your putts and you'll enjoy this course. 6. [7/85]

***Canoe Brook CC**, Summit. South course by Charles Alison, North by Alfred Tull, with lots of revisions.*

I only saw the composite course set up here for the 1983 Women's Amateur, which I'm assuming was mostly Alison's work, although I never asked. It struck me as a pretty good layout, but I can hardly remember any of it today; I was distracted by one of the contestants. Still, if I can't remember the holes, they couldn't have been that great. 4. [8/83]

***Essex County CC**, West Orange. Charles Banks, 1930, with revisions by A.W. Tillinghast and Frank Duane.*

Another hilly layout, Essex County struck me as a fairly good course when I walked it, but in retrospect there's only one hole that really stands out in my memory—the par-3 11th, across a gorge and uphill over a narrow stream rushing down the hillside, which has to be one of the best par-3 holes in the Metropolitan area. 5. [3/90]

***Forsgate CC**, Jamesburg. East course by Charles Banks, 1931; West course by Hal Purdy, 1974.*

At one time, the old *GOLF Magazine* book, *Great Golf Courses You Can Play*, suggested that Forsgate was in the peer group of Pine Valley and Baltusrol. Guess what? It wasn't. The West course, a Hal Purdy contraption, is completely forgettable. But the East course is quite a different kettle of fish. Banks was a Macdonald protégé, and apparently was not bound by the general set of dimensions to which Macdonald limited himself: Forsgate East has deeper bunkers and more daring mounds within the contours of the green than any course I can think of. Steep and deep aside, there are several wonderful holes, including the punchbowl 5th, the long 8th, and the par-3 3rd, with its very severe green. However, the new ownership was proceeding with a plan to commandeer the 5th through 7th holes for housing space, and the replacements they were preparing would ruin the continuity of the course. East course: 6. West course: 3. [9/89]

**Hollywood GC**, *Deal. Walter Travis, 1899, with modifications by Dick Wilson, 1953.*

A super sleeper. I had seen old pictures of a couple of the short holes here from way-back issues of the USGA Green Section Record, but I didn't even know whether the course still existed until Rees Jones mentioned it to me a couple of years ago. It is not a long course, but the detail work to the greens and bunkers is some of the neatest I've stumbled across in a long time. Travis' huge, finicky fairway bunkers are just plain neat, and Wilson's work blends well. Among the holes I enjoyed were the wild par-3 4th, with its outlandish bunkering; the par-5 7th, with its four-tiered green; the 9th with its great back-left pin placement; the extremely long par-4 12th, followed by the short par-4 13th; and finally the long par-3 17th, with another fantastic green. 7. [10/89]

*The 7th green at Hollywood.*

**Lawrenceville School GC**, *Lawrenceville. Original nine by John Reid, c. 1895, with revisions by William and David Gordon, 1953.*

A private school layout whose tattered condition belies the wealth of the school's benefactors. The sedate property limits the possibilities, but the lack of fairway irrigation makes for hard summers. Several holes still follow the routing of John Reid, who laid out the original American course, St. Andrew's. 2, but the students can't make the most of this rating. [4/95]

**Medford Village GC**, *Medford Lakes. William Gordon, 1964.*

I first heard of this course in the middle of a discussion of great courses in the USA with some members of Riviera, when out of the blue the "Sunny Jim Golf Course" came up. The member described it as "like Pine Valley, only narrower." It was my duty to check it out.

Turns out that "Sunny Jim" (whoever he was) sold his course to the members, and it is now a member of that elite group of good courses which nobody knows about: top Jewish clubs. Because these clubs are generally out of the loop of golf course rankings, a good one can easily slip by undetected for years. Franklin Hills, in the Detroit suburbs, is probably the best example, along with Hollywood and Lake Merced; Medford Village is another. Designed by Gordon, whose work I know little about, it is a classic parkland course in the Tillinghast mold. Except for the lack of good fairway conditions and a somewhat too aggressive planting program (there are a lot of narrow dogleg holes), this could be of Quaker Ridge caliber. Instead, it's just a very good course that will probably continue to escape notice. 6. [10/89]

**Metedeconk National GC**, *Jackson Township. Robert Trent Jones and Roger Rulewich, 1987.*

I don't understand how this has become recognized as one of the best new courses; apart from the peace and quiet it enjoys as an ultra-private club (there are only 100 members, and they're building a third nine to handle the play), it doesn't have that much going for it. Much has been made about the thick undergrowth to the sides of the holes, which is supposed to be like Pine Valley, but here it's so thick you can't find your ball to attempt recovery. Inside the grassed area, I thought the golf course was fairly

dull, though tougher than it looks from the tees—the exact opposite of MacKenzie's ideal that players enjoy a hole that looks impossible, but is not really so difficult. At least it's not busy: I whizzed around the back nine in 45 minutes to go check out Hollywood, and I made the right call. 5. [10/89]

***Mountain Ridge GC**, West Caldwell. Donald Ross, 1929.*

A well-kept, well-heeled course on the western outskirts of the metropolitan area. There are several fine holes, perhaps the most memorable being the downhill par-4 1st, with a severe mound in the back right portion of the green, making for some tough pin placements. No weaknesses, but nothing really special. 5. [10/90]

***Pine Valley GC**, Clementon. George Crump, 1912–18, with advice from H.S. Colt, and finished after Crump's death by Hugh and Allan Wilson.*

See the "Gourmet's Choice." 10. [6/80]

***Pine Valley GC**, Clementon. Short Course by Tom Fazio and Ernie Ransome, 1992.*

Consciously deciding not to try and compete with the best 18 holes in the world, the Pine Valley brass came up with an intriguing concept for this ten-holer: to try and recreate some of the big course's most interesting second shots, making the "tees" of the par-3 course full fairways so that the approaches could be tackled from any length or kind of lie. The latter concept is terrific, and makes the course as interesting as the player wants it to be. However, the former doesn't really work, since the main thrill of Pine Valley is the threat of the jungle off the tees and the unique recovery shots required if one strays. (If you really want it to play like Crump's masterpiece, let your opponent chuck your ball in the bushes on every tee, and see if you can break 50.) I would have tried to build some original holes in the Pine Valley mold, but in fact some of the copies are terrific, and the two original holes are only marginally interesting. 6. [7/92]

***Plainfield CC**, Plainfield. Donald Ross, 1903.*

The architect and date listed here are misleading; the club swears the only changes from the original Ross layout were made by Ross himself, but those little ponds scattered around the course and the sweeping bunker lines don't look like Ross' work to me. Whatever its origin, it is a really good course, with plenty of length and some treacherous greens for championship speeds, and there are a host of good holes headed by the long par-5 12th. 7. [8/87]

***Ridgewood GC**, Ridgewood. A.W. Tillinghast, 1929.*

One drawback of having 27 good holes is that it's tough for visitors to figure out which two nines form the "championship" configuration, and thus such courses are often overlooked in rankings of the great ones. Fortunately, the rankings have finally caught up with this, one of Tillinghast's finest efforts. The West and East nines form the "regular" course, but each of the three nines has a couple of holes to recommend it; personally I'd have to rank the par-4 South 9th with any hole on the property. The Tudor-style clubhouse is a beautiful bonus. 7. [4/84]

***Somerset Hills CC**, Bernardsville. A.W. Tillinghast, 1918.*

A quiet little club just a few miles from the USGA headquarters, this course is a terrific example of Tillinghast's early work, using every corner of a tight property well. It is somewhat short by modern standards, but the tiny, treacherous greens suppress any thoughts of very low scores. The short holes are an excellent set, and the longer holes are made by the contouring of the greens. The club spends far less on course upkeep than most in this class, if that bothers you. 7. [8/87]

***Stone Harbor GC,*** *Cape May Court House. Desmond Muirhead, 1988.*

Without a doubt, this is the most ridiculous golf course I have seen to date. Muirhead has an absurd interpretation of how to employ psychological hazards; he thinks that a bunker in the shape of an ax, say, will induce fear in the player's subconscious, instead of a normal bunker located in a strategic spot. The tees are built up unusually (and uncomfortably) high, so you can see all the goofy bunkers. In short, it is a golf course that makes no effort at all to blend into the landscape, and the only golfing value it possesses is probably an accident.

Muirhead likened his island green/island bunkers par-3 7th hole to the legend of Jason and his ship the *Argo* passing between clashing rocks; if there were any justice, the first hurricane to visit the Jersey shore would have sent the Argo crashing into a bunker and sunk it. I understand that the members have since filled in the gaps between bunkers and green to make the hole more playable, but Muirhead takes great pride in the fact that pictures and posters of the hole still circulate—as if that validates its design more than its usefulness for golf.

A lot of people who have met him think Desmond is a genius, and he may be, as a land planner and art critic—but he doesn't understand golf. His success in the business is the ultimate proof that salesmanship is more important than golfing knowledge (but it's funny that some of the mainstream architects who laugh loudest at Muirhead pretend that statement doesn't also apply to them). As for Desmond, I hope that somewhere he can find room on one of his courses for a duck-shaped bunker, to symbolize what a quack he is. (quack *n.* any person who pretends to have knowledge or skill that he or she does not have in a particular field - *Webster's.*) 0. [6/89]

***Upper Montclair CC,*** *Clifton. Robert Trent Jones, 1956.*

Another 27-holer, but with none of the majesty of Ridgewood. The 415-yard West 3rd, doglegging to the left with water beside the right of the long narrow green, is a tough but slightly awkward hole (I'm not fond of hitting shots through the green into a water hazard, which a player is likely to do off a short drive here), and there aren't any other holes here as interesting. 4. [11/81]

***White Beeches G & CC,*** *Haworth. Walter Travis, c. 1917.*

A fairly blah country-club layout that was one of the more celebrated metropolitan courses fifty years ago: it must've been changed some since. The short par-4 4th hole, zigzagging between large oaks, is neat, but otherwise there's not much to brag about. 3. [4/84]

*—Gossip—*

The Knoll, in the northern town of Boonton, is a Charles Banks layout featuring all the old favorite holes; and someday I'd also like to see the old-fashioned Spring Lake CC, by George Thomas with revisions by Tillinghast. Among more recent courses, Arnold Palmer's Laurel Creek has gotten some surprisingly good reviews. There are also a couple of new-money ventures near Atlantic City, but you'll find better odds at the blackjack tables.

## PENNSYLVANIA

***Aronimink GC**, Newtown Square. Donald Ross, 1928, with revisions by Dick Wilson, George Fazio, and Robert Trent Jones.*

I was glad to get back here to play the course; my only prior visit was the afternoon after I'd seen Pine Valley and Merion for the first time, when the course had no chance to impress me. In excess of 6,900 yards, it plays to a brutal par 70 unless you hit it as long as member Jay Sigel. Even then, it's difficult because Mr. Jones pinched the long driver's landing areas down to nothing with new bunkering, built for the PGA Championship, which the club had to forego; now they're talking about "restoring" the Ross course, just five years after they spent a million dollars destroying it! Thankfully, the club has not tinkered with the original Ross greens, which start out fairly subdued but get really interesting on the back nine. 6. [9/92]

***Fox Chapel GC**, Pittsburgh. Seth Raynor, 1925.*

Just another ho-hum excellent Raynor effort, which I knew about because a friend of mine almost won the U.S. Women's Amateur there in 1985. The rolling Raynor greens have been outstandingly preserved, and looked pretty quick to me. Several holes make use of a small brook that meanders down the middle of the valley in which the course sits. Best holes: the short par-4 12th and 15th, both with the magnificent clubhouse as backdrop, and the short par-5 8th, with a downhill tee shot along the brook followed by an approach to a high platform green hanging out over a severe drop to the right. But the quality of this hole, like several others, is muted by overzealous tree-planting; the "arboretum look" of the various species detracts from an outstanding course. 6. [4/93]

***Gulph Mills GC**, Gulph Mills. Donald Ross, 1919, with revisions by William Flynn, Perry Maxwell, Wayne Stiles, William and David Gordon, and Robert Trent Jones.*

The premier old-money club in Philadelphia, Gulph Mills has made innumerable revisions to its course over the years, so today it is something of a collection of different designs. There are some excellent holes—the short 4th over a deep valley, and the 6th and 11th with their distinctive greens (Mr. Maxwell, I presume)—but some of the supporting cast are fairly dull, and a couple are radically overdone (the 10th in particular). Most amusing hole: the drastically uphill 421-yard 18th, the shortest par-5 of my acquaintance. 5. [8/92]

***Hershey CC**, Hershey. West Course by Maurice McCarthy, 1930.*

They were "too busy" to let me walk around this course, which was once in *Golf Digest's* 100 Greatest. But a quick drive around the perimeter led me to believe that it's not in that class, though many in eastern and central Pennsylvania swear by it. A 5 or maybe a 6, tops. [8/92]

***Huntingdon Valley G & CC**, Abingdon. Howard Toomey and William Flynn, 1927.*

Around Philadelphia, HVCC is considered by some to be the third best golf course in town, on the basis of its difficult back nine and an unusually strong playing membership. For my money, it's not quite the best of the Toomey and Flynn Philadelphia collection. Set in a wooded bowl that bottoms out just a bit too abruptly, the front nine goes around the exterior of the property like it was routed by Richard Petty—all left turns with high right-to-left banks. The back nine, crisscrossing the bottom of the valley and the stream that runs through it, is much better stuff, with several excellent par-4 holes and completing a good set of par-3's. 6. [6/92]

***Kahkwa C,*** *Erie. Donald Ross, 1915.*

A stately old club and a pretty good course, but not worth a special trip. The rolling terrain is put to good use, but the golf course is pretty uneven. It appears that three different guys built the greens: a few are just simply constructed plateaus, a few are more crafted, and three or four (the 9th, 12th, and 18th, in particular) are beautifully sculpted at the original grade, with bowled pin placements ranging from gentle to severe. The big par-5 12th is certainly the most memorable hole. 5. [6/95]

***Lancaster CC,*** *Lancaster. William Flynn, 1920, with revisions by William and David Gordon, 1959.*

See the "Gourmet's Choice." 7. [10/92]

***Laurel Valley GC,*** *Ligonier. Dick Wilson and Bob Simmons, 1960.*

A championship course with only a modicum of character, Laurel Valley occupies gently rolling bottomland in the valley below Ligonier. The elite membership consists exclusively of corporate CEO's, most of whom fall well short of the course's demands: it weighs in at over 7,000 yards, with medium-sized greens vigorously defended by bunkers and mounding, and a variety of water features emanating from a small stream. Thirty years of tree growth have transformed the fairly open site, but it's still far from a trek through woods. A solid and well-manicured test, but boring and over-shaped for my tastes. 6. [10/92]

***Manufacturers G & CC,*** *Oreland. Howard Toomey and William Flynn, 1925.*

A good parkland layout on fairly hilly terrain; it's scary to think that it doesn't always make lists of Philadelphia's top 10, but it makes my list with room to spare. The entire course lies in a valley and on a sidehill that faces the massive stone clubhouse above; a creek through the middle of the property comes into play on five holes, and the bunkering is well-placed but a bit less stylish than Flynn's best. The five par-3 holes are particularly noteworthy, ranging from the strongly uphill 199-yard 6th and the stiff 233-yard 13th down to the "pocket quarry" 117-yard 8th; there were also several excellent mid-length and longer par-4's. Only downer: the landscape committee has gone berserk, supplementing giant native sycamores with newer nursery trees that narrow the course and obscure the full-frame view of the holes from the tees. 7. [5/92]

*The classic Manufacturers.*

***Meadowink Municipal GC****, Murrysville. Ferdinand Garbin, 1969.*

Never expect much from a golf course architect named Ferdinand. 2. [9/74]

***Melrose GC****, Cheltenham. Perry Maxwell, 1927, with revisions by Robbie Robinson.*

During my tenure in Philadelphia, no one even mentioned this course as worth seeing, but I had to look it up after seeing a letter from Alister MacKenzie to Maxwell commending his fine work here. I discovered it's only 5800 yards and somewhat overgrown, hence the lack of local reputation, but there are still a handful of super-wild Maxwell greens, and I'd like to play the roller-coaster par-5 2nd once in my lifetime. 3. [5/94]

***Merion GC****, Ardmore. East and West courses both designed by Hugh Wilson, 1911; East course revised by Wilson, 1925.*

See the "Gourmet's Choice." East course: 10. West course: 4. [10/90]

***Montour Heights CC****, Coraopolis. Original nine holes by Dutch Loeffler and John McGlynn, c. 1920; expanded to 18 by James Harrison, c. 1960.*

This course is now a commercial development, torn up and replaced by a new P.B. Dye layout on very hilly terrain, which has been quite controversial among the members. At least they can't claim they lost much: the older course consisted almost entirely of parallel par-4 holes playing from a ridgetop tee down into a valley of fairway and back up to a ridgetop green. [9/85]

***Moselem Springs GC****, Fleetwood. George Fazio, 1964.*

The project that vaulted George Fazio into architectural prominence, its fairways cruise across the landscape of a country estate north of Reading. There are beautiful parts and silly parts, as you might tell from the club entrance itself: you come in across a steel bridge past a beautiful mill, and then make an awkward sharp right to circle around the practice tee uphill to the clubhouse. The golf holes are straight from the sixties, with very large bunkers and greens, and three of George Fazio's favorite kind of hole: downhill short holes from hilltop tees. I might have liked it better but for a handful of incredibly long holes like the 576-yard 12th and the 442-yard 14th, both uphill all the way; apparently Fazio was worried that by the turn of the century everyone would hit the ball like John Daly. 6. [4/95]

***Mount Airy Lodge GC,*** *Mt. Pocono. Hal Purdy, Malcolm Purdy, and Chandler Purdy, 1981.*

A hilly Poconos resort layout with a couple of really good holes—the par-3 17th, across a deep valley to a narrow shelf of green, is outstanding. But there are also some real doozies: for example, the first hole is a short, double-dogleg par-5, about eighty feet uphill, with a pond in front of the green that you can't see until you're up there. 3. [10/91]

***Oakmont CC,*** *Oakmont. William and Henry Fownes, 1903.*

This must be considered as one of the classic American courses because of its place in the history of American course design, but it was probably my least favorite of the classics until the most recent Open, which cemented my fondness for it. It has all the charm of an S.S. commandant the way it is set up for a tournament, but the more everyone whined about it the more I grew to appreciate it: it kept the best players in the world in check without resorting to the water and out-of-bounds that modern designers employ. I've never understood why water to the right of a green is acceptable, but rough and a tilted green that make it impossible to get up and down from the right are "unfair."

Hole-by-hole, I like the 3rd and 4th (though I dislike the Church Pews), the 12th, 13th, the 15th, and the 18th, and the 9th solely for its combination

green and putting clock; but I hate the 1st hole as a par-4 opener, plus the 2nd, 8th, and 17th. I'm also disappointed that the club has placed such emphasis on excessively fast greens; their contour would hold plenty of interest without it, but the attention they've given to speed has led other courses to overdo it, too. But you can't really hold that against the layout itself. 9. [10/94]

**Philadelphia CC**, *Gladwyne. Spring Mill Course by Howard Toomey and William Flynn, 1927; Centennial Nine by Tom Fazio and Jan Beljan, 1991.*

The original Spring Mill course is one of my favorites in Philadelphia—not quite as tough for the low-handicapper as Huntingdon Valley or Philadelphia Cricket Club, but a good test, and a bit more pleasant of a round. There is an outstanding set of par-3's, including the downhill over-the-pond 5th and the strongly uphill 220-yard 15th, which has been aced only twice in sixty-five years of play; but the whole round is full of good holes, with an emphasis on interest rather than sheer difficulty, and the greenside bunkering is outstanding from both an esthetic and strategic point of view. The new Centennial nine, on an inferior piece of sloping ground, could hardly have been expected to live up to the test—there's nothing wrong with it, but very little to recommend it, either. Spring Mill: 7. Centennial: 4. [9/92]

**Philadelphia Cricket Club**, *Flourtown. A.W. Tillinghast, 1922.*

Some observers favor this course as one of Philadelphia's top five, but only to break up William Flynn's monopoly. It wouldn't make a list of Tillinghast's best work: the front nine is pretty cramped in spots, especially at the par-4 2nd (where I casually pushed my approach shot onto the roof of the men's locker room) and the dueling par-3 3rd and 10th holes. But there is a good stretch of two-shot holes in the middle of the back nine, and the 9th and 18th are both backbreakers: the 9th is just uphill and difficult, but the 18th is something special, sweeping downhill and to the left, with a creek crossing in front of the green and defending against the slice. 6. [7/92]

**Philmont CC**, *Huntingdon Valley. North Course by Howard Toomey and William Flynn, 1924; South Course by Willie Park, Jr., 1907.*

There's a bit of character here, as the courses are a bit scruffier around the edges than most of their brethren in the metropolitan area, but unfortunately, the architecture isn't quite as exciting. The more-acclaimed North course is another Toomey and Flynn design, but somewhat more cramped than their other nearby works. The hook-shaped, tree-lined and untouchable par-5 9th hole made my *GOLF Magazine* list of the top 100 holes in America a few years back, but I wouldn't have voted for it; I actually preferred the straightaway, uphill/sidehill par-5 12th. Mean-

*Philadelphia Country Club.*

while, the South course occupies mostly flatter terrain below the clubhouse. There is a fairly difficult set of short holes (though a half-dozen Philadelphia courses have better), but probably the best of the South is the opening hole, a drive and pitch dogleg left over a rushing brook. Not a bad 36 holes of golf, but I'd be hard-pressed to place either course in Philadelphia's top ten. North course: 5. South course: 4. [9/92]

***Phoenixville CC,*** *Phoenixville. Hugh Wilson, 1913, with modifications by Bill Kittleman.*

This nine-holer is noteworthy simply because it's one of only three remaining Hugh Wilson designs. (The fourth, Cobb's Creek Municipal, has been raped for the sake of speeding up play.) There are some steep gradients to be negotiated, with a deep ravine behind the clubhouse to be crossed from the 1st, 4th, and 8th tees, and containing the 9th green. It's certainly not the conventional layout, topping out at just over 2,800 yards, and with back-to-back par-3's at the 6th and 7th, but the 3,500-square-foot greens are sharply canted, leaving no substitute for pinpoint accuracy on the approaches. Most of the bunkering is fairly basic, but Merion pro Kittleman has added some remarkable-looking fairway bunkers at the 5th and 8th, restoring the Hugh Wilson flair to a course that may not have had much to begin with. 4, but it could go up as the restoration work continues. [5/92]

***Pocono Manor Resort***, *Mt. Pocono. East course by Donald Ross, 1919.*

Could Ross ever have set foot on this goat-hill site? If so, he had more of a sense of humor than I ever knew. The sharply downhill, 77-yard 7th has become famous: club pro Greg Wall advises you to "take it back about hip high with a sand wedge, and if it feels like you're going to chip it in the water, you'll probably be on the green"; I blew it over and off a rock outcropping. But the 200-yard blind 3rd, with a tiny green at the bottom of a V-shaped cut, is almost as strange.

There aren't any sand bunkers left, just odd little knobs and grassy hollows around the greens; there's no fairway irrigation, either, so the turf can be nonexistent, and the tiny greens almost impossible to hold. You need some imagination in order to get around in reasonable figures, but it's hard to believe they can charge resort-course prices for these conditions. 2. [10/91] P.S.—The "putting course" adjacent to the 5th tee (near the Lodge) is wonderful; it's even more severe than my lost putting course at High Pointe.

***Rolling Green GC***, *Springfield. Howard Toomey and William Flynn, 1926.*

A very hilly layout with flashy greenside bunkers reminiscent of Merion's "white faces," not surprising from Flynn, the Hugh Wilson disciple. (I wouldn't be surprised if Wilson himself had a small advisory role in this design.) The most memorable holes are the par-4 13th and long par-3 14th, which cross and re-cross a deep gully to cliffhanger greens, and the par-4 8th, with its landing area in the arc of a small brook. The five par-3 holes are all rather memorable in the best sense of the word, but the 614-yard uphill 9th seemed longer than all of them put together. 7. [2/92]

***Rolling Rock C****, Ligonier. Donald Ross, 1917.*

Built within the 1,300 acre preserve of the Mellon family, Rolling Rock is one of the best nine-hole courses I've seen, and surely the only one I know with an international membership of 2,500. (At that, they only play 9,000 rounds per year on the course.) The nine holes occupy sloping parkland, which makes for an occasional blind tee shot, but it is the greens that really make the course. Some of them look more like Pine Valley greens than anything else I've seen of Ross, with high shoulders at the edges and fairly steep levels running from side to side. The par-3 3rd green is one of the wonders of the world, but really all the greens from the 2nd through 8th are pretty wild stuff. At a shade under 3,000 yards, with par of 35 or 34 depending on which alternate tee you use for the finishing hole, Rolling Rock is not exactly championship stuff, but it is quite a place. A second nine is now underway, but there isn't an architect alive who can improve upon the nine they've got. 7. [10/92]

***Royal Oaks GC****, Lebanon. Ron Forse and Bruce Hepner, 1992.*

These young designers have quickly achieved a reputation as lovers of the classics and restoration specialists, but hopefully their original work will show more flair in the future—especially since Bruce works with me now. They were handicapped by an owner who wanted "modern-style" features, and a property divided into three separate, oddly shaped parcels, but still their mounding and green shaping left a lot to be desired. Proof to me that no matter how big a fan of the classics you are, you've got to have creative talent in the field, and not rely on just any shaper to get things right. 3. [8/92]

***St. David's GC****, King of Prussia. Donald Ross, 1927, with revisions by A.W. Tillinghast.*

For a course of such noble pedigree, St. David's is very much a plain Jane by Philadelphia standards. The terrain is only moderately interesting, the scenery basic parkland, and there aren't any holes that get the blood pumping. 3. [8/92]

***Saucon Valley CC****, Bethlehem. Old Course by Herbert Strong, 1922, with revisions by Perry Maxwell and William Gordon; Grace Course by William and David Gordon, 1953–58; Weyhill Course by William and David Gordon, 1967.*

A huge 54-hole facility, which I toured in a head-spinning two-hour ride in the superintendent's pickup truck; forgive me if I'm a bit loose on the details.

In a popular election there's as much division on the issue of which is the best course here as the 1992 Presidential election. For now, my own vote would go to the Old Course, which has a handful of breakneck greens that give it a bit more character. They renumber the holes for tournaments to avoid finishing on the short par-4 18th, but its wild Maxwell green makes it one of the premier holes.

The Grace Course, weighing in at 7,051 yards from all the way back, has for years been rated highest by *Golf Digest's* panel, but except for a few moments along Saucon Creek it's got less character than the Old. The small greens are pretty well conceived for a course of this vintage, but the double-dogleg par-5's seem to try too hard, and some holes, like the long par-3 3rd over a pond, lack inspiration.

Most difficult of all for me to remember is the Weyhill Course, which has just been taken over by the club after being operated privately by Bethlehem Steel for years; now that it will operate from a small separate clubhouse instead of the steel company's impressive hospitality house, they were in the middle of arguments about how best to renumber the holes, and I don't know the final order. The property is certainly the most dramatic of the three courses, with a couple of big hills at the far end and a deep quarry that comes into play twice on the front nine; and it may be the hardest of the three courses, or at least

the most likely one on which to register a snowman on your card. But its popularity among visitors may rest on its previous exclusivity, since it also struck me as very uneven in character. Of the three courses, I'd probably be most curious to play Weyhill first. Old Course: 7. Grace Course: 6. Weyhill Course: 6. [4/95]

***Stonewall,*** *Elverson. Tom Doak and Gil Hanse with Jay Sigel, 1993.*

It's hard to evaluate one's own work, but as my first opportunity to build a private club course, I'm lucky to have the reviews of members who have come to know it, and they're enough to make me blush. We were fortunate to have had property with great character and founders who understand the ambiance of a great club, so its success as a place worth visiting was all but assured; luckily we also came up with some golf holes I relish playing.

From the beginning, there was a question of whether the golf course could be made long enough and hard enough for the best players, but by the end we were being encouraged to tone it down a bit, so I suspect our combination of small, sloping greens and strong two-shot holes will do well. The five par-3 holes are probably the cream of the course, especially the three on the front side. But the two great holes are the par-4 6th, an alternate-fairway design around "Jay's Creek" that allows all golfers to play to their strengths, and the downhill par-4 18th, where I really went out on a limb by locating the green precariously close to the old stone dairy barns that serve as the clubhouse and offices. The several sidehill approaches, which allow you to bounce a ball in if you plan to in advance, but kick away low screamers, also lend the course a character of its own. If they like it in Philadelphia, we'll have succeeded in a very tough neighborhood. 8. [9/95]

***Waynesborough CC,*** *Paoli. George and Tom Fazio, 1964, with revisions in 1978.*

A classic early Fazio parkland course, with characteristic sweeping greens, sprawling bunkers, and plenty of length. Not my type, exactly, but pretty good if you like the style. 5. [9/92]

***Whitemarsh Valley G & CC,*** *Lafayette Hill. George Thomas, 1908.*

A really tightly packed course bordered by busy roads, which gave the novice architect Thomas little opportunity to test out any of the complex alternate-route holes he favored in his book. It's hard to believe they ever found enough room to host a PGA Tour event here (the now-defunct IVB-Philadelphia Classic). Best holes are the widely varied par-3's, but even these don't hold a candle to the local competition. 3. [8/92]

*—Gossip—*

I was very fortunate to spend a summer in Philadelphia, for it gave me the chance to explore all the fine courses there; although I never did get to Donald Ross' Torresdale-Frankford course near downtown. I doubt Pittsburgh's hillier ground contains such wealth, but I know I haven't done it justice until I see Sewickley and Pittsburgh Field Club, which is right next to Fox Chapel; a new Nicklaus course called Nevillewood is also getting outstanding reviews, but I can't tell if they are from Jack-lovers or Jack-haters who are now overrating his most recent, understated work. Several others in western Pennsylvania have been recommended by Dr. Cal Waisanen, including New Castle GC and Sunnehanna (both by Tillinghast)—but be forewarned, Cal's into sporty holes even more than I am. Lehigh CC, a Flynn design up near Bethlehem, is also on my play list.

## MARYLAND

***Baltimore CC,*** *Baltimore. Five Farms East course by A.W. Tillinghast, 1922, with restoration by Brian Silva, 1991*

This is surely the standout course in the Ocean State, but not, in my opinion, one of Tillinghast's top five. The parkland layout is somewhat similar to Somerset Hills in contour, but lacks the severe greens that make that course outstanding. There are some really good holes, including the par-4 opener and the "Barn hole" 6th, a par-5 that can be reached in two if the drive carries the maintenance barn (which is out of bounds), but some of the long par-4's near the finish are dullards, and the only interesting landscaping on the course is at the short par-4 10th, with a Japanese scene too close to the left side of the green. (Maybe they should furrow the bunkers here.) I've heard very complimentary things about the recent restoration of the greens, which might revise my opinion of the course upward. At least, I hear it's way better than the West course, which Bob Cupp and Tom Kite totally remodeled a few years ago. East course: 7. [6/82]

***Columbia CC,*** *Chevy Chase. Various artists, including Herbert Barker, 1910, Walter Travis, William Flynn, and George and Tom Fazio.*

The Mall and our national monuments were built on flat ground—probably a wetland, if the truth be known—but I had forgotten just how hilly the rest of the District is. Like Columbia, for instance. It's laid out within tight boundaries on a roller-coaster property of hills and deep valleys, making for some wild shots. It's an uneven test, with the back nine presenting most of the good golf, and the turf didn't look too appetizing, although December is not the best time of year to judge. But I'd like to play it someday, anyway. There are several very interesting shots to be played, and a couple of the greens are terrific—especially the "Split Level" 10th, with the left third of the green a punchbowl dipping three feet below the right-hand plateau. However, most observers would agree that the par-4 11th is the class of the course. 5. [12/91]

***Congressional CC,*** *Bethesda. Original 18 by Devereux Emmet, 1924; expanded to 27 by Robert Trent Jones, 1960, and redesigned by Rees Jones, 1989; fourth nine (holes 6–14 on Gold course) by George and Tom Fazio, 1975.*

If it weren't Washington's most fashionable club you'd have never heard of Congressional's Blue course, which is of championship length but whose reputation is largely inflated by Beltway hype. The layout I played years ago was just a modestly above-average Trent Jones layout that happens to be in DC, although I hear that Rees' redesign has made it substantially better. (The notion that he *could* improve it goes a long way toward confirming my opinion of the previous version.) However, the new greens have been problematic, as you might have discerned while watching USGA Green Section personnel tap down the spike marks with their tennis shoes between groups at last year's Senior Open. The Gold course is just the Fazios' version of the same story. Blue course (pre-redesign): 6. Gold course: 4. [10/80]

*18th green at Congressional, site of the 1997 U.S. Open*

***Gibson Island CC,*** *Gibson Island. Charles Blair Macdonald and Seth Raynor, 1922.*

There are only nine holes here, and what's left is so decayed that it's not worth seeing. Located on an island at the tip of a peninsula into Chesapeake Bay, you'd think it ought to have a Fishers Island-type setting, but from the looks of what's left I doubt it was much of a course to begin with. 1. [6/82]

### —*Gossip*—

Maryland has become one of the toughest states in the Union as far as environmental permits to build golf courses are concerned, so it appears that the Baltimore area is stuck with Five Farms, the public Hog's Neck, and Caves Valley, the new Tom Fazio course whose reputation to date rests more on visits by George Bush and Dan Quayle than on reports of interesting golf holes. In the suburbs of Washington, DC, the only older course that I've heard favorable things about is the ultra-private, notoriously all-male Burning Tree; the one new contender, the Robert Trent Jones International GC, is in Virginia.

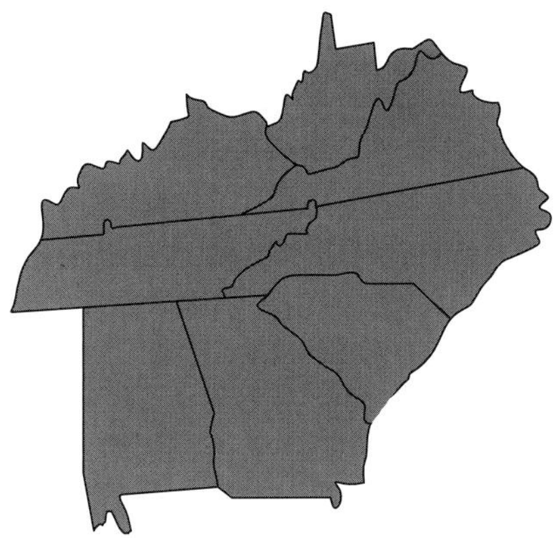

## SOUTHEAST

The former Confederacy has been one of the highest-growth areas for golf in America over the past 30 years, due to the lucrative combination of golf and resort/second-home communities. Indeed, it was here, on Hilton Head Island [which then had only four golf courses], that my own golfing adventures began 25 years ago.

While there are some classic Donald Ross courses in the hills of North Carolina and Tennessee and around Atlanta, the majority of courses in this region are of newer vintage, and most are fairly flat — they don't call it the "Carolina Lowcountry" for nothing. Ellis Maples and George Cobb are among the architects who made their homes here, but the Carolinas are better remembered as the proving grounds for today's legends, Pete Dye and Tom Fazio. Indeed, it was Pete's groundbreaking work at Harbour Town and Long Cove which raised expectations for Southern golf.

## WEST VIRGINIA

***Pete Dye GC,*** *Clarksburg. Pete Dye and company, 1994.*

Begun in 1978, this should have been one of Pete's most original and memorable designs; but by the time it was finished, after legendary battles between architect and developer, and then financial problems, most of the innovations had already been seen elsewhere. The developer, a strip coal miner named Jim LaRosa, became obsessed with building the best golf course in the world, even though he's not enough of a golfer to understand what that meant—but when he found out Pine Valley took ten years to build, he decided to top it, and keep all his heavy equipment operators busy while the strip coal industry sagged.

The property is gorgeous—bisected by a winding river and surrounded by tree-covered hills, 1000 acres of it dedicated to the golf course. There are some gimmicks, such as a waterfall coming out of the 10th green and some relics of the coal-mining origins of the site. (On the way to the 7th tee you go through the entrance to a deep mine, while the par-5 8th has a huge bunker with a 60-foot quarry wall on the far side.) But there are also some great holes, including the par-4 2nd and 18th, with spectacular across-the-river tee shots, and the par-5 5th, with its second shot up a bluff along the river's edge. Undoubtedly, though, your opinion of it will hinge on your opinion of Pete Dye's monumental 1980s style, which is too bad, because if they'd finished this course on time it would have been a true original. 7. [7/93]

—*Gossip*—

I didn't get around to see any of West Virginia's other courses during my stint in Clarksburg (not even the Bridgeport CC, which is right on the road to the new course and no more than a mile away), but the Old White and Greenbrier courses at The Greenbrier are probably worth checking out; Old White is the only remaining C.B. Macdonald layout I haven't seen.

## VIRGINIA

***Elizabeth Manor G & CC,*** *Portsmouth. Dick Wilson, 1951.*

A very unassuming, flat layout that was most likely built early in Wilson's career, and on a low budget. It's not a bad course at all—they play the Eastern Amateur here every summer, and the good players keep coming back, but that's probably a better testament to the greens conditioning than to the architecture. There's not much change of elevation to set off the fairways, and the bunkering is Spartan in design, with none of the flair for which Wilson later became famous. There are a few interesting features, such as a tiny green on the par-4 10th, but overall it's pretty bland. 4. [4/91]

***Golden Horseshoe GC,*** *Williamsburg. Gold Course by Robert Trent Jones, 1964.*

Brian McCallen at *GOLF* had told me he believed this was the best course that Trent Jones ever built; he must not think too much of Trent's work. The course is crammed into 125 acres of woodland, and it would be downright dangerous if the trees between holes weren't really thick. But they are, so instead the course is simply too narrow, especially when the sloping fairways are taken into account. The focus of the course has always been its four par-3 holes, all of which play across a couple of small ponds in a deep ravine at the center of the property; the 16th, with its wide, shallow island green, is the most famous of the four. But even though they are somewhat different in terms of green setting, I didn't think any one of them was really outstanding in other than visual terms; I've played dozens of courses with a better set of short holes. Some of the greens are very small or skinny, and the bunkering is very basic. The Williamsburg Inn, which is adjacent to the course, looked like a 9; but this golf course doesn't begin to achieve the same level of quality. 5. [6/91] P.S.—Rees Jones has just completed a second 18 here; no reviews available at press time.

***Hell's Point GC,*** *Virginia Beach. Rees Jones, 1982.*

Another good but basic public layout. There is a creek, which divides the golf course into two sections, but it doesn't figure into any of the golf holes, even though it was perhaps the only natural feature of a low-lying site covered with substantial but nondescript trees. Instead, there are a couple of holes revolving around man-made ponds, including the 320-yard 17th threatened by water on the right its entire length (one of Rees' personal favorites); but there's nothing here to write home about. 4. [2/91]

***Kiln Creek G & CC,*** *Newport News. Brian Ault and Tom Clark, 1991.*

One of the worst courses I've ever seen. The architects were instructed to "lose" 2.5 million cubic yards of dirt that was excavated from a canal around the development after construction on the course had begun. So, they simply filled most of the holes about 8-10 feet above natural grade, and contoured to their original plans from there. The worst part is that the course is routed through potential development land, which is wooded now; so throughout the

course there are steep banks from the fairways and greens down to the property line. Nothing blends in, and the fairways are so high that it would require a three-story house to get any decent golf course view. When you also consider that they spent $9 million in construction on this—by definition, it's a 0. [6/91]

***Sleepy Hole GC,*** *Suffolk. Russell Breeden, 1972.*

A good municipal layout that hosted an LPGA event during the early 1980s. Most of the routing is fairly mundane, but the practice range sited at the river's edge must be a breath of fresh air in summer, and the par-4 18th hole is one of the most difficult finishing holes I've ever seen—a good carry across a valley off the tee with a marshy inlet off to the left, and a very long second shot downhill to a green site with the river left and behind, the clubhouse too close for comfort on the right, and a patch of cattails in front of the green. There's no room at all to bail out. 4. [4/91]

***Two Rivers GC*** *(Governor's Land), Jamestown. Tom Fazio, 1992.*

I only got a glimpse of this course, wheeled around by a real-estate guy while the course was just being planted. It's carved out of a nice wooded site with some good gentle rolls, and frontage on the James River for the last three holes. However, compared to the bulk of Fazio's recent work it seemed rather uninspired. The routing doesn't make much use of the ground—the fairway contours are all bulldozer-born, and the county is so strict on wetlands preservation there's 50 feet of trees separating a couple of the holes from nice marsh views. But I can't rate it, because when I saw the course there were still only 17 holes—the 18th was pending a decision on whether the archaeological site by one green site or the wetland by the other was more significant. [6/91]

***Virginia Hot Springs G & TC,*** *Hot Springs. Cascades course by William Flynn, 1923.*

I probably ought to reserve judgment on this course until I play it. On the one hand, it's not a striking course, with only subtle contouring on and around the greens, modest bunkering, and no overpowering holes; but on the other it's probably one of America's purest esthetic golf experiences, beautifully contained in a Shenandoah valley with practically no outside distractions except for the two-lane highway that passes through it, and the variety of hilly lies and dogleg holes might provide a perfectly balanced test. I doubt it's one of the 50 best courses in the world, as *GOLF Magazine* once ranked it, but I'd like to let it grow on me a little more first. 7. [9/85]

*—Gossip—*

There are definitely some others to explore here. I've already mentioned the Robert Trent Jones International GC in Manassas, which has quickly earned a reputation as one of Jones' very best—but I haven't yet established if it's the politics or the design. Kingsmill, in Williamsburg, is the only celebrated Pete Dye course I haven't seen (although Pete doesn't recommend it), and just for fun I'd also like to look up the old Cavalier Golf & Yacht Club in Virginia Beach, a Charles Banks original. The James River course at the CC of Virginia, Richmond, is another Flynn layout that gets good reviews. Up in the hills, I'm told that the Farmington CC course in Charlottesville (near the University) is especially good, while a new Rees Jones course at Wintergreen is also getting a lot of ink from the locals. But, when we finally get it going, the best course in the state may be the one I've laid out for Harbour View GC on the banks of the Nansemond River in Suffolk, which features some drop-dead gorgeous holes laid out on low bluffs looking over fingers of tidal marsh.

## NORTH CAROLINA

***Black Mountain GC,*** *Black Mountain. Ross Taylor, date unknown.*

Not to be confused in any way with Tom Fazio's Black Diamond, this course on the eastern fringe of Asheville has won fame for having the longest golf hole in America, the 747-yard, par-6 17th. (It measures 692 from the white tees, and a comfortable 634 from the reds.) I should add that this prodigious hole pushes the total blue tee length of the course to 6,181 yards, and that there is almost no fairway turf to speak of. 2, just for novelty. [9/89]

***Carmel CC,*** *Charlotte. North Course by George Cobb, 1950, with minor modifications by Rees Jones.*

The South course at Carmel, modified by Rees Jones about ten years ago, is the championship track here; I only walked around the North, which the club is thinking about modifying. The property is pleasantly rolling in nature, and the small undulating greens present more than their share of tricky recoveries. But the layout itself is far from ideal—there are four par-3's on the front side, including the first hole, and though the course is fairly compact the ordering of the holes is so convoluted you need a map to determine which follows which, with some substantial walks from green to tee so that the 9th will return to the clubhouse. 4. [2/93]

***Charlotte CC,*** *Charlotte. Fred Laxton, 1912, with modifications by Donald Ross in 1926 and Robert Trent Jones in 1963.*

A rare success story of redesign—so I'm most surprised to hear that Brian Silva is in the process of restoring it to the "original Ross plans." Of course, I never saw the Ross layout, but Jones' modified greens had some of the best subtle contours I've ever seen: you never got stuck with a death-defying downhill putt between tiers, but there were places on the greens where a putt could get away from you, and they were usually near the middle of the greens, so there were two kinds of difficult pin placements—those on the wings of the greens, and those near the steeper contours in the middle. The greenside bunkering was also excellent, narrowing the target considerably when one drives to the wrong side of the fairway. There weren't any bowl-you-over holes—the par-3 11th, which has been featured in several places, didn't really deserve singling out—but they were all of a high standard. 7. [10/90]

*Highlands, Bobby Jones' favorite place to get his game in shape.*

***Charlotte Golf Links,*** *Charlotte. Tom Doak and Jim Urbina, 1993.*

This isn't my proudest moment in the design business; the developers started the project behind schedule, got delayed by weather, and were in such a rush to plant it that they didn't have time for little details like floating out the fairways to eliminate puddles. In concept it's supposed to have the flavor of a British links, though there are occasional patches of woodland to break up the scenery. Still, there are a few holes I'm fond of, including the short par-5 6th with a large oak overhanging the approach, the long par-5 12th with a gauntlet of mounds 120 yards in front of the green, the reverse-Redan 16th and the stern par-4 17th, which is reminiscent of the 8th at Muirfield. I just hope they get the place looking right someday, instead of simply beating the players through with a stick; but I hear they're going to build another course nearby (without an architect) instead of fixing this one. 4. [7/93]

***Club at Longleaf,*** *Pinehurst. Dan Maples, 1988.*

A schizophrenic layout if ever I saw one: the front nine lays out across open ground, with more than half the holes tangling with the remains of a horse track, while the back nine runs around hilly property reserved for housing. Maples must have inherited a bad developer's routing for the back nine—no way any architect would have put three par-3's in the space of four holes, sandwiched around the absolutely awful double-dogleg par-5 14th. 4. [6/94]

***CC of North Carolina,*** *Pinehurst. Dogwood course by Ellis Maples, 1963.*

I really don't understand the popularity of this course; it's just another well-landscaped course among the pine trees and a housing development, not much different than Grandfather or quite a few others. Too many of the greens are elevated, so you can't even see your ball land on them, and there are no great holes as far as I could see. 6. [4/83]

***Highlands CC,*** *Highlands. Donald Ross, 1926.*

The mountain retreat of the Palm Beach winter crowd, Highlands is a billy-goat Donald Ross layout in immaculate condition, which zealously guards its privacy as much today as when it was Bobby Jones' summer retreat. In places it becomes a bit too narrow, particularly on the front nine, where the combination of sideslope and precarious width rivals that of the Olympic Club; but the back nine widens out somewhat to better holes. There are some excellent two-shot holes, notably the severe 5th and the long dogleg 10th, which is pinched by a brook to the right of the landing area, at a distance such that you have to gamble a bit on the tee shot if you want to reach the green in regulation. However, the greens are not as beautifully conceived as Mr. Ross was capable of, and the lack of length (6,266 yards from the tips) will prevent some strong players from holding an affection for the course. 6. [8/89]

***Landfall Club,*** *Wrightsville Beach. Pete Dye, P.B. Dye, and Bobby Weed, 1987.*

A fine layout on gently undulating ground, one of the better housing-development courses I've seen. The bentgrass greens had to be slightly larger in this climate than the Pete Dye standard of late, and this forced the architects to spend more time developing interesting contours, which then flow nicely into the variety of waste bunkers and smaller pots, which add strategic interest. The split-fairway 9th is the most interesting hole, but perhaps a bit gimmicky, too; it's the solid, unflashy holes like the par-4 8th and 16th that really make the golf course. 6. [11/87]

***Linville GC,*** *Linville. Donald Ross, 1929.*

A beautiful little layout in a tranquil mountain valley just outside the town of Linville. I happened past at the peak of fall color season, which at Linville is about three weeks after the club closes up shop for the year: it is apparently a summer resort in more than name only, though the course was still playable (sans flags) in mid-October. The renowned par-4 3rd is indeed one of the best holes in America, but I had no idea that the winding brook which makes that hole could be brought into play on so many others—I think it is a factor in 12 holes all told. In short, the course is everything I hoped it would be. 6. [10/88]

***Maggie Valley G & CC,*** *Maggie Valley. William Prevost, architect.*

A small, quiet hotel-operated course near the entrance to Great Smoky Mountains National Park, which I remember from all the little ads it used to run in *Golf Digest.* It's just a basic layout. 2. [4/75]

***Marsh Harbour GL,*** *Calabash. Dan Maples, 1980.*

Close to Oyster Bay (it actually straddles the border between the two Carolinas), this course occupies a slightly better piece of property than its younger sister, with a bit more elevation change and marsh frontage to use. Choosing the better layout is difficult: I think I prefer the longer holes of Marsh Harbour, although I'm still undecided on the "signature" island-hopping par-5 17th, but the lack of variety among the par-3's (all five are more than 200 yards from the back tees!) and the poor finishing hole detract from it. 5. [9/88]

***Ocean Harbour GL,*** *Calabash. Clyde Johnston, 1989.*

A very pretty property: the course guide gushes that "throughout the 500 prime acres you will find grass bunkers, wind-sculpted trees, saltwater marshes, groves of live oaks, pine, maples, gum, dogwoods, holly, and cedars, gently contoured and rolling fairways, along with sand bunkers and multiple ponds." But the course looks much better in plan than on the ground, where the combination of narrow clearings and abrupt banks down to the marsh keep the used-ball business at the Beach humming. 4. [3/92]

***Old Town C,*** *Winston-Salem. Perry Maxwell, 1928.*

Be forewarned that this is the kind of club that wants you to have permission from the Board of Governors just to take a walk around—but fortunately, I had walked around most of it at dusk the night before I asked. Just a couple of minutes away from the Wake Forest campus, it's prime-time real estate, and there's plenty of it reserved for the golf course, which is on fairly hilly property. There are only a couple of truly arresting holes in the routing plan, but the key feature is those Maxwell greens—in this case, almost all of them sited into a significant slope, giving plenty of scope for the architect to design severe rolls into them. Worth seeing just for the greens—if they'll let you on the property. 7. [7/93]

***Oyster Bay GL,*** *Sunset Beach. Dan Maples, 1983.*

Located at the northern end of the Myrtle Beach "Grand Strand," this is one of the most popular of the publicly available courses, and is indeed a very fine public facility. There are a couple of holes on the flashy side, namely the island 17th and the drive-and-pitch 13th with its oyster-shell retaining wall above the marsh; but the better part of the course is sounder, if less than spectacular. 5. [11/88]

***The Peninsula CC,*** *Charlotte. Rees Jones, 1990.*

A large-scale development course on a very good piece of property—rolling wooded ground which goes down to a huge lake created by Duke Power. I'm less impressed with the golf holes—the green complexes are all too similar (there aren't any rolls off the sides to blend back into the natural contours), and some of the mounding Rees has done to keep drives out of the trees looks *very* out of place (grass depressions might have fit in better). The routing is also stretched out unmercifully to maximize development frontage, making for a very long ride around, and there are a couple of par-3 holes featuring a dozen or more tee boxes apiece so they can be played from radically different angles of approach—a bit much for me. 5. [9/90]

***Pine Needles GC,*** *Southern Pines. Donald Ross, 1927.*

I was quite pleasantly surprised by this course, because it was not in the least pretentious. The layout wanders over fairly hilly terrain, with a brief span of flat holes near the finish. The par-5 holes are very weak, with the exception of the 1st, but there is a good variety of short and medium-length two-shotters. The short 3rd hole across a pond has been photographed for years and is documented to be wholly unchanged since Ross' day, but it is the long par-3 5th over a deep valley that stands out as the best hole. 5. [4/92]

***Pinehurst CC and Resort,*** *Pinehurst. Nos. 1 through 4 courses by Donald Ross, with revisions to No. 4 by Richard S. Tufts and Robert Trent Jones; No. 5 course by Ellis Maples and Richard S. Tufts, 1961, with modifications by Robert Trent Jones; No. 6 by George and Tom Fazio, 1978; No. 7 course (unreviewed) by Rees Jones, 1986.*

See the "Gourmet's Choice." Doak ratings: No. 1: 3. No. 2: 10. No. 3: 4. No. 4: 5. No. 5: 4. No. 6: 5. [5/94]

***Pinehurst National GC,*** *Pinehurst. Jack Nicklaus, 1989.*

Jack supposedly spent quite a bit of time over at Pinehurst No. 2 and tried to capture the same flavor in his greens design here; maybe he should have taken the shapers over there with him. There's more short grass and fewer bunkers around these greens than a typical Nicklaus product, but that's where the similarity to Pinehurst No. 2 ends. The shapes of the Pinehurst National greens are too contrived to blend successfully into the surrounding contours, and the contours are nowhere near as intricate as those of No. 2.

Like most of the new courses in town, Pinehurst National is hillier than Pinehurst itself, and doesn't lend itself as well to golf—no surprise, since Donald Ross and the Tufts family clearly had first dibs on all the land in town, and put their own golf courses where it made the most sense. The reachable par-5 10th, around a pond on the right, is the standout hole—to get there in two you pretty much have to flirt with the pond off the tee, as at The Dunes #13, although the green is perhaps not of suitably receptive shape even if you've accomplished the first objective. But most of the rest of the design is eminently forgettable, in spite of its eye appeal. 5. [4/91]

***The Pit GL,*** *Aberdeen. Dan Maples, 1984.*

This site, in the bowels of an old sandpit, was an inspired choice for the location of a golf course; the spoil piles are covered by trees, giving it a uniquely mature look that cannot be created from scratch. There are also several good holes, including the par-4 9th and 10th, that play through the quarry and then along its rim; but in working around the quarry's leftovers there are also some goofy holes, in particular the short par-5 8th and 15th with their narrow entrances and ridiculous tucked pin positions. The short 16th, just 100 yards from the back, is another issue: I like short par-3's to small greens, but you can't have a postage-stamp green on a course this busy, so they went for the big and blah model. It's not the pits, but neither is The Pit a diamond in the rough. 5. [10/88]

*The 7th tee at Roaring Gap.*

***Roaring Gap C,*** *Roaring Gap. Donald Ross, 1925.*

A wonderfully relaxed summer club set atop the eastern continental divide in the northern part of the state; the first few and last two holes drain toward the Atlantic, and the middle of the course toward the Gulf. Members' homes are scattered along the course, but completely unobtrusively à la Crystal Downs, as many of them actually face away from the course and off the top of the ridge. The greens are small and of the more subdued Ross period, but the routing is excellent across a hilly property, with several holes of great character, particularly the par-five 7th, 11th, and 16th, and the wild par-4 12th. It is quite short overall at just 6,200 yards, but there are still holes of interest and fun for the good player, and for the connoisseur it's a real hidden gem. 6. [5/94]

***Providence CC,*** *Charlotte. Dan Maples, 1990.*

I only got around twelve holes of this course before we got rained out, but I never went back for the finish, even though we later built a course next door to it. Carved out of low-lying land, this has "development course" stamped all over it, although a couple of the water holes are rather too severe for the clientele—you can't tell where the pond starts until you see the splash. 4. [9/90]

***Renaissance Park GC,*** *Charlotte. Dr. Michael Hurdzan, 1988.*

Built on top of a reclaimed landfill and bisected by high voltage power lines, this municipal course is one of the most unappealing sites for golf this side of Seaton Carew, England. Nevertheless, they're lining up to play it. Since there was plenty of real estate available, they decided to make the course an enormous 7,465 yards from the back tees, which only an idiot would play—but it only takes one foursome of idiots to hold up everyone. The uphill, 600-yard 1st hole is an especially forbidding opener. 0. [2/92]

***Seven Lakes CC,*** *West End. Peter Tufts, 1976.*

The only architectural effort of Peter Tufts, of the famed Pinehurst family, and a creditable job for a one-time effort. The holes are stretched out in a single loop over fairly hilly property for the benefit of the surrounding development, but the layout is okay, and the greens are modestly interesting, with a few fall-away green sites early on. However, after the first few holes the detailing of the bunkers starts to slip away, and on several holes there are semi-blind ponds necessitating forced carries or lay-up shots. 4. [5/94]

***Talamore GC,*** *Pinehurst. Rees Jones, 1991.*

Yet another tough, fair, and pretty dull layout by Rees, which generated a lot of publicity for its bag-toting llamas. The property is overly hilly, requiring wall-to-wall shaping, which makes me want to spit like the caddies. 4. [6/94]

*Chimney Top looms over the 17th at Wade Hampton.*

***Wade Hampton GC,*** *Cashiers. Tom Fazio, 1987.*

One of the very best of this generation of new courses. It is a development course, but the golf course is entirely self-contained in two mountain valleys, with no interior housing lots; the majority of houses will be on a ridge facing away from the course, leaving the golf experience uninterrupted by road crossings and such. The layout makes use of a couple of winding streams, and though Chimney Top Mountain looms closely overhead there is hardly any severe climbing to be done while playing the course. Three of the four short holes are postcard material, but the best holes are in the stretch of two-shotters from the 13th to the 16th, capped off by the long, downhill par-3 17th across a brook to a huge green guarded by large pines to either side. The only down side is the wet climate: they've put in tons of drainage since the course opened, but it's still apt to be soggy. 7. [8/89]

This is another state where I ought to do a lot more exploring: the soil and native vegetation seem ideally suited to producing good golf courses, and there are a lot of minor Ross works lying around that might be pleasant surprises. I'm also interested to see Ellis Maples' Grandfather G & CC in Linville, which we drove into years ago when I was a kid, and looked quite pleasant; I hadn't heard anything about it for years until it suddenly and quite unexpectedly popped up on the *Golf Digest* top 100 list. The nearby Linville Ridge also has strong supporters, but the pictures I've seen cast it as more pretty than good. Most of the newer courses are over-hyped, but perhaps Rees Jones' Bryan Park, in Greensboro, is different.

## SOUTH CAROLINA

***Arcadian Shores CC,*** *Myrtle Beach. Rees Jones, 1974.*

I shouldn't include this because I never actually got out and walked it, but I did drive by it about 20-30 times while living in Myrtle Beach, and you can see all but a couple of holes from the road. It's a flattish property and the design is "early Rees," with lots of sand and slightly elevated greens with bunkers immediately adjacent and mounding outside the bunkers, but no real fairway mounding. Makes you wonder what kind of pull the Myrtle Beach advertisers must have had at *Golf Digest,* back in the days when this was rated among the 100 Greatest Courses in the USA. 5, tops. [4/92]

***Beachwood CC,*** *North Myrtle Beach. Gene Hamm, 1968.*

Basic fare for the low-budget Myrtle Beach golfer; eat calabash when you're through here for the true NMB experience. 2. [4/92]

***Camden CC,*** *Camden. Donald Ross, 1934.*

A crude little Ross layout built during the Depression, which is a good enough course to have quite a local following. There are a couple of neat holes, such as the downhill par-3 2nd and the long par-5 which follows it (from an island tee, no less!), but the whole interest of the course is in the greens, which are about as small as I've ever seen on a golf course: Harbour Town size, and often crowned to boot. It may look small and cramped, but play the course once and you'll have to respect it. 4. [8/89]

***Cane Patch Par-3 GC,*** *Myrtle Beach. Ed Ault and the General Electric Co., 1982.*

Ever wonder how they can light a golf course well enough so you can follow your ball in flight? Make the longest hole 94 yards, that's how! Truthfully, these green complexes wouldn't be bad at all if the grass weren't so furry; but I was still unable to resist the temptation to ignore the mat tees provided, and start playing to the greens under or over trees from the back of the previous green. We even stretched out one hole to a full 9-iron! 2. [3/89]

***CC at Callawassie,*** *Callawassie Island, near Beaufort. Tom Fazio, 1986.*

A nice development and entrance set-up, with just a little gate-house guarding a causeway to the island; the golf course is typical late-'80s Fazio—narrow with some interesting featuring, but just another in his string of islands. Perhaps Al Haig was right about the Domino Theory: first Fazio took over the islands, from Wachesaw in Myrtle Beach to Wild Dunes, Kiawah, Dataw, Callawassie, Moss Creek, Long Point, and Hammock Dunes near Palm Coast, and now he controls the world. 5. [12/88]

***CC of Charleston,*** *Charleston. Seth Raynor, with revisions by Hurricane Hugo and John LaFoy, 1989–90.*

One of the most unusual Raynor layouts I've seen; while it does have the unmistakable Raynor style, it doesn't have some of the trademark holes he used everywhere else, such as the Biarritz or Alps. But there are a couple of truly bizarre holes: the par-4 16th, with a horseshoe-front plateau green fronted by a deep "lion's mouth" bunker, and the par-3 11th, a Redan gone crazy with an eight-foot-high false front that has been cursed by the likes of Ben Hogan. The site is plainly flat, and not as pretty after Hugo took out 600 trees in late 1989. The club traces its roots to a group of golfers who organized on Charleston green in 1786, though its continuous history dates only from the early 1920s. 5. [6/95]

***De Bordieu Club,*** *Georgetown. Pete and P.B. Dye, 1987.*

A very good layout on flat ground along lagoons and marshes, somewhat reminiscent of Long Cove, although Hurricane Hugo did its worst to wreck the maturity of the landscape. This is the type of ground where P.B. is at his creative best, cutting shallow bunkers with steep lips and siting greens in between native stands of trees, and it really impressed me how much could be accomplished with features only four or five feet high. Best holes include the two-shot 5th and 17th. The only resort to gimmickry is at the short 8th, where the patented railroad tie bulkhead lining the lagoon from tee to

*A fortress of bunkers protecting the 16th green at The Dunes.*

green is raised at the far end to hide the substantial part of the putting surface from the back tee: all I can figure is that P.B. wanted everyone to understand how it feels to be short. (Recently they've built an elevated tee to make the green surface visible, but from there it's just another hole: I'm ashamed to admit it, but I think I actually prefer the original design.) 5. [5/89]

***Devil's Elbow GC's, Moss Creek Plantation,*** *Bluffton. North course by Tom Fazio, 1979; South course by George and Tom Fazio, 1974.*

I think this is a super name for a golf course—it was stolen from a hairpin bend on the A-93 road between Braemar and Blairgowrie in Scotland, if you weren't aware—even though I can't figure out what it has to do with Moss Creek. I also think these are two of the better housing-development courses I've seen, although probably partly because the housing wasn't very far developed the last time I saw them. (P.B. Dye remarked to me that the lot stakes were so tight that they needed a local rule to allow a free drop away from them within a fairway.) The front nine of the older South course is sort of dull, but the back side has several interesting holes around open marshes. The newer North course was constructed on somewhat less promising land, but the use of natural grasses and some interesting bunkering makes it a more sophisticated piece of design. These were also the best-kept courses around Hilton Head when I lived there. North course: 6. South course: 5. [8/81]

***The Dunes G & BC,*** *Myrtle Beach. Robert Trent Jones, 1949.*

Of all Trent's courses, this is my favorite; for some reason, his familiar style looks at home here. I was surprised to find the course is modestly hilly, whereas I had assumed that everything in Myrtle Beach was dead flat. (I was only 90% right.) The stretch from the 10th to 12th holes is a very good one, and the par-5 13th is a much more interesting hole than my first impression of it: its heroic angles of play and prodigious length are such that a well-placed tee shot and second shot can mean the difference between a 3-iron and wedge approach. However, they just got finished rebuilding the greens for bentgrass, and word is they took out the character of the most interesting greens (13, 16, 18) to do it. 7. [4/92]

*Pete Dye and Jack Nicklaus' partnership gave us Harbour Town.*

***Fripp Island GC,*** *Fripp Island. Ocean Creek course by Davis Love 3d and Bob Spence, 1996.*

I only saw a few holes of this yet-unfinished course in a reconnaissance effort. It's a nice piece of property, with lots of small rolls in among the trees, but the course is squeezed a bit too tightly together to give much latitude for interesting fairway bunkering. The greens had broad, gentle undulations like a Tour pro would do it; a handful of holes I didn't see have marsh prominently in play. Pleasant, but not a showstopper. [6/95]

***Haig Point GC,*** *Daufuskie Island. Rees Jones, 1986.*

I like the design of this course: there's a nice set of small, elevated greens, and two extra holes for weaker players who did not want to confront two greens placed along a narrow strip of land between the marsh and sea. Adding to the fun is the fact that the course is secluded from the rest of Hilton Head by a 35-minute ferry ride, and private enough that there are few disturbances or other groups to slow up play. However, I think that the ferry ride has caused it to be drastically overrated by those comparing it to Hilton Head's best: it's a neat, low-profile course, but there aren't any holes I'd want to steal for Long Cove or Harbour Town. 6. [10/87].

***Harbour Town Links,*** *Sea Pines Plantation, Hilton Head. Pete Dye and Jack Nicklaus, 1969.*

Harbour Town holds a special place in my heart, because it was the first really good golf course I saw, and it gave an impressionable youth a taste for golf architecture. It is rightly famous among American courses for marking a turning point in the history of golf architecture, away from the Trent Jones school to the Pete Dye school, and there are an enormous number of good strategic holes despite the flattish ground and lack of total length. There is indeed a fine set of short holes, although I do not agree that they are the *best* set in the world—they're much too similar.

However, I would be inclined to agree with Pete that the course is somewhat overrated by many critics. The Tour players still love it for its tiny greens, which demand precise iron play, but these proved to be less than functional at a resort which does 70,000 rounds of golf annually, and I understand that criticism over the condition has caused some of the greens to be enlarged and changed in character. I hope I get to build a course like the original Harbour Town someday, but it will have to be at a private club with very restricted play. 8. [12/88]

***Heather Glen GC,*** *Little River. Original 18 by Willard Byrd and Clyde Johnston, 1987; Third nine by Clyde Johnston, 1989.*

All the public relations material about how this course is reminiscent of the ancient Scottish traditions of the game makes me want to just throw up. Pot bunkers simply do not occur naturally in the faces of small, pimply mounds; and contrary to the firm and fast-playing character of Scottish courses, Heather Glen drains like a rice paddy. Like many other new courses, the "feature holes" are all the worst holes. I can't believe this course is highly regarded, even in the design wasteland of Myrtle Beach. The new nine accomplishes something I didn't think it could—some of the new holes are even worse than the old. Worst of all is the new 4th, a straightaway par-4 with a sunken green site hemmed in by railroad ties set into the downslope. Ugh. Old 18: 3. Third nine: 0. [10/89]

***Heritage Club,*** *Pawleys Island. Dan Maples and Larry Young, 1986.*

I think I know why Heritage Club doesn't stand up architecturally to Larry's other operations at Oyster Bay and Marsh Harbour: Larry was around too much. The property is quite pretty, but the profusion of pot bunkers cut into conical mounds at the back of several greens isn't Scottish—it's ugly. Those who rate it highly must put a lot of stock in the clubhouse and facilities, which are truly first-class. 4. [11/88]

***Hilton Head GC,*** *Shipyard Plantation, Hilton Head. Willard Byrd, 1970.*

I'm not sure they still use this name for the first course built at Shipyard; it's been ages since I saw it. However, I remember it as somewhat better than the average low country layout, thanks to a resident pro who spent some time overseeing the shaping of the greens and bunkers. But it's still flat and over-saturated with lagoons. 3. [4/74]

***Hope Plantation GC,*** *Kiawah Island. Clyde Johnston, 1990.*

There's no hope for this course, or for the attached housing development; only one house got built before the developer went under. 2. [3/92]

***Kiawah Island Resort,*** *Kiawah Island, Charleston. The Ocean course by Pete Dye, 1991.*

It would be unfair to describe this course as "PGA West by the Sea"; though as controversial as its California cousin because of the marketing decision by Landmark and the PGA of America to hold the Ryder Cup here before the course was a year old, it will ultimately be more well-liked than PGA West simply because of its gorgeous beachfront site.

The comparisons to a links course are inevitable, even though all of the contours in the fairways were constructed from fill so that all the drainage water generated by the course could be recycled into a central pond, protecting the surrounding marshes from contamination. In fact, though most of the greens are unguarded by bunkers in front, several are elevated to such a degree that a bounced-in approach is impractical; but because the banks of the greens are shaved down to collar height, it is possible to play a variety of running shots around the greens, as you might on a links, though these are harder.

My favorite holes are the first few, where the marsh and the sand dunes are often in play, and the fairways are not built up so high that they seem unnatural—though some of the greens are. The weathered oaks at this end of the strand also add a great deal to the picture. On the back nine, the elevated fairways at 11 and 12 do provide a different perspective of the background for the greens (and afford nice views of the ocean), but the steep bank down to grade on the right makes them obviously contrived, as are the 16th and 17th. The 17th,

heretofore known as the Mark Calcavecchia Memorial Choke hole, is a great do-or-die hole that provided high drama during the Ryder Cup, but doesn't look like it belongs here. Indeed, all the par-3 holes (except the 14th) look like Pete was trying too hard—it's tough to make an arresting par-3 hole without a severe natural green site or some exotic bunkering, and Kiawah has neither. Interestingly, neither do most links courses, and most of the par-3 holes are rather ordinary, except for the "Postage Stamp" holes, where the golfer is required to be accurate in the wind. Pete should have built one of those at Kiawah.

Overall, though, I think The Ocean Course is one of Pete's most original designs in the last 15 years. I love some of the contouring around the greens, particularly the few green sites (nos. 4, 7, 10, 12, 13, and 18) that blend right into the dunes. I also admire the effort Pete has put into landscaping the out-of-play areas back into dunes covered with beach grasses, although it certainly didn't make viewing easy for the Ryder Cup crowds. The flexibility of teeing grounds, which allows the course to be stretched to 7,752 yards, is fine with me, as long as they mix up the tee markers so that different holes play long on different days. If you play this course from the tips, you'll spend a week in traction. 7. [3/92]

***The Legends Golf Complex,*** *East Conway. Heathland Course by Tom Doak, 1990; Moorland Course by P.B. Dye, 1991; Parkland Course by Larry and Danny Young (started by Tom Doak and Gil Hanse), 1992.*

I must first apologize for the misnomer "Heathland" for a course that is modeled after a British links: developer Larry Young changed it from "Linksland" because his reservation operators couldn't pronounce it. What makes it work is that it is a contiguous golf course, without housing beside the holes, so that the "sand dunes" could run obliquely to the holes rather than strictly parallel; then we could afford to build one big hill for three holes, instead of needing three separate ones. We created the site first—stripping 175 acres of pulp pines off the flat site, digging two deep ditches (disguised as "burns") into the middle of the site for drainage, and then creating as much undulation as we could for the budget—and then designed holes over it.

The best part of the Heathland is the contour of the ground, which in places actually begins to have the variety of linksland, and the width of the course, which allows the hapless Myrtle Beach golfers to get around in four hours. The greens, unfortunately, had to be extra large to handle the volume of golf traffic, but like St. Andrews they have enough contours to make for interesting pin placements when you want to find them. On reflection, the fairway bunkering could have been a little sterner, but Heathland still has all the elements of a Scottish course (open feel, open fronts to the greens, deep bunkers, and capricious winds), and none of the waste bunkers or bulkheaded ponds that characterize other pseudo-Scottish modern designs.

When I parted ways with Larry after completing the Heathland course, I just about challenged him to hire P.B. Dye to design the Moorland—they wanted something modern and hard, and I figured P.B. would get so car-

ried away that my course would wind up looking better by comparison. Actually, though, I have to say that P.B. did better than I would have with the concept. The driving areas are about as wide and as playable as anything the Dyes have done recently, and while there are "steep and deep" bunkers sprinkled liberally about, it's very playable for the average golfer; in fact, my wife consistently scored better here than on my course next door. The only two holes that gave her fits were the par-5 11th, with a small elevated green surrounded by steep banks mowed at fairway height—a great hole, which isn't too difficult as long as you keep straight, but gets really hard once you miss wide of the green—and the par-5 15th, which has a forced carry on the second shot beyond the means of most Myrtle Beach golfers. The finishing holes get a little weird, because of wetlands restrictions that were being imposed while the course was underway, but overall it's a fun course and a good effort.

I guess I should have known better than to expect a free hand from Larry in designing the Parkland course, but I thought after the success of the Heathland I'd get a little more respect and leeway. Turned out I was wrong; he believes the first course was a success because we moved a lot of dirt and because he developed it, instead of because we got the details right. Anyway, we were trying to build a very-low-profile layout with some flashy bunkers in small clusters, but Larry thought it looked *too* plain, and all his suggestions were 9th-grade design-class stuff ("movement" around the greens—meaning mounds) that would have made it look like any other stupid Myrtle Beach course. A couple of our holes survived—the short par-5 11th, and the stretch from the 14th through 16th, which featured our best low-profile work—but sadly, Larry blew up some other pretty good work, and the goofy 5th, 9th, 10th, and 18th were all his idea. This could have been the most interesting of the three Legends courses for the serious student of design; instead, it was headed down the tubes, so I had to let it go. Heathland: 6. Moorland: 5. Parkland: 5. [10/93]

***Long Bay Club,*** *Wampee. Jack Nicklaus, 1988.*

This is about the lamest of Jack's designs that I've seen: it's very low-lying ground, and even with a lot of earthmoving there isn't much definition to it except where they've built rows of goofy mounds. Worse yet, Long Bay has four or five driving holes that force you either to lay up from the tee or attempt some difficult carry that a first-time player cannot judge with any degree of accuracy. (It is supposed to go private someday, but it's still indefensible when you've contrived the land to make it so; blind shots over hills I don't mind.) Still, it's highly ranked among South Carolina courses—proving either that it's better than I think, or that Jack's name carries a lot of weight with the voters independently of the merits of his designs. 4. [3/89]

*Pete Dye's splendid Long Cove.*

***Long Cove Club,*** *Hilton Head. Pete Dye and crew, 1981.*

I must admit to being predisposed to like this course because it was the first at which I worked on the construction crew, but I thought from the beginning that it would be one of Pete's best, and I love the result. The beautiful, fluid contouring of the greens is something of a knee-jerk reaction to the controversy of the TPC at Sawgrass; Pete kept telling us we had to keep it soft because of the older clientele who would be playing the course, but its quality of design has attracted a much more sophisticated audience. Though there are waste bunkers, the holes are well differentiated by the variety of terrain, which includes lagoons, live oaks, salt marsh, and Pete's artificial sandhill ridge, designed to obscure the power line paralleling the 6th through 8th holes.

Though I want to emphasize the fact that 100% of the design credit here belongs to Pete Dye, I was deeply impressed by the correlation between a sharp construction crew and a great product—most of the guys thought it was hilarious that I was training to be a golf architect, but five Long Cove alumni are now golf architects in their own right. 8. [12/85].

***Myrtlewood GC,*** *Myrtle Beach. Palmetto course by Ed Ault, 1972.*

This is a little better than the typical Myrtle Beach layout, just because it finishes with a good par-4 hole along the Intracoastal Waterway. The other 17 holes aren't anything earth-shattering, but they're playable without being as dull as the earliest courses in town. 3. [4/90]

***Palmetto Dunes GC's,*** *Hilton Head. Robert Trent Jones course, 1970; George Fazio course, 1978; Arthur Hills course (n.r.), 1986.*

The original Trent Jones design is the quintessential sixties-style development golf course, arranged more for airspace between the condos than for interesting play: I've seen more of it than I need to just from driving past on the highway. The Fazio course is better, but they still must have paid *Golf Digest* a hefty sum to get it ranked among America's best golf courses, as it was not so long ago. Some of the bunkers do sprawl out of George Fazio's usual cookie-cutter lines, but the course was given a lot of points for "classic styling," which I never saw. Jones course: 2. Fazio course: 4. [7/81]

***Palmetto GC,*** *Aiken. Herbert Leeds, 1896, with revisions by Alister MacKenzie, 1933.*

Here's a real sleeper of a course not far across the river from Augusta, although you can see from the architectural credits that its quality is no accident. The property is hilly and there are a couple of weak, goat-hill holes within the routing, but much of MacKenzie's genius in contouring is in evidence around the greens, although the bunkering is unusually subdued. My favorite holes were the uphill par-4 2nd with a tough approach, the good two-shot 4th, the long 10th, and above all the short 7th to a shelf of green that reminded me of Dornoch. The club is also a treat, a very friendly place once you get to know the members. 6. [2/86]

***Prestwick GC,*** *Surfside Beach. Pete and P.B. Dye, 1989.*

For the Dyes, this is a dull affair. It's a beast from the back tees as always, and they didn't spare much in the dirtmoving department—several of the holes are bounded by a long, high berm in the manner of the 7th at Long Cove, though none as ele-

gantly. But there is a stretch of several really mediocre holes on the front nine, and the back nine, though better, still falls short of having any great holes. There *is* a fine set of greens, contour-wise, so P.B. blew my theory that if you build an interesting set of greens, you automatically have a pretty good golf course. Prestwick is only fair, or maybe I still hold the Dyes to a higher standard. 5. [3/89]

***The Sea Pines Club,*** *Sea Pines Plantation, Hilton Head. Frank Duane and Arnold Palmer, 1979.*

A private course for Sea Pines residents, a bit more sophisticated than the two courses at the Plantation Club, but still nothing special. Very tight driving in places, unless it was just my horrible day off the tee. 3. [7/81]

***Sea Pines Plantation Club,*** *Hilton Head. Ocean and Sea Marsh courses by George Cobb, 1959–60.*

You couldn't have imagined what Hilton Head would become when these were the first two courses on the island: but the place certainly wouldn't have taken off like it did if all the courses were like these. The Ocean course is more popular because of the view off the back of the 15th green, but that is about all it has going for it, while the Sea Marsh course may someday become famous for being the first I ever played. (At least, it is unlikely ever to become famous otherwise.) I will never forget the 1st hole at Sea Marsh, which requires a 150-yard carry over a pond for the opening tee shot—dubious for a resort course, and very intimidating for a ten-year-old beginner. Both courses: 3. [1/79]

***Secession GC,*** *Beaufort. Bruce Devlin, from a routing by Pete and P.B. Dye, 1992.*

A national membership club founded on the mantle of traditionalism, this course occupies Gibbes Island, a low-lying island in the tidal marsh about three miles from historic downtown Beaufort, where the Articles of Secession were drafted. The Dyes were originally given the assignment, along with a prescription for a very-low-profile design with virtually no rough and minimal mounding throughout the course; but then they were booted from the job when the founders decided they wouldn't follow orders, and Bruce Devlin was brought in to finish the job using the Dyes' routing.

The end product is a mixed success. The routing is solid, with the surrounding marsh in play to the left on the first six and last six holes, and the small island 17th green makes for a terrific panorama. The low-profile, all-fairway concept is noble, but they needed Donald Ross instead of Devlin to pull it off, especially once it was decided to go with big and relatively flat bent greens instead of small Bermuda surfaces, which might have worked. Nearly all the mounding looks artificial, because it had to be done with fill dirt; they couldn't create any shallow depressions to tie the contouring together because there was no elevation to drain them. Finally, the shaved sod-wall bunkers used near greens are quite attractive, but I don't know how they'll weather southern summers, and the developers had no idea they would have to be rebuilt every 3–5 years.

Dumbest gimmick: the four-foot-tall flagsticks. (You could put an eye out getting the flag out of the hole.)

Bottom line: it's a very pleasant and secluded place to play golf, but it's nowhere near a good enough course to pull off the Pine Valley retreat concept upon which it was founded. Anyone who tells you otherwise probably knows better, but the part owners can't stand to admit it to themselves. 5. [3/92]

***Spring Island GC,*** *Spring Island. Old Tabby Links by Arnold Palmer and Ed Seay, 1993.*

Another pretender to the throne of "the first really good course that Arnold's done," and perhaps this is it. Certainly, it's a most relaxed and genteel atmosphere, with only 21 homes in three thousand acres, and hidden past the gates of the adjacent Callawassie development. The property is quite nice, with native low country forest between many of the holes, beautifully landscaped lagoons in play on the front nine, and a bit more openness on the back, culminating with the beautiful par-3 17th across a dike at the edge of the marsh. (You've no doubt seen the hole in their advertisements, but there's much more elevation than you can see.) There are, however, some over-landscaped waste areas, quite a few pointless bunkers and mounds, and an island-green short par-4, and there's not a lot of interest to the green complexes. A pleasant retreat, but not a classic. 6. [6/95]

***Surf G & BC,*** *North Myrtle Beach. George Cobb, 1960.*

The Surf Club is very reminiscent of the Dunes, its sister to the south, though not as good. Its principal weakness is the plethora of dogleg holes, which insist on making their turns at all sorts of awkward (and hard-to-judge) distances from the tees: I played here in the Golf Writers' annual tournament, and club selection at the tee was a bitch. I will say, however, that for that tournament the greens were as good as any over-seeded Bermuda greens I have ever putted on—firm, true, and nearly perfect. 4. [4/89]

***Tidewater Plantation GC,*** *Little River Neck, North Myrtle Beach. Ken Tomlinson, 1990.*

Almost anyone could design a golf course; the two keys to being a professional at it are to design good holes, and to do it with a minimum of waste. Ken Tomlinson has succeeded well at both at Tidewater. Apparently he parted ways with the original designer, Rees Jones, over his selection of a routing plan. If so, Tomlinson cannot be faulted too much, because although his routing has the logistical problem of having to cross a public road four times, it does bring both the inlet and the Intracoastal Waterway into play on each nine.

Instead of building mounds to form his features, Tomlinson chose to keep all his bunkers and greens of the low-profile variety, with fairly good results. Most of the greens are interestingly contoured, although a couple look like Nicklaus leftovers, while the bunkers are large, although I don't like his flash bunkers around several greens, which lack any value as a hazard (you can putt out of them). There are also several holes that will be hell on the pace of play—the concept was to limit play by charging a higher green fee, but some of the golfers most able to afford such fees are some of the worst players. I'm also sure that Tomlinson wasted a fortune during construction moving things around until he had them just right, but that's his prerogative as long as it was his money. (Most everyone in the business makes mistakes in planning. Some correct them in the field at enormous expense, while others just let them be.)

Overall, I think the course has been overrated by the golf magazines—though it was nice to see them applaud something different, just once—and because of the inevitable power of Myrtle Beach mass publicity; but it certainly is a refreshing alternative to Dan Maples' or Tom Jackson's ninth course in Myrtle Beach. 6. [10/89]

*The late afternoon sun highlights the 11th at Wachesaw.*

***Wachesaw Plantation Club,*** *Murrells Inlet. Tom Fazio, 1986.*

A private club laid out on perhaps the best piece of land in the Myrtle Beach area: nice pine groves, white sandy soil, modest undulation, and an overlook to the inlet at the finishing hole. Some of Fazio's waste bunkers here are really spectacular—a real elevation of a form that is not generally my favorite—but some of his mounding and other bunker work goes too far, especially at the alien-looking par-3 7th. It's still about as good as Myrtle Beach has to offer. 6. [9/89]

***Wild Dunes G & RC,*** *Isle of Palms. Links course by Tom Fazio, 1980; Harbor course also by Fazio, 1986.*

Wild Dunes has been remarkably patched up after serving as ground zero for Hurricane Hugo in September 1989. I've always liked the routing and the land itself, which would probably rate a 9 on my 1-10 scale, but the steep contours of some greens (like the 10th and 11th, where an approach shot six feet below the hole may well be worth *two strokes* more than an approach six feet above the hole, if you try to do more than lag the downhiller) are a bit much. Otherwise, it was a beautiful course, but the corridors through the development were always on the narrow side, and the destruction of trees by the hurricane has brought much more of the encroaching homes into view. The holes in the sand dunes (with the exception of the 11th) all have exciting golf to offer, with the shortish par-4 17th (not the 18th) the best of the lot.

The Harbor course is a real puzzle to me: a couple of club pros whom I respect tell me that the back nine here is one of the best nine holes they've ever played, but aside from one fine hole (the long par-4 13th, across and along the marsh) it just looked hard and contrived to me, typified by the 18th, which is 470 yards long and about 20 yards wide in the landing area, between ridiculous peaked mounds on the right and the entrance road for the development on the left. The front nine is like Long Point at Amelia Island: it's so narrow, and there's so much marsh in play, they should give you an airboat instead of a golf cart. Don't know if it survived Hugo, and I don't much care. Links course: 7. Harbor course: 0–4. [2/89]

***Wild Wing GC,*** *East Conway. Wood Stork Course by Willard Byrd, 1991.*

Slightly more than basic Myrtle Beach golf, even though the Japanese ownership has lavished its attentions on trying to make it so. It tries to be a "classically styled" course, but that just means you

can see some sand and there's a lot of green grass; the green complexes are pretty dull, and there's no terrain to make up for them. 4. [4/92]

***Yeamans Hall Club,*** *Hanahan. Seth Raynor, 1925.*

The bad news first: the sad neglect that plagued much of golf course maintenance during the Second World War ravaged Yeamans Hall, as nearly all of the greens were shrunk inside their original shapes and sizes. Forty years of topdressing later, the existing greens are uninteresting, slightly raised mounds inside the shells of their former selves.

Except for that, which spoils the course completely, Yeamans Hall is one of the neatest places I've ever visited—and one of the weirdest. Like Seminole, the club was built by old northern money, and in its heyday the course was closed entirely during the summer: all of the residents of the small housing development integrated with the course leave for the Hamptons or the mountains. But when the miracle of irrigation occurred, the club decided it might as well let the citizens of Charleston play during the summer for a modest membership fee. This lower class of members has to park behind the barns, isn't even allowed to enter the clubhouse, and slams beers after their rounds in the pro shop/snack bar. And they can't understand why they're considered one of the snobbiest clubs in the U.S.

The course was pretty neat, too: it's a very good piece of property for Charleston, rolling from the edge of the marsh up to the clubhouse, surrounded by some unbelievable trees. There are the standard Raynor par-3's (with an especially good and simple Redan, the 6th), but the two-shotters, though some of them are pretty strong, are not especially memorable. The ambience of the place is the real attraction, particularly the old gatehouse and the entrance drive, which combine to make the best entrance I've seen to any golf course anywhere. The melding of the golf course with secluded homesites is also unsurpassed. Too bad about the greens; fixed up, Yeamans Hall would be terrific. 5. [6/95]

*—Gossip—*

There are still a lot of courses I didn't get around to seeing during my year in Myrtle Beach, but I don't think I missed any of the good ones. So many of the old courses (Beachwood, Robber's Roost, Seagull, etc.) are so flat and dull that I think you could blindfold the chief P.R. man for *Golf Holiday* and take him out in the middle of one of them and he would have about a 1-in-25 shot of identifying the course he was on. The new Caledonia course, the first solo effort by former Fazio assistant Mike Strantz, looks pretty good in the ads—junior Fazio—but I wish him more luck with his new patron, Larry Young, than Dan Maples or P.B. or I had.

Elsewhere in the state is the Chanticleer course at Greenville CC, which has always been ranked well by *Golf Digest,* though we've been known to disagree; and the obscure Musgrove Mill, a very difficult Pine Valley-like layout by Arnold Palmer, where Tidewater founder Ken Tomlinson played a role in construction. Along the coast, there's Rees Jones' Charleston National, denuded by Hurricane Hugo just days before its grand opening; and on nearly every island between Charleston and Savannah there is now a golf course or two to explore: the Trent Jones "Crooked Oaks" course at Seabrook, Nicklaus and Fazio layouts at Kiawah Island, Tom Fazio's Dataw Island, Nicklaus' low-profile Colleton River just off Hilton Head, which has spent liberally on its advertising budget to distinguish itself as different than other Nicklaus designs; and the new hopeful is the next-door Tom Fazio course at Belfair. As a general rule, however, better go without reading the developers' advertising claims unless you want to be disappointed.

## KENTUCKY

***The Champions GC,*** *Nicholasville. Art Hills, 1987.*

The architect whose success puzzles me most is Art Hills: I can't figure out how his career has taken off without ever having done a single course that the press or public has taken to heart. I'm told that his two best courses are Bonita Bay, which I haven't seen, and The Champions, where he was given a fairly good piece of rolling ground and exceptionally wide corridors to route his course through the development. Overall, this is a pretty good course—it has a pleasant, open feel to it, and it fits the land pretty well, although most of the mounding around the greens is a bit finicky, and out of scale with the sweeping contours of the ground. The course was also noticeably well-conditioned, in a tough area of the country for grass-growing. But the use of several forced water carries is uninspired—more trouble for the weak player than interesting for the good player—and the finishing holes are a bit overdone. 6. [4/91]

*—Gossip—*

The pride of Kentucky is Jack Nicklaus' Valhalla, outside Louisville, which ranked among the top 50 in America in the last *Golf Digest* poll; but I think they're getting a lot of credit for spending the money to spray their bentgrass fairways, because the one picture of the course I've seen (of a par-4 green set atop a pile of boulders) looks like Jack at his innovative worst. But you can't get good fairways out of bluegrass, and this is the Bluegrass State.

## TENNESSEE

***Belle Meade CC,*** *Nashville. Donald Ross, 1921, with revisions by Robert Trent Jones and Gary Baird.*

One of the premier social clubs of my experience, with ballrooms and formal dining rooms to beat the band; but as a golf course, it's well landscaped, instead of an interesting layout. The ground is fairly flat, and the flashy white-sand bunkers don't make up for its lack of interesting topography. 4. [6/88]

***Cherokee CC,*** *Knoxville. Donald Ross, 1915, with revisions by Dan Maples.*

A good layout across a steep sidehill site, definitely in prime real estate. The back nine is much better, with a run of excellent holes beginning at the par-5 11th. But they did have to cheat a bit with six short holes, including two strongly uphill one-shotters (the 6th and 8th) with heavily sloped greens, and the "restored" bunkering isn't very Ross-like. 5. [10/95]

***Gettysvue Polo G & CC,*** *Knoxville. Bland Pittman, 1995.*

One of the first solo design efforts of Pittman, a land planner by trade who has worked extensively on the land plans for many of Jack Nicklaus' and Tom Weiskopf's development courses. So, it's ironic that he would hang himself with a poor golf course routing as he did here. Actually, there may not have been any good solution for this site: the clubhouse provides a great view, but the ridge is so high and so close to the main road that the starting holes look like toboggan runs, and the finishing holes look like corkscrews from the bottom up. However, the other holes aren't very well conceived either: on the long sidehill par-5 17th, if you fail to hit it within 15 yards any side of the perfect spot in the fairway, you'll be flying blind off a sidehill for your next shot. 3. [10/95]

***Holston Hills CC,*** *Knoxville. Donald Ross, 1933.*

A terrific, well-preserved example of Ross' work, this is a stately and broad-shouldered layout on the east edge of town. The stretch from the 9th to 14th holes is the meat of the challenge, but my three favorite holes are the "Cape"-type par-4 2nd, the very long par-5 5th, and the split-fairway short par-5 7th, none of which require 12-foot-deep waste bunkers for punctuation. Unfortunately, as this is now the "wrong" side of town, they don't have a lot of money to spend on it—but maybe that's one factor that has helped to preserve the design intact. 7. [10/95].

***The Honors Course,*** *Ooltewah. Pete and P.B. Dye, 1983.*

I think a lot of the praise for this course comes because, like Shoal Creek for Nicklaus, The Honors is a lot more traditional-looking than most of Pete's work, thanks to the sidehill forest setting and superintendent David Stone's work in naturalizing the roughs. In a way it reminds me of a course like Oak Hill (with more severe hazards, of course) because of the homogeneous look to the holes: there is nothing but woods, lakes, and rock walls for landscape. But look closer, and there are an awful lot of green complexes with some silly-looking mound or pot bunker which the hole would have been better off without. More important, there aren't many notable holes: only the par-4 7th, a neat solution to putting a hole along the dike of the irrigation pond, but otherwise one of the most gimmicky-looking holes Pete Dye ever built, and the 9th, which is a very good drive-and-pitch hole to a narrow green perched over a pond front left. That keeps it from being Pete's best in my mind.

I must admit, though, that much of my disdain for the course is due to the attitude the club presents. It's one thing to aspire to be Augusta, but you can't create tradition overnight, and you certainly shouldn't be complaining about rival new courses being less traditional than your own. I don't think you ought to be able to have it both ways, seeking high rankings and national tournaments while trying to remain extremely exclusive at the same time. 7. [10/95]

*The 9th at The Honors requires a perfect pitch.*

***Richland CC,*** *Nashville. Jack Nicklaus, 1988.*

Surprise! This isn't the same Richland course on which Amy Alcott sweated out the field to win the U.S. Women's Open in 1980. That course has been dozed over after a real-estate swap deal for a new property on the south end of town, where Jack has shoehorned the new layout into a tight, hilly property. The members are bound to be antagonistic about the change, since the new course is nearly impossible to walk 18 holes; but the layout is probably as good as or better than the old one. 5. [6/88]

***River Islands GC,*** *Mascot. Arthur Hills, 1991.*

A poor man's Blackwolf Run, built for the "upscale daily-fee" market in Knoxville. The setting on the French Broad River is fabulous, with golf holes on both sides of the river and one three islands within, but the holes themselves are a mixed bag: some are heavily shaped, others very low-profile with the occasional eruption of a feature. The grass bunkers and chipping areas are interesting, but *not* designed for the bump-and-run game, with odd bounces at the front of many greens. It's also a very different course depending on where you play from—for example the par-5 6th is 639 yards from the blacks across the river with a pot bunker in the landing area, but 482 from the next markers, while the par-3 3rd is 195 and 154 across the river for the men, but 65 yards from the red tees, from which I could two-putt for a birdie. The rocky backdrops of the river, the requisite humidity, and the trees also make it nearly impossible to grow grass on the island holes—they had fans laying on the greens on my visit. 5. [10/95]

*—Gossip—*

The only strong newcomers to the fray are Tom Fazio's Golf Club of Tennessee near Nashville, said to be one of his better recent designs, and Bob Cupp's 36-hole Legends Club, plus the "Little Course," which is the most complicated combination short course and turf nursery ever conceived. Just across the state line from Chattanooga is Lookout Mountain, Georgia, while Highlands CC (see North Carolina listings) is not far over the ridge to the east.

## ALABAMA

***CC of Birmingham,*** *Birmingham. West course originally by Donald Ross, 1927, with major revisions by Robert Trent Jones, 1959, and Pete and P.B. Dye, 1984. East course by Donald Ross, 1927, with revisions by George Cobb, 1964.*

If you're headed for Birmingham expecting to see any of Donald Ross' work, you might as well forget it. In the late fifties and early sixties, the club brought in Trent Jones and George Cobb to "update" the master's work, and they redid just about all 36 Ross greens between them. The West course was still ranked as one of the top 100 in the country in 1984, when the green committee got restless again and decided to bring in Pete Dye. At the start of the project the discussion centered on tearing up the Jones greens (which weren't growing any grass, because they'd been smothered by thick woods) and "restoring the Ross look to the course," but they gave Pete too much money and equipment, and I'm told he made the course way too severe. That wouldn't surprise me, knowing the crew that worked down there. I've always been afraid to go back and see it for myself. East course: 3. West course: ? [5/84]

***Shoal Creek Club,*** *Shoal Creek. Jack Nicklaus, 1976.*

Of all the golf courses I've seen since I began working on the *GOLF Magazine* rankings, none was a bigger disappointment than Shoal Creek, which by some phenomenon of mass hysteria was named the 26th best course in the world in 1983. I believe the course's high ranking is an overreaction to the trend in modern architecture (particularly by Nicklaus and Pete Dye) toward very difficult, artificial, and borderline gimmicky designs. Shoal Creek is none of those things, and I think some people were so relieved to see a "no-gimmick" golf course that they were too enthusiastic in support of it. The par-five holes aren't bad, but surely aren't the best set in the world either, as some made them out to be before the PGA Championship; and there isn't a single par-4 on the golf course that is really memorable.

Some people defend the golf course on the grounds that it allowed the players to score in the

PGA, and that it "yielded to a great round of golf" or two, but penal design isn't Shoal Creek's problem: it's too dull and too easy. 6. [5/84]

*—Gossip—*

The two hot topics among new courses in 1994 were both in Alabama: Tom Fazio's Old Overton and the seven-location, multi-course Robert Trent Jones Golf Trail. I still haven't figured out what's supposed to be special about Old Overton—it's very private and the construction was immaculate, but the few photos I've seen make it look wide open and dull. The Jones Trail takes the opposite tack, mass-producing courses on severely hilly sites throughout the state. If they were going to spend this kind of money, you'd think they would have wanted to hire several different designers, or at least someone who could build different-looking courses for different sites. Word is the Grand National courses, at Auburn/Opelika, are the best of the bunch by far.

## GEORGIA

***Atlanta Athletic Club,*** *Duluth. Highlands course designed by Robert Trent Jones, 1967, and extended to 18 by Joe Finger, 1971, with modifications by George and Tom Fazio.*

This is one of those early seventies "championship" courses that is more difficult than charming, but since it has the facilities for big tournaments and the drawing power of the deep South behind it, you can expect it to remain on the roster of major championship venues. But don't expect the players to love it: it's oppressively hot in the summer, and the last four holes give players the unwelcome opportunity to choke away a championship. (Ask John Mahaffey or Tom Weiskopf about that.) 6. [8/81]

***Atlanta CC,*** *Marietta. Original layout by Willard Byrd and Joe Finger, 1965, with major revisions by Bob Cupp/Golforce, Inc., 1980–81.*

Like the Athletic Club, this course is well out in the boonies, so it's not the choice for a late game after business in town. I saw the course in the middle of Nicklaus & Co.'s renovations, so I'm not entirely qualified to rate the course as it looks today, but generally I imagine the course to be tougher, more manicured, and more expensive to belong to. 6. [8/81]

*Atlanta Athletic Club (Highlands).*

***Atlanta National GC,*** *Crabapple. P.B. Dye, 1988.*

For openers, this is one of the worst names I've heard yet for a new course, especially when the town name had such a great ring to it. But it's entirely fitting, since everything else at the Atlanta National is similarly overdone. This was probably the best piece of property any of the new Atlanta clubs had to work with, with nice contour and some unbelievable specimen trees, and they just ruined it by trying to make a course in the image of PGA West, with deep bunkers, island greens, and the rest. Pete Dye is rumored to have said that "once you play the first two holes here, you might as well turn around and head in, because you've seen it all"—supposedly in reference to its severity—but after seeing the gimmicky start I wouldn't be surprised if he was being a bit sarcastic as well. P.B. would be a lot better off without clients telling him to build a "U.S. Open course"; he needs encouragement to make his courses hard like Madonna needs a dating service. 0. [10/87].

***Augusta CC,*** *Augusta. "Hill" course by David Oglivie, with revisions by Donald Ross, Seth Raynor, and Bob Cupp.*

Although the clubhouses are miles apart, Augusta's two most famous courses touch borders, where the downhill 8th at the Country Club runs into the fence behind the 12th green of the National; it's about the only common ground the clubs share. For good local golfers, the Country Club is the place to belong—the National is impossible for locals unless you're a member of the old Augusta society, in which case your membership would have been handed down from granddaddy. But, no need to feel sorry for the locals, who have a pretty good golf course here. The par-3 6th is especially memorable: a bit like the 6th next door, with a pond at the bottom of the hill. 5. [8/81]

***Augusta National GC,*** *Augusta. Alister MacKenzie and Bobby Jones, 1933, with so many subsequent revisions that MacKenzie might not recognize it today. Par-3 course by George Cobb, with revisions by Tom Fazio.*

There's not really much new to say about this course: the major golf magazines exhausted the possible topics in their Masters preview articles about ten years ago. But words and photos will never do justice to the severity of Augusta's hills: I was *amazed* to see the hill on the 10th and 18th in person for the first time. Augusta is a terrific study in how interesting one can make a course without long grass or long carries, but there's so much interest in the course they feel like they have to be downright rude to all those who enquire. Someday you really ought to read MacKenzie's description of the golf course, just to see how completely it's changed from his vision. Holes to study: 2nd, 5th, 7th, 10th–13th. Holes I could do without: 1st, 9th, 15th, 18th.

The par-3 course also deserves a mention: only three of the eleven holes require more than a 9-iron (and a couple are only 70 yards), but it's a great addition to the facility, and a lot of fun on Masters Wednesday. Main course: 9. Par-3 course: 4. [2/86]

***Brunswick CC,*** *Brunswick. Donald Ross, 1936.*

Just back on the mainland across the bridge from Jekyll Island. I thought I should check it out because of the architectural credit. But it's probably one of those topo-map Ross routings done in two days in Pinehurst and built by some local yokel, because the layout is pretty bland. 2. [1/81]

***Cobblestone CC,*** *Acworth. Ken Dye (Finger-Dye-Spann), 1992.*

A tough one for me to judge—it's nothing at all like anything I would design, but at least it was different, and a couple of good players I know really

like it. The property itself was full of pluses and minuses—nice lake frontage, nice trees, extremely hilly, no soil—and all of the above comes across clearly in the end product. There's a lot of mounding about, but it was done so thoroughly that it wouldn't bother me, except that the buffalo grass they used on the mounds is starting to wear out from the combination of foot traffic, steep slopes, and poor soil. There are also several oddly shaped greens, where an average golfer may not be able to hold the ball in some shallow pin placement areas, and could wind up three-putting around a grass bunker to get at the hole. I'll have to play it before I'm comfortable with a rating, but I'd rather try this than White Columns. 5. [4/95]

***CC of the South (or is it The South?),*** *Alpharetta. Jack Nicklaus, 1987.*

An unusually mundane effort for Nicklaus' recent work, but predictable since its main function was to serve as a backyard for two-million-dollar homes: Jack's name in this market had sold $27 million worth of real estate by the time of the Grand Opening. There's nothing really wrong with the course other than its high maintenance budget, and the one gimmick (a par-3 hole with a double green bisected by a stream) works a lot better than I thought it would; but it's not an overly impressive course either. 5. [10/87].

***East Lake CC,*** *Atlanta. Tom Bendelow, 1910, with revisions by Donald Ross and George Cobb; restored by Rees Jones, 1995.*

There is a major effort now underway to restore East Lake, which had become run-down as its members abandoned what has become a seedy neighborhood. Only 18 holes are left of the 36 the young Bobby Jones grew up on, but the course and the old brick clubhouse (formerly home to the Athletic Club) are still very much alive with the ghosts of yesteryear, and it's the only course in Atlanta that has a classic feel. The par-3 6th hole, downhill to a skinny green surrounded by water and lily pads, is the most memorable. 5. [8/81]

***The Farm GC,*** *Dalton. Tom Fazio, 1989.*

Built just a couple of years before he was elected the Pope of design, this course is a fine example of what I used to not like about the Fazio camp's work, and what I miss about it today. It's a stern test for anyone, chock-full of long, difficult par-4 holes with greens tilted off the mountainside. I was never a big fan of these "classic Fazio" greens, but at least back then he wasn't afraid to take a chance in building something difficult. There are some top-notch holes, including the long par-5 2nd with water left, the par-4 6th with its green on a knoll, and the short par-5 15th with a stream in front of the green; but the best part may be the secluded atmosphere of the club, a world away from Atlanta just 90 miles up I-75. 6. [4/95]

***GC of Georgia,*** *Alpharetta. Lakeside course by Art Hills, 1990; Creekside also by Hills, 1992.*

Named the best new private course in the nation a couple of years back, the first 18, Lakeside, is one of the most overrated I've seen. The Japanese-developed course is intended to be an homage to Augusta National, with wide fairways through the woods and minimal bunkering, but the bunkering is some of the most awkward I've ever encountered. Indeed, were I to look at the lay of the land and circle one place around the green not to put a bunker, that's where the only greenside bunker will be found on many of the holes—right where the entrance ought to be, forcing you to fly the ball all the way to the target. And the greens, well, they aren't MacKenzie's contours. If this is the project that rocketed Hills to prominence, he should be forced to give it all back.

The Creekside course, stretched out around the perimeter of the Lakeside, is simply horrible. The property is laced with wetlands, which make for lay-ups or impossible carries, and the design solves none of the problems. The par-5 5th is one of the worst holes ever, and the par-4 8th isn't much better. Lakeside course: 5. Creekside course: 0. [4/95]

***The Harbor Club,*** *Lake Oconee. Tom Weiskopf and Jay Morrish, 1991.*

I played this course the week after it opened, and it went through bankruptcy soon after, so conditioning is questionable; the layout is interesting, but like all development layouts, it lacks variety because it saves most of the high ground for homes. There is one outstanding hole—the 326-yard seventh, by far the best of the design team's compulsory driveable par-4 holes that I've seen so far, because there's a diagonal carry to be made by the player going for the green, and a hook is history—but there are also some bland holes. Overall, I think it's only a medium effort for Weiskopf and Morrish, but not a mediocre course. 5. [4/91]

***Jekyll Island CC,*** *Jekyll Island. Oleander course by Dick Wilson, 1961. (Didn't see the other courses.)*

A far cry from the days of the millionaires, the three Jekyll Island courses appeal mostly to the retirement and cheap golf vacation set. I was told the Oleander was the flagship course, and it is a pretty decent test, but there aren't many memorable holes, and I was totally turned off by the forward-tee solution: every hole had one tee, 60 yards long, with the blue markers at the back, the white markers in the middle, and the red markers right up front, which only serves to make you feel like a nerd to tee it up in the middle. Obviously, then, there isn't much contour to the ground or variety between tee positions. 3. [1/79]

***Jones Creek GC,*** *North Augusta. Rees Jones, 1985.*

A layout that has been heralded as "a great public course," but just another one that requires the "public" qualifier. The back nine, which wanders partway along the line of a creek, is the more interesting of the two; on the front side the surrounding development competes for attention with the golf architecture. 5. [12/87]

***Lookout Mountain GC,*** *Lookout Mountain. Seth Raynor, 1926.*

In a spectacular mountaintop setting high above Chattanooga, this course sports some of the most severe terrain ever taken on by Raynor, with rock outcroppings and some steep sideslopes. But it's not as dramatic as you'd expect from an architect famous for "steep and deep" bunkers, for a host of reasons: minimal soil coverage over the rock, Raynor's death during construction, and washouts before planting that eliminated much of the fairway bunkering. Most memorable hole: the short 6th, with its tee atop a chimney rock. 5. [10/95]

***Oceanside GC,*** *Jekyll Island. Walter Travis, c. 1900.*

Once upon a time, around the turn of the century, Jekyll Island was a winter retreat for the wealthiest industrialists, and when golf began to become popular the "millionaires" commissioned Walter Travis to design them a nine-hole golf links in the true Scottish style—which it remains to this day: a very rudimentary layout just a bit removed from the seafront, with five holes out in a line and four back, and not even 3,000 yards long. It made me giggle trying to imagine the Vanderbilts scraping it around out there, but it might be the only course in the USA where you'd feel at home playing a gutty ball. 2. [1/81]

*Peachtree—another of Bobby Jones' favorites.*

***Peachtree GC**, Atlanta. Robert Trent Jones and the real Bobby Jones, 1948.*

This is a golfers' club, much closer to town than the others in Atlanta. The concept was to use the heavy rolling topography of the site as the principal tee shot hazard, and design everything around huge, rolling greens in a furthering of the Augusta National style. But I think Jones (as in Trent) took the style too far by totally eliminating fairway bunkers except at the 1st hole (coincidentally my favorite hole on the course), and by building greens as big as any I've seen this side of St. Andrews, complete with some very severe contours—the 2nd green really *does* look like it has an elephant buried in the middle of it. *USA Today,* in its laughable ranking of great courses a few years ago, listed this as one of the "three most important designs prior to 1962" (the result of Trent Jr., who wrote most of the list, trying to give his father credit for the Augusta look); fortunately, however, the course didn't have that much influence. 7. [8/81]

***Pine Island Club (a.k.a. Tifton Family Golf Center),** Tifton. Paul Massey, 1991.*

A nice par-3 layout built by the owners of the Tifton Turf Farm. Nothing's more than 170 yards, but the green complexes have a fair amount of detail, and there's plenty of scope to work on shotmaking when the wind blows. 3. [5/95]

***Pine Isle GC,** Buford. Ron Kirby and Gary Player, 1972.*

A resort 30 miles north of Atlanta in the Lake Lanier Islands, Pine Isle is designed mostly for visual appeal, as many "resort" courses are. The site is one of the most severe I've ever seen for a golf course: treacherously hilly, terrible soil, and water (in the form of Lake Lanier) to contend with on several holes. Therefore, the mellow curves of the fairways, convoluted green shapes, and shallow cookie-cutter bunkers placed miles to the sides of the greens seem all the more out of place. (I hate having to putt off the green and through the fringe to attack the hole, and you'll be lucky not to have to do it three times a round at Pine Isle.) There are some memorable holes, thanks to Lake Lanier, including the long 5th, the down-and-up par-4 13th, and the double-water-carry 18th, but it seems like there ought to be more good ones. 4. [8/81]

***Port Armor Club,** Lake Oconee. Bob Cupp, 1986.*

A very nice development/retreat located south of the main interstate about halfway between Atlanta and Augusta. It is laid out over hilly ground that becomes steep in places, and Cupp's bunkers do not stir the same passion in me that MacKenzie's or Thomas' do, but there are a lot of excellent holes and very few mediocre ones. It is also an especially pretty course, except in winter when the Bermuda grass is not over-seeded and the trees are bare. 6. [12/87]

***Reynolds National GC,** Lake Oconee. Plantation Course by Bob Cupp with Hubert Green and Fuzzy Zoeller, 1988; Great Waters Course by Jack Nicklaus, 1992.*

The original course is a textbook development routing—all the holes run through the bottom of wooded valleys, with homes up high to both sides, so there's no chance for the topography to influence the play. There's also an unfortunate signature hole, the short par-4 2nd, with a shallow hourglass green backed up by a rock outcropping in the hillside behind.

Great Waters, oddly, is several miles' drive around the other side of the lake—they bought the property to preserve the views from the main plantation, and since the development of this side was secondary to their plans, they gave Jack a lot of latitude to route parts of eight holes along the lakefront. The design is the "new Nicklaus"—extremely wide and gentle—but on many holes there's little to do except

bust it off the tee, and even on several of the waterfront holes (like the par-5 18th) the fairway is so wide that you'd be nuts to get within throwing distance of the lake. There are a couple of neat holes, including the downhill par-4 9th, with its approach over a cove, and the short par-4 11th with a double-wide fairway offering two angles to attack the green. High marks for playability, but not much punch. Plantation Course: 4. Great Waters: 6. [4/95]

***Sea Island GC,*** *St. Simons Island. Four nine-hole layouts: Plantation by Walter Travis; Seaside by Colt and Alison; Retreat by Dick Wilson; Marshside by Joe Lee.*

An excellent example of old-fashioned and modest modern design in one place, almost like a museum; still, the "championship" layout of Seaside and Retreat has enough continuity to save its character. There are several excellent holes along the marshes on two nines, particularly the 4th and 7th holes of Seaside, which tend to overshadow the rest of the holes; but nowhere in the 36 do the holes get really mundane. The 5-star Cloister Hotel nearby has a Southern plantation society appeal that is more for Barbara Bush than me, but the golf at Sea Island is rewarding and completely unstuffy. Championship layout: 6. Other nines: 5. [1/81]

***The Standard Club,*** *North Fulton County. Art Hills, 1987.*

This is Art Hills' take on the go-go '80s—a difficult layout over rolling terrain with lots of native grasses about, but not much interest to the bunkers or greens. The weakest element of the design is the green complexes, with the same set-up (set at an angle to the fairway, the flank guarded by a steep drop or other hazard) at damn near every hole. 5. [10/87].

***Sterling Bluff GC,*** *Richmond Hill. Pete and P.B. Dye, 1986–89.*

One of those crazy Dye projects where I was in residence briefly while doing planning work. I only ever saw the front nine through the woods, which has one or two outstanding holes (including a marvelous green at the par-5 3rd), although it's a bit of a ball-buster in the P.B. Dye tradition; the back nine, which was supposed to be an artificial links dredged from the plantation's old rice paddies, was finished years later. The course lies just three miles off I-95, but I don't know anything about how it's being run; it was supposed to be the private stomping grounds of a wealthy Arab, but he turned out to be one of the major players in the BCCI bank scandal. 5. [12/85]

***White Columns GC,*** *Alpharetta. Tom Fazio, 1995.*

Remember those courses you heard about in college, where everyone passes and nobody has to think too hard? We called them "gut" courses, and White Columns is golf's closest approach yet. Clearly designed to impress the worst stereotype of the typical Atlanta yuppie golfer, it's long and green and immaculate enough to please the Japanese ownership, but totally devoid of interest. The greens say it all—huge, mostly flat, with an occasional tier or false front, beautifully manicured (the brand-new Crenshaw bent surfaces were as pure as anything I've putted on), but absolutely vapid. 4. [4/95]

—*Gossip*—

The only two growth areas in recent years have been the suburbs of Atlanta and the lake district halfway between Augusta and the capital; I saw most of these in my last trip down, though I'll be back to see Coore and Crenshaw's Cuscowilla GC when it's built. The other big pretender is Rees Jones' private Ocean Forest layout near Sea Island, which I hope is less predictable than Rees' recent award-winners.

## FLORIDA

Growing up in New England, spending a year in the British Isles, and traveling all over the world, I've become convinced that undulating topography is the soul of great golf courses. The variety of undulations created by God is infinitely more complex than anything possible to man, and so the complexity of golf holes laid out over the natural terrain.

It follows, then, that the golf courses of Florida are anathema to my own tastes. As the capital of the Flat Earth Society, very few Florida courses have any significant undulation, and worse still, because the ground is so low-lying, there often has to be lots of water in play simply to get a golf course to drain properly. On top of everything else, the grass choices in the state are pretty much limited to strains of Bermuda; the only other grass native to the state is St. Augustine grass, a coarse-bladed variety that withers under the feet of the day's second foursome.

Yet, because of its popularity as a retirement capital, there are more than 1,000 golf courses in Florida today. I'll take Seminole; you can have the other 999.

***Adios GC,*** *Deerfield Beach. Ed Seay and Arnold Palmer, 1985.*

Certainly the ambiance of this all-male club is first-class: the landscaping is plush, and the clubhouse is one of the most striking I've seen. The greens are quite severe in places, but they putt well, and elevate what would otherwise be a narrow and drab layout. But whoever did the routing should be shot, as there are a couple of 90-degree doglegs around interior holes; and all the moguls in the fairways and along their edges are a bit much for me. 5. [4/89]

***Amelia Island Links,*** *Fernandina Beach. 27 holes by Pete Dye, 1973.*

One of the narrowest golf courses I have ever played, with huge live oaks draped in Spanish moss overhanging the fairways. The Oakmarsh and Oysterbay nines comprise the main drag, but the most exciting holes on the property used to be the three along the shore on the Oceanside nine, which are rapidly being eaten away by the Atlantic surf. The course is only about 6,100 yards from the back tees because the resort owners want to move people around quickly, but they'd have a better course if they added some back tees and thinned out the trees. 5. [1/84]

***American Golfers Club,*** *Fort Lauderdale. Robert Trent Jones, 1958.*

The blandest of the bland of public tracks, built strictly to generate revenue out back of Coral Ridge. I wonder how that paid off, as opposed to just covering it with wall-to-wall housing? 1. [1/86]

***BallenIsles CC,*** *Palm Beach Gardens. East course by Dick Wilson, 1964.*

The former national headquarters of the PGA, which hasn't built a winner yet. (At least they had the sense to leave Landmark alone at PGA West, so their name isn't completely mud.) There are three courses, but the only one I've seen is the East, which hosted the PGA and Ryder Cup in 1971—a very long course with lots of water and Bermuda rough in the driving zone, perhaps *the* course that set the stereotype for Florida. The 18th hole is particularly noteworthy, a long par-4 with an alternate fairway to the

left if one can carry a large expanse of water. (Even Nicklaus, at the height of his skills, laid up safely when he had a two-shot lead in the PGA instead of risking the water with his second shot.) 5. [1/86]

***Bay Hill Club,*** *Orlando. Dick Wilson, 1961, with revisions by Arnold Palmer.*

One of the favorite courses on the pro tour, with long, difficult holes and immaculate grass, but like everything else in Florida, about a zero in the "character" category. The two finishing holes are impossible, the other 16 just forgettable. Admittedly, I had only a cursory look around, but anyone who thinks this is a "great" course is in dire need of deprogramming. 6. [3/83]

***Black Diamond GC,*** *Lecanto. Tom Fazio, 1988.*

By now you have probably already seen photos of the five quarry holes, which play over and around two eighty-foot-deep rock quarries: spectacular holes of the highest order, and quite playable, although only one of the five holes has any real strategic interest. The only one of these holes I didn't like was the long par-3 17th, at which a slight pull of a 220-yard tee shot can rebound to disaster, and even a rocket from the tee can hit the downslope of the green and run away against the quarry wall at the back.

Equally important, Black Diamond's other thirteen holes are also good ones, with 20- to 40-foot elevation changes throughout the hilly routing. It also has some of the best Tifdwarf Bermuda greens (over-seeded with bent) that I have ever putted on—maybe too good, because there are some steep putts, particularly at the 18th, which is just too small and severe for its own good. This may be because Fazio's assistants direct the shapers primarily through sketches rather than detailed grading plans, so they have to exaggerate the contours of the green in order to get their point across in sketch form. Even with the three-putts, it's still a hell of a course. 7. [4/89]

***Boca Rio GC,*** *Boca Raton. Robert Von Hagge and Bruce Devlin, 1967.*

This course got a lot of press when it opened—the mounds that define the bunkers were as daring for their time as Grand Cypress' are today, and in fact Boca Rio was actually called "the Troon of the tropics" in one magazine of the day. Today, it seems almost impossible, with the same low mounds and bunkers looking much less dramatic in comparison to those on other modern layouts. 4. [1/81]

***Coral Ridge CC,*** *Fort Lauderdale. Robert Trent Jones, 1956.*

The ultimate Trent Jones Florida course—long, difficult, and giving new depth to the meaning of the word 'flat.' The only relief, relief-wise, is a couple of terrifically severe greens. There is one hole worth remembering—the short 12th, which I believe is a tribute to the 11th at St. Andrews, with just as much fall to its green. 4. [1/86]

***Fort George Island GC,*** *Fort George Island. Bill Amick, 1962, with revisions by Robert Trent Jones.*

Not much of a golf course—it's too tightly confined by trees, and never breaks out onto the marsh as one would hope for. But the clubhouse—a group of fine white buildings left over from the Rockefeller plantation days, with a beautiful center courtyard containing some huge oaks—is one of the best anywhere. 2. [2/84]

***Frenchman's Creek GC,*** *Jupiter. North and South courses by Gardner Dickinson, 1975.*

Gardner Dickinson is one of those Hogan disciples, a brilliant ball-striker who hates putting, and Frenchman's Creek reflects that mind-set, with two long and difficult courses with very little interest around the greens. A couple of par-4 holes on the North course have alternate "hard" and "easy" greens, leaving the option to the players of playing for either—which I'd never seen before, but have seen a few times since. Still, the flat terrain and resulting poor visibility are a serious handicap to the courses. North course: 4. South course: 3. [3/83]

**Golden Ocala GC,** *Ocala. Ron Garl and Bob Spence, 1986.*

The first attempt, I believe, to build replicas of holes from around the world, with surprisingly good results, even though the development has gone bust. Eight holes are near duplicates of great holes from Augusta, Baltusrol, St. Andrews, Royal Troon, and Muirfield, and amazingly accurate duplicates at that, which raise a couple of questions—like what's so great about the 4th at Baltusrol, and why reproduce the new 13th green at Augusta instead of the old one? The ten "original" holes are less well-conceived strategically, of course, but they do a fair job of bridging the gap between the several divergent architectural styles of contouring and bunkering. I'm not sure I want to see more courses like Golden Ocala, because no matter how close the holes are copied they lack the natural appearance of their models, not to mention originality. Still, a course I would recommend seeing. 6. [2/86]

**Grand Cypress GC,** *Lake Buena Vista. Old course (North and South nines) by Jack Nicklaus, 1983; New course by Nicklaus, 1988.*

To my tastes, Grand Cypress' original layout was one of the most offensive courses built in recent times—though as much for the marketing of the course as for the actual design. The site was a flat orange grove with a major road cutting across it, and Jack decided to pile up huge mounds covered in Bahia grass beside the fairways to enclose the golfers' views. Fair enough, if he'd just said he was building a fantasyland course on unpromising terrain. But Jack routes the course to include two double greens, and then goes and tells the world that this is a "Scottish-style" course, as if it is a replica of Dornoch or something. It's one thing for some P.R. stooge to do that, but when Nicklaus does it, it sets back golf architecture another five years, because so many people take his word for things that they never bother to learn the true lessons of Scottish courses.

From the shot-value standpoint the old course isn't so bad, although I don't think there are any great holes here, either; but from an artistic standpoint Grand Cypress is pretty schlocky, and from a maintenance standpoint (requiring fly-mowers around nearly every bunker on the course) it's the worst nightmare ever built. On balance, that doesn't put the course very high on my scale.

When Brian Morgan (who lives in St. Andrews) told me he thought the New course at Grand Cypress had the feel of St. Andrews, I knew it was worth investigating. It is. Provided you don't have the time or money to visit St. Andrews, the New course is a wonderful simulation of the wide-open look and links contouring of the Old Course at St. Andrews. But, considering you have to stay at Grand Cypress Resort to play the New course, St. Andrews is about as affordable, so why settle for this?

I also can't understand the modifications Jack made to the holes he imitated from the Old Course. Why would you want to lengthen the 12th at St. Andrews so it's a full wedge to the green, instead of the unique short running approach the shallow plateau green is made for? Or why flip-flop the Road hole to accommodate a faded second shot, with the major driving hazard still on the right? Neither version is nearly as good as the original hole, which they apparently had the ability to copy exactly if they had wanted to. Meanwhile, the 8th through 10th holes of the New course (both fronted by burns) completely blow the concept of the St. Andrews style of approaching greens, while the 3rd and 12th are just plain awful par-3's. Old course: 5. New course: 5. [4/89]

**Grenelefe G & Racquet Club,** *Haines City. East course by Ed Seay, 1974; West course by David Wallace; new course by Ron Garl and Andy Bean, which I haven't seen.*

Every year, *GOLFWEEK* magazine conducts a reader poll to determine the most popular golf courses in Florida, and every year Grenelefe West comes out no. 1, ahead of Seminole, the TPC, and all the rest. If I didn't suspect this has something to do

with *GOLFWEEK's* advertising revenues, I would be more despondent over public appreciation of golf architecture in Florida, because Grenelefe West isn't much better than Grenelefe East—long, dull, and terribly overrated, even though it does have some elevation to it. The new course, which I've heard includes imitation church-pew bunkers, promises to be even worse. West course: 4. East course: 3. [1/81]

***Gulf Stream GC,*** *Delray Beach. Donald Ross, 1926.*

An old Ross layout in the posh Gulf Stream section, spread out between the Intracoastal Waterway and the Atlantic Ocean, which makes a hell of a backdrop for the par-4 18th. A couple of the shorter holes were diagrammed as exemplary in George Thomas' book on design, but neither hole would have struck me if I hadn't remembered they were in the book. 3. [1/81]

***Harder Hall GC,*** *Sebring. Dick Wilson, 1958.*

Wilson must have just come out of detox to design this course, which is dead flat and has no particularly memorable holes. It does, however, host a women's amateur tournament every January, and I enjoyed the scenery a couple of times. 2. [1/86]

***Indian Creek GC,*** *Jupiter. Lamar Smith, architect.*

There is a very good William Flynn course called Indian Creek just north of Miami Beach, which Ray Floyd calls home; this one is just a low-budget muni down the street from where I lived one winter. I include it only for the sake of completeness. 1. [1/86]

***Innisbrook CC,*** *Tarpon Springs. Island, Copperhead and Sandpiper courses all designed by Larry and Roger Packard, 1970–72–74.*

Of all the resorts I have seen, this one should be the model for golf operations. The two championship layouts have both done time among the 100 Greatest Courses in America (though neither is really quite that good), and the Sandpiper course is an excellent complement for the shorter hitter. Always well-maintained and well-run, Innisbrook might be the best resort destination in the East for winter golf. Island and Copperhead courses: each 6. Sandpiper course: 3. [5/84]

***John's Island Club,*** *Vero Beach. North and South courses by Pete Dye, 1974.*

One of Pete's lesser-known designs, probably because he built it in such a hurry—the South course was open just eleven months after groundbreaking. The two courses have distinctly different characters, with the South course hemmed in by trees, while the North course is fairly open and runs out to the Intracoastal Waterway, but their common strength is a set of excellent short holes, and their common weakness is in fairly dull longer holes. Thus both courses rate 4. [1/81]

***Jupiter Hills Club,*** *Tequesta. Hills course by George Fazio, 1970; Village course by Tom Fazio, 1980.*

Since this is the architects' home stomping grounds, you might expect that both courses have undergone several revisions through the years. The Hills course was an immediate focus of attention in the architectural world for its hilly terrain (unique to south Florida) and its three "wasteland" holes, in imitation of George Fazio's former home club at Pine Valley (his ninth hole would have been too severe even for George Crump's taste.) The Hills remains one of the few courses in Florida that is unencumbered by surrounding development—a huge plus—but I think it gets too many brownie points from Florida critics just because it isn't flat. Ironically, it's too hilly.

Meanwhile, the newer Village course is exceptionally pretty at its far end, with white sand in the roughs and a few excellent holes, but it looks more manufactured than the original, and much more like Tom Fazio's other recent Florida efforts. Hills course: 6. Village course: 5. [4/89]

***Jupiter Island Club,*** *Hobe Sound. Bill Diddel, with revisions by the Fazios and P.B. Dye.*

This is the winter retreat of the Fishers Island summer crowd, thus also one of the most exclusive

clubs in the country. (In a recent edition of the *New York Times Magazine* fashion section, I was reading that nowadays a white tuxedo in summer is considered acceptable almost everywhere, except in ultra-ultra-conservative places "such as Hobe Sound, Florida.") The course is for the most part short and tight, but there is one great short hole, P.B. Dye's latest version of the 14th, which plays out to the tip of a peninsula into the Intracoastal Waterway. 4. [1/86]

***Lake Nona GC,*** *Orlando. Tom Fazio, 1986.*

An exclusive development slightly to the east of the Orlando airport that has become a very fashionable hangout since David Leadbetter set up shop here. When it debuted it had a bit of a new look, with lots of white sand left open around the trees in the rough, some very steeply flashed bunkers around the greens and occasionally in the fairway, and four finishing holes that border on 800 acres' worth of lakes. I wasn't really impressed with the contouring of the greens, but it seems like I never am anymore. (The par-5 15th is an excellent example: a beautiful long hole from tee to green around a huge bunker and a lake to the left, ruined by a very artificial-looking green that suddenly jumps up onto a high plateau and bends back to the right around a grass bunker. It works strategically, but looks terribly out of place.) The course in general and the par-5 holes in particular are worth seeing, but it will be squeezed out of top 100 lists by newer Fazio designs. 7. [2/86]

***Loblolly Pines GC,*** *Hobe Sound. P.B. Dye, 1988.*

This may be P.B.'s best work, a widely varied golf course where enough dirt was moved so it doesn't look or play Florida-flat. The variety of native plantings around the inevitable waste areas is particularly interesting. But I can't recommend it to anyone if there remains a chance you'll be treated as rudely by the staff as we were. It would take a full nine points on the Doak scale for a course to be worth sacrificing your dignity in order to get a game, and whatever else it is or is not, Loblolly Pines ain't no 9, unless you're standing on your head. 6. [4/89]

***Long Point GC,*** *Amelia Island. Tom Fazio, 1986.*

Owned by Amelia Island Plantation and operated out of a separate clubhouse just down the road from the main gate, this course is a good example of just how far environmental restrictions have come since Pete Dye built the first course here in 1973; most of its 18 holes are threaded along narrow stretches of high ground between protected marshes. The course is quiet and the architecture pleasant, with a good variety of golf holes, but this layout is even skinnier than I am, which makes it very tough going for a resort. 5. [11/87]

***Loxahatchee Club,*** *Jupiter. Jack Nicklaus, 1985.*

I prefer this over-mounded course to Grand Cypress (at least there aren't any double greens), but it's much too conspicuous that Jack tried anything and everything to fight the dull terrain he inherited, and that he lost the war. The "signature" holes are the par-4 11th, where you either lay up or try to drive over a cross-bunker and maybe through the dogleg into a lake, and the button-hook par-5 16th, which Jack has since replicated on at least five other courses; neither one is very good. And the mounds are *horrible.* Their insistence on bentgrass greens, even when they were dirt, has also been a minus, and it's rumored that great changes are afoot.

The one thing the course did have going for it is a fair amount of interest around the greens—a surprise from Jack, who didn't appear to value the subtleties of chipping and recovery play in his early designs. 6. [4/89]

***Marsh Landing GC,*** *Ponte Vedra. Arnold Palmer/Ed Seay/Harrison Minchew, 1986.*

A new layout just north of the TPC, which I saw before it actually opened. The number of bridges will give you some idea of how far the wetland conservation service has come since the construction of the TPC, but the forced carries lend it a respectable measure of difficulty. I wasn't all that impressed, but I'll boost it a bit purely on the recommendations of a couple of friends who say it's turned out well. 4. [2/86]

*The approach to the 10th at the Medalist Club.*

***Mayacoo Lakes CC,*** *West Palm Beach. Jack Nicklaus and Desmond Muirhead, 1973.*

This course is way out in the sticks to the west of the Florida Turnpike—it seemed at the time like it would be twenty years before civilization gets out to it, but the way Florida's growing, Mayacoo might be downtown now. The course is very atypical for Nicklaus, because it's so flat that visibility is poor, and generally there's too much water in play. The sixth hole, a par 4 with two alternate island greens in a waste bunker after a forced carry over a pond, is one of the all-time worst; but now that I think about it, maybe it was one of Desmond's first symbols crying out to me. 4. [1/81]

***The Medalist C,*** *Hobe Sound. Pete Dye and Greg Norman, 1994.*

This new layout has received instant attention because of its famous collaborators, and it deserves its share of attention. The property is typical southeast Florida—very flat land divided by large expanses of open marsh—and in places the course plays very severely because of the carries involved, but at the same time if you can make the carries there is a much greater variety of holes than at Old Marsh, where the water is always there laterally, too.

As is often the case with Pete's work, the difficulty of the course has overshadowed everything else, and with only three sets of tees at 7200, 6600, or 5900 yards, it is very difficult to finish unless you play one set of tees further forward than normal (which women, of course, cannot opt to do). But the course is noteworthy for its green complexes, which beautifully incorporate chipping areas better than anything else south of Pinehurst, and also for its unique brand of sod-wall bunkering. Once the construction of the adjacent housing pod is completed, it will also be a marvelously secluded place, despite its proximity to the A1A highway.

There are a couple of holes that border on gimmicky—especially the short fourth, with its green perched high in the air above a mess of man-made horrors—but after this the course settles down, and the interesting play around the greens makes up for the lack of real terrain. 7. [1/95]

***Mountain Lake C,*** *Lake Wales. Seth Raynor, 1922.*

A very old-money development and course that cuts a low profile in central Florida, about an hour from Disney World: not even the secretary of the Florida PGA knew of it. It's a great atmosphere—quiet, relaxed, and fun to play—but not one of Raynor's best efforts. There are all the standard holes, including the Redan 11th with a deep pit left of its green, and a neat par-4 coming back up over the pit and then down to a green with a steep lateral tier, but other than these two holes it's fairly flat and dull. Tour guru Rick Smith was just breathless about the course, but he must never have seen Shoreacres, Camargo, or Yeamans Hall. 4. [1/95]

***Old Marsh GC,*** *Jupiter. Pete Dye, 1988.*

The first thing I have to say about this course is that Pete Dye is very proud of it, which leads me to believe that there must be a lot to it. I respect the man's opinion.

But water comes into play on 27 shots at Old Marsh, which is not my favorite concept at all. There wasn't much else Pete could have done here—there was barely enough land for 18 fairways to begin with—but if you're having an off day or playing from too far back, the marsh can get old very quickly, and you'll be reloading often.

Despite all the water, there's much to like about Old Marsh. It's a unique setting amid the hustle and bustle of the Palm Beaches; even though it's just west of the Florida Turnpike, the marsh is secluded and quiet, apart from the teeming wildlife. The golf course is a masterpiece of engineering, the ultimate in low-profile courses (apart from the inevitable 5th hole); yet all the drainage water is captured and pumped back into the irrigation storage to make Old Marsh an environmentalist's dream (though some would have preferred the course not be built in the midst of a wetland sanctuary to begin with). Pete has put an awful lot of variety into the recovery play around the greens, considering that the front and back of all 18 greens are set at the same elevation throughout the course, and that all the character derives from small internal rolls. I like these greens a lot.

I wish I liked the driving game as much. All the tee shots present the same problem of water carry or lateral water to contend with, and there isn't a lot of variety built into the distances of carries required: if you're playing from all the way back, they are all 180-220 yards, and from the next tees they're mostly 140-180 yards. Everyone would enjoy the course more if Pete hadn't built the back tees on about six holes, so there would be a greater variety of carries. Of course, there's no law that says you can't play the "combo" tees, moving up where a hole plays into the wind, and playing back on the downwind holes; on this plan, I think Old Marsh becomes a much less harsh and more enjoyable golf course. But it's still a weakness you don't find on classic layouts without water on the brain. 6. [4/89]

***PGA National GC,*** *Palm Beach Gardens. Champions course by George and Tom Fazio, 1980; revised by Jack Nicklaus, 1990.*

I've lost track of exactly how many courses there are here now—I think it's up to four, but the only one I've seen is the Champions course, and that was before Nicklaus changed it. Its original greens were tiny and heavily contoured, with bunkers of all shapes and sizes scattered about, not to mention several blind water hazards. My first glimpse of this course and the brand-new TPC at Sawgrass were days apart, and at the time PGA National struck me as the more severe of the two. 5. [1/81]

***Pine Tree GC,*** *Delray Beach. Dick Wilson, 1962.*

The penultimate Dick Wilson layout: longer, flatter, more heavily bunkered, and possibly the most difficult of all his courses. Ben Hogan thought this was one of the best courses he'd ever played, but Ben Hogan was a lot better at carrying a high 2-iron shot over a sprawling bunker to an elevated green than mortals like me, and Pine Tree calls for that shot about half a dozen times in 18 holes if you want to break 80. Maybe in plan view the holes are more varied, but it all looks too much alike from the landing areas. 6. [1/81]

***Ponce de Leon Lodge & CC,*** *St. Augustine. Donald Ross, 1916.*

A fun course, though none too difficult. The front nine isn't much, but the back side is out between the marsh and open water, and there are several good holes. 4. [3/83]

***Ponte Vedra Club,*** *Ponte Vedra Beach. Ocean course by Herbert Strong, with revisions by Robert Trent Jones; Lagoon course, first nine by Trent Jones, expanded to 18 holes by Joe Lee.*

Just a few years ago, this was one of the poshest places around, but it has been severely overshadowed by its neighbors in the last fifteen years. The Ocean course is still somewhat interesting, with some of the earliest holes ever shaped by heavy dirtmoving. Check out the par-5 3rd, and the short 9th with an early forerunner of the 17th hole at the TPC Ocean course: 4. Lagoon course: 2. [1/81]

***The Ravines GC,*** *Middlesburg. Ron Garl and Mark McCumber, 1982.*

A super piece of ground for a golf course stranded in the middle of nowhere. This has to be the only land in Florida transsected by 50-foot-deep ravines in several places. But instead of using the ravines as diagonal hazards, the designers stuck to using them as forced-carry hurdles, with awful holes such as the 2nd and 4th the result. There are a couple of shots that make the heart beat faster, such as the drive to the 9th, but overall this was a big disappointment. 4. [6/84]

***Sawgrass GC,*** *Ponte Vedra Beach. Ed Seay, 1971, with revisions by Gardner Dickinson.*

Remember the days before the Tournament Players Club, when the pros thought that Sawgrass was too difficult? Actually, it can be a monster when the wind is up—there's a lot of water in play, and no trees to hide behind as there are across the highway. (My favorite story about the course is from the 1975 tournament, when one contestant withdrew while his ball was still in the air, well out over a lake.) There are a few arresting holes, all of them involving water, but in the end it's still a Florida course. 5. [6/84]

***Seminole GC,*** *North Palm Beach. Donald Ross, 1929, with some revisions to greens by Dick Wilson.*

One of the true aristocrats among golf courses, Seminole is cast by some critics as horribly overrated because of its status in the golf world; others think it's one of the ten best simply because Ben Hogan used to practice here. I reject both arguments. My friends Ron Whitten and Pete Dye both swear that most of the present-day Seminole is the work of Dick Wilson, who secretly rebuilt much of the course after World War II. That may be, but the real genius of Seminole is the routing, which uses the limited topography of the site brilliantly. There is essentially just a low dune ridge along the shore and a higher ridge near the inland boundary of the course, but Ross somehow managed to utilize one or the other in fourteen of the eighteen holes, many to dramatic consequence. Though the green contouring is fairly subtle and the bunkering is not all that tight up against the greens, those who criticize the course must consider them in light of the wind, an ever-present factor at Seminole.

I've lately been turned off by the way the club is run, partly because I was treated so nicely by the late president Allan Ryan on my first visit that the present exclusiveness seems just an excuse for snobbery. But if anybody tries to tell you this isn't a great course, either they've been treated like riffraff, or they just don't know what good is. 9. [4/89]

***Stonebridge G & CC,*** *Boca Raton. Karl Litten, 1985.*

A typical modern development course, which the architect tried too hard to jazz up. There's too much water in play, and the green-to-tee walks are awful, one being so long that they had to shuttle players in a station wagon for the LPGA event, which the course twice hosted. You can tell that the LPGA is in trouble as long as it keeps moving its tournaments around for any real estate developer who'll put up a few bucks for the advertising. 3. [1/86]

***Summer Beach GC,*** *Fernandina Beach. Mark McCumber and family, 1987.*

A fairly basic new resort development whose course just touches the dunes along the Atlantic beach. 4. [11/87]

***TPC at Eagle Trace,*** *Coral Springs. Art Hills, 1983.*

This is a course that became lost in the conceptual stage. On the one hand, Deane Beman wanted it to be like the TPC at Sawgrass, complete with waste bunkers and bulkheaded ponds and severe holes; on the other, the publicity people tried to convince us that "when you stand on the porch of the clubhouse, you could easily think you're at Muirfield or Troon"; and then the developers decided that they would like to plant a bunch of northern-type trees for landscaping—all on a typical flat south Florida landscape where you had to dig lakes to generate dirt to make the golf course! The result is predictably awful, complete with a colonial-style clubhouse that looks like the Americana exhibit at EPCOT Center. The combination of wind exposure and plenty of water to the sides is a disastrous recipe, and the course became so hated by the players that the Tour ultimately abandoned it in favor of a non-TPC layout. Don't necessarily hold the design against Art Hills, who was doomed by backseat designers before he broke ground here. 5. [1/84]

***Tournament Players Club at Sawgrass,*** *Ponte Vedra. Pete Dye (with Deane Beman and David Postlethwait), 1980, with a couple of informal suggestions from the boys on Tour.*

A sentimental favorite of mine, because it was at the center of the universe just as I became involved with the design business in general and its architect in particular. Today, it is harder to defend, because it is no longer a once-in-a-lifetime proposition, and the progression of bastardized imitations it has fostered have done little to advance modern golf architecture, while undermining the originality of the TPC itself.

It's not the course it was designed to be, either, and while some players applaud that, I'm saddened to see it. Pete's original design was meant to be a low-maintenance torture track that would make the pros sweat, and draw out all their heroic talents. But the Tour didn't like the idea of its home headquarters looking "scruffy," so they've Augustatized the course, even though I vividly remember Pete saying at the first event in 1982 that "everything here is the dead opposite of Augusta—on purpose." But the TPC is still one of the wonders of the golfing world: a torture track that illustrates the differences between Tour pros and the rest of us. On my first trip, I shot 102 from the back tees and 78 from the whites, a fairly accurate accounting of the psychological terrors the back tees hold for a ten-handicapper.

There are still a lot of excellent holes here, and they aren't the best-known: the three-shot par-5 9th, the drive-and-pitch 4th, and the great 14th, to name three. It's certainly a course worth seeing; but it should have made its mark like Pine Valley, as an example of what most courses cannot be like, instead of as a prototype for the architects of the eighties to try and outdo. 8. [2/86]

***Walt Disney World GC's,*** *Lake Buena Vista. Palm, Magnolia, and Lake Buena Vista courses all by Joe Lee, 1971.*

I haven't seen the new courses here by Pete Dye and Tom Fazio, both of which have gotten lukewarm reviews, but I'm sure I will soon, with my son approaching age five. As for the original courses, they're not quite poor enough to describe as "Mickey Mouse design," thanks to some fairly good bunker shaping, but they're not terribly interesting, either. The Magic Kingdom is a bigger attraction, and I could live without it. Palm course: 4. Magnolia course: 3. [1/81]

*World Woods Pine Barrens course—*
*a Pine Valley imitation in Florida.*

***World Woods GC**, Homosassa. Pine Barrens, Rolling Oaks and Short Courses by Tom Fazio, 1993.*

A golf-only mega-complex built by Japanese money in the boondocks northwest of Orlando; 90% of the players drive more than an hour to get here, but it's certainly worth the drive. You've got to wonder what other supporting facilities they're considering, but it's also possible that the owner just decided he'd rather give Fazio an unlimited budget to go wild with 45 holes in the Florida sand, as it's still cheaper than blowing down a mountainside in Japan to yield one bad 18-holer.

Pine Barrens is certainly the show-stopper of the complex, a public-access homage to Pine Valley, and the most believable knockoff of the New Jersey classic to date. A few of the holes are overdone, particularly the alternate-fairway short par-4 15th, which has been featured everywhere; but there are also some classics, including the heroic par-5 4th and the long par-4 13th, with a big carry off the tee followed by a running approach through a valley.

Rolling Oaks has been declared by some as a superior 18 holes, but my quick ride around it wasn't so inspiring. There are some nice open vistas and big flashy fairway bunkers, and several holes are downright hilly, but it's neither as stylish nor as memorable as Pine Barrens.

The Short Course, with seven 3's and two short par-4's, was a terrific complement to the two main courses and the humungous practice facility—back in the opening year when the daily green fee for the place included all the golf you could play. But now that they're charging $25 for the Short Course alone, practically nobody plays it—probably because it's not too severe, and they don't lure many "B" players to drive this far to play it. In downtown Chicago it'd score big, but not out here. Pine Barrens: 8. Rolling Oaks: 6. Short Course: 4. [1/95]

*—Gossip—*

I never have gotten down to Doral to see the famous Blue course, but the way things are going in south Florida, Royal County Down is not only a hell of a lot better, but maybe safer. If you're looking for something really good down that way, though, I would be more prone to bet on Indian Creek near Miami or the Country Club of Florida, two older layouts that shun the spotlight and aren't tourist-laden targets.

Elsewhere in Florida, where there's always something new going on, I've been neglectful in not getting over to the Gulf Coast to see all the new developments between Tampa and Naples, including Bonita Bay (reputedly Art Hills' best, although they keep changing it for expansion), Hills' Sanctuary, and Mike Hurdzan's Naples National. I should also get to the Florida panhandle someday, although I haven't heard of any particular course there worth the trip. Sprinkled elsewhere around the state, there's Seville GC (a low-budget layout among natural sand dunes that may really be Hills' best), John's Island West (which Tom Fazio has volunteered as his most underrated course), and the new LPGA International by Rees Jones near Daytona Beach. But I never get too excited about anything in Florida—after all, it is the world capital of the Flat Earth Society, and I still haven't seen a flat golf course I'd consider a great one.

## GREAT LAKES

The Great Lakes region of the U.S. is blessed with an unusual number of outstanding golf courses, considering its relative lack of scenic splendors. Remember, though, that the soul of a golf course is topography and vegetation, and the combination of rolling farmland, fertile soils, native hardwoods, and cool-season grasses bodes well for golf development.

I'm not a big fan, though, of the two most well-known golf capitals of the Great Lakes, Chicago and northern Michigan. With a couple of exceptions, I find the Chicago school of golf courses much too similar, with limited topography and little variety of texture. (They have a fetish for pure bluegrass roughs.) And most of northern Michigan's new courses are clichés of ski hill topography and north woods vegetation, even though other sites of beautiful undulation and native grasses go unused.

Most every architect has created at least a couple of golf courses in this region, from C.B. Macdonald right down to the present-day big names, but no one worthwhile has really dominated the region. The one unsung design team is the Chicago pair of William Langford and Theodore Moreau, who created some spectacular greens and bunkers in the twenties when the land afforded them the opportunity.

## OHIO

***Brookside CC,*** *Canton. Donald Ross, 1922, with minor revisions by Jack Kidwell and Mike Hurdzan.*

Some Ohioans would have you believe that this course is a hidden gem on the order of Crystal Downs, but let's not get carried away—Brookside is a very good course, but it's nowhere in that league. It's an expensively manicured course in the classic parkland setting, and a moderately hilly layout with a few interesting holes, in particular a set of inordinately difficult par-3 holes. The one feature that deserves discussion is Brookside's greens, which are some of the most severely sloping greens I've ever seen. They're fairly big for Ross greens—bigger than Pinehurst No. 2, anyway—but they have some tremendous back-to-front slopes and some real moguls in them, and the club maintains them at such consistently fast speeds that they must rank right up there with Augusta National, Oakland Hills, and Somerset Hills in terms of putting difficulty. I didn't have a chance to play here; maybe those greens make the course play a notch better than my rating, but not more than that. 6. [8/90]

***The Camargo Club,*** *Indian Hill. Seth Raynor, 1923, with alterations by Bob Von Hagge, 1963, and long-term restoration by Tom Doak.*

I don't think there can be much question that this is Cincinnati's premier golf course, though I haven't seen the other contenders. The short holes, of the typical Macdonald/Raynor models, are all superb, and the two-shotters are very strong as well. A great example of what can be done on interesting ground without much grading work, and a must for fans of Macdonald and Raynor's work. 7. [10/89]

***Canterbury CC,*** *Cleveland. Herbert Strong, 1922, with some modifications by Jack Way and Geoffrey Cornish.*

Another parkland layout, and an overrated one in my opinion. The finishing holes are undeniably strong, but overall I think the course is less interesting than The Country Club, and I doubt the course would be considered in such high esteem today had it not hosted several major championships in its past. 6. [8/81]

***Chagrin Valley CC,*** *Chagrin Falls. Stanley Thompson, 1925.*

This is a spectacular golf course if it's fall foliage you're after; for great golf holes, though, it falls short of my expectations. The dramatically sloping site, which falls away from the clubhouse along several narrow ridges, unfortunately forced the designer to route three rather dull uphill holes for every one strong downhill par-4, such as the long 12th. The greens hold little interest, and although it's a bit more woodsy than the classic parkland course, the course does not possess the kind of character that would make it outstanding. 5. [10/89]

***Coldstream CC,*** *Cincinnati. Dick Wilson, 1963.*

The prototypical Dick Wilson layout—long, strongly bunkered, but somewhat dull due to the gentle topography of the site and the sixties-style large greens. There are some difficult holes, in particular a couple of long par-3's over water, but nothing very original. I'd rather play NCR. 6. [9/94]

***The Country Club,*** *Pepper Pike. William Flynn, 1930.*

A very good layout, typical of Flynn. Spread out over rolling parkland terrain, it features wide fairways and just enough bunkers to delineate preferred lines of play, with greens of subtle contour. The par-3 9th and short two-shot 17th are its most outstanding holes. I'm worried, though, that it might be getting a boost in the rankings from a couple of panelists who think they're voting on Brookline; it didn't look any better than four Flynn courses around Philadelphia that have very little top 100 support. 6. [9/86]

*The 17th at The Country Club, Ohio.*

***The CC at Muirfield Village,*** *Dublin. Jack Nicklaus, 1982.*

Muirfield Village wasn't originally planned for 36 holes, and only a couple of the holes on the newer course are on good golfing terrain. The rest of the property is pretty dull, and the Country Club is all the proof you need that you can't force a great course onto lousy land. 4. [5/82]

***Double Eagle GC,*** *Galena. Tom Weiskopf and Jay Morrish, 1991.*

This is the kind of club we'd all like to belong to, if we could afford it, or find someone like John McConnell to subsidize it for us—300 acres of nothing but golf, and just 50 members, so it's never busy. But I'm still trying to decide if it's as good a course as advertised. The bunkering is the best feature work, attempting to imitate the look of George Thomas or Tillinghast at San Francisco Golf Club, although I don't think they quite captured the 3-D sweep of its models in worrying about maintainability. The greens are fast and true, but I've never seen so many 40-foot straight putts in my life. Finally, what are supposed to be some of the feature holes—the 9th and 18th in particular, which profess to exemplify the theory of alternate routes to the green—instead seem just a bit overdone, although I did think the obligatory driveable par-4 17th was an interesting example of the type. I liked it, but since I don't add points for the Stimpmeter reading of the greens (or the tees!), I'm not ready to proclaim it a Top 100 test just yet. 7. [10/92]

***Firestone CC,*** *Akron. South course by Robert Trent Jones, 1960, with revisions to greens by Jack Nicklaus, 1986. North course by Robert Trent Jones, 1960.*

The only time I've been to Firestone was on the eve of the World Series of Golf, and they didn't want me to walk around the South course. Too bad: I've never figured out from watching on TV why everybody thinks it's so good, and now that Nicklaus has redone all the greens I may never know.

I did, however, walk around the North course, which borders the reservoir across Warner Road, and I was most impressed. Some of the holes, particularly the 225-yard 17th to a peninsula green, are overdone, but in general it's a beautiful course with probably the two most memorable holes of the entire 36—the beautiful dogleg 14th, and the par-5 16th with a lake threatening those who go for the green in two. North course: 6. [8/81]

***The Golf Club,*** *New Albany. Pete Dye, 1967.*

Perhaps the highest praise anyone has paid to The Golf Club comes from the architect himself. A man who cannot resist tinkering with his past creations, Pete Dye has been content to leave this course the way he built it thirty years ago, a sure sign that it's one of his very best.

When the late Fred Jones hired Pete, still a relative unknown in the design business, he gave him 400 acres and instructions to build it so that it would "look like it's been there 200 years." Predictably, Pete ran out of land, anyway—Jones had to buy an additional two acres to put the 12th tee just where Pete wanted it—but he certainly succeeded at the second objective. The use of high, rough grasses at The Golf Club is unmatched by other courses of that era, and had much to do with shaping the look of modern design.

As always on a Dye course, the short holes are excellent (although the 16th, my favorite, has reportedly been sabotaged by a club committee since my last visit). But the four superb three-shot holes are what set this course apart. They're among the best in the country, with tremendous variety between the narrow, sloping approach to the 7th and the zigzagging fairway of the "untouchable" 14th. The two-shotters are no slouches, either.

Unfortunately for the general public, The Golf Club is one of the most difficult courses to gain access to, with only about 150 members from the inner circle of Columbus golf. 9. [5/82]

***Granville GC,*** *Granville. Donald Ross, 1920.*

This was a picturesque public course featuring a fine Ross routing plan, which worked its way uphill for a couple of breathtaking holes before the turn. But I've just heard an ugly rumor that there have been changes to eliminate these holes, in which case my rating probably no longer stands. 5. [8/81]

***Inverness Club,*** *Toledo. Donald Ross, 1919, with modifications by Tillinghast and Dick Wilson, and four new holes by George and Tom Fazio in 1975.*

The charm of Inverness, like Merion, is that it manages to pack so much into a small property. The routing of the back nine is much like the procession of targets in a shooting gallery, back and forth without a break, and yet the major contours of the ground fall in a different place on every hole, so that no two holes are very much alike. Throw in its tiny, severely canted greens, and Inverness is a great challenge.

I don't think much of the changes that were made here by the Fazios in the 1970s: even Tom Fazio now says he wouldn't do them today if he had it to do over again. They simply don't fit in with the rest of the golf course at all, and in trying to eliminate Ross' historic short par-4 7th hole (which was deemed unsatisfactory because players were likely to shortcut the dogleg), Fazio and the USGA created the Hinkle Tree incident, not to mention the awful par-4 5th, where one often drives through the dogleg into trouble. Inverness and Oak Hill are the two major reasons I'm opposed to doing redesign work for a living, especially when the motivation for such work is to host a single tournament. Leave well enough alone. 8. [8/89]

***Muirfield Village GC,*** *Dublin. Jack Nicklaus with Desmond Muirhead, 1974.*

When Jack built this course it was going to be his home, his answer to Jones' Augusta National, rather than a springboard into the golf architecture business. Though I must say he has dedicated himself to the business more than most practicing architects, it's obvious that Muirfield Village came out better because he didn't have to divide his time among ten or twenty concurrent projects; and I think it's one of the few he's done whose reputation is based on the golf course, rather than on hype and expensive maintenance.

Nicklaus began this project as a developer should: he spent a lot of time looking at property around Columbus until he found a piece of ground with nearly ideal contours for the building of a golf course. The course's most exceptional virtue is the perfect sightlines from fairway landing areas to the target areas and to all hazards around the greens, for which no expense was spared. There are also several great holes, including the 5th, 8th, 9th, 12th, and 14th; my personal favorite is the roller-coaster par-five 15th.

So why isn't the course one of my #1 choices? Well, the curse of Jack's approach is that he puts perfect sightlines and perfect turf ahead of any consideration of natural character, which to me is the most important part of golf architecture. On most of the courses which comprise my "Gourmet's Choice," you're constantly marveling at the terrain over which the holes were laid out. At Muirfield Village, even though it's laid out over a great piece of ground, your attention is drawn to the architecture and maintenance—and if there's even one divot in the fairways, it stands out so much that it bothers you. On the great courses overseas, a divot just looks like part of the course, so you're more inclined to accept a poor lie in one instead of letting it affect you.

I have always felt, too, that Nicklaus' courses often didn't give me a realistic shot to approach the hole. You can't simply put a tee up forty yards so I can hit a 7-iron to the green, and then expect me to hit a miniature version of Jack's 7-iron: trajectory and consistency just aren't comparable. Of course, this fault isn't confined to Jack's work: in fact it is symptomatic of all modern design. I just tend to notice it more on a course like Muirfield Village, where if I play

*NCR South, the 12th*

it from the back there are several shots I just can't hit, and if I play it from the whites it's as unexciting as professional golf itself. 8. [10/88]

***National Cash Register CC,*** *Kettering. South course by Dick Wilson, 1953.*

This is one of the better Wilson layouts I've seen, but I have to confess that doesn't place it as highly in my overall scheme of things as it does in most other critics'. Its strength is in the longer two-shot holes, and there are also some interesting par-5 holes to be found here; but the shorter holes are disappointing, as is generally true for nearly all courses built in this expansion era. Favorite hole: the 434-yard 12th, which made a great short par-5 for the U.S. Women's Open, and is a searching two-shotter for the members the rest of the time. On the other hand, the opening hole, a long, semi-blind two-shotter with out-of-bounds all the way down the right side, is not an inspiring start. 6. [8/86]

***New Albany CC,*** *New Albany. Jack Nicklaus, 1992.*

Much more subdued than the Nicklaus of five years ago—so much so that you'd have to be one of those players who wholeheartedly ascribes to Jack's interpretation of "shot values" in order to get much out of it. Otherwise, you'd call the front nine dull, and the bulkheading on the back nine ugly. 5. [10/92]

***Ohio State University GC's,*** *Columbus. Scarlet and Gray course both by Alister MacKenzie, 1939.*

MacKenzie died in California in 1934 after he had drawn plans for this course but before it was built, and my friend Terry Buchen sent me some fascinating letters from the OSU archives about all the politicking that occurred over who would get the commission to complete it. (Among the tidbits, Bobby Jones, through an intermediary, recommended Robert Hunter or the young Robert Trent Jones ahead of Perry Maxwell, whom he had not met as of 1935.) MacKenzie's concept is enough to make the Scarlet one of the premier university courses in the country. Still, I wonder whether the course is coasting on its famous connections: Weiskopf and Nicklaus rate it highly (and it was strong enough to contain them in their college years), but neither the bunkering nor the greens are up to the standard of those built under the Doctor's watch. The Gray course is shorter and less challenging, but a good game for the novice player, for whom it was intended. Scarlet course: 5. Gray course: 4. [8/80]

***Scioto CC,*** *Columbus. Donald Ross, 1916, with revisions by Dick Wilson & Co., 1963, and Jack Nicklaus.*

Now that I've played Scioto, I'm more convinced than ever that its reputation hangs on its connections to Donald Ross, Bob Jones' 1926 Open victory, and Jack Nicklaus' boyhood. The present course has more to do with Dick Wilson & Co. than with Ross, as a lot of the green complexes were overshaped in the 1963 redesign. The par-4 second is a very tough driving hole, but far from the best #2 in golf, and other holes that had impressed me before are too tough to play, particularly the par-4 5th with its killer back right pin placement. It is one of the best-conditioned club courses in America, but even more so than Inverness or Oak Hill, Scioto is resting on the laurels of a designer whose work is long gone. 7. [10/92]

***The Sharon GC,*** *Sharon Center. George Cobb, 1965.*

This all-male club, southwest of Akron, was built at the height of the architectural trend toward big greens in the mid-sixties, and has on average some of the biggest greens that I've ever seen. But the course is generally wide open and boring from tee to green, and three-putting is the principal hazard. The par-3 12th is the most memorable hole. 5. [8/81]

***Urbana CC,*** *Urbana. Paul Dye, Sr., 1925.*

This "goat-hill" nine-hole layout was built by Pete Dye's father on a small patch of farmland, and was the foundation for Pete's interest in turf and design. The routing plan is pretty much back-and-forth out of necessity, as the course is wedged into a tight, hilly property, but the 2nd and 8th holes stand out in my memory for their death-defying sidehill contours, and it's evident where Pete got his affection for long par-3 holes and short par-4's, not to mention trouble around the greens. It would have made my list of top nine-hole layouts, but P.B. Dye has just produced a second nine—I wonder what that will be like? 4. [7/89]

*—Gossip—*

I still haven't really explored the Cleveland area at all. Pepper Pike, the all-men's club, is #1 on my list of suspects, because it's a Flynn layout and because I was in the parking lot once and the terrain looked good, but there wasn't anyone around with authority to let me walk it. Acacia, Kirtland CC, and Mayfield also deserve to be checked out. Overall, there are a hell of a lot of good golf courses here for an inland state.

## MICHIGAN

***Antrim Dells GC,*** *Atwood. Bruce and Jerry Matthews, 1971.*

A well-liked public course, featuring a nice set of rolling greens and a few good holes, particularly on the back side. The strategic design, however, leaves much to the imagination, with flanking greenside bunkers on nearly every hole. 4. [9/87].

***Belle Isle Park GC,*** *Detroit. Ernest Way, 1922.*

A dull nine-holer in the middle of the Detroit River. The island/park was landscaped by Frederick Law Olmsted, the "father of landscape architecture," so this is sort of his closest approach to golf course design. 1. [5/82]

***The Belvedere Club,*** *Charlevoix. Willie Watson, 1917.*

Another fairly quiet club with a fine little course by an unsung designer. Three of the holes were diagrammed in George Thomas' book on course design, the best of which is the par-4 11th to a green in a small natural amphitheater—but only because the club has tinkered with the bunkering at the 16th. There isn't much in the way of fancy trappings, but stop by if you get a chance. 5. [5/82]

***Birmingham CC,*** *Birmingham. Donald Ross, 1916, with alterations by Wilfrid Reid, Robert Trent Jones, and Bruce and Jerry Matthews.*

A fairly uninspired Ross creation, tightly packed into a small, hilly property. Though the bunkering is unmistakably Ross' style, it isn't as well placed as on some of his better works, and the greens are dreadfully dull by comparison with Detroit Golf Club. The one standout hole: the short par-3 11th, tight between two huge trees to a sharply sloped elevated green. 4. [5/87].

***Blythefield CC,*** *Grand Rapids. Bill Langford and Theodore Moreau, 1927, with revisions by Jay Riviere, 1973, and Bruce and Jerry Matthews, 1973–85.*

Probably the most respected older course in Grand Rapids, Blythefield is a solid but unspectacular test. The meat of the course is in some substantial

par-4's on the upper plateau, but the five holes down by the Rogue River are the most memorable, in particular the long par-3 13th across the rapids. 5. [11/92]

***Boyne Highlands GC,*** *Harbor Springs. Heather course by Robert Trent Jones, 1960; Moor course by Bill Newcomb, 1975.*

After breaking up Jones' original Black course to expand to 36 holes, the new clubhouse of the Ross course has been utilized as the starting point of the newer holes so that the original course is once again playable as the "Heather." In truth, though, the secluded north woods atmosphere probably had more to do with the original course's high ranking than a special design effort by Trent Jones, whose par-3 holes all look alike here. Neither course is really very memorable. Heather course: 6. Moor course: 5. [7/88]

***Boyne Mountain GC,*** *Boyne Falls. Alpine course by Bill Newcomb, 1969; Monument course also by Newcomb, 1986.*

These two courses feature a most unusual routing plan, with the starter's shack and first tees a mile and a half uphill from the clubhouse, and the two courses zigzagging down the mountain like ski runs. The original Alpine course was a fairly modest layout on which Newcomb included an amazing collection of bunkers in all shapes and sizes, though mostly well wide of the line of play. The Monument course is Newcomb's attempt to compete with 1980s "signature" courses, with predictably gimmicky results. Features such as a railroad-tie ha-ha wall guarding the left side of the 4th green, a 60-foot-wide fairway at the 11th, and a split-fairway design at the par-4 16th are destined to live in infamy. The huge boulders designating tees and 150-yard markers are another sideshow attraction. The first hole isn't bad, but it's all downhill from there. Alpine course: 4. Monument course: 2. [6/86]

***Briar Downs GC,*** *Mesick. Designer unknown, 1989.*

I turned down a chance to design this course, because the property was too cramped by wetlands and boundaries, and because the owner didn't have high expectations; he just wanted to build a short course that would bring in some play. Good move: the owner wound up being sentenced to a year in jail because of wetlands violations. It's not much of a track, although the greens are so small it wouldn't necessarily be easy. 2. [8/89]

***CC at Boyne Highlands (Donald Ross Memorial Course),*** *Harbor Springs. Reconstruction of Donald Ross holes by the Boyne staff, with advice from Jim Flick and Bill Newcomb, 1989.*

I didn't think I was going to like this course much; the advance publicity stated the owner's love for Ross' "flair for using the existing ground to create exciting golf holes," so they moved mountains to try and recreate holes which Ross had fit into the ground on their real sites. Seems to me they were more interested in cashing in on the name of Ross, instead of Newcomb; I wonder if the old man's estate could get any royalties from this?

The course turned out very well, though. The holes they have chosen don't represent Ross' absolute best (I will try and do that list in the gazetteer); in fact, several represent a redesigned and changed version of a Ross hole, and two (from Bob O'Link and Royal Dornoch) weren't even designed by Ross to begin with. But in taking so much time to do detail work around the greens, even if they didn't get them all just right, they got better results than 90% of modern courses. The course is also very wide open off the tee, making for a pleasant resort test. Low marks for originality, and a "B" for authenticity, but a good golf course nonetheless. 6. [10/89]

***CC of Detroit,*** *Grosse Pointe Farms. H.S. Colt and C.H. Alison, 1927, with modifications by Robert Trent Jones, Bruce Matthews, and Geoffrey Cornish.*

One of the better flat courses I've played, in the highest-rent suburb of Detroit. The greens are still mostly the Colt/Alison originals, and there are some super ones among them, particularly in the first few holes; and during my last visit a bunker cape-

and-bay renovation project was underway, which the course needed badly. For quite a few years, the club managed to preserve its stately elm trees while others were succumbing to the Dutch elm disease, but sadly now the trees are also dying off rapidly at the Country Club, and they are starting just that much further behind in relandscaping the course. 6. [10/86]

***Crystal Downs CC,*** *Frankfort. Alister MacKenzie and Perry Maxwell, 1929.*

See the "Gourmet's Choice." 10. [9/95]

***Crystal Mountain GC,*** *Thompsonville. Bill Newcomb, 1977.*

Just your basic tight, tree-lined golf course, at the foot of the ski hill. Newcomb has added a new, reportedly more interesting nine since my visit. 3. [10/88]

***Detroit GC,*** *Detroit. North course by Donald Ross, 1916, with greens rebuilt by Art Hills, 1991, and again in 1993.*

An otherwise modest parkland layout that became something special thanks to a fabulous job of contouring the greens: if this wasn't the work of Ross himself, I would like to know who did the greens shaping. Some greens are abrupt, and some more mellow, but there is none that could fairly be described as ordinary, and a couple (such as the 2nd) turned ordinary holes into world-class stuff. North course: 6. [10/86]

***Drummond Island GC,*** *Drummond Island. Architect unknown.*

This isn't The Rock, which I hear turned out fairly well; the only time I was on Drummond was to interview for that job, and I told Mr. Monaghan's people I thought it would be a waste of his money. The only course on the island then was this one, a real low-budget nine-hole layout around the Drummond airstrip, along flat ground with nothing to recommend it. 1. [8/87].

***Dunes GC,*** *New Buffalo. Dick Nugent, 1991.*

Built by a small group of Chicago golfers just across the border from Indiana (and within commuting distance of Chicago), this nine-hole layout should quickly ascend to the short list of outstanding nine-hole courses in the world, especially as many of the best old nine-holers are in the midst of expansion. All I had seen of Nugent's work previously was modernistic, manicured Chicago layouts like Kemper Lakes, but the Dunes shows a great deal of attention to detail. The landscaping is exceptional, with many low plants and shrubs around the edges of the bunkers, giving it a distinctive look (a bit like Pine Valley in places); there are also some excellent holes, particularly at the finish. I'd sure rather play it than Point O'Woods, but the club is so exclusive I'm not sure they'll let us on. 6. [7/91]

***Dunmaglas GC,*** *Charlevoix. Larry Mancour and Dean Refram, 1991.*

This difficult new course was designed by an accomplished club professional, and his lack of previous architectural experience, combined with the severe site, makes for some interesting holes—some spectacularly beautiful, some spectacularly severe.

The choice of the clubhouse site is perhaps the most spectacular feature. It commands a high ridge with tremendous views of Lake Charlevoix, the town itself, and Lake Michigan and the Fox Islands—but it simultaneously ensures that the golf course is saddled with some unappealing uphill holes. (The fifth green is more than 300 feet below the first tee, and the ninth returns to the clubhouse!)

Its weakness is playability. Mancour is such a straight driver that he sometimes doesn't give the other 95% of us enough room off the tee, and his choice of green sites is too severe, especially at the 5th (a long par-4 with a forced carry over 100 yards of marsh in front of the green), and on the finishing holes for both nines. But there are several holes here that are a cut above what most of Michigan's

professional architects can produce, and the difficult slope rating will attract golfers like moths to a flame. Indeed, these factors combined to give the course a fourth-place ranking in the state by the ridiculous *Golf Digest* rating system; the reality check says that it's interesting, but not nearly that good. 5. [4/91]

***Egypt Valley CC,*** *Ada. Valley course by Art Hills, 1991.*

A new 36-hole complex built as part of a land-swap deal for the old Green Hills CC, and very much like the similar deals at Austin (Texas), Richland (Tennessee), or The Standard Club (Georgia), it has not been a popular move for the members, going from a walkable, forgiving 18 to a torturous, hilly, carts-only new layout way across town. The part of the golf course I walked was way over-shaped, over-dramatized, and just plain overdone for average players. I'm becoming convinced that all such deals are doomed to failure: when they're playing with a third party's money, neither the architects nor the club committees can resist the temptation to over-design. 0-5. [10/93]

***Elk Ridge GC,*** *Atlanta. Jerry Matthews, 1990.*

I interviewed for this job a ways back, but I was less than confident that a course this far removed from the mainstream could be successful—there really *are* elk wandering the property. It's a nice piece of land, although the contours alternate between a bit too flat and (around the clubhouse) a bit too steep, and the course has more outstanding trees around its perimeter than any I've seen in northern Michigan. Unfortunately, they saved too many trees. (How narrow is it? My friend Dave Richards hit a tree on the left of the fairway with his opening tee shot, and it caromed across the fairway and stuck a tree on the right *while still on the fly.*)

There is one first-rate hole, the heroic par-4 16th across and along a duck pond; but there are a couple of horrible holes, too, and the six sharp dog-leg-right holes on the front nine don't add much variety to the course. If you decide to go, take along a chainsaw, and do them a favor. 5. [7/90]

***Elmbrook GC,*** *Traverse City. Architect unknown, with modifications by owners.*

Your typical daily-fee golf course, with a little bit of interest, but mainly designed to get you around quick. The 4th has some rugged undulations, but they'd be much more interesting if one could see where one was going. 2. [9/87].

***Frankfort Public Golf Club,*** *Frankfort. Designed by an unknown troubled soul.*

Just two miles from Crystal Downs, but light-years away where quality is concerned: here the contour creates a lot of blindness. Interesting feature: the par-4 1st and par-3 9th utilize the same tee! 2. [9/86]

***Franklin Hills CC,*** *Franklin. Donald Ross, 1930.*

A very private Jewish club, which therefore is not very well known in golf-architecture circles, but it's a fine Ross layout that stands comparison with any of the better Detroit clubs. Sort of a cross between Oakland Hills and Detroit Golf Club: not quite as challenging as Oakland Hills, thanks to the lack of fairway bunker overkill, but with a very good (and pretty severe) set of Ross greens. Play this one if you can get on. 7. [5/94]

***Garland GC,*** *Lewiston. Ron Otto, 1980.*

They've built a lot more holes here in the last few years, and I think that the East course I saw has since been broken up—but it's no matter, since all the golf at Garland is the same. The owner/designer believes in giving the public what it wants—lots of water, pretty trees, minimal bunkering, and bland design. The lodge is gorgeous, but the corporate philosophy applies better to interior decorating than golf design. 4. [6/86]

***Grand Haven GC,*** *Grand Haven. Bruce Matthews, 1965.*

A very good and well-maintained public track, but the pine trees to the sides are thicker than mo-

lasses, with the result that several holes are straight-jacket-narrow. Otherwise, it's got some good two-shot holes and a fairly interesting set of greens. 4. [9/86]

***Grand Hotel GC,*** *Mackinac Island. The Jewel course substantially remodeled by Jerry Matthews, 1986.*

The hotel is big, posh, and stuffy; the golf course is very short (2,335 yards), all landscaping and very little golf. And can you believe they allow golf carts on Mackinac Island? For a flat nine-holer? 2. [5/88]

***Grand Traverse Resort,*** *Acme. The Bear course by Jack Nicklaus, 1984.*

A classic mid-eighties artifice, The Bear has achieved a big-name reputation in the Midwest, for all the wrong reasons. Artistically, it's one of the worst courses I've seen: all those mounds and strange greens are suspended in between flat decks of fairways and natural stands of fescue rough or trees, so that no one in their right mind could think this course was for real. (The 5th green complex is one of the ugliest of all time.) To make things worse, the resort developer decided what he wanted was the hardest course in the country, and goaded Jack into building something that isn't any fun for anybody from the back tees: the shortest of the par-4 holes is 393 yards. If the same course were in Florida I might be more generous, but when you could go two miles in any direction and find really good land for golf, an artificial course like this is a joke. 0-5. [9/91]

***High Pointe GC,*** *Williamsburg. Tom Doak, 1988.*

See the "Gourmet's Choice." 8. [9/95]

***Indianwood G & CC,*** *Lake Orion. Old course by Wilfrid Reid and William Connellan, 1928, restored by Art Hills and, later, Bob Cupp. New course by Bob Cupp and Jerry Pate, 1988.*

I love the look and feel of Indianwood's Old course; it's much like Shinnecock, only the topography is a bit more undulating. But I can't quite agree with Frank Hannigan and those who want to put it in the first tier of American courses—the green contours create short-game interest, but the first 17 are basically the same, and the 9th and 18th holes are too bizarre for this to be one of the few. In fact, Hannigan's review polarized opinions so much that I have since heard well-informed people say that the New course is better than the Old, which is ridiculous. Why can't they just be satisfied with calling the course different than the mainstream American parkland course, and a lot more fun, and leave it at that? Wilfrid Reid would have been happy with that judgment.

Down the road, Aldridge has built his New course, a Jerry Pate/Bob Cupp design that is destined to take its place somewhere between Pine Valley and PGA West in the realm of super-difficult courses. That's what Aldridge wanted; I don't mean to say that makes the course any good. The architects had a good piece of land to work with, and they've built some great (if contrived) holes, but the "Scottish-style" mounding here has nothing to do with the site, and if Aldridge keeps the rough knee-high the way it was for the grand opening, the course will be unplayable for many. There are some excellent two-shotters and some beautiful green sites, but there are also crossover holes to a double green à la St. Andrews, which takes imitation to new limits of stupidity. Old course: 7. New course: 6. [8/89]

*Indianwood—another gem in Michigan.*

***Michaywé GC,*** *Gaylord. Lakes course by Jerry Matthews and Mike Husby, 1988.*

I've only played the newer of the two courses here, a pretty but claustrophobic layout that starts and finishes around Lake Michaywé. It's a nice course, geared more toward the senior set because of its shortness and many tight holes, but I think the trade-off of elbow room for reduced construction cost was a mistake, and there are three or four terrible holes (the 8th, 9th, and 12th) that spoil the beauty of the rest. 4. [6/88]

***Mistwood GC,*** *Lake Ann. Jerry Matthews and Ray Hearn, 1993.*

Another basic Matthews effort, with little originality in bunker placement or greens contour. The land was modestly good for golf, but they tore up a lot of the attractive native areas to build it, such as a natural valley between the 10th and 18th, which they turned into a pond. The front nine still wasn't open when I saw it, but everyone who's seen the course complains about the par-4 7th. 4. [7/93]

***Oakland Hills CC,*** *Birmingham. South course by Donald Ross, 1917, with major revisions by Robert Trent Jones, 1950 and 1983. North course by Donald Ross, 1923.*

Jones' redesign of 1950 turned the South course into one of the world's most severe tests of driving, with wasp-waisted landing areas hemmed in by fairway bunkers on both flanks on most of the longer holes. This is not my favorite concept: for a short hitter consigned to the back tees, many of the long holes revert to driver-spoon-wedge affairs, with none of the bunkers coming into play. Of the two-shot holes, the humpbacked 11th and the dogleg 15th, with a bunker inside the margin of the fairway near the corner, appeal to me most.

As for the 16th hole, the sharp dogleg to the right around a willow-lined pond, which is the standard choice for golf writers' lists of great holes, I don't understand all the fuss: it's a good hole, but it's just a water hole. However, if you're looking for impossible holes, by all means include the 14th at Oakland Hills, with its nasty fall-away green, on which not a single birdie was recorded over four rounds of the 1951 U.S. Open. No wonder Hogan called the course a monster! But many positives also stand out. The back nine is absolutely outstanding, although I like the "other" holes more than I like the last three. So are the greens, which are among the most severe throughout 18 holes that I have seen. They are just the opposite of those at Prairie Dunes: the most severe pin placements are at the wings of the greens, which are folded up like gull-wing doors, while the center section of many greens is a deep hollow that tends to gather balls. Of course, if your ball doesn't gather you're left with a breakneck downhill putt, but most of the members can handle a two-putt in this situation, and if you stick the pins in the corner placements at holes such as the 1st, 5th, and 9th, the course quickly becomes difficult enough for anyone, even if the rough isn't at four inches. 9. [5/94]

***Old Channel Trail GC,*** *Montague. Robert Bruce Harris, 1926 (nine holes), with revisions and nine holes added by Bruce and Jerry Matthews.*

Forget the Matthews holes: they're dishwater dull. The only reason to see Old Channel Trail is the unique, overgrown grass fairway bunkers that Harris left over on his remaining holes (now the 10th through 16th), plus the two practice holes, which were also part of his original nine. I've never seen hazards like these anywhere, and though I am not sure I would want to copy them, they are worth seeing. There are also some interesting green complexes (with severe folds in the putting surface) on the old course, and a couple of good two-shotters. It baffles me why they didn't try to copy the style on their new nine; it would have been easy to do, and more interesting. 3. [5/89]

***Plum Hollow CC,*** *Southfield. Wilfrid Reid and William Connellan, 1925, with alterations by Bruce Matthews and Bill Newcomb.*

Another parkland layout on terrain similar to Toledo's Inverness, intersected by several deep swales. There is a good set of short holes (although none of them is that short), and the par-4 13th is probably the best hole on the course. 5. [5/81]

***Point O'Woods G & CC,*** *Benton Harbor. Robert Trent Jones, 1960.*

One of Trent Jones' most respected works, which has held the young and strong at bay for 30 years as annual host to the Western Amateur. The old man has been back recently, making a few minor alterations (lengthening tees further back, adding a few fairway bunkers) that make the golf course harder, but not better. They've also added wall-to-wall irrigation, to compete turf-wise with Chicago area clubs. It's certainly a tough course, but I don't think it's head and shoulders above Trent's others, and that doesn't rate so highly. 6. [5/89]

***Polo Fields CC,*** *Ann Arbor. Bill Newcomb, 1995.*

A development course slightly behind its time; it was built about 1988, but only revived this year after going bankrupt before opening. Apart from some gross over-mounding, the only memorable features are the back-to-back horseshoe-shaped greens at 17 and 18, Newcomb's tribute to a MacKenzie gimmick at the U of M course. One such green is horseshoe, two is horseshit. 3. [6/95]

***Radrick Farms GC,*** *Ann Arbor. Pete Dye, 1965.*

This is one of Pete's earliest courses, back when he was imitating Trent Jones: it features large, undulating, and somewhat awkward greens that look nothing like Harbour Town or the TPC at Sawgrass. Pete has said that he wishes he had this rolling piece of farmland to work with again, and I'm sure he could have done a better job. 4. [8/89]

***Scalawags GC,*** *Mount Clemens. Reggie Sauger, 1986.*

A new public course northeast of Detroit, constructed on ground of very little promise, and with predictable results. 2. [9/86]

***Schuss Mountain GC,*** *Mancelona. Warner Bowen, 1977.*

This is about the kind of course I expected to see from the second line of Michigan resorts—modest design, not too rolling terrain, several holes cut through dense woods, and above all, affordable to build and maintain. But they'll still charge you $40 to play it: and since the property's mediocre and Warner Bowen is no Hugh Wilson, it's not worth the cash. 3. [6/86]

***Shanty Creek GC,*** *Bellaire. Legend course by Arnold Palmer, Ed Seay, and Bob Walker, 1985.*

A pleasant resort layout routed mostly through deep, wooded valleys, widely spoken of as the Palmer company's best course when it opened. (Whenever they open something promising these days, the word of mouth is that it's the first really good one they've done.) Anyway, I don't think that's saying too much. The routing lacks variety, and I thought the only really memorable stretch of golf holes on the course was from the 10th through the 13th; the atmosphere of woods and seclusion probably has more to do with the course's reception than the holes themselves. Still, it's less gimmicky than a lot of the other new entries in the design world, so that's not all bad; and I hear they've finally got healthy grass on the greens. 5. [6/86]

***Sugar Loaf Resort,*** *Cedar. C.D. Wagstaff, 1966.*

They didn't waste a lot of money here like at Grand Traverse, but they didn't accomplish very much, either: just another golf course. 2. [6/86]

***Sylvan Resort,*** *Gaylord. Treetops course by Robert Trent Jones, 1987; Treetops North Fazio course by Tom Fazio (Dennis Wise), 1992.*

You can't talk about Treetops without talking about Rick Smith, the director of golf/Tour guru (and now, golf course architect) who has been the main P.R. man since its inception. He makes everyone who visits Treetops feel they have been someplace special, and has had a lot more to do with giving the golf courses a far-reaching reputation than the actual designs.

Rick has done so well for himself the past few years, you wonder how he might have done working for Michael Milken; but the answer is obvious, because he managed to hard-sell the original Treetops layout, which is golf's closest equivalent to a junk bond. The sad part is that its problems are things that Mr. Jones never used to screw up: it looks like

he's lost touch with his own style in trying to keep up with the eighties. Whether you liked his "Howard Johnson" period or not, all of Jones' courses were flexibly difficult through multiple pin placements and huge tees, but always broad and playable for the amateur. At Treetops (as at Ballybunion New) he has suddenly developed a penchant for small greens with severe drops to unplayable areas at the sides, and the routing plan eschews the playable for the spectacular. I pissed off Rick Smith by choosing the 1st and 8th holes for my original "worst 18" list, but other holes at Treetops (the 5th and 10th) also could have been chosen.

Tom Fazio had a decided advantage over Mr. Jones when he came here to build course #2—a great piece of property with some deep, sweeping natural valleys the perfect width for resort fairways. The product is a very good course well suited for resort play, which the first Treetops course was emphatically not. But I can't help feeling they could have done much better with the property: they moved 150,000 cubic yards of dirt where I wouldn't have moved any, and broke up some of the sweeping valleys that grace the property for the sole purpose of hiding cart paths from view. (A classic example of the cart driving the course.) Several of the greens blend severe level changes into adjacent banks, making it almost impossible to play certain approach putts anywhere near the hole, and the greens of two short par-4 holes (the 5th and 15th) are downright gimmicky, which is rare for Fazio. It's very good, but it should have been something unique. Jones course: 5. Fazio course: 7. [9/92]

***Traverse City G & CC,*** *Traverse City. Tom Bendelow, with substantial revisions by Bill Newcomb, 1985–90.*

A short, modest layout on perfect sandy soil on some of the highest ground in Traverse City, which stays so dry that Noah could have gotten his money's worth out of a monthly pass here. Unfortunately, the club got halfway through a master-planned redesign before it came to its senses, so the present course is a bizarre mix of basic straightaway holes with oval bunkers, and ridiculous modern stuff with amoeba-shaped greens and sharply defined grass depressions. 3. [9/95]

***Twin Birch GC,*** *Kalkaska. I've met the designer, but don't remember his name. 1988.*

I'm blushing; I forgot to include this course in the underground edition of the *Confidential Guide.* It's not much to remember; the nine holes I walked were somewhat tight and had specimen trees saved in just the wrong places on a couple of fairways, while the new nine was only notable to me because they were trying the same blend of fescue fairways we tried at High Pointe. But I should have remembered to include it. 2. [5/88]

***U of Michigan GC,*** *Ann Arbor. Alister MacKenzie and Perry Maxwell, 1934, with revisions by Bill Newcomb; "restored" by Arthur Hills, 1994.*

There's been much hullabaloo in my home state about the restoration of the U-M course, and certainly it's good news that they're taking it more seriously now than in the mid-eighties, when its #1 service was as parking lot for Michigan Stadium just across the street. It's also a much better layout than I had noticed in my first walk-through, on which I missed several of the early holes due to fading light. However, I'm not terribly impressed with the $3 million restoration. They did an excellent job of preserving some of MacKenzie's wilder greens, but the construction of everything else (tees and bunkers in particular) is efficient and sterile, with none of the flair or naturalized look that are MacKenzie's hallmarks. 5. [6/95]

***Warwick Hills CC,*** *Grand Blanc. James Harrison, 1955, with modifications by Joe Lee.*

Harrison was a student of Donald Ross, and his design here has a certain charming simplicity—but the routing plan may be a bit too simple, as the two parallel loops of holes result in "paired" holes that mimic one another, instead of adding variety to the course. The huge, immaculate greens and bunkers for which the course is best remembered are Joe Lee's work. Twenty years ago, this was considered one of the more difficult courses on Tour, thanks to sheer length and

speedy greens; now you have to shoot 15 under to finish in the top ten, one of the best indicators of how much better these guys are today, and/or how much easier the game has become. 5. [7/86]

**Wilderness Valley GC,** *Gaylord/Mancelona. Valley course by Al Watrous, 1970, expanded to 18 holes by Bruce and Jerry Matthews, 1979. Black Forest Course by Tom Doak and Gil Hanse, 1991.*

When I asked what his goals were for the Black Forest, Wilderness Valley developer Dave Smith told me he "just didn't want anybody coming in and complaining it was too easy," as they did with the original Valley course. He hasn't had to worry about it yet, but I must admit I'm still suspicious of a course where I haven't broken 80 yet. We may have committed the cardinal sin of the eighties here: overdoing things.

A lot of my mixed feelings about this course come from the fact that it has helped to overshadow High Pointe, which I think has a greater variety of shots. Black Forest is undeniably beautiful and spectacular—the dark woods and the magnificent bunkers give it an epic feel, which can turn downright intimidating if you're off your game—but there are a couple of greens here I'd really like to fix, and it worries me that people rate it more highly just because it's more difficult and because it better fits the cliché of northern Michigan—18 holes through the trees.

But there are some terrific golf holes. The par-5 opener is a great mood-setter, and the 13th a fine short par-4 that can be played in several different ways; but my favorite is the par-5 10th, which runs downhill through a narrow valley and forces you to play the second shot through a narrow gap between two maple trees. Maybe one day I'll play a decent round here and I'll feel better about the whole thing. Valley course: 2. Black Forest course: 6. [6/95]

**Wawashkamo GC,** *Mackinac Island. Alex Smith, 1898, with revisions/restoration by Larry Grow.*

I'm not much into Indian names for golf courses, but this one—"walk a crooked path"—is more appealing than most. So is the course, a beautifully restored nine-holer laid out over an old farm in the middle of the island. It is the genuine, 19th-century article: unirrigated fairways that nevertheless provide a playable lie, teeny greens that make approach play and chipping difficult, and a short but well-conceived layout that has alternate tees for the front and back nine. They even have antique clubs and gutty balls for rent, in case you want to see how difficult golf was in the old days. Even with modern equipment, though, the club is a quiet and enjoyable place for golf, and the small clubhouse is more homey than most. 4. [5/88]

**Wequetonsing GC,** *Harbor Springs. Architect unknown, 1899.*

A very private small club dating to the turn of the century, set high up the slope overlooking Lake Michigan. The course is modest but features a couple of spectacular elevated tees, particularly for the dropping shot to the tiny 17th green. The club is a summer haven for Masters chairman Hord Hardin, and Tom Watson used to spend summers here as a boy. 3. [7/86]

*—Gossip—*

Having lived in Michigan the greater part of the past nine years, I'd like to say I've seen everything worth seeing, but new courses are being built at such a clip that it's impossible to keep up, and there's so much hype about every newcomer that I can't sort it out. (Neither can the writers.) I also have difficulty in rating these new ones because in some instances I have been interviewed for the job, and can't set aside my own preconceptions about how the course should have been designed. I am most curious to see Rick Smith's architectural debut at Treetops; he really has a great feel for shotmaking so I'm sure it's interesting, but the Michigan scribes treat him like the Christian Broadcasting Network treats Pat Robertson. The other big project up north is Art Hills' Bay Harbor, which starts with a magnificent frontage on Little Traverse Bay and a huge promotions budget.

Further south, I've got to see the Gailes GC at Lakewood Shores in Oscoda, modeled after a British links and designed and built by Kevin Aldridge, the son of the owner of Indianwood (and The Gailes), because friends tell me it really plays firm and fast like a links. And someday I'll have to see Robert Trent Jones, Jr.'s daily-fee Orchards GC, the toast of the Detroit media, and the old Donald Ross–designed Rackham GC, which my partner Bruce Hepner has slowly helped to restore. However, I must confess that when I have time to play golf around home, I'm quite happy limiting myself to Crystal Downs and High Pointe; they're the kind of courses you never get tired of.

## INDIANA

***Brickyard Crossing GC,*** *Indianapolis. Pete Dye (Jason McCoy), 1993.*

Pete's redesign of the old Speedway Golf Course is sure to be a boon to the owners' pocketbooks; it's a difficult but very playable public course with big greens contoured to make it difficult to get close to the pins. And the four holes within the famed oval are a unique setting, even though Pete apparently ran completely out of ideas at the par-4 9th, where for some reason he put about 20 round bunkers. For Pete, though, the layout is quite undramatic—you shouldn't go out of your way to see it. 5. [9/93]

***Crooked Stick GC,*** *Carmel. Pete Dye, 1964–85.*

Except for Casa de Campo, this may be Pete's favorite of his own designs—it has little touches of Macdonald, Tillinghast, Ross, and MacKenzie, plus the classic Dye look. The front nine demands solid shotmaking, and includes the postcard par-3 6th; yet it is the back nine that stands out in my memory, and especially the stretch of holes 13–16.

Unfortunately, Crooked Stick has recently become another example of a club that couldn't leave well enough alone, and most of it is Pete's fault. When the club lost its putting surfaces to C-15 bentgrass decline, Pete seized the opportunity to make some major design changes to the layout while the place was torn up, in preparation to host the 1991 PGA Championship. The subtle changes he made to the course's undulating greens are fine, but the few holes to which he made major modifications look more like they belong at PGA West than at Crooked Stick. "The Stick" used to be a great example of Pete's "early period"; now, it's a mixed bag. 7. [8/90]

*Pete Dye's earliest masterpiece, the 6th at Crooked Stick.*

***Culver Military Academy GC,*** *Culver. William Langford, 1920.*

A rip-snorting design suited to a military school—if you get out of line in class, it would be a bitch of a hike with a full pack. Four of the holes traverse valleys 20 to 30 feet deep, and though there is no sand in Langford's deep "bunkers"—the fairway hazards are much more plentiful here than on any of his other designs I've seen—the jungly grass on their faces is plenty of hazard for anyone. The greens ought to be expanded back to their original size so that pins could be placed closer to the brink of disaster, and fairway irrigation would make it more appealing to country-club visitors, but hopefully they'll resist any temptation to take out the blind shots or otherwise "improve" it. 4. [7/95]

***Evansville Country Club,*** *Evansville. William Diddel.*

The best in town, but that's not saying too much; its only real attractions are a fairly hilly property and good zoysia fairways. 4. [2/95]

***Harrison Hills CC,*** *Attica. Original nine by William Langford and Theodore Moreau, 1923; expansion to 18 holes by Tim Liddy, 1996.*

A wild layout I just happened to drive past short-cutting from Terre Haute to West Lafayette. The terrain is fairly hilly and so is the course, with wildly undulating greens dramatically perched above deep bunkers on the scale of Fishers Island or PGA West. Every one of the original nine holes deserves praise for daring design. Especially memorable are the par-3 2nd, with its small artificial green pushed out into a semi-blind bowl; the driveable par-4 14th, with deep bunkers chiseled away at the sides and back of the green; the drive-and-pitch 15th, with PGA West bunkers to both sides on the uphill approach; and the convex, roller-coaster short par-5 finishing hole, with a wonderful blind approach daring you to go for it in two.

When I stopped in five months later to see how it actually played, they were in the midst of expanding to 18 holes. The new work was still too raw to review, but except for two holes by the new irrigation pond, it fit in better than I imagined it would—hats off there to Liddy, a Pete Dye protégé whom I've never

met. (Unfortunately, to make returning nines he had to destroy the old par-5 3rd, one of the most heroic driving holes I'd ever seen—the last half of the fairway now becomes the practice range, but you used to tee off from beside the 2nd green, choosing either to lay up to the base of the hill or blast it around the corner up top.)

Despite the success of blending new with old, I have to question the wisdom of expanding the course at all. I'm worried that we have gone so far toward standardizing what qualifies as "quality golf" that anything different is under pressure to conform, even in a small town so far off the beaten track that no one else knows or cares about it. The original nine at Harrison Hills was golf as it was invented to be—wild, fun, and full of challenge. But I suspect that 18 holes of this bent will be too much for some golfers, and will somehow discredit the terrific golf holes left over from the original nine. It was probably easier to enjoy when you could choose at the turn whether the round was done. 6. [7/95]

***Hulman Links***, *Terre Haute. David Gill and Garrett Gill, 1977.*

A first-class public facility built on land donated by the estate of Indianapolis Speedway owner Tony Hulman. The course is interesting but has several features you wouldn't generally plan for an ideal public course: lots of small bunkers speckled across the landscape, wide fairways that tighten up just where the weak player might fall short with the second shot, and the narrow par-5 11th hole where a wayward driver might lose an entire bucket of balls in the surrounding woods, all of which contribute to a very high slope rating. 5. [2/95]

***Maxinkuckee CC*** *(formerly East Shore CC), Culver. William Langford and Theodore Moreau, 1922.*

A private nine-hole country club for 84 members with summer cottages on Lake Maxinkuckee, most famously one Alice O'Neal Dye, who spent part of her youth here. Now I understand one of the main things she and Pete had in common when they met—they both grew up playing wild little nine-hole courses (see Urbana, Ohio). This property is much flatter than Culver Academy just up the road, but there are still four greens with near-vertical six- to ten-foot banks down the sides and back, which helps to explain why neither of Alice's sons think that their own "steep and deep" designs are all that radical. Because of the flat site there's only one really outstanding hole—the par-5 8th—but it's a doozy. 4. [7/95]

***Sand Creek Club,*** *Chesterton. Ken Killian and Dick Nugent, c. 1975.*

A stylistic modern course just a couple of miles from the Lake Michigan shore. The one very memorable hole is the par-5 16th, with a Pine Valley–like plan concept of several island landing areas separated by sandy wastes; but the definition and visibility of the hole don't approach the model's. Otherwise, this is just a fairly good modern course. 5. [7/85]

***Wolf Run GC,*** *Zionsville. Steve Smyers, 1987.*

Artistically, this is one of the best-looking modern courses I've seen: it really has a distinct quality about it, combining the natural hazards, the undulations of the property, artificial mounding covered in fescue, chipping areas in locations that actually make sense, and bunkers placed with reckless abandon. There are also some memorable golf holes, including two (the short par-4 4th, and the alternate-fairway par-5 10th) that are completely manufactured, but wouldn't look it to the untrained eye. Overall, this puts Smyers in the very small group of modern designers whose work I will now seek out.

Unfortunately, because they were playing for a men's club audience and had to compete with nearby Crooked Stick, owner Jack Leer and Smyers turned up the difficulty meter about ten degrees too far for anyone over a 4-handicap. It's virtually impossible for anyone less accomplished to finish with the same ball

with which they began the round, as several holes leave no room for error on the approach, and no place to hedge if you doubt you can pull off the shot. Witness the 240-yard 13th over the shoulder of a hill peppered with bunkers, with only a tiny straight-in approach fairway, or the 435-yard 14th, with a forced carry of 150 yards over a pond to the green, hemmed in by flanking bunkers and the long fescue roughs. These are the heart of what Smyers' new design partner, Nick Faldo, designated as the "most difficult four consecutive holes" he had ever played—and I'd be hard-pressed to nominate anything tougher. Definitely worth seeing once, but only those who are supplied their golf balls for free could enjoy it on a regular basis, even after they've cut back the rough significantly over the years. 7. [7/95]

*—Gossip—*

The only top-rated track I've missed is Sycamore Hills in Fort Wayne, which looks from the pictures I've seen like fairly dull parkland terrain (with mid-1980s vintage Nicklaus-style terraced greens). There's also Otter Creek in Columbus, a great public facility but probably just another long and difficult Robert Trent Jones track. I'd rather see Broadmoor CC in Indy, a Donald Ross course whose greens Pete Dye studied intently before starting on Crooked Stick.

## MINNESOTA

***Edina CC,*** *Edina. Tom Bendelow, with some revisions by Geoffrey Cornish, and more in planning by Roger Rulewich.*

We interviewed here for the job of redesigning the course, but weren't selected, possibly because we liked the layout a bit more than the members did. The hilly property has many good features, although the course is crowded onto about 120 acres so that not all the landing areas could be positioned on ideal vantage points; there are a couple of small blind ponds in play on the par-5 1st and 4th. The opening run of par 5, par 3, par 5, par 5 is unique in my experience, though hardly ideal; the best holes were the strong par-4 7th and 10th, and the very short par-4 13th; and the weirdest hole the par-3 16th, with an unbelievably sloped green fronted by a pond. I can't really imagine what they'll do with it. 5. [4/94]

***Golden Valley CC,*** *Golden Valley. A.W. Tillinghast, 1924, with revisions by Geoffrey Cornish and Brian Silva.*

One of the best players I know, Jody Rosenthal (now Anschutz), grew up here, and now I know how she got to be such a good putter—these greens are slick and tilted pretty sharply in the best Tillinghast tradition, so you don't want to play from above the hole. It's also an above-average property, as far as the topography is concerned, and there is some modestly nice bunkering. But the choice of holes is weird—five pretty good par-3's, but all between 168 and 179 yards, and six par-5's, which Minnesotans seem to have a fetish for. (Every course I saw in the Minneapolis area had at least five par-5's, even though some of them were so short they were only 5's by club convention.) The one excellent hole was the short par-5 6th, reachable in two with a drive to the left and a long second over a stream seventy yards short of the well-bunkered green. Footnote: I've seen courses divided by a major public road, a power line, and a railway line—but all three? 5. [11/93]

***Interlachen CC,*** *Edina. Willie Watson, 1910, with revisions by Donald Ross in 1919, Willie Kidd in 1929, Robert Trent Jones in 1962, Gerry Pirkl in 1968, and Brian Silva and Geoffrey Cornish.*

A historic course, thankfully not substantially changed from that Saturday in 1930 when Bob Jones skipped his second shot across the lake at the par-5 9th, on his way to the third leg of the Grand Slam. Other holes impressed me more: the par-5 4th, where you have to flirt with a pond short right to go for the green in two; the short par-4 10th, with its uphill approach to a severe green; the 187-yard 13th downhill toward Mirror Lake; and the par-4 18th through a valleyed fairway and uphill to a green with a severe false front. But I think the place gets some brownie points for its history and stature in the community; I'm not sure the course is really as exciting as its advance billing. 6. [11/93]

***Midland Hills CC,*** *St. Paul. Seth Raynor, 1919, with revisions by Paul Coates.*

One of the less well-preserved Raynor designs of my acquaintance; it's a fairly nice piece of property, but these holes are less dramatic than other versions, and in some places they've grown in considerably. The Redan par-3 16th is on a grand scale, but a lot of other holes, like the Cape 8th, with a severe uphill second shot, are below the Macdonald standard. 3. [4/94]

***Minikahda Club,*** *Minneapolis. Willie Watson and Robert Foulis, 1906, with expansion to 18 holes by Robert Taylor and C.T. Jaffray; and revisions by Donald Ross in 1917, Ralph Plummer in 1962, and Michael Hurdzan in 1990.*

A stately club with a fine course, but it's gotten a bit short for the modern day. There are some good holes in the middle of the course, including the short 3rd over a valley paralleling the main road, and the par-5 7th and 13th, both fine two-and-a-half shotters. But the course is sorely handicapped by a weak finish of four par-4's, none of them over 400 yards. 5. [11/93]

***Northland CC,*** *Duluth. Donald Ross, 1921.*

Set into a steep hillside just north of the city, the course's higher reaches provide majestic views of Lake Superior. It's a relatively unchanged example of Ross' work, but a bit like Capilano: aside from the dramatic level changes there aren't many interesting small-scale undulations, except for those at the par-4 7th hole. But the greens do have a lot of tilt and speed, so it's far from easy. 6. [8/95]

*The 15th tee at Northland, with Lake Superior beyond.*

***Rochester G & CC,*** *Rochester. A.W. Tillinghast, 1922, with revisions by Geoffrey Cornish, 1988.*

A fairly subdued Tillinghast layout set among pine trees. The routing is good across hilly terrain, although a couple of the holes feature steep banks in front of and behind their shelved greens. The par-3's are a little weak for Tillinghast, with the exception of the tiny 11th; but the two-shotters are excellent, and the par-5 holes are unusually good for Tillie. The greens are more subdued here than Golden Valley or certainly Winged Foot; conventional wisdom is that Tillie didn't want to make it too hard for his daughter, who lived here. Cornish has added two new holes to create room to expand the clubhouse, but they don't fit in at all, and the club is still debating whether to change them or return to the original holes and forget about expanding the facilities. 6. [8/94]

***Somerset CC,*** *West St. Paul. Seth Raynor, 1919, with revisions by Stanley Thompson, Robert Bruce Harris in 1958, George Cobb in 1976, and Geoffrey Cornish in 1979.*

A very nice, quiet club, but I wasn't as impressed by the layout as many Minnesotans are; a lot of the holes are so rudimentary in bunker and green construction that I'm surprised to find so many architects have fiddled with it. There is one really high hill at the southeast corner of the property, with a couple of good holes working around it, including a Redan; but too many parallel holes spoil the broth. 5. [11/93]

***White Bear YC,*** *Dellwood, White Bear Lake. Donald Ross, 1915, with minor revisions by Don Herfort, Geoffrey Cornish and Tom Doak.*

A walk on the wild side, with fairway undulations of holes like the par-4 5th reminding me of the north Atlantic in a very bad mood, and greens that would make Perry Maxwell blush. The back nine includes some of the wildest Ross features I've ever seen: for example, the par-3 11th with its green tilted right-to-left and flared up high in the back to return balls; the par-4 12th with green tilted sharply away; the short par-4 14th with a sharp tier running through the green at an angle; and the skinny green of the long par-4 15th with a bowl to the left and a plateau on the right separated by a narrow ridge. Whew! The story goes that they had Pete Dye come in a few years back to advise on rebuilding the 14th green; after looking at it for a few minutes in silence, he lamented, "Man, I wish I could get my guys to build greens like this," and the green stayed put.

There are some poor drainage areas, and at least a couple of blind shots—there could be many more if you're not hitting your drives solidly, particularly on the par 5's. It has the makings of a cult course: you're either going to love it or hate it, but I guarantee you won't see anything else like it in the Midwest. 7. [8/95]

*Ross's wild White Bear Yacht Club.*

*—Gossip—*

I was impressed by the high standard of architecture in Minnesota and, in most of the above cases, pretty good property devoted to golf. I still haven't gone out to see Hazeltine National, which didn't pique my interest while watching the 1991 U.S. Open on TV; the superintendents around Minneapolis also speak highly of the very exclusive Wayzata CC. I would also be curious to see The Pines at Grand View Lodge in the northern part of the state, an unconventional design by former golf pro Joel Goldstrand—the reviews have been very mixed.

## WISCONSIN

***Blackwolf Run GC,*** *Kohler. River and Meadow Valleys courses by Pete Dye (Scott Pool), 1988–89–90.*

The unusual expansion of this course from 18 holes to 27 and 36 has made it difficult to keep track of; the original 18 holes are now holes 1–4 and 14–18 of the River Course, and the back nine of the Meadow Valleys. A lot of the Meadow Valleys course is artificially created from a field, with the exception of a handful of fine natural holes at the 14th, 15th, 17th, and 18th.

But the really outstanding holes at Blackwolf Run are those that utilize the river, and most of these are now part of the River course. The fourth nine was welded into the middle of the original front nine to produce the new River Course, which may well be an improvement on the original Kohler 18. The new nine starts with the par-4 5th from a high tee overlooking the river, and is all contained within a loop of the Sheboygan River downstream from the original golf course, which Mr. Kohler had reserved as off-limits for the original layout. Several dramatic holes follow, including the short par-5 8th from a high tee above the river, the unique short par-4 9th with three distinct routes to the green, the right-angle dogleg par-5 11th around a sharp river bend, and the par-3 13th along the river yet again. This is an especially difficult nine holes, and Pete really went to town on it with alternate-route fairways, dramatic deep bunkers and difficult rolling greens, so you're bound to either love it or hate it, but I think that most must agree that it has a lot of character to it. River Course: 7. Meadow Valleys Course: 5. [9/95]

***Blue Mound G & CC,*** *Wauwatosa. Seth Raynor, 1924, with revisions by David Gill, Killian & Nugent, and Bob Lohmann.*

Another Raynor franchise effort. On the plus side there is some goodly contour to the greens, and an excellent rendition of the "Punchbowl" (the par-4 8th). But the greens have shrunken considerably, the first three holes are now bordered by the back lot of a shopping mall, it's still as short as the day it was built (6,300 yards), the property is gently rolling but unmemorable, and the club's landscape committee over the past sixty years should be lined up and shot for planting so many trees of so many varieties. 5. [5/94]

***Green Bay CC,*** *Green Bay. Dick Nugent and Tim Nugent, 1995.*

An impressive new course on prime property just south of the Green Bay bypass. The combination of mature hardwoods, dramatic elevation changes, and a looping river create the foundation for some outstanding holes on a big scale. But there are some strange design features, too, including an island-green par-3, a dreadfully manufactured 650-yard par-5, and chipping areas in some of the most awkward places imaginable around the greens. 6. [9/94]

***Lawsonia Links,*** *Green Lake. Links course by Bill Langford and Theodore Moreau, 1929; Woods course added by Rocky Roquemore and Joe Lee, 1983.*

The steep-walled bunkers and elevated greens of the Links course dominate the natural topography; so why do I find this course charming, and Blackwolf Run contrived? Well, Pete had a better piece of ground in Kohler than Langford had to work with here, and there are fewer examples of Lawsonia's style left in the world than of Pete Dye's. But I guess another part of the reason is that it's easier to accept an older course's design as a given, whereas on a brand-new course one can always find something that could (or should) have been done differently. I wish I could remember whether the greens here were as good as at Harrison Hills.

The Woods course was only nine holes when I

saw it but has been expanded to eighteen: it incorporates the edge of the cliff down to Green Lake in the routing, but it looked rather narrow and rugged at a glimpse. Links course: 6. Woods course: 4. [8/86]

***Milwaukee CC,*** *Milwaukee. Charles Alison and H.S. Colt, 1929, with revisions by Robert Trent Jones, 1975.*

A vintage Alison layout on a magnificent property on Milwaukee's north side. The front nine occupies mostly higher ground, while the back side descends to the Milwaukee River, which comes into play at the 12th and 14th. There are some very strong fours at the start, and the variety of the one-shotters is very good, but the single most memorable hole for me was probably the short par-4 9th to the back of the clubhouse, with a dramatic false front at the entrance to the green. Perhaps the only weakness is the set of par-5 holes: the green complexes and the bunkering on the approaches are admirable, but still none of the four is longer than 515 yards. 7. [5/94]

***Oneida G & Riding C,*** *Green Bay. Stanley Pelchar, 1928, with revisions by Bob Lohmann, 1985–91.*

Packerland's old-guard standard, mostly because it's in terrific shape unless the river has flooded the lowest-lying four holes. The members swear by it, but the design is pretty straightforward, with many flattish holes, large blobby bunkers, and fast but flattish plateau greens. Even the two most interesting holes, the short par-4 7th and 15th, are both 90-degree doglegs to the left. 5. [9/93]

***Ozaukee CC,*** *Mequon. Bill Langford and Theodore Moreau, 1922, with revisions by David Gill and Bob Lohmann, and more underway by Ron Forse.*

I only got through nine holes here before we were put off by rain and sleet (I'm getting to be quite a wimp in my old age) but I liked what I saw. The greens were especially interesting, with a couple of difficult shelves at the sides, and some sweeping contours in the middle—I'd hate to putt them at 10 on the Stimpmeter, but at 8 1/2 they were a lot of fun. However, the club's tree-planting program is classic overkill, spoiling the vast scale of the bunkering and the layout. Hopefully they'll allow Ron Forse to fire up a chain saw as part of his program. 5. [10/91]

***Sheboygan CC,*** *a.k.a. Pine Hills, Sheboygan. Harry B. Smead, 1928.*

An exceedingly pretty, rolling layout featuring several good short holes and two gorgeous par-4's that prominently feature a swift-flowing stream. The course measures out rather short, but the contours add to the challenge, particularly in the form of narrow, elevated greens, which make recovery difficult but detract from the otherwise natural feel of the course. 4. [9/87]

*—Gossip—*

The two courses I'd most like to see are both in Madison: Maple Bluff CC, another old Seth Raynor layout, and the new University Ridge GC by Robert Trent Jones, Jr., which has gotten some good reports. If you like flower arrangements, you should also go and see Sentryworld, the insurance giant's answer to Versailles, and Bobby Jones' flower child. But, the really big news is going to be Pete Dye's new Whistling Straits GC, on a bluff overlooking Lake Michigan north of Kohler—even veterans of Pete's operation are rolling their eyes at its awesome scale.

## ILLINOIS

***Alton Municipal GC,*** *Alton. Architect unknown.*

I played this with my uncle Gus when I was about 11 years old, and am including it only for the sake of completeness. About all I remember about it is that it's nine holes long (with a front four and back five, or perhaps it was the other way around), the 9th hole is a 110-degree dogleg, 300-yard par 4, and the course condition struck me as "ratty" even at that age. 1. [±1973].

***Beverly CC,*** *Chicago. Donald Ross, 1907.*

A very well-done parkland course crammed onto a tight property, with a few drastically tilted greens and a fine set of par-5 holes. But nothing new. 5. [7/86]

***Bob O'Link GC,*** *Highland Park. Donald Ross, 1916; C.H. Alison/Colt/MacKenzie, 1926.*

Known more for the atmosphere of the club (which one member described to me as "a fraternity house with a golf course") than for the golf course itself, I was pleasantly surprised by the quality of the Bob O'Link course. Classic parkland in character, its main advantage over other courses of this genre is the expansive property, which (although heavily planted) never gives the impression that the holes are packed together in a parallel routing. The golf holes themselves are also quite good, thanks mostly to the work of Mr. Alison: somewhat reminiscent of the Country Club of Detroit, though the high Chicago edge is a disgrace to Alison's bunkering. There is a superior stretch of holes from the turn through the 15th. 6. [7/89]

***Butler National GC,*** *Oak Brook. George and Tom Fazio, 1973.*

The brainchild of the late Paul Butler, the all-male Butler National club was the permanent home of the Western Open and one of the most golf-oriented memberships in the country. Unfortunately, the golf course, even though it provided one of the toughest tests on the PGA Tour, doesn't possess the same kind of character. Many of the individual holes are less than memorable, and a couple of the ones that are, are so because they're impossible. (The all-water 240-yard 5th leaps to mind.) I played here from all the way back after a 4-month winter layoff, which was a definite mistake, but I don't believe the course would be terribly inspiring even if you did confine yourself to the right set of tees. Most interesting holes are the 617-yard 7th, which is a whale of a par-5; the short 8th; and the very tough par-4 finisher. 6. [7/86].

***Chicago GC,*** *Wheaton. Charles Blair Macdonald and Seth Raynor, 1895–1923.*

The first golf club founded west of Pennsylvania, Chicago possesses a genuine old-course atmosphere, from its colonnaded white clubhouse to the artificial mounds that delineate many of Macdonald's hard-line bunkers. Few golfers would identify this as a pretty course, as it sits in fairly open parkland with only a few ancient oaks dotting the terrain, yet the course provides a difficult test and still manages to exude a certain charm. As with all Macdonald/Raynor designs, Chicago features several familiar prototype holes—the "Road" 2nd, "Biarritz" 3rd, "Redan" 7th, "Punchbowl" 12th, and "Cape" 14th among them—but several of these are among the best examples of their types the two architects produced. For the golf historian, Chicago is a must-see; for the rest, it's still a good trip. 8. [7/86].

***Cog Hill GC,*** *Lemont. No. 4 (Dubsdread) course by Dick Wilson and Joe Lee, 1964.*

I believe that Cog Hill, with four courses in all, is unquestionably the finest municipal course facility in America, a testimony to Mr. Joe Jemsek, who operates it (and several other courses in suburban Chicago). The course that receives all the attention is the "Dubsdread," which is the only public facility ranked among America's 100 Greatest Courses, even though Pasatiempo and Bethpage Black surely ought to be ahead of it if design were the primary criterion. The back nine is laid out across the sidehills, instead of from ridge to ridge like the front side, and constitutes the more memorable part of the course. In general, Cog Hill No. 4 is a long, strong course, and one not to be taken lightly. 6. [5/81].

***Hinsdale GC,*** *Hinsdale. Donald Ross, 1913, with revisions by Roger Packard, Dick Nugent, and Bob Lohmann.*

A nice old club with a straightforward, unspectacular parkland course. The class of the course are the short holes, especially the short 13th across a pond to a steeply sloping green, and the long 16th with the "Andy Gump" bunker off its right shoulder. But it's not a hidden Ross gem—he was never on-site in the first place, and the bunkering has been bowdlerized by decades of committees and consultants. 4. [5/95]

***Kemper Lakes GC,*** *Hawthorn Woods. Ken Killian and Dick Nugent, 1979.*

Here's the corporate approach to giving the public-course golfer what he wants: fast greens, high-dollar maintenance, lots of water hazards, and a premium price. The bottom line says it's a winning formula in Chicago, but the course leaves me cold—the lines of the fairways look like they came straight out of the blueprint machine. 5. [8/88]

***Medinah CC,*** *Medinah. Number 3 course by Tom Bendelow, 1928, with modifications by Harry Collis, 1932, George and Tom Fazio, 1974, and Roger Packard, 1986.*

In his foreword to *The World Atlas of Golf,* Alistair Cooke neatly summarized Medinah No. 3 as "a claustrophobia of woods." Actually, it's not quite as tight as the Olympic Club, but at 500 yards longer, it is definitely a maximum-security prison—poor compensation, in my book, for its lack of strategic challenge. If you believe in the test that great golf courses produce great champions, it would be wise to reflect on the career of Lou Graham—or Mike Donald, who was one swing away from becoming a national champion here.

After the 1975 fiasco, when most of the world's best players bogeyed home from the 16th on Sunday afternoon, the USGA vowed not to hold another Open at Medinah, at least as long as its poor, claustrophobic finishing hole remained in place. But we all knew that they couldn't keep the Open away from Chicago forever, and no other club has comparable parking or tournament facilities, so the club managed to convince the "blue coats" that some Roger Packard revisions to the course would make it a worthy Open venue again.

The Open was a success, but I'm not fond of the changes to the course. The new par-5 14th is a real beast, and by swallowing up the old short par-4 15th it has usurped the only respite on the back nine. The new 17th is a clone of the old 2nd and 17th, a third short hole straight across Lake Kadijah distinguished only by its corrugated-metal bulkhead in front (hardly a selling point to me). And the new 18th is a tougher hole than the original finisher, but it does not solve any of the old problems of gallery flow. Since the course has already been altered several times, the club cannot be faulted for screwing up the original design character of the course, but the new routing has succeeded only in making Medinah No. 3 even tougher than it was, and does nothing to address what I consider to be the course's weakness—the total lack of finesse play required. No. 3 course: 7. [7/86].

***North Shore CC,*** *Glenview. Charles Alison and H.S. Colt, 1924, with revisions by Killian and Nugent, then Roger Packard.*

Like many others of the Chicago elite, this was a big disappointment to me. It fell from the magazine rankings and the public consciousness several years ago with the loss of many elms, but they must have been some trees to gain respect for the otherwise dull design. I suspect that stretching the course to 7,000 yards impressed the voters more than it did me. 5. [5/95]

***Old Elm C,*** *Highland Park. Donald Ross.*

This has the reputation of being an "old men's club," and the design is well suited to that set, with interesting run-up approaches to many greens—but this same characteristic makes it interesting for all but low-handicappers, who may find it a bit squatty to present a strong challenge. 5. [9/94]

***Olympia Fields CC,*** *Olympia Fields. North course by Willie Park, 1922; South course by Tom Bendelow, 1916, with modifications by Jack Daray and Larry Packard.*

In its heyday during the Roaring Twenties, Olympia Fields was the greatest golfing community in America, including four golf courses in all, not to mention its own school system and fire department. Only two courses are left today, and of the two the North, which hosted the 1928 U.S. Open, is the standout, with a good variety of holes on rolling parkland. The long par-4 14th is especially memorable.

However, the South is one hell of a good golf course, too. It has a few really dull holes, but there are several top-notch holes, including one of the best I've ever seen, the drive-and-death-defying-pitch par-4 6th. It could use a few more back tees and a few other touches, but if you go to Olympia Fields, don't settle for playing the North course twice and skipping this one. North course: 7. South course: 6. [5/89]

***Onwentsia C,*** *Lake Forest. James Foulis, Robert Foulis, H.J. Tweedie, and H.J. Whigham, 1895, with revisions by Dick Nugent, 1969–present.*

A landmark course—it hosted the U.S. Amateur of 1899 and the U.S. Open of 1906—with no sense of history at all, its appearance almost entirely that of a Dick Nugent design for the Chicago public park system. The club facilities and the conditioning are absolutely first-class, but the course suffers from a flat and uninteresting property, not to mention the loss of 800 elms over the past 25 years. I've been retained as consultant to the club, but our mission is unclear—even in its heyday it was more noteworthy as a prestigious club than as a great course, so it appears to be more a question of creating new features that look old, rather than restoring the original design. 4. [9/95]

***Pine Meadow GC,*** *Mundelin. Joe Lee and Rocky Roquemore, 1985.*

I confess to harboring some ill will for this course, which beat out my work at Riverdale Dunes for top new course honors in 1985. But this is a very posh public facility: it looks like an old country club, because the trees are from an old country club that was abandoned on the same site a few years earlier. The layout is good, but nothing earth-shaking: big greens, typical Chicago look. 5. [8/88]

*Shoreacres is laced with ravines.*

***Shoreacres,*** *Lake Bluff. Seth Raynor, 1921.*

One of Raynor's finest layouts, and a must-see for fans of the Macdonald style. The property is intersected by several deep ravines that drain into the adjacent Lake Michigan, and the designer used these ravines ingeniously in the routing to create a number of outstanding holes. There are all the prototype Raynor holes (most noteworthy are the Cape 4th, the Redan 14th with an oddly artificial banked green that nevertheless plays perfectly, and the Short 12th which plays down into the bottom of another), but there are also some magnificent originals like the short par-4 11th, and the par-5 15th. Alas, the overall yardage is quite short, but it's still a real gem. 7. [9/93]

***Skokie CC,*** *Glencoe. Tom Bendelow, 1904, with substantial revisions by Donald Ross, William Langford, and Rees Jones.*

A good parkland course with some difficult greens and some unusual bunkering, the product of several different designers. Credit for some of the most intriguing work belongs to Langford, including the arresting 220-yard par-3 3rd hole, across water to a high platform green. It's also pretty difficult and well-maintained, but I was still surprised to see it recently added to the *Golf Digest* top 100—I'd have picked Bob O'Link or Shoreacres well ahead of it, just among its near neighbors. 6. [8/88]

***Westmoreland CC,*** *Wilmette. Joseph Roseman, 1917, with revisions by William Langford, A.W. Tillinghast, Bill Diddel, and Ken Killian.*

I understand that the club has had Arthur Hills totally remake the course I saw in 1988, which was not a particularly difficult or interesting test of golf, thanks to too many parallel holes. The only hole I remember distinctly is the long par-4 3rd hole with its blind second shot and stoplight signaling system, which they wanted to tear up, but I didn't have the heart to carry out their orders. 4. [9/88]

## —*Gossip*—

Suburban Chicago is reputed to have one of the outstanding local collections of golf courses in the world, but they all look rather of a kind to me. Maybe Knollwood or Ravisloe will be different. New additions are coming every day as Chicago's real estate boom continues; Nicklaus' Wynstone and Tom Fazio's Conway Farms are the most celebrated, and fairly typical of their styles, while there are a gaggle of new ones from the "Chicago four" of Killian, Nugent, Packard, and Lohmann, all of whom are interchangeable as far as I'm concerned: just give them all a big 4-5 sight unseen, and write me if you discover anything better. (Lohmann's new Merit Club in Libertyville may be considerably better than this estimate, or it may just be getting a lot of brownie points because there are only 38 members: see Double Eagle.) Finally, somewhere out in the boondocks in a place called Galena there is Eagle Ridge, which has two courses I've heard good (not great, good) things about.

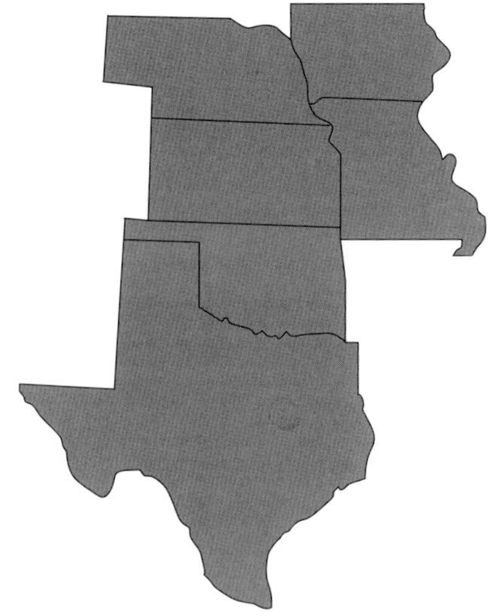

## GREAT PLAINS

Okay, so the image of a great plain doesn't conjure up dreams of golf. The nation's Middle West has always been devoted to agriculture, a way of life which doesn't leave much time for golf anyway. But Iowa, Missouri, Nebraska and Kansas are hillier than Easterners imagine, and they're also the windiest part of the United States, which adds value to every golf course in the region.

While great courses don't run in packs across the Plains, there are a few gems dotted across the landscape, like the great cavalry forts of the mid-1800's. The most famous outposts are the work of Perry Maxwell, an Oklahoma banker who apprenticed under Alister MacKenzie, and was the one great practicing architect during the Depression era—any course which has preserved Maxwell's original rolling greens is automatically worth a game. But there are some spectacular properties in this region, and as the economics of "destination golf" continue to grow, there will be more noteworthy projects from the Dakotas to Texas.

## IOWA

***American Legion CC,*** *Shenandoah. Original nine by Chic Adams, 1956; recently extended to 18 holes.*

A fairly plain layout across a rolling field, although the older part of the course is partly treed and includes some fairly radical greens—fortunately, they never get too fast. Best hole is the first, a 305-yard par-4 where you lay up short of a ditch in the fairway, but have to be careful to place the tee shot so as not to be stymied by a large tree at the left front of the green. 2. [7/91]

***Essex GC,*** *Essex. Designer unknown, 1982.*

Originally this was eighteen holes, but only nine survive; there's not much golf revenue in a town of 977 citizens devoted to their farms. It's a pretty natural course, with 1,500-square-foot greens, steep hills, and rock-hard fairway conditions when it's dry; so it's not exactly easy, either. This might be true natural golf, Scottish-style; but if Scotland's terrain were all like this, golf would never have become popular there. 2. [5/93]

***Wakonda Club,*** *Des Moines. Bill Langford and Theodore Moreau, 1922, with revisions by Dick Nugent, 1987.*

The "best course in Iowa" turned out to be more interesting than I expected; it's a rollicking, old-fashioned layout across a decidedly hilly in-town property. Mature oaks have added grace to the land, but they've obscured the wonderful original fairway bunkering, which was built short and wide of the present landing areas, and the club has chosen to grass in the bunkers rather than remove the trees—a real loss. Still, there are several interesting holes, including a set of wild par-5's and two different short holes that feature alternate greens, some severe putting greens, and one of the toughest opening par-4's I've encountered, all of which make it worth seeing before the green committee ruins it. 6. [6/94]

My wife's family hears that Sidney CC has the reputation of being the best golf course in the southwest part of the state; that probably just means they've got irrigation. The Amana Colonies GC is a possibility—a high-end daily-fee course on dramatic property, rumored to be a bit severe for the average Iowa golfer. And Tom Fazio is working on a course in suburban Des Moines which is sure to please, even if it's just another generic 1990s Fazio product.

## MISSOURI

***Old Warson CC,*** *Ladue. Robert Trent Jones, 1955.*

A fine example of Trent Jones' work at the peak of his career: still plenty long for Open qualifying (in fact, it's probably one of the toughest local qualifying sites in the country), and featuring very large, undulating greens, and bunkers that sprawl with a flourish. My favorite hole is the Cape-type 14th, but most of the holes on the back nine qualify in the "memorable" category, and the front side is certainly no pushover. 5. [8/81].

***St. Louis CC,*** *Clayton. Charles Blair Macdonald and Seth Raynor, 1914, with revisions by Robert Trent Jones.*

A classic Macdonald layout. Many of the bunkers are invisible from the field of play, but as one of the members I played with put it, "You know where they are—anytime you hit a bad drive, you're in one." In addition to the standard Macdonald repertoire, there are two superb three-shot holes (the 9th and 13th), and a fine par-3 (no. 3) that doesn't fit any of the known Macdonald types. Definitely worth playing. 6. [8/81].

***Tan-Tar-A GC,*** *Osage Beach. 27 holes by Bob Von Hagge and Bruce Devlin: Hidden Lake nine, 1969, and 18 holes added in 1980.*

I haven't seen the place since the summer of 1973, when my Dad attended a convention here in August, but even though I haven't seen the new 18, I can safely tell you that no golf course in the world would be worth playing in the Lake of the Ozarks in August—the heat and humidity were so unbearable that some of the players couldn't even finish nine holes. I remember the 4th was a good par-5 hole looking down toward the lake, and then you walked half a mile through the woods to get to no. 5, which was only a 95-yard drop shot over a skinny pond to a 40-foot-deep green. (I guess the site must have been pretty severe, for any architect to come up with a routing like that.) 2. [8/73].

The "Show-Me" State hasn't shown me very much variety of golf courses so far. Around St. Louis, there is of course Bellerive, the Trent Jones monster that ate the field in the 1965 U.S. Open, and put most of them to sleep in the 1992 PGA; and everything I've heard about in Kansas City is on the wrong side of the river.

# NEBRASKA

*The 11th hole at Firethorn.*

***Firethorn CC,*** *Lincoln. Pete Dye (Scott Pool), 1985.*

Pete Dye rarely deals with low construction budgets or good pieces of land nowadays, but at Firethorn he had both, maybe just to prove he could still work that way. I think it's one of Pete's better efforts in recent years, and even though it hasn't made any lists of the best courses in America, it's a huge standout in Nebraska.

Until I played Firethorn, I don't think I really understood just how severe Pete Dye's style of golf architecture really is. Lincoln is a very windy, very dry climate in the summer, and when this course is dried out and the wind picks up, it's as difficult as any I would care to play. Pete's new technique of routing the longer holes *into* the prevailing wind (to combat the length of the modern golf ball) is very conspicuous here, and the playing surface gets so fast in summer it can be hard to keep the ball between the lines. They used to pride themselves on letting the roughs grow wild, but they're cutting a lot more grass these days.

The routing includes a couple of short two-shot holes that won't strike everyone's fancy, and for my money a very uninspiring finish; but the stretch of outstanding holes through the middle part of each nine more than compensates. 7. [5/93]

***Heritage Hills GC,*** *McCook. Dick Phelps and Brad Benz, 1981.*

Not your typical Phelps course at all: but there isn't much of a market in McCook for condos thirty feet to either side of the fairways of an 18-hole golf course, and that, to me, is a typical Phelps effort.

This course is the very antithesis of Muirfield Village: instead of setting up perfectly from the tees and landing areas, all the holes at Heritage Hills look better from some completely different angle. If you could just move a few of the tees, there might be some pretty good holes here, but you'd have to move them into the fairways of other holes in order to make it work. My guess from looking at this course is that neither Phelps or Benz is better than a 20-handicap, because the placement of the hazards only makes sense at that level.

This is an exciting piece of ground (if a bit too hilly) and it takes a good picture, but that's the only reason to go. 4. [8/85]

***Highland CC,*** *Omaha. William Langford and Theodore Moreau, 1924, with revisions by David Gill, 1973.*

As of the time I saw it, this was rated the second-best course in Nebraska by *Golf Digest,* but, in the club champion's words, "That's mainly because there's only one outstanding course in Nebraska." Indeed, this parkland layout is only modestly interesting, though the smallish and severely pitched greens present some difficulty. The club plans significant modifications, but there wasn't enough potential in the land to interest me. 4. [4/93]

***Mullen GC,*** *Mullen. Architect unknown, converted to grass greens in 1991.*

A little nine-holer with green fees on the honor system and maintenance by local contribution, but not all bad, since it lies on rolling terrain in the sandhills; if it weren't for the next course listed, I might have been more impressed. But there isn't much small-scale interest to the terrain, and the guy who added the grass greens was no artist. 2. [5/93]

***Sand Hills C,*** *near Mullen. Bill Coore and Ben Crenshaw, 1995.*

See the "Gourmet's Choice." 9. [10/94]

***Willow Green GC,*** *North Platte. Architect unknown.*

A routine nine-holer I visited when my car broke down on one of my cross-country runs. Its only memorable feature was the green of the par-4 8th hole, which was shaped like the ace of spades, with the base of the blade actually coming to a point at the front sprinkler head, and a nasty crown shedding approaches into grass hollows on both sides in back. 1. [8/85]

*—Gossip—*

There are a couple of new courses around Omaha—The Champions Club and Woodland Hills—both designed by Jeff Brauer, that have quickly jumped to #2 and #3 in the state; but the Sand Hills in the dirt has to be way better than either.

## KANSAS

***Alvamar CC,*** *Lawrence. Bob Dunning, 1968.*

This course has achieved some notoriety, but I'm not sure why: the ground is modestly hilly, the holes mediocre. The highly rated public course next door looked no better, but I suppose that still makes it a fairly good public course. 4. [10/86]

***Crestview CC,*** *Wichita. 27 holes by Robert Trent Jones, 1969, with nine added by Robert Trent Jones, Jr., 1977.*

A telltale example of Trent Jones' later work, when he spent more time in the air than doing the designs. Pretty monotonous. 3. [9/84]

***The Highlands GC*** *(formerly Paganica GC), Hutchinson. Leo Johnson, 1972.*

A housing-development course on the wrong side of Hutchinson, golf-wise. When first built, the course might have been attractive because of the rolling terrain and native grasses that surrounded it; but now that the turf has declined and the hills are starting to be cluttered with housing, I would not recommend a visit. By the way, the original name for the course is supposedly derived from an ancient Roman game that resembled golf, but the only other reference I've ever seen to it was in the first paragraph of the original *GOLF Magazine Encyclopedia of Golf,* which came out about 1970; my guess is the developers didn't look very far to find it. 3. [8/86]

***Kansas City CC,*** *Shawnee Mission. Tom Bendelow, 1922, with revisions by Floyd Farley, Bob Dunning, and Rees Jones.*

A parkland layout reminiscent of those back East, though it's decked out in Bermuda grass and occupies much hillier terrain. The strength of the course is a number of excellent two-shot holes, but the best individual hole is probably the long, downhill one-shot 12th. The course still benefits from some majestic elm trees, but will sorely miss them when they inevitably decline. 6. [10/86]

***Macdonald Park GC,*** *Wichita. James Dalgleish, 1911, with revisions by Orrin Smith, Bill Diddel, and Bob Dunning.*

I was proudly told by Wichita members that this was a Perry Maxwell layout, but Mr. Whitten does not concur. In any case, while I don't think this is a great course or anything, it has a lot more character than the other courses in town, because it uses a couple of stream valleys to great advantage on several holes. It hasn't been too well maintained since the country club moved uptown, and the clubhouse is reminiscent of Project Mercury mission control, but it's a pretty nice golf course. 3. [9/84]

***Pine Bay GC,*** *Wichita. Architect unknown, 1985.*

A low-budget, nine-hole layout by a self-taught golf course designer who evidently has a lot to learn. The clearings for the holes are ludicrously narrow, which makes for a couple of the most severe holes I've ever seen; and the capper is a short hole with a near-island green in imitation of the 17th at the TPC, which is a ball-eating monster for players of the caliber this course attracts. 1. [8/85]

***Prairie Dunes CC,*** *Hutchinson. Nine holes (1-2-6-7-8-9-10-17-18) by Perry Maxwell, 1937; extended to 18 holes by J. Press Maxwell, 1956; some modifications by Bill Coore.*

See the "Gourmet's Choice." 9. [8/86].

***Southwind CC,*** *Garden City. Donald Sechrest, 1980.*

This is another course that I'd heard compared to Prairie Dunes for its use of native roughs and dune-like terrain, a rumor that gained credence from the course's being so remote that no one had seen it to dispute the description. Well, part of the course does get into some exciting terrain, and there are native grasses everywhere, but generally they're well wide of the playing areas, and more important, these aren't Perry Maxwell greens. But if you're ever stuck in Garden City, Kansas... 5. [8/85]

***Tallgrass GC,*** *Wichita. Art Hills, 1982.*

When this course was being built, it showed a lot of promise, with native grasses in the roughs making it look like it grew up out of the prairie. But then the development around the course sold out about 200% faster than expected, and most of the wild grasses were transformed into tract housing, and we discovered how many of the sharp dogleg holes had condos close on the inside corner. Also, Hills' "pseudopod" landing areas work a lot better on paper than on flat ground—generally, those complex touches only work when they're added in the field, rather than contrived in the design office. The pampas-grass 150-yard markers are terrible, and have been known to cause nightmares for girls preparing to go through LPGA Tour qualifying over the course. 4. [9/84].

***Terradyne GC,*** *Andover. Don Sechrest and Craig Schreiner, 1987.*

In direct contrast to his first course, Stillwater CC, this latest design of Sechrest's is everything I have feared in modern golf design: it attempts to combine elements of Prairie Dunes, PGA West, and the greens of Desert Highlands into one "super course," and the result is a disaster of epic proportions. Six different greens feature two high plateaus with a three-foot-deep swale dividing them into multiple "pin areas," and all the greens are in the range of 9,000 to 15,000 square feet, including two outlandish double greens.

How bad is it? On the first hole, a 465-yard par-4, you play to the right half of a double green, and although the left half of the approach is open they frequently tuck the pin behind a bunker on the right, from which the green runs straight away from the shot to a "burn" at the back edge, with bushes behind so that it is difficult to find a legal place to drop.

The rough is a mixture of ryegrass and wheat (the crop, not the grass), which makes finding and playing the ball difficult to impossible, and the fairways are much too narrow considering the nature of this rough and the presence of the wind. Finally, the monumental clubhouse is unbelievably overdone for the outskirts of Wichita, and I'm still trying to figure out why they built an exact replica of the water-tower halfway house at Pine Valley in the middle of a cornfield. As David Letterman would say, yeeeech! 0. [11/89]

***Wichita CC,*** *Wichita. Bill Diddel, 1950.*

The town's premier club, but hardly a classic course: in fact, their decision to move from Macdonald Park to this new site was not well received by some of the members. The design is forgettable except for a handful of severe greens, and the superintendent and green committee have changed their minds about fairway turf so many times that it's hard to tell which is their current favorite. The club's conspicuous location along the main glide path into McConnell AFB, and the frequent opportunity to inspect B-52's up close from underneath, is the icing on the cake. 4. [9/84].

***Willowbend GC,*** *Wichita. Jay Morrish and Tom Weiskopf, 1987.*

A good public track built by my friend Johnny Stevens over some unpromising (flat) Kansas terrain. Certainly I couldn't visualize doing more with the flat and relatively barren site; but that doesn't make the course outstanding, either. The holes are fairly well thought out, although a lot of the reason people will like it has more to do with the landscaping (rock walls lining large ponds) than outstanding strategic design. 4. [11/89]

***Wolf Creek GL,*** *Olathe. Dr. Marvin H. Ferguson, 1972.*

An all-male club about an hour's drive west of Kansas City, and the second-to-last sort of layout you'd expect to find in Kansas. The drive from the first tee and the one-shot 11th hole constitute two of the steepest dropping shots I've ever seen on a golf course (see Carmel Valley Ranch, California, and Strathpeffer Spa, Scotland), but there are also some good strategic holes to contend with, like the short 5th and the heroic par-5 7th. 5. [8/81].

*—Gossip—*

For a long time, Kansas City was sorely lacking for good golf courses, but two new courses on the scene, Hallbrook Farms (by Tom Fazio) and Shadow Glen (by the trio of Morrish, Weiskopf, and Tom Watson), have improved the picture considerably. I'm betting I will like Shadow Glen more, because I've heard that Hallbrook Farms is just impossibly difficult. Ron Whitten has also mentioned a relatively pristine nine-holer by Perry Maxwell in Coffeyville.

Elsewhere in the state, I've tried to check out all the courses that claim to be "another Prairie Dunes," without finding anything worth a second trip. If a similar course is ever built, it will probably be right next door to the original course: in fact, the club owns more of the duneland and has considered building a third nine.

## OKLAHOMA

***Cedar Ridge CC,*** *Broken Arrow. Joe Finger, 1970.*

My friends on the University of Tulsa women's golf team all swore to me that Cedar Ridge is a great course, but I'll write that off to home-course loyalty. Cedar Ridge is a difficult golf course from the back tees, but the routing is a monotony of back-and-forth, up-and-down holes that makes it impossible to remember them individually, and if the place has any character at all, I missed it. All I got from walking it was heat prostration. 4. [10/84].

***Dornick Hills CC,*** *Ardmore. Perry Maxwell, 1913–1923, with revisions by Dick Nugent.*

Not a bad layout for the locals, but no longer a classic—the "modernization" of the course a few years ago under CCA's stewardship removed much of the character around the greens. But it's still worth the drive from Dallas to see Maxwell's "Cliff Hole" 16th, a natural wonder. This short par-5 is reachable in two shots, but only if the long second can scale a 50-foot cliff with a sheer rock face running at an angle about 30 yards short of the green. Just to keep the long hitters honest, a long shot to the "safe" left side will carry back off the far side of the ridge. 4. [11/86]

*The 3rd at Golf Club of Oklahoma.*

***The GC of Oklahoma,*** *Broken Arrow. Tom Fazio, 1983.*

Another in the recent glut of one-man's passion/megabuck clubs (the Augusta National of the Midwest?), this one founded by John Williams. It's probably only because I am friendly with a couple of the members, but the exclusivity here (which, at $100 grand per membership, is pretty exclusive) doesn't bother me as much as at Shoal Creek or The Honors Course. You still can't get past the main gate without a member, but at least they don't go to the extreme of maintaining an overall-clad caddie force or an overdone clubhouse complex; the atmosphere is far more informal, like that of The Golf Club in Columbus.

I also liked the golf course, except for its collection of short holes, any of which might cause you to walk off the course. There's the 5th, which looks great from the tee, but the green must have six feet of fall to it from front to back, so you're absolutely dead on sidehill or downhill putts; the 7th has too severely tiered of a green; the 15th, a short drop shot to an unbelievably long green in three tiers going away from you, with a swampy lost ball haven short right of the green; and the 17th, which would be a great dropping shot except that the green looks very artificially concocted, with steep falls to all sides and the front left side pockmarked with deep sod wall pot bunkers.

But it's not all weird: the routing plan wanders the property beautifully, and most of the longer holes are superbly designed, even if the greens are overly steep. (Maybe the solution is simply to let the grass grow a bit.) The 3rd hole, across open land, is as good an imitation of rolling linksland as any new course I've seen, and a great par-4 to boot; the 4th, with its two-tiered green, makes a marvelous strategic hole; and the 1st, 10th, 13th, 14th, 16th, and 18th are all top-notch holes as well. The club also has one of the best-designed practice facilities I've ever seen, with multiple tees, target greens, and practice bunkers on the main range, and three entire practice holes with a couple of greens apiece circumnavigating the central range. In fact, you could have a pretty good golf match without ever leaving the range, but you'd be missing out on plenty of good holes if you did. 6. [10/84].

***Oak Tree CC,*** *Edmond. 36 holes by Pete Dye (John Gray and Russell Talley), 1981–85.*

The men's club across the street proved so successful that Landmark wound up building a full-fledged Country Club next door so as not to offend the families. The West course, made up of the back nine of the original 18 plus the third nine (which are now holes 8 through 16 West), is strong enough to have hosted one of the two qualifying rounds in the recent U.S. Amateur, but it is not that visually striking; the East course, recently completed, is a strange mixture of open holes surrounded by cornfields and some in very rolling terrain with water to contend with. It's a very interesting design, but for club members it's way too much from the back tees, and some of Pete's high-lipped pot bunkers within grass islands within waste bunkers are other-worldly: in the red clay they must have looked like Mars. West course: 5. East course: 5. [9/84].

***Oak Tree GC,*** *Edmond. Pete Dye (David Postlethwait), 1976.*

There are lots of courses where the duffer can get into more trouble, but for the pro game today (sheer brute strength off the tee, and difficult putting) there isn't a test of golf in the world more difficult than Oak Tree, and the owners wouldn't have it any other way. It seems like half the guys on Tour play out of the club, but none of them can play this course from the back tees in even par more than half the time, even if the greens weren't cut down to lightning speed. Every single hole on this golf course is a potential double bogey, and some of them (the 3rd, 4th, 14th, and 17th, especially) are downright intimidating, even with a camera in your hands.

But as for artistry in golf course architecture, I'm afraid that Oak Tree doesn't rate so highly with me. I think Pete overshot the mark in building a variety of holes here—the changes of scenery are so

*The 16th & 17th at Oak Tree Country Club (East), where many professionals honed their skills.*

abrupt that the course seems more like a collection of holes than a single entity, a problem reinforced by naming the holes after other courses (Muirfield, Augusta, Prairie Dunes, etc.) and trying to suggest their looks. The only character the holes have in common is that the greens are severe and they never let up on the difficulty meter.

On the other hand, practically every member of the club is a real character (an Oklahoma trademark), and I doubt you could have more fun at a member-guest anywhere else in the country. Just don't expect anyone in your foursome to break 85 from all the way back. 6. [9/84].

***Oklahoma City G & CC,*** *Oklahoma City. Perry Maxwell, 1930, with minor revisions by A.W. Tillinghast, Press Maxwell, and Donald Sechrest.*

The general run of the course is rather dull, but it owns two classic holes: the delayed-dogleg 2nd, and the one-shot 11th across a slashing stream more sinuous than the Barry Burn. There is also one of the weirdest holes in the world to contend with: the short par-4 12th, which can be played either by laying up a 4-iron to a narrow landing area and knocking a wedge onto the green, or by attempting to reach the green with a power-faded blind drive over a stand of trees. (I'd need a half-dozen balls to figure it out for sure.) 4. [8/81].

***Quail Creek G & CC,*** *Oklahoma City. Floyd Farley, 1961.*

The story goes that Dan Jenkins named the par-4 17th at Quail Creek as one of America's 18 greatest holes for *Sports Illustrated* by mistake: he wanted to include the par-5 8th, which isn't that great a hole either, but they had switched the nines a year earlier and he got stuck with the other hole. Or else this is just an excuse floated by Jenkins in an attempt to save his reputation as someone who knows something about architecture, because the 17th is just a hard, crummy hole.

As for Quail Creek in general: it's difficult, all right—there are a lot of trees to contend with, and the stream on the 17th intrudes on several other holes—but I can't think of any reason I'd want to go back and play it. 4. [8/81].

***Silverhorn GC,*** *Oklahoma City. Randy Heckenkemper with Scott Verplank and Willie Wood, 1991.*

An "upscale public course" which plays the part too well: they seem more concerned with service and a well-stocked pro shop than with providing anything more than adequate golf. The course isn't easy; the back nine is quite narrow and menaced by two slashing streams, while the front side is completely exposed to the Oklahoma winds. Plus, the pro/consultants insisted on several small greens, particularly on the par-5 holes, which are excellent for a Tour pro but outrageous for everybody else. There is some good native rough, but in most places the "containment mounds" around fairways and greens hide it from view. 4. [11/91]

***Southern Hills CC,*** *Tulsa. Perry Maxwell, 1935, with slight modifications by Robert Trent Jones and George Fazio. Third nine added by Bill Coore and Ben Crenshaw (not reviewed), 1993.*

This course is a favorite of several higher-ups in the USGA, which guarantees its stature as a championship site; but I must admit that without having played it, I can't see why they think it's *that* good. With its ever-present trees and wiry Bermuda rough, Southern Hills is very demanding of the driver, but there is next to no variety in the parkland scenery, and the fact that the sand in the bunkers has the texture of dust, guaranteeing buried lies, is hardly sporting. The par-4 12th is one of the most difficult two-shotters in America—the approach is quite similar to the 13th at Augusta National, but they call this one a par-4—and yet it is far from a classic hole, since the stream crossing in front of the green is invisible from the landing area for the poorer player. Maybe I would have a different idea of the course if I got to play it a couple of times. And Ray Floyd's 63 in the PGA here a few years ago was a great round, but just because "a great course will occasionally yield a great round" does not mean the inverse is also true.

Southern Hills also has to be one of the most oppressively hot places in the world in midsummer, making major championships played over it more of an endurance contest than a golf tournament. 8. [8/81].

***Stillwater CC,*** *Stillwater. Don Sechrest, 1966.*

This was Sechrest's first course, and it shows that he was obviously a decent player who had some understanding of the game when he devoted enough time to his work. It can be a fairly tight course when the wind is blowing, and the green complexes, while not intricate, are well-conceived, enough to make it worthwhile to place your approach below the hole. This is no "hidden gem," but suffice to say it contains the OSU golf team reasonably well at only 6,455 yards on the card. 5. [11/89]

***Tulsa CC,*** *Tulsa. A.W. Tillinghast, 1920, with revisions by Floyd Farley and Jay Morrish.*

A misleading genealogy if I've ever seen one; if this course was ever an interesting one, the maintenance crew must have dragged it all down and top-dressed it to death. I walked it in a hurry (I'd already done Cedar Ridge and Southern Hills that day), and the only holes I remember are the par-3 6th across a pond (and more for its old stone bridge than for the golf hole) and the back-to-back par-5's to finish, just like Baltusrol, though the holes are nowhere near as good. 4. [8/81].

***Twin Hills G & CC,*** *Oklahoma City. Perry Maxwell, 1926.*

An old layout on the east side of town which the locals seem to prefer to those below, although I didn't see much to separate it from the Oklahoma City G & CC. It's on hillier ground than the other courses in town, yielding some better holes and some poorer ones, but I don't remember the greens being anything special—my guess is they were rebuilt and softened. 4. [8/85]

*—Gossip—*

The new Karsten Creek course at Oklahoma State University, by Tom Fazio, has gotten some impressive reviews; they've even called it "minimalist," though Fazio got into some rugged terrain I would have avoided.

# TEXAS

***Austin CC,*** *Austin. Pete Dye (Rod Whitman), 1984.*

The eighth wonder of the golf world, this course was hewn out of the side of a rocky mountain by the only man in the business who would even have conceived of such a project back then. It is not really defensible as a members' course, even for a club whose members include Tom Kite and Ben Crenshaw: it is geared toward the spectacular instead of the playable, but the property left little choice. The holes down by Lake Austin are eminently forgettable, but the stretch beginning with the 8th is one of the most memorable and difficult in golf, including a couple of holes that might have been painted by Loyal H. Chapman instead of built by Rod Whitman.

One thing I must say in defense of this course: I've found it much less difficult to play than it appears, and I think the primary reason is that the targets are so well defined (and the only alternative to a good shot is such complete disaster) that I am able to put everything but the target out of mind, and play right to it. If you play badly the course will give you nightmares, but I can attest that it will reward great shots with great success. 6. [10/84].

***Barton Creek Club,*** *Austin. Tom Fazio, 1986.*

Another course on very severe hill country terrain, it can't seem to make up its mind whether it's supposed to be playable or spectacular, and winds up in an awkward place somewhere in between. If they'd built it before Austin Country Club, I would probably like it a lot better. The long, uphill par-5 finishing hole, where you can actually lose your ball in a natural cave just short of the green, is pretty silly. 6. [11/86]

***Brook Hollow GC,*** *Dallas. A.W. Tillinghast, 1919, with reconstruction by Bill Coore and Ben Crenshaw, 1993.*

A fine, old, eastern-style parkland course on the outskirts of Dallas whose recent revision has dramatically improved conditions after decades of deterioration. (Contamination of the irrigation supply forced the club's hand on a complete overhaul.) It was decided to work with the mature trees current to the property instead of returning to Tillinghast's original design, which had scores of bunkers separating fairways, but Coore and Crenshaw's graceful bunkering and greens contouring make for an impressive course. The land is gently contoured, with a valley near the clubhouse providing interest for several holes. No spectacular holes, but many good ones, including three wonderful short holes (8, 10, 16) and the par-4 7th and 17th. 7. [2/94]

***Champions GC,*** *Houston. Cypress Creek course by Ralph Plummer, with suggestions by Jack Burke and Jimmy Demaret, 1959; Jackrabbit course by George Fazio, 1964.*

Champions was the first club to get the idea of trying to establish an "Augusta of the region," and as you know by now I'm not impressed by the type; my main interest in Champions is in trying to decide which course is worse.

Cypress Creek hosted the 1969 U.S. Open, and gave us Orville Moody as national champion. The fairways are wide and the greens huge, like the Augusta National's, but there the similarity ends: there are no hills, no magnificent views, and—oh, by the way—no great holes to set it apart. The hole that has most often been held up as exemplary is the 228-yard 4th, which calls for a long carry across a bend of Cypress Creek itself; but the creek is so overgrown by scrubby vegetation that you can't even see the huge green, which is full of unpredictable ripples. The only things I remember about the course are bad features.

Meanwhile, across the road, the Jackrabbit

course is one of George Fazio's least stylish designs. Again, the flat ground makes for a boring layout, and again, the most-praised hole on the course is one of the worst: Dan Jenkins named the par-5 18th (then the 9th—he didn't pick it ahead of the 18th at Pebble Beach) as one of his 18 greatest, but it isn't so thrilling on the ground as in plan, with the ditch crossing the fairway and the pond beside the green both invisible from the driving zone. The par-4 with the pine tree in the middle of the fairway is another real winner.

Jimmy should have gotten a few demerits for having anything to do with this place. Cypress Creek: 5. Jackrabbit: 4. [8/81].

***Colonial CC,*** *Fort Worth. John Bredemus, 1935, with three holes (nos. 3-4-5) added by Perry Maxwell, and revisions by Golforce, Inc., 1980.*

Considered one of America's classic courses when local hero Ben Hogan was the best player in the game, Colonial's reputation has faded somewhat in recent years. At 7,066 yards in length and a par of only 70, it has to be about the last course in the world you would want to try and shoot in the red on (except for Rye, England); quite a few holes demand tight long iron approaches to slightly raised, well-guarded greens. But when you set difficulty aside, there aren't that many classic holes. The banana-shaped 5th, certainly the toughest hole on the course, borders on the criminal since a non-faded drive sufficiently long to get you home in two winds up in a grassy swale through the fairway on the left; and the prettiest hole on the course, the 9th, necessitates a long drive for a clear look at the approach to a green ringed in front by water and behind by pecan trees. The 18th is an excellent finishing hole, but for me it doesn't redeem all of what comes before. 7. [8/81].

***Great Hills CC,*** *Austin. Don January and Billy Martindale, 1974.*

An aptly named course, since walking around it is a strenuous test. The front nine is hilly and difficult, but the back nine wanders up and down through the valleys and is very well conceived, particularly in the stretch of holes 11–15. However, there are a few places where a longer hitter can drive it through the fairways into serious trouble, and the course condition was very poor when I saw it: the development has changed hands a few times, and course condition fluctuates with how long the new owner has been in. 3. [3/84].

***The Hills of Lakeway GC,*** *Lakeway. Jack Nicklaus, 1981.*

This course has become semi-famous for one hole in particular, the waterfall par-3 7th, calling for a shot across a deep gorge and the face of a moss-hung waterfall to a green bulkheaded in front by stone. Most of the rest of the course also follows the course of this water feature, which begins life as a small brook at the upper end of the site but becomes a yawning chasm after the waterfall; the prevailing winds also follow this direction, with the result that some of the longer par-4's can be harder than hell. The club also features Jack's first golf "academy," with not only a range but three entire practice holes, an idea recently imitated (and carried off even better) at The Golf Club of Oklahoma. 6. [10/84].

***King's Crossing GC,*** *Corpus Christi. Bill Coore, 1987.*

This has to be one of the least promising sites anyone has ever tried to build a golf course on: heavy clay, with only the surrounding overhead wires and telephone poles to break up the views. I'm sure building houses around the holes will have helped it immensely, and just as sure that Bill isn't going to look for any more jobs like this one. 2. [11/86]

***Kingwood CC,*** *Houston. Island course by Joe Finger, 1971.*

The lengthy, water-infested island course is memorable for its odd variety of three-shot holes, especially the infamous 586-yard 18th—the two-shot route to the green requires massive hits to island landing areas almost completely surrounded by

water. In plan, the hole is somewhat similar to MacKenzie's award-winning design for the *Country Life* competition in 1914 (except much more penal); but on the ground it is much too flat and too long to be any fun for the average player. The rest of the course is lost in the memory of this one catastrophic hole. 4. [8/81].

***Lochinvar GC,*** *Houston. Jack Nicklaus, 1979.*

One of Jack's earliest and dullest courses, before his mounding period. The property was nothing to brag about, a nearly dead-flat piece of ground out near the airport with a few trees on it; they dug a bunch of lakes for hazards, but didn't achieve much visual relief. Claude Harmon gives lessons here, and maybe it's a good place for that—at least the golf course wouldn't distract you from your swing thoughts. 5. [8/81].

***Northwood C,*** *Dallas. William Diddel, 1946, with revisions by Jay Morrish, 1991.*

Trivial pursuit: Julius Boros won the U.S. Open here in 1952, the only blot on Ben Hogan's run of Opens from 1950-53. Site selection must have had a lot to do with some Texan on the USGA Executive Committee, because the then-six-year-old golf course must have been remarkably unremarkable. The recent revisions have improved it somewhat, though predictably, with soft "definition" mounding beside fairways and corralling errant approaches. Two pretty good holes: the par-4 10th, along the line of a gully with the fairway banked left and the approach and green on the opposite bank, and the par-5 14th with a pretty drive across the chasm of White Rock Creek. 5. [2/94]

***Pecan Valley CC,*** *San Antonio. J. Press Maxwell, 1963.*

A former host to the PGA Championship, but certainly don't make a side trip to the city just to see it and the Alamo, as I did. Lots of pecan trees (you were expecting cypresses?) make the course a wild driver's nightmare, but there's nothing else to recommend the place; the architecture is eminently forgettable. 3. [8/81].

***Rockport CC,*** *Rockport. Bill Coore, 1985.*

This is one of the best new courses I've seen in a long time, and it's a shame it's so isolated that it doesn't get the credit it's due. Coore overcame a fairly dull and restricted site by building a great set of greens, and did such a thorough but subtle job in contouring the remainder of the course that it's hard to imagine the site was once pancake-flat. The course takes the natural windy climate into full account, planned with the prevailing winds in mind but wide enough to remain playable even when the winds blow from odd directions. There ought to be more in Texas like it. 6. [11/86]

***Stonebridge Ranch GC,*** *McKinney. Pete Dye (Rod Whitman), 1988.*

Seen during construction. The course is as big as Texas, and though a couple of holes make good use of natural features, others are entirely concocted. The course must have some of the biggest, rollingest putting surfaces Pete's built since Crooked Stick—the result of Rod's having rebuilt all the Indiana course's greens just prior to moving here. [11/86]

***Trophy Club CC,*** *Humble. Joe Lee with advice from Ben Hogan, 1974.*

A slightly run-down club north of the Metroplex, which apparently lost out in the competition to establish a premier golf community for the 1970s. Hogan's influence is evident in the wide fairways (ironically, for such a great ball-striker, he detested trees anywhere near the line of play) and modestly contoured greens. But clearly neither party had much artistic flair, with large greens on substantial fill pads, and Lee's trademark flashed bunkers have, if implemented to begin with, been subdued with grass faces in the interest of maintenance. All the proof you need that golfing talent does not necessarily translate into talent for golf architecture. 4. [2/94]

***Waterwood National CC,*** *Huntsville. Roy and Pete Dye, 1974, with revisions by Bill Coore.*

A rare piece of land for Texas, featuring plenty of undulation and teeming with natural growth in the roughs. From the back tees, the course is also one of the toughest you're likely to find: before the revisions, in fact, nobody could break par over it for the extent of the Tour qualifying school. There were several gimmicks in the original Roy Dye layout, but the worst of these were remedied by Bill Coore while he served as superintendent—so well in fact that the 3rd is now one of the classic holes on the course, reminiscent of Pine Valley. Other superb holes are the long par-4 4th and 5th, and the downhill par-4 13th, which for some reason suggests Bermuda (the island, not the grass) to me—quite a feat for a course in the middle of Texas. There are few holes in the world as frightening as the par-3 14th from the seldom-used back tee: 225 yards of pure carry across a corner of Lake Livingston to a green perched atop a sandstone cliff, with no real lay-up option. A word to the wise: don't go on a Monday, because that's when every assistant pro in Houston heads north to play something interesting. 6. [8/81].

*—Gossip—*

Ben Crenshaw's interest in architecture was first sparked by a trip to Brookline for the U.S. Junior; the contrast with dreary Texas courses must have been shocking. Among older courses, the slim pickings include Shady Oaks, Hogan's home course in Fort Worth; Preston Trail, the exclusive all-male club in Dallas; and River Oaks in Houston, a 1924 Donald Ross design. But I'm grasping at straws; all have been rated behind Champions.

The future looks considerably brighter. Five- and ten-year-old layouts like Horseshoe Bay CC in Marble Falls (54 holes in all) and Crown Colony CC in Lufkin get decent approval ratings; but the new wave includes Barton Creek's Coore & Crenshaw course (which some people don't like or understand), Weiskopf and Morrish's La Cantera, and Keith Foster's exciting first solo project, The Quarry in San Antonio.

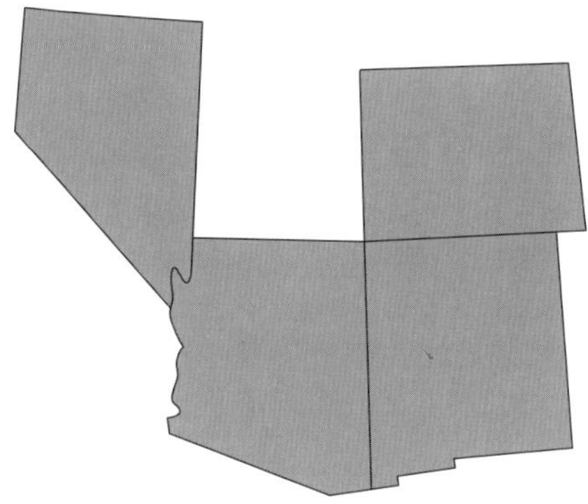

## ROCKY MOUNTAINS

You'd think that all that spectacular mountain scenery would provide instant fodder for great golf courses, but until recently this has been the most disappointing section of the country for golf courses. Colorado, New Mexico, and Arizona weren't highly developed during the boom of the 1920s, and even the few courses built in that "classic" age are fairly tame. Up until 1980, the combination of rocky soils and the droughty climate [which includes Denver as well as Phoenix] confined most golf development here to dull, sensible properties.

Recently, though, the boom in high-profile, mega-budget golf courses has ushered in a new age for the American West, an age tailor-made for Tom Fazio and Jack Nicklaus to exploit. Desert Highlands was the beginning, and Shadow Creek the epiphany, but the turn of the century will see spectacular layouts like these in places like Aspen, Idaho, Montana and Santa Fe — anywhere the new-money west is headed.

## COLORADO

***Arrowhead GC,*** *Littleton. Robert Trent Jones, Jr., 1979.*

I used to believe that if you built a good golf course in a beautiful setting, even if it was in the middle of nowhere, it would have to succeed because golfers would seek it out. Guess I was wrong. Set back in the foothills of the Rockies and surrounded by the jagged Red Rocks, Arrowhead is one of the most visually stunning courses I've ever seen and a decent layout to boot, and yet in its short life it's gone bust twice during construction, bankrupted a development, and been forced to go public, and it still doesn't make any money because they're liable to have to close it anytime from October to June because of snow.

In actuality this is a pretty blah design, but nobody notices that because of the scenery. There *are* two world-class memorable holes: the long par-4 4th with a small rock outcrop in the fairway and a shelf of green set behind a pond with the rocks behind, and the short 13th, a drop shot through a gap in the rocks. But how good might it have been had they started out with higher expectations? 5. [11/83].

***Beaver Creek GC,*** *Avon. Robert Trent Jones, Jr. and Don Knott, 1982.*

This course is routed along a concept I've always fancied: it follows the line of Beaver Creek, which unfortunately comes into play in all the wrong places on the opening holes. The other problem is the fall of the property from one end to the other, which must total between 500 and 1,000 feet. After you make the turn, it's a mighty tough grind up the hill coming home (especially if you've already walked three other courses that day). It's a lot better on paper than in a golf cart. 4. [8/84]

***The Broadmoor GC,*** *Colorado Springs. Original 18 by Donald Ross, 1918; divided and expanded to 36 holes by Robert Trent Jones, 1954-65; South course added by Arnold Palmer and Ed Seay, 1976.*

All the best holes at The Broadmoor are from Ross' original 18, but since they've been split up, the best 18 you can play is the East course, which doesn't ride quite so high up on the mountains. The first six holes of either the East or West courses represent a substantial climb, but a necessary one which is best gotten out of the way early; after that, you're pretty much coasting the rest of the way, if your game is good enough to handle the golf courses. Since both the men's and women's Amateur championships have been held on the East course (not to mention the annual men's and women's Broadmoor Amateurs, among the most prestigious of amateur events), you know you're dealing with a basically solid course. The West isn't far behind in quality, but its uphill holes seem a little more mundane. On either course, the difficulty of reading putts this close to the Continental Divide complicates scoring.

Meanwhile, the South course is a private club with separate clubhouse further up the hill, but it was clearly built for real estate's sake rather than because the land demanded a golf course—they practically denuded the entire mountainside in order to terrace the holes in. There are some picturesque holes, but on others you can see the valley a lot better than you can see where you're supposed to hit it.

One word of warning: the thunderstorms come over the mountains very fast and almost every afternoon in the summer at the Broadmoor, and anytime you start after noon you are risking getting caught out on the course in the lightning, which is not one of my favorite experiences. East course: 5. West course: 4. South course: 4. [7/84].

***Castle Pines GC,*** *Castle Rock. Jack Nicklaus, 1982.*

Another installment in our Augusta-clone series, this one is oilman Jack Vickers' Augusta National of the West. Its rankings among the best courses in America by *Golf Digest* (42nd) and *GOLF Magazine* (about 110th) are so widely divergent that Mr. Vickers is frustrated; and though there is no official reason why—just voters' opinions—I would like to explain the difference as best I can.

From the paint-by-numbers *Golf Digest* viewpoint, Castle Pines has to rate very highly. It's one of the most difficult courses I've seen from the back tees; it's in immaculate condition; and the holes are memorable. But from an artistic point of view, I think it fails in two key respects. First, the holes are memorable because so many different landscape treatments were used on them that the course lacks continuity—like Oak Tree, it is more a collection of golf holes than a homogeneous golf course. There are never more than two holes in a row that feel like they belong on the same course, nor for that matter do you ever come back to an area that reminds you of an earlier hole. While I like several of the individual holes (especially the 3rd, 4th, 6th, 9th, and 10th), the total picture is something less than the sum of its parts.

More important, I think, there is one "signature" element of the course that sets it apart from other Nicklaus courses—the so-called "collection bunkers," which can sweep a ball off the putting surface on three holes, most conspicuously the 16th. These are so gimmicky to play and so unnatural in appearance that they spoil the course for me, and I think that other well-traveled critics tend to look at them as putting the course behind some of Jack's other work. Realistically, there are only so many open spots on a top 100 list for new courses, and the *GOLF Magazine* panel is more apt to single out some of Jack's less gimmicky work, such as Shoal Creek. Meanwhile, *Golf Digest* has had to change its definition of greatness to add tradition (which has nothing to do with the quality of a course), simply to counteract the ugly consequence that the rest of their definition favors hard, expensive modern designs. 6. [9/83].

***Cherry Hills CC,*** *Englewood. William Flynn, 1923, with slight modifications by Arnold Palmer and Ed Seay.*

Once without rival as the premier club/golf course in the Rockies, Cherry Hills is now being pushed to maintain its status by some of the new de-

velopments going on in the region. The property is certainly nothing like I imagined—only marginally hilly and very tame parkland, with the Rockies well in the distance—and neither are the famous holes. The par-5 17th, with the moat around its green which cost Ben Hogan the 1960 Open, is one of the worst holes I've ever seen, because you can't see the water from the landing area for the drive; and the 14th and 18th, while very good golf holes, somehow aren't as striking as I thought they'd be. On the other hand, the short par-4 3rd, the par-5 5th, and the par-4 16th holes all looked like sleepers to me. If this course were in Philadelphia, it wouldn't be famous. 7. [7/84].

***The CC at Castle Pines,*** *Castle Rock. Jack Nicklaus (Scott Miller), 1986.*

This new course at the north end of the exclusive Castle Pines development is the kind of course I kept hoping to find in Colorado: a rugged course with fantastic mountain vistas. It is a major departure for Nicklaus, with less goofy contouring around the greens to make the course more playable for the members, and nice bluegrass fairways to keep the maintenance budget within reason. Throw in some first-class golf holes and stunning views of the entire Front Range, and you've got the kind of golf course Jack ought to be building, even if there is one *awful* uphill hole (the par-4 9th) in the routing, and some of the fairways aren't cleared wide enough. Scorecard trivia: to compensate for the altitude, the front nine, par 37, weighs in at *4,003* yards—surely a record. 6. [10/86]

***CC of Colorado,*** *Colorado Springs. Pete Dye, 1971.*

Between the goofy nature of a few of the holes and the look of the development which surrounds it, I think this is one of Pete's poorer courses. While there are many individual elements of the design that I really like—the native grasses in the roughs (which were kind of new that many years ago), the small bunkers to the right of the 6th green, the waste bunker in front of the 17th, and some of the bulkheading work around bunkers—I don't really remember very many of the holes as being that great. 4. [7/84].

***CC of the Rockies,*** *Edwards. Jack Nicklaus, 1984.*

I'd heard rumors that the owners of this course (which was originally to be called Arrowhead at Vail, until the other Arrowhead objected) had spent a fortune building it, so naturally I expected to see a very severe mountain course; but with the exception of four holes that border on Vail Creek, the course is all within a fairly flat highland meadow. (I'm reminded of Andrew Kirkaldy's description of Muirfield.) The course was built at the height of Jack's shelved-green, collection-bunker, double-green period, so it will come as no surprise that I didn't like it much. 5. [8/84]

***Denver CC,*** *Denver. A host of architects: James Foulis, Donald Ross, William Flynn, Harry Collis, Ed Seay, and recent modifications by Bill Coore.*

A well-heeled in-town club, considerably improved over the last decade by some beautifully detailed re-bunkering. The majority of the property is flattish, but the hillside along one edge of the course and the creek that runs through its center feature into twelve of the eighteen holes. Best of the bunch: the "Cape" 6th along the creek, and the short dogleg 16th with a pretty dished green on a natural plateau. 6. [12/94]

***Glenmoor CC,*** *Cherry Hills Village. Pete and Perry Dye (Rod Whitman), 1985.*

This golf course never should have been built to begin with—there simply wasn't enough land to make it work with the housing density the developer was insistent on, but he would have gone ahead with it and gone completely bust with another architect. Perry decided he could do better than that, so Rod Whitman (whom I have a lot of respect for) devoted a year and a half of his life to attempting to build a

great golf course here, which he couldn't have done even if he had Peter Graves, Martin Landau, Barbara Bain, *and* Greg Morris on the crew. I just hope it hasn't ruined him for life.

At its best, Glenmoor could be a very fun place to go out with a couple of friends and have a Skins Game–type match; some of the holes are brutally hard and a lot of them are interesting. (Then again, you could do the same without a $6 million course.) But Pete would die an early death if he had to play the rest of his golf here. 4. [12/84].

***Green Gables CC,*** *Lakewood. William Tucker, 1928, with second nine by James Haines.*

If you had to pick *the* stereotypical country club setup, Green Gables might be a good selection, except for the fact that the clubhouse burned down in 1983 and they were using a tent last time I saw the course. But the golf course, on fairly flat ground (except for the clubhouse site, which of course sits up on a hill) with long lines of nice trees separating the fairways, is exactly what most Americans form in their mind's eye when you mention a golf course. 3. [8/84].

***Heatherridge CC,*** *Aurora. Dick Phelps, 1973.*

Condo golf at its worst—they've been known to have fist fights between property owners and golfers over errant drives. Add the fact that the greens, while interestingly molded, fall way too steeply from back to front (I hit the back of the first green in two, and four-putted), and you have the makings of a good disaster movie. 1. [4/84].

***John F. Kennedy Municipal GC,*** *Aurora. Henry Hughes, 1968.*

Seen in winter, as was my experience with it, Kennedy is one of the bleaker public golf landscapes around; but the course is long enough to present a challenge, and at least you can swing the club without condophobia. 2. [3/84].

***Keystone Ranch GC,*** *Dillon. Robert Trent Jones, Jr. and Don Knott, 1980.*

For my money, this is one of the better Colorado courses, ranking just ahead of the other mountain courses I walked in my one-and-only road trip while working in Denver. There is a very nice variety of terrain here, from thick pine groves to open low-

*Skiing or golf at Keystone.*

land prairie to lakeside and hillier holes, although the transitions between areas are too abrupt to give the course the flow it needs. Individually, very few holes stand out in my memory, however. 6. [8/84]

***Lake Arbor GC,*** *Arvada. Clark Glasson, c. 1960.*

One of many courses in Colorado where the condos were built much too close together to try and squeeze in a golf course, but someone tried anyway. Some of the holes are downright dangerous, and none of them are really memorable. However, the course is in unusually good shape for a well-trodden public track. 2. [8/84].

***Perry Park CC,*** *Larkspur. Dick Phelps, 1974.*

An exclusive housing-development course set in the majesty of the Red Rocks, about halfway between Denver and Colorado Springs. The course is pretty short (especially in the thin Colorado air) and very tight on some of its wooded holes, and there is really no standout hole, although the par-4 7th and par-3 17th are both in the shadow of the Rocks. But the peace and quiet make the scenery that much better. 4. [8/83].

***Plum Creek GC,*** *Castle Rock. Pete and Perry Dye (David Postlethwait), 1984.*

A good argument against building a course specifically for tournament players, this former TPC course failed to meet the Tour's growth projections, and has now reverted to a public course under private ownership. (If Perry Dye hadn't found foreign investors who would honor the memberships the Tour sold, this would have been a legal battleground.)

The course is good and tough, but perhaps too predictably so. The fairway target areas are really narrow and the greens small and sloping, the location of the course leaves it at the mercy of the strong winds that can blow along the Front Range, and the fescues and prairie grasses in the rough add to the difficulty. It seems like, although some of the better holes give you room to bail out, all the nondescript holes (particularly on the front side) are just brutally tough.

The short holes, as on most Dye courses, are nearly all good (I don't especially like the 2nd hole, but the narrow 7th is a good one); and among the longer holes, the par-4 4th, 13th, and 16th are all favorites, plus the uphill par-5 11th. The only thing that really bothers me about the course is that Pete's long par-4 holes in the finishing stretch, with railroad tie–lined ponds on one flank or the other, became the TPC's answer to McDonald's golden arches. Word to the wise: if there's a wind coming up out of the south, stay in the clubhouse. 5. [8/85].

***Riverdale GC,*** *Brighton. Knolls course by Henry Hughes, 1965; Dunes course by Pete and Perry Dye (Tom Doak), 1985.*

Owned and operated by Adams County, these two courses are about as different as you'll ever find operating out of one clubhouse. (I once suggested they be named the "Good" course and the "Other" course, but they thought I was kidding.) The original Knolls course is just your typical municipal track, with concrete drainage ditches forming the principal hazards, though it has come a long way in the past few years with tree growth and a modicum of manicuring.

The Dunes course, which was really the first course in which I played a major role on the bulldozer, is a much different story. It began life as a flood-irrigated onion field, so it still suffers from being open and on the flat side, but we moved enough dirt so it doesn't play flat. I didn't get to design it all, because Perry allowed some of the other crew members some input (I'm not to blame for the 15th hole), but I am very proud of the midsection of the course, which includes my tributes to the Burmah hole at Royal Troon and the Dell green at Lahinch. The greens are some of the largest "Pete Dye" has ever built, to allow maximum flexibility in the day-to-day setup of the course, but from the back tees it's still no pushover. Knolls course: 2. Dunes course: 6. [9/93]

*Tall prairie grasses accent Riverdale Dunes.*

***South Suburban GC,*** *Littleton. Dick Phelps and Brad Benz, 1974.*

A decent, well-kept public course serving the metro south Denver area at incredibly reasonable rates for residents. Some of the holes are extremely tight in the landing areas, which, as in all Phelps designs, tend to be located too close to the tees—I hit what I thought was a horrible slice off the 3rd tee, but the hole doglegged so soon off the tee that I actually wound up around the corner and over the ravine, and was left with just a 75-yard pitch to the green on what is supposed to be a solid par-4. Even with greens on the goofy side, this is still a step above the average muni. 3. [8/83]

### —*Gossip*—

Even though I lived in Denver for about a year and a half, I never got around to see some of the better courses in the state; if I had any real time off I'd go to California to see courses. And there's been a lot of activity in the ten years since I left.

Up in the mountains, the hot new course is Tom Fazio's Maroon Creek in Aspen, a mega-budget project that one friend (who is not a Fazio groupie) reports is "Fazio's best work." Tom Weiskopf is also working on a course at Steamboat Springs, and Fazio on another at Cordillera, where I've heard fabulous reviews of the Lodge at Cordillera, but not of their original Hale Irwin layout. I'd rather see Hiwan, a long, difficult course which is the annual host to the Colorado Open (and never gets shot up).

Finally, in the southern part of the state, there is the Eisenhower GC at the Air Force Academy (long and flat, I believe), and Tamarron, a difficult and severe layout way out in Durango. But don't expect any of these to be any better than the courses listed above, none of which would make my short list of courses worth seeing in the U.S.

***Singletree CC,*** *Edwards. Golforce, Inc. (Jay Morrish and Bob Cupp), 1982.*

This development is just across I-70 from the CC of the Rockies, but occupies a much hillier site, and the hills come very much into play in the routing. In fact, only a stretch of flatter holes in the middle of the back nine prevents the course from ranking highest among the Colorado mountain courses in my ratings. 5. [8/84]

## NEW MEXICO

*—Gossip—*

I've never spent any time in New Mexico, but my shaper Jim Urbina has gone down there a couple of times to check out what's new. His favorite is the South course at the University of New Mexico, which another source once described as "with grooming, another Shinnecock"; that guy must have had altitude sickness, but Jim says the course does have some great greens. Lyle Anderson's money will continue to keep Nicklaus' new Las Campanas (in Santa Fe) in the limelight, but though it's interestingly different for the Nicklaus camp, the photos look no more like a MacKenzie design than Pinehurst National looks like Pinehurst No. 2. Finally, there's Ken Dye's Pinon Hills, a daily-fee desert layout that *Golf Digest's Places to Play* has ranked on an equal footing with Pinehurst No. 2 and Pebble Beach—of course, these are the same judges who rated about 40 Michigan courses above High Pointe.

## ARIZONA

***Anasazi GC,*** *Phoenix. Original design (Mummy Mountain GC) by Roy Dye, c. 1979; revised by Gary Panks, 1984.*

Arthur Hills has totally redone this course since I saw it, so the review is just for posterity. The course had its share of detractors, but the one thing you could say for it is that it didn't look like the other courses around it; nothing built by Roy Dye ever did, though. At least it was a real estate success story—Dye took a very wide wash area, of practically no real estate value, channelized the wash into a very narrow path and built a golf course on both sides of it, thus greatly enhancing the value of the surrounding land. But the greens, built on high plateaus to prevent flooding, were very poorly blended into the surrounding earthworks—the par-3 5th hole, with the back part of its banana-shaped plateau green hidden behind the mound that guards its inner left flank, was a really strange bird. Thus Anasazi, while a visually striking course (especially near sunrise or sunset), wasn't a very good one. 3. [4/85].

***The Boulders,*** *Carefree. North and South Courses by Jay Morrish, 1984 and 1991.*

A more playable version of desert golf amenable to resort play, the original 18 of The Boulders was split in two to expand the resort to 36 holes. The latest nine, which is part of the North course, is much more severe: in fact, the very first hole is a killer par-4 into a funneling fairway reminiscent of my own 2nd hole at Black Forest. The North course definitely has more feature holes. North course: 6. South course: 5.

*Desert Highlands is literally at the foot of Pinnacle Peak.*

***Desert Forest GC,*** *Carefree. Red Lawrence, 1962.*

A better course than I recognized in my original *Confidential Guide,* Desert Forest is the only "natural" desert layout ever done, and deserves high marks for originality. The fairways aren't artificially contoured, as on the modern desert designs; instead, they are laid out on ridges and through valleys in the foothills of Carefree, making this a great tee-shot golf course, rewarding accuracy first, and then length. Only the large, plain greens keep it from being my favorite desert layout. 6. [1/92]

***Desert Highlands GC,*** *Scottsdale. Jack Nicklaus, 1983.*

See the "Gourmet's Choice." 8. [11/86]

***El Conquistador CC,*** *Tucson. Sunrise Course by Jeff Hardin and Greg Nash, 1982.*

The Tucson resorts have banded together to place major advertisements in golf magazines, and one of the biggest investors is Sheraton, which owns the El Conquistador courses. They have to go for the big ads, because their golf courses don't compare with Ventana and La Paloma in terms of scenery or difficulty, and they're not much more playable, either, thanks to water restrictions. I'm told this course has come a long way in recent years from a horrible original layout, but it's still not much to write home about. 3. [11/90]

***Foothills GC,*** *South Mountain Park, Phoenix. Tom Weiskopf and Jay Morrish, 1988.*

What you get when you combine a predictable low-profile design with a dull site: a dull course. Strategically it's fine, although by now the obligatory double green and driveable par-4 are starting to wear thin, but the course is all confined to a broad valley and will all be surrounded by housing development, which won't improve it. No saguaros here—just flat expanses of decomposed granite soil to scuff your clubs on. 3. [1/88]

***Forest Highlands GC,*** *Flagstaff. Tom Weiskopf and Jay Morrish, 1988.*

See the "Gourmet's Choice." 8. [9/89]

***Gambel Golf Links,*** *Carefree Ranch. Roy Dye (Gary Grandstaff), 1982.*

I can't say this was a great golf course, but while I spent time working in Phoenix I had the chance to play it about once a week, and I really enjoyed it in spite of its several goofy holes.

To appreciate "The Ranch," you have to know a little about the history of the development. Roy Dye bought a total of 7000 acres of desert on the eastern edge of Carefree, which was to be the Carefree Ranch development; but he had so overestimated the market that a few years later he sold out to the developers of Desert Highlands, with a grand total of two houses having been built. (The course has since been torn up and replaced by the Desert Mountain development.)

With his cash-flow problems quickly becoming apparent, Andy (as the Dyes called him) decided to build the course under the most austere budget imaginable. He cleared only enough ground for tees, fairways, and greens (a total of 22 acres on the nine holes, all carpeted in bentgrass), leaving 200 yards or more between the back tee and the start of the fairway on every one of the longer holes; in this regard it was the true forerunner of the modern desert layouts. He also moved as little dirt as possible even in the playing areas, just smoothing them down to their broader contours before planting them. Then the pump station could only provide enough water capacity for nine holes, so only the back nine was ever in play, even though several holes on the front side were grassed and the irrigation lines installed at one point.

The result was one of the most natural courses I ever played—it fit the ground perfectly, which was an undeniable charm. But it was also one of the most severe courses ever, because where the ground *didn't* make a great natural golf hole it stuck out at you like a sore thumb, and there was so little grass around the greens that the bold contours of several greens literally shed balls into the desert. It was also terribly long from the back tees (3,674 yards!), because apparently nobody could resist adding another back tee here, and still another there; it was only fun if you played mix-and-match from different tees every lap around. There were some really awful holes in the nine, but I will mourn the loss of the 10th, 13th, and 18th—three excellent two-shotters.

And you should have seen the beginnings of the front nine! Some of the strangest stuff in the history of golf course architecture was out there: a cactus in the middle of a green, a par-3 with a narrow 3-leaf-clover-shaped green, and a great blind drive at what was to be the 9th hole. No matter how goofy Gambel Golf Links was, I had some very good times playing golf there, and I'm sorry to see it go. R.I.P. [3/85]

***The GC at Desert Mountain,*** *Carefree Ranch. Renegade course by Jack Nicklaus (Scott Miller), 1987; Cochise course by Nicklaus and Miller, 1988; Geronimo course, 1990.*

I don't know exactly how to rate Renegade, which achieved instant notoriety for its radical concept, allowing players to choose between two target flags (one easy, one hard) on each hole. It's certainly a visually striking course, with a similar look to Desert Highlands minus the poor uphill holes, and the concept allowed them to go crazy contouring around the green areas, just as long as they left one relatively easy pin position for each hole. The concept was executed much better than I thought it could be carried off, in that you can play with a friend who's using different tees and playing to the other set of flags and still enjoy his company. But whether you're playing to the easy pins or the tough ones, after a while it gets monotonous and you wish there were a hole where the shot values were different—an easy hole in the middle of the hard course, or a hard hole in the middle of the easy one. I suppose you could decide with your companion to play it this way, but I don't think an architect should abdicate this part of the design. I guess in the end I've got to wonder why golf needs new concepts like this.

The newer Cochise course, from a separate clubhouse higher up on Carefree Mountain, is contained in a gorgeous desert valley. It's the least severe of the three Desert Mountain courses, but with Arizona's water restrictions limiting architects to 90 acres of turf, long carries from the back tees across the desert are still the rule. The par-5 18th is a super hole, but there are gimmick elements here, too—the island double green that serves the short 7th and par-5 15th is a real joke, and Jack must have built the alternate greens at the short par-4 6th because he couldn't decide which one of the two green sites was *worse.*

Geronimo is definitely one of the hardest courses I've ever played—I played my butt off from the "green tees" (which feature four par-4's in the 480-yard range) and shot 87, in the company of fringe Tour player Danny Briggs, who played a perfect round and shot a course-record 67, which is sure to last a while. There are a few stunning holes here (and also a couple of very uncharacteristic holes for Nicklaus, such as the short par-4 14th with a blind green hidden in a bowl in the desert), but like many modern courses the real problem is the deafening crescendo of difficulty, and here it is elevated by the severe terrain. To my mind, the best super-hard course is the one where you run up your score trying to recover: it's one thing to miss a green and wind up deep below, à la Pine Valley, but it's another to find your ball down there lying up against a rock, with a cactus in the way of your stance. Renegade: 0–5. Cochise: 6. Geronimo: 0–6. (Renegade 1/88; others 4/90]

***Karsten GC at Arizona State University,*** *Tempe. Pete and Perry Dye, 1989.*

These holes are packed together like sardines, but the steep mounds between holes prevent you from seeing the balls coming at you from adjacent tees and fairways. It's also one of the most visually unappealing sites I've ever seen, surrounded by high-voltage lines, a major power station, and busy roads. Its only merit is that it's right smack at the edge of campus, across the street from the baseball stadium; but it hardly matters, since the Sun Angel Foundation spent so much on the course that they must cater to outside green-fee business instead of student play. The green complexes are very tricky, as they should be on a course confined to a small acreage, and the finishing holes are difficult in the Dye tradition—the par-3 16th is borderline impossible—but overall this course is a horrific waste of money and effort. 0. [4/90]

***La Paloma Resort,*** *Tucson. 27 holes by Jack Nicklaus, 1985.*

There are some really spectacular holes here, because the terrain is hillier than most of the other desert courses, and it's been used to advantage. But, like my own Black Forest, one has to question the wisdom of building such severe green complexes (not to mention desert carries) for a resort course. If it weren't for the energetic forecaddies, it would take seven hours to play 18 holes here—for those who didn't give up totally on the 7th and 8th holes of the Canyon nine. 5. [11/90]

***Mountain Shadows CC,*** *Paradise Valley. Jack Snyder, 1961.*

An "executive-length" course at the foot of Camelback mountain, well-maintained but very blah architecturally, and squeezed too tightly between the condos in several places. 2. [3/85].

***Phoenix CC,*** *Phoenix. Harry Collis, 1910, with revisions by Gary Panks, 1984.*

The oldest extant course in the southwest, the city of Phoenix has since grown around it, putting the Country Club almost smack in the middle of downtown and putting a great refresher at the fingertips of local businessmen. Unfortunately, the city grew a little too tightly around it—I would be surprised if the golf course occupies more than 100 acres. The old Phoenix Open was the Tour's equivalent of jamming 15 frat brothers into a Volkswagen, so it's no wonder that the Tour built a new TPC development in Scottsdale to move into.

Still, the old Country Club course has some character to it. I have mixed reactions to the recent modifications by Gary Panks—I really like the mounding he did on the 9th, 16th, and 17th holes, but I hated the bulkheading work on the par-3 2nd. And even though the size of the site demanded the routing of a lot of parallel holes divided by rows of trees, the course has a real sense of place to it, probably just because of the maturity of the vegetation. 4. [1/85]

***Pima CC,*** *Scottsdale. Billy ("The Kid") Bell, 1959.*

The new desert courses are all of a certain standard; they may scuff your clubs around, but they're all unique and memorable courses. All the courses of the previous generation in metropolitan Phoenix and Scottsdale are more like Pima Country Club—flat and architecturally depressing. Pima does have the slight advantage of being long enough (at 7,000 yards, maybe too long) to be of some challenge to a good player, but aside from that fact it's a real yawner. 2. [11/84].

***Red Mountain Ranch GC,*** *Mesa. Pete and Perry Dye (John Harbottle and John Gray), 1987.*

A housing-development course in the desert that was ruined by the town's flood-control retention requirements; then again, the narrow playing corridors and goofy greens didn't help it much, either. Not a Dye classic, but at least they keep the greens in great shape. 3. [4/87]

***Scottsdale CC,*** *Scottsdale. Lawrence Hughes, 1954, with major revisions by Arnold Palmer and Ed Seay, 1983.*

The problem with this one is just the opposite of Pima Country Club—instead of being long, wide

open, and architecturally bland, the new Scottsdale CC layout has some very nicely shaped bunkers and greens, but it's squeezed into the site so badly that even at 6,000 yards it appears to be too long. Several of the dogleg holes make their turns too early and too sharply around the housing development within. We used to have fun with these before the development was finished, playing "Lee Trevino rules"—play everything down, no out-of-bounds or other penalties—and trying to cut the corners of the doglegs by bouncing drives off the cul-de-sacs. 2. [11/84].

***Starr Pass GC,*** *Tucson. Bob Cupp and Craig Stadler, 1986.*

This defunct TPC attempted to combine the concepts of desert golf and Stadium golf, which weren't that compatible. The holes I remember best are from the beginning of the course, especially the uphill par-5 5th. I thought the par-3 holes were particularly uneventful, which seems to be a weakness of desert courses in general, since most modern architects have relied on water to make short holes interesting. 5. [11/86]

***Tatum Ranch GC,*** *Cave Creek. Bob Cupp, 1987.*

What happens when you build a low-profile golf course on flat desert scrub? In this case you wind up with Tatum Ranch, a flat, boring layout with low-profile but still artificial-looking green sites (especially the two stupid double greens) and nary an interesting golf shot. 3. [1/88]

***TPC at Scottsdale,*** *Scottsdale. Tournament course by Jay Morrish and Tom Weiskopf, 1987; Desert course by Morrish and Weiskopf with Jim Colbert, 1988 (I haven't seen it).*

The Tournament course succeeds in two out of three respects, and fails miserably in the third. As a stadium course, it's a winner, with the CAP flood control berm itself providing good views for thousands (although some of the spectator mounds are too steeply sloped to stand on comfortably). From the Tour players' standpoint, it is perhaps their favorite of all the TPC courses to date because it flatters their games: it's possible to shoot a high score if you're struggling or get impatient, but it also gives them a chance to shoot 62 or 63 if they get rolling. But from an artistic standpoint, the course is a dismal failure, with absolutely zero natural character unless the "desert revegetation" project makes drastic progress over the course's opening. 5. [11/86]

***Troon G & CC,*** *Scottsdale. Tom Weiskopf and Jay Morrish, 1985.*

Tom Weiskopf has been quoted as saying that this piece of land was so good, his only problem as golf course designer would be to not get in the way of it. It didn't look like *that* good of a piece of land to me; but then again, I've only seen it after Tom had already cast his shadow.

The obvious temptation is to compare the course with its neighbor across the street, and the general consensus seems to be that Troon is a better course, largely because the greens aren't so severe. I agree with the point, but disagree with the conclusion. For my money, Troon is just another pretty good course which happens to be in the desert, but lacks the style and inspiration of Desert Highlands, just as Troon's clubhouse provides more amenities but fails to impress design-wise.

Troon does possess some spectacular holes, such as the "Cliff" 14th (which is no match for Dornick Hills), but I'm not sure that there's a hole on the course with much strategic interest to it, and that's a major negative from my point of view. The greens appear simple, but be sure to look for the mountain when lining up a putt: some of the breaks can make you look like a fool. 7. [11/86]

***Troon North GC,*** *Scottsdale. Jay Morrish and Tom Weiskopf, 1989.*

This course has amassed a considerable following in a short time, particularly from Brian McCallen at *GOLF,* who admires its resort-style playability amid the desert landscape. But I don't think it's the best of the desert courses. It is very playable, be-

cause the architects assigned a large portion of their 90-acre turf allowance to providing fairway-height chipping areas around the greens. But the chipping isn't very interesting, because the greens are so big (to allow for the onslaught of players) that there's always ample room to pitch the ball onto the green and stop it, so there's no urgent reason to pitch and run. Meanwhile, the narrow transition areas between fairway and unplayable desert don't provide enough buffer for the average golfer's drives, and don't provide the illusion that you're playing out of the desert. Overall, it's a good routing, but there aren't that many holes I remember . 6. [4/90]

***Tucson National GC,*** *Tucson. Robert Bruce Harris, 1963, with revisions by Bob Von Hagge and Bruce Devlin, 1979.*

Not a desert course at all, because it predates the local restrictions on water usage by a generation, Tucson National is therefore automatically more playable than the newer Tucson resort courses, even though it does get narrow in places between trees and development. More playable, yes, but certainly not more interesting; there are enough long holes to make it a "championship layout," where a round of 67 loses ground to the field (and five or six shots to Johnny Miller at his peak). The bunkering modified by Von Hagge and Devlin is silly: they took flash bunkers behind the greens, flattened the bottoms, and backed them up with pointy mounds. You can see the non-over-seeded faces behind the greens quite clearly, but often it's just a grass bunker, and even if it is sand it hardly makes a difference, since the face of the bunker is behind the golfer as he plays out to the green. A few of the greens are steeply pitched, and the drive between double-diagonal ponds at the finishing hole is arresting, but as a whole the course is rather dull. 5. [11/90]

***Ventana Canyon Resort,*** *Tucson. Mountain and Canyon courses by Tom Fazio, 1985, 1987.*

The Mountain course quickly achieved fame for its tiny 3rd hole, a 105-yarder sculpted almost entirely out of rock and surrounded by saguaro cactus, which looks more like one of those "Great Golf Holes of New Zealand" holes than a real golf hole. A course with a bunch of holes like that would be ridiculous, but only the tee shot to the 4th has a similar aura to it: the rest of the course is on ground more like Desert Forest, with Fazio's distinct style of shaping to the bunkers and greens. There are a lot of design elements at Ventana that I really like individually, but somehow as a whole it's not very memorable.

The Canyon course has the most contrived "cart golf" routing I've ever seen, because the initial plan only allowed for 27 holes: so the new back nine starts and finishes at Loews Resort, more than a mile away from the base of the other three nines. In addition to the long ride from one side to the other, the severe terrain requires several excruciating cart rides between green and tee. There are some very good holes on the new course, and one in particular (the very short par-4 10th) that is strikingly original; but there are also some very severe green complexes, and the par-5 18th with the green sticking out into a pond backed by a large waterfall in front of the Loews Resort is spectacularly overdone. But it's impossible to get into any rhythm for playing golf, and you have to deduct a point for that. Mountain Course: 6. Canyon course: 5. [11/90]

*—Gossip—*

New projects abound in Phoenix, including the second Troon North course, which is Tom Weiskopf's first project independently from Jay Morrish, and the Gary Panks/David Graham design at Grayhawk, which got a couple of very poor reviews from friends of mine. Good, bad, or indifferent, it's all still desert golf, and therefore has its limitations.

## NEVADA

***Edgewood Tahoe GC,*** *Stateline. George and Tom Fazio, 1968.*

One of the most overrated golf courses I've ever seen. The landscape is breathtaking, close to the lakeshore, and mostly covered by towering pines: but it is not particularly conducive to golf, because the trees branch up so high that effectively they play like telephone poles, and the shore of the lake curves so imperceptibly that it doesn't make for interesting holes along its border. The 17th and 18th holes are drastically overrated, and there aren't any sleepers to make up for them. I can't believe this has been rated in the Top 100 courses in America. 4. [10/86]

***Emerald River GC,*** *Laughlin. Tom Clark and Brian Ault, 1990.*

I helped convince *GOLF Magazine* to name this one of the "Top Ten New Courses You Can Play" in 1990, strictly on the basis of a second-hand description; and maybe it was, because the competition is typically weak in the public/resort sector. But then I went to see the course the next spring, and I can't say I was very impressed. The course does border on the river, which comes into play on three or four holes. But the primary hazard is the lack of a sufficient irrigation budget: the course is very narrow, and golfers frequently tangle with the rocky scrub that constitutes desert in this part of the country. 4. [2/91]

***Las Vegas CC,*** *Las Vegas. Ed Ault, 1965, with substantial revisions by Ron Garl.*

Basic Vegas golf—which is pretty basic, although at least the club is less afflicted by tourist golfers than the hotel courses. 4. [2/91]

***Shadow Creek GC,*** *North Las Vegas. Tom Fazio and Steve Wynn, 1989.*

See the "Gourmet's Choice." 9. [2/91]

*—Gossip—*

Until about 5 years ago, Las Vegas was a wasteland for golf, but now that's evolving toward a "family resort." There are several new developments, incuding Bobby Weed's TPC at Summerlin. Otherwise, the golf picture in Nevada is one of the bleakest in the lower 48, although I'd be curious to see Northgate, the Benz/Poellot design near Reno, and my friend John Harbottle's first solo design, Genoa Lakes.

## PACIFIC COAST

In many ways, from politics to antismoking campaigns to any number of other social trends, California serves as an indicator for the nation to follow. Let's hope this is not true of golf course environmental permitting, since they've made it practically impossible to build a golf course on beautiful property here anymore.

Seventy years ago, the situation was much different. California was the land of opportunity, and two architcts in particular, Alister MacKenzie and George Thomas, capitalized on its rich natural beauty and emerging wealth to create some of the most exciting golf courses in the world. Both made their homes here in the boom twenties: Thomas in Beverly Hills, right in the middle of his great triumvirate of Los Angeles courses, and Mackenzie at Pasatiempo in Santa Cruz, just up the road a bit from Monterey. With the help of Billy Bell and Robert Hunter, respectively, and with their friends Max Behr and H.Chandler Egan, they set a standard which three generations of architects have been unable to surpass.

Hawaii has finally started creating worthwhile golf courses, after years of pandering to resort developers' narrow opinion of their guests' needs. But in Washington and Oregon, there is currently a great race to see whether California's migrating wealth can outrun its environmental restrictions.

## WASHINGTON

***Lakeview Par-3 Golf Challenge,*** *Vancouver. Duke Wager, 1988.*

This little layout boasts of being the "hardest par-3 in the Northwest," and was written up glowingly a couple of years back for its guerrilla-type difficulties, so I expected to find some extraordinary terrain. Instead, it's a virtually flat 10-acre lot around the owner/operator's house, with ten greens and alternate tees for front and back nines, and only one hole over 130 yards. It is kind of an interesting study in how hard you can make a course with greens that are nastily crowned or unusually shaped. But on most holes you also have to pitch over or through small trees, and a couple of greens (particularly the 8th, with a concrete birdbath water hazard inside of it) reek of miniature golf. I keep hoping to find a little course on rugged terrain with a couple of all-world short holes, but this ain't it. 2. [5/93]

***Port Ludlow GC,*** *Port Ludlow. Tide and Timber nines by Robert Muir Graves, 1975, with Trail nine added by Robert Muir Graves, 1992.*

The original course here is widely heralded as the best resort or public course in the Pacific Northwest. It's playable and pretty, but there are also blind water hazards, bad uphill finishing holes to both original nines, and Graves' trademark squiggly-shaped greens. Leftover old-growth pine stumps do add native character, but also the specter of unplayable lies.

The new Trail nine is entirely another story; my wife, Dianna, bestowed upon it the first-ever "Hiking Boot Award" for its ridiculously severe terrain. They were nuts to build a course here, much less to try and integrate the result with the other nines at Port Ludlow. Six of the nine holes are serious candidates for worst-hole honors, and on a couple Dianna (handicap: 22) had to hit a nine-iron off the tee to avoid going through the landing area into a wetland or off a cliff, only to be rewarded with a full-

blooded long iron or more to the green. The P.R. men describe it as "toughest in the state," and "memorable." How about "awful"? Tide/Timber: 5. Trail nine: 0. [5/93]

*—Gossip—*

Try Sahalee in Redmond, Semiahmoo near the Canadian border, or the vintage Indian Canyon in Spokane; but don't expect miracles. Or for a real adventure try the spectacular new Desert Canyon GC in the inland valley of Orondo: some love it, others detest it as being too severe.

## OREGON

***Eugene CC,*** *Eugene. Original layout by H. Chandler Egan, 1926; totally remodeled by Robert Trent Jones, 1967.*

One of history's most interesting redesign projects: Trent Jones reversed the direction of all 18 holes, and enlarged small water hazards in front of the original tees so they present difficult approaches over or skirting the water. There are some very nice, very subtle rolls to the fairways, but rarely more than 3–4 feet in height, so it's not especially memorable or troublesome. It could only have been rated one of the best courses in America as a token Oregon selection. 5. [3/95]

***Ocean Dunes GC,*** *Florence. Nine holes by Fred Federspiel, 1960; expanded and remodeled by William Robinson, 1990.*

Here's the property you were hoping to find at SandPines—gargantuan inland sand dunes barely covered with native vegetation. But even though the dunes go on for miles, the course is crammed into about 110 acres, with some housing around the original nine. Because the architect had little room to maneuver, there are several awkward or blind shots around the steep hills, and at 5,670 yards par 70 it's hard to get very excited. But most of all, it's hard to enjoy the expansiveness of nature when you're busy ducking stray shots from other holes. 4. [3/95]

***Pumpkin Ridge GC,*** *Cornelius. Ghost Creek and Witch Hollow courses by Bob Cupp and John Fought, 1992.*

I had to go out of my way to see these two courses, which *Golf Digest's* course raters and the USGA brass (by scheduling the 1996 U.S. Amateur here) have made into instant celebrities. Cupp's work here reminds me a bit of Robert Trent Jones' "Howard Johnson" period of solid, fair, difficult, but uninspiring design; and the land is fairly pretty but lacks any real topographic interest.

What I found most difficult to believe was that nobody could choose between the public Ghost Creek and the private Witch Hollow courses—which are the only co-owned courses I've ever seen separated by a high chain-link fence. Ghost Creek has the

benefit of medium-to-small greens (which I would have expected on the private side instead), but the rest of the layout has "playability" written all over it, at the expense of character and interest: a year later, I can't remember the details of a single hole. Witch Hollow was more appealing to the eye, with some variety of bunkering patterns (and a bit more shape to the bunkers also), and more "native" look, as opposed to Ghost Creek, where everything is gang-mowed. But it also included several of those trademark Cupp greens (wide and shallow, left two-thirds guarded by hazard) brought over from Jack, which are a pet peeve of mine; and only one of the five short holes was outstanding. Considering the reviews, I expected more. Ghost Creek: 5. Witch Hollow: 6. [5/93]

***SandPines GC,*** *Florence. Rees Jones, 1993.*

One of the most disappointing courses I've seen, because of its buildup by *Golf Digest* when it won the Best New Public Course award a couple of years back. I was hoping to find stretches of open sand, but there's only a sandy bluff at one edge of the property; the course itself is totally manufactured from a huge mass of sand without much interesting contour. Take Rees' Atlantic Club, add a big lake for the last three holes à la Perry Dye, widen it out for public play, and take away nearly all of the grass contrast, and here you have it—tough but fair, but artistically barren. It may be a reasonable escape for the Eugene crowd, but it's certainly not worth going out of your way to see. 4. [3/95]

*—Gossip—*

It's hard to know whom to believe here: their standard-setting "classic" courses, like Columbia Edgewater and Waverley CC in Portland, are so weak by comparison to Eastern or California classics that a 7 in my book is a 10 as far as anyone in Oregon or Washington knows. (I'm convinced this has something to do with the plethora of recent *Golf Digest* award-winners from Oregon.) But with half of California considering moving here, Oregon is now one of the centers of new-course construction, and the scenery is exciting enough to hold some promise. There's Peter Jacobsen's Oregon Golf Club, on a very severe riverside site in the south suburbs of Portland—some rave reviews, but also one unenthusiastic one. I'm more intrigued by Broken Top GC in Bend, one of the last Morrish and Weiskopf collaborations. But the two prime prospects take advantage of the Oregon coast—the old Astoria CC, which Peter Jacobsen gushes over, and Mike Keiser's Bandon Dunes property, a bluff of linksland above a desolate stretch of beach that has the potential for some Ballybunion-class holes, if it ever comes to fruition.

## CALIFORNIA

***Bear Creek GC,*** *Temecula. Jack Nicklaus, 1982.*

This course marked Nicklaus' first heavy involvement in the development end of the golf course business, and I don't think it's a coincidence that the course marks a turning point in his design career as well. At Muirfield Village, Shoal Creek, and Glen Abbey, regardless of whether I like them or not, I'm convinced that Jack was still designing courses to his own perception of the "best" possible design; but at Bear Creek, his architecture suddenly takes a turn toward the marketable, including features that would sound good in the brochures or take a good picture for the cover, whether or not they suited good golf. Jack has managed to convince himself that this style of architecture *was* "best," but I still think Bear Creek is where he sold out. The bottom line on Bear Creek is that if you hang on Jack's every word, you'll love the course; if you're suspicious of him, you'll hate it. 6. [11/86]

***Bel Air CC,*** *Los Angeles. George Thomas, Billy Bell, and Jack Neville, 1927; with subsequent tampering by Dick Wilson, George Fazio, and Robert Trent Jones.*

Nestled among the canyons and palatial homes of Bel Air, this club is the epitome of "Beverly Hills posh," and an ideal case study of how a club can ruin its course by trying to keep up-to-date.

In plan, Bel Air might be the most spectacular golf course in the world. From the small, modern clubhouse perched high atop a hill at the approximate center of the course, the first hole (a short par-5, the standard Thomas opening gambit) fires straight out toward the skyscrapers of Westwood, and the next four wind their way along the bottom of a canyon until they reach a dead-end. Where next? You simply tunnel under Ronald Reagan's retirement home, and re-emerge in another canyon containing four more holes. From the 9th green, it's into another tunnel and up in an elevator to the clubhouse, from the porch of which you play your shot to the spectacular 190-yard 10th across another canyon, and head off across to the green via suspension bridge. The back nine, with a par of 34 and one more tunnel, provides most of the better golf.

But what Bel Air lacks is continuity of character. Thomas was the most imaginative bunker-shaper of our time, yet only three of his whirly-gigging, impressionist masterpieces (which always seem ready to grow a new lobe and swallow your approach) remain in their original form. The rest of the bunkers, and several of the golf holes themselves, have received plastic surgery from one or another of the top architects of the last thirty years, even though it probably wasn't necessary at all: none of the guys who have been here since was a better designer than Thomas himself. The upshot is that Bel Air ought to be an 8 or 9 on my scale, but in tinkering around they've reduced it to a 7. [2/84]

***Bodega Harbour GC,*** *Bodega Bay. Robert Trent Jones, Jr., 1977–86.*

Just expanded to 18 holes even though there is only room for about 12, Bodega Harbour is something like Perry Dye's Glenmoor on the sea. The last three holes, part of the original nine, are wedged beautifully between tidal marsh and oceanfront dunes, but the newer holes comprise the really wild stuff. The 430-yard uphill 4th looks like a hole from the mountains of Wales (or the Moon), while the par-5 5th is really crazy, a downhill double-dogleg with two 90-degree bends around prodigious bunkers. The golf course gets high marks as a visual attraction, but for playing golf it's looney tunes. 4. [11/87]

*Bodega Harbour.*

***The California GC of San Francisco,*** *South San Francisco. A.V. Macan, 1926, with revisions by Alister MacKenzie and Robert Trent Jones.*

A fairly simple hillside layout with some excellent holes amid the pines and eucalyptus. The back nine, though laid out in shooting-gallery routing, is especially good, with the long 14th at the top of the list. 6. [11/87]

***Carmel Valley Ranch GC,*** *Carmel. Pete Dye (David Pfaff), 1981, currently under revision.*

Until recently, all I had to do to get a look around a golf course was walk in the front door and tell them I worked for Pete Dye. But in Northern California, that approach only gets you a look of sympathy, because the only Pete Dye course they're familiar with is Carmel Valley Ranch, the most preposterous course Pete ever built.

Like Spyglass Hill, the Ranch is divided into two distinct parts: 13 holes crammed onto the floor of the valley, and the other five in more of an alpine theme. Spiritually, the course begins at the 10th tee and ends at the 14th green. A couple of those are actually quite good holes—the uphill par-5 10th and the drop-shot 13th—but the other three belong in a Ripley's cartoon, featuring a switchbacking cart path up to the elevated tees at the 11th, a weird split fairway banked by railroad ties at the crest of the 12th, and the five-tiered putting surface at the 14th, which nobody else would have had the guts to build on a *miniature* golf course, much less a "championship" layout.

If it were on another planet, I might be able to convince myself that Carmel Valley Ranch was a lot of fun—in the same class as Nefyn, Wales—but when you're five miles from Pebble Beach and eight from Cypress Point, it's a poor substitute for golf. 4. [10/86]

***Claremont CC,*** *Oakland. Jim Smith, c.1910, with revisions by Alister MacKenzie, 1929.*

These 18 holes are amazingly shoehorned into a hilly 100-acre site in Oakland, surrounded by urban neighborhoods. The MacKenzie touch is plainly evident in the contouring of several greens, and the routing must have been MacKenzie's idea—no one else would ever have had the guts to build crossover holes in two separate instances, but damned if they don't make the most out of the contours of the site. Many of the holes are too narrow, since the trees have grown up between them, and the bunkers admittedly do not show much of the MacKenzie flair. But the simple fact is that Claremont plays well, a fine testament to its designer's genius. 5. [2/91]

***The Club at Morningside,*** *Rancho Mirage. Jack Nicklaus and Associates, 1982.*

This is undoubtedly one of the dullest Nicklaus layouts I've seen, despite its polished look and plush maintenance. The front nine, which is a backyard for some condos, looks exactly like a backyard for some condos; meanwhile, the back nine is much prettier thanks to the distant mountain backdrop, but the golf holes still lack inspiration. The two alternate holes, which were designed for use when the flood basin is under water and can't be crossed, are a neat touch, but the cookie-cutter pot bunkers and two double greens cannot be mistaken for originality. 4. [2/84]

***Coto de Caza GC,*** *Laguna Hills. Robert Trent Jones, Jr., 1987.*

I played this one a couple of months before it was open, and don't remember it very well today. It lays along the line of a deep, tree-filled gulley which runs lengthwise through the course; but for environmental reasons most of the gulley could not be cleared, and a lot of the holes play toward it on the tee shot and then turn awkwardly away (against the slope of the ground) for the second, instead of going on across. There were a number of interesting holes, but in the end this will be a better housing development than golf course. 5. [11/86]

***Cypress GC,*** *Cypress. Perry Dye (Matt Dye and Jim Urbina), 1992.*

Yet another of Perry's futile attempts to turn 102 acres into a full-scale golf course. The mounding around greens and tees is ridiculously high in an attempt to provide safety, so the greens contouring (which isn't bad, in itself) is doomed not to blend at the margins. What's worse, the course has garnered great publicity for its sophisticated, isolated irrigation design and its use of new buffalo grass roughs on mounds and bunker faces, but some combination of heavy traffic and poor maintenance was trashing these high-tech low-maintenance areas. 0. [1/93]

***Cypress Point Club,*** *Pebble Beach. Alister MacKenzie, 1928.*

As good as it gets. There's not a single hole beyond the abilities of the ten-handicapper, but there's good golf throughout, even though the 18th is about as anticlimactic as the credit reel of a movie. The variety of terrain is stunning, and the routing of the course makes for a moving experience. My favorite holes, other than the obvious ocean views: 2, 4, 6, 9, 11, and 12. A perfect 10. [10/86]

***Desert Dunes GC,*** *Palm Springs. Robert Trent Jones, Jr., 1989.*

One of the courses that beat out my beloved High Pointe for *Golf Digest's* list of "Best New Public Courses" in 1989, so naturally I'm somewhat biased against it. Not that it's not a good layout—the holes are all okay, and the windy site just east of the Palm Springs wind energy project adds a lot of difficulty. (How windy? Well, it blew the door off the superintendent's pickup truck one day while he was shutting off the irrigation.)

However, with the notable exception of the par-3 5th, there was little effort to utilize the beautiful natural desert vegetation within the golf holes. All the ground between back tees, fairway, and greens was cleared and grassed, so the desert only comes into play if you're way off line. They could easily have brought more of the native vegetation into the field of vision, if anyone had tried; but obviously the contractor just took the grading plans and bulldozed a clear path from tee to fairway, with no one from the architect's office stopping them. Another example, I guess, of equating a "public course" project with a prescription for blandness. 5. [2/90]

***Fort Ord GC,*** *Monterey. Bayonet course by Major Robert McClure with Lawson Little, c. 1940.*

Compared to its neighbors on the Monterey Peninsula, the Bayonet course hardly rates a mention, but it is a very good test of golf, and much more interesting than it looks at first. Mr. Little knew a thing or two about how the game is played, and surely his input had a lot to do with the strategic nature of the bunkering and provision of easy and difficult pin placements on every green. Still, I wouldn't choose to play here instead of another round at Pasatiempo or elsewhere on the Peninsula. 4. [2/85]

***Green Hills CC,*** *Millbrae. Alister MacKenzie, Robert Hunter, and H. Chandler Egan, 1930.*

A real goat-hill layout which overlooks the runways of San Francisco International Airport from the ridge to the west. There is a neat assortment of MacKenzie bunkers, but the mature trees and bay views cannot neutralize the handicaps of the topography. 4. [11/87]

***Half Moon Bay GL,*** *Half Moon Bay. Frank Duane and Arnold Palmer, 1972.*

Strictly a one-hole golf course: the par-4 18th, playing south along a cliff overlooking the Pacific, being one of the better holes in California. The other 17 holes are mostly Hamburger Helper. 3. [8/80]

***Harding Park GC,*** *San Francisco. Willie Watson and Sam Whiting, 1925, with revisions by John Fleming.*

A picturesque, broad-shouldered layout that is one of the busiest public courses in the nation, and has a great history from San Francisco city championships featuring the likes of Ken Venturi, Bob Rosburg, and Harvie Ward. The Monterey pines and eucalyptus frame the holes beautifully, and the back nine has some great topography for golf holes, best of all the run home from the strong par-4 14th. The 337-yard 16th is another gem, with a picket line of cypresses tightly guarding the right side for its last 100 yards. Unfortunately, though, the heavy traffic, heavy soil, and wet San Francisco climate make it almost impossible to keep the course in shape, and the smallish greens really take a beating—restored, it would easily be the third best course in the Bay Area. 5. [2/95]

***Hillcrest CC,*** *Los Angeles. Willie Watson, 1920.*

This is L.A.'s most elite Jewish club, directly across the street from the studios of 20th Century Fox. What little I've seen of Watson's work is impressive, although subtle to the eye; but after a tour of L.A.'s Great Triumvirate, I didn't see that kind of sophistication in Hillcrest. Could be I missed something. 3. [8/80]

***Hunter Ranch GC,*** *Paso Robles. Kenneth Hunter and Mike McGinnis, 1994.*

A layout designed by the developer and professional to give the public what they want—wide, lush fairways, lots of sand in not-too-threatening locations, and big greens with modest contours. But it was a really nice piece of property, with some fine stands of oaks and some shallow washes like at Los Angeles Country Club, and a professional golf architect could have gotten a lot more out of it. 4. [3/95]

***Industry Hills GC,*** *City of Industry. Eisenhower and Zaharias courses both designed by Billy Bell, Jr., 1978.*

A municipal-course complex built on top of a mountain of reclaimed garbage, east on the Pasadena Freeway from L.A. Both courses are memorable for the thick wildflowers and undergrowth that was hydroseeded into out-of-play areas, but some of which comes into play anyway. The Eisenhower course is also notable for its back (black) tees, which turn it into a 7,600-yard monster no one can play. Eisenhower course: 4. [8/80]

***La Cumbre G & CC,*** *Santa Barbara. Original nine by Tom Bendelow, 1918, with major changes and expansion by George Thomas and Billy Bell, Sr., 1920; revised by Billy Bell, Jr., about 1960, and totally rebuilt again since my last visit.*

Still a prestigious club, but little is left of the marvelous holes illustrated in Thomas' 1927 book—the pond they're designed around was dry on my last visit! There's also precious little left of the old par-4 16th (now the 8th), which from the diagram and picture in Thomas' book had to have one of the great second shots of all time; the ravine which was the

principal hazard has been filled, and the hill that supplied the sideways bounce on the approach has been carved up to weave a cart path through. 4. [2/84]

***La Jolla CC,*** *La Jolla. Billy Bell, Sr., 1927, with modifications by Ted Robinson and Rees Jones.*

One of the most exclusive clubs in the San Diego area, but hardly much of a golf course by California standards. The only really interesting holes are the 11th and 12th, two-shotters playing up a narrow canyon running away from the clubhouse; but their interest is offset by the fact that they flood out when it rains. The other 16 holes are crammed onto higher ground on either side of the canyon, with mediocre results. 4. [3/85]

***La Purisima GC,*** *Lompoc. Robert Muir Graves and Damian Pascuzzo, 1986.*

A good modern daily-fee layout, long enough and tough enough for a scratch player from the back tees, and with only a couple of holes on the back nine becoming too severe for the average golfer. The layout is expansive across a fairly hilly site, and in good condition. 5. [2/90]

***La Quinta Hotel GC,*** *La Quinta. Pete Dye: Mountain course, 1977; Dunes course (with Lee Schmidt), 1980; Citrus course, 1987.*

The private Mountain course, with several holes butting up against the Santa Rosa Mountains, is unquestionably one of the most beautiful golf courses in the world. You would hardly imagine that the overriding objective of the design was to create a flood basin to protect the town of La Quinta from the stormwaters coming down off the mountain, but that is exactly the case, and in designing all the greens to stay above flood level, Pete had to build more small, elevated greens than really suited the golfer. Consequently, the golf course is very unforgiving to approach play, and rates only a 6. [2/84]

The Dunes course was designed to be just as difficult a test as the Mountain, but is confined to unpromising ground away from the mountains. Several holes lie in the flood drainageway, giving the impression of playing down the bottom of a long, green bathtub with condos along the rim looking down—not a pretty picture. But the holes at the east end of the property touch the desert, and those on the clubhouse side of Eisenhower Drive are more worthwhile. 4. [2/84]

*The Mountain Course at La Quinta.*

The Citrus course is much more recent, and Pete spent a lot of time on it trying to prove to his critics that he could build a "typical development course" surrounded by condos with a smaller budget than PGA West, which was still superior to everyone else's. Pete gave me a quick tour of the course just before it was open (tracking about two pounds of sand inside my Porsche, to the disbelief of the car-wash guys in Indio who helped me clean it up), and I was favorably impressed with the contours of many of the greens, but thought his bunkering still relied too much on the steep banks familiar to PGA West. It's more polished than the Dunes course, but not as tough. 5. [11/86]

***Lake Merced G & CC,*** *Daly City. William Lock, 1922, with revisions by Alister MacKenzie, and major changes by Robert Muir Graves, 1960.*

A nice layout across several ridges and valleys on the Pacific slope, just south of San Francisco Golf Club. Unfortunately, eleven of the holes had to be changed when the freeway bordering the east side of the property was built, and the members instructed the architect to build the new greens flat. So, while the routing falls across the ridges and valleys quite nicely with lots of variety, the detailing of the bunkers and greens is just average. The front nine suits better players, with several strong par-4's, while the back side has more variety but lacks length. 5. [9/93]

***The Lakes CC,*** *Palm Desert. Ted Robinson, 1982.*

Perfectly tailored to the average Palm Springs retired couple; but if you hit your drives 230 yards or more, you'll have to lay up to avoid going through the innumerable doglegs. This was where Robinson pioneered the extensive use of those artificial waterfall features (22 in 18 holes, if I remember right), and I'll never forget watching P.B. Dye laughing hysterically after he was unable to get the attention of our playing companion at the back of the green: he was yelling at the top of his lungs, but the "white noise" of the water drowned it out. 4. [2/84]

***Links at Spanish Bay,*** *Pebble Beach. Robert Trent Jones, Jr., with Sandy Tatum and Tom Watson, 1987.*

I liked Spanish Bay when I first saw it; I admired the audacity of the designers to try and simulate links conditions, I liked the sweeping greens contours, and I am still amazed by the apparent naturalness of the contours on what is, in fact, a totally created landscape from a barren site.

As of my last visit, the playability of the course was totally disrupted by the "dunes restoration" that was undertaken as part of the project, under the auspices of the California Coastal Commission. The native grasses and plants have not taken off as anticipated, even with drip irrigation in place, so much of the area between the holes is fenced off, with signs imploring golfers not to trample the dunes looking for their balls, and instead take a free drop. Such local rules are incompatible with the spirit of links golf, and are particularly disruptive when the fenced-off area was intended to shape the strategy of the hole: for example, at the par-5 10th, instead of deciding whether to make a long carry to the right or play more safely to the left, you simply bomb away and take your drop if you go too far to the right.

I was one of the few admirers of the fescue fairways and greens, an especially appropriate choice, considering the drought that California has experienced the past few years. I thought they played just fine: if Dornoch was in this kind of shape, you'd kiss the ground, and you wouldn't have to worry about what they'd sprayed that day. But I guess another standard applies when visitors are paying $125 per round, and to cater to their clientele, Pebble Beach Company has now completely abandoned the links turf concept—I couldn't find a blade of fescue in the 11th fairway on a quick reconnaissance last fall. 7, when they take the fences down; 5, until they do. [11/92]

***The Los Angeles CC,*** *Los Angeles. North Course by George Thomas and Jack Neville, 1920.*

I hadn't played this course in more than ten years, and I didn't remember just how hard it was from the back tees—or maybe that's an indication of how far my golf game has slipped. The washes on the front nine are still the most interesting feature of the terrain, but the most interesting design is to be found on holes like the 10th and 12th, where Thomas planned entirely different approaches depending on the length of one's drive. But, the bunkers weren't as spectacular as I remembered them, and the 1st and 18th holes are hampered by fairly dull ground and by playing straight into the rising and setting sun. Still, of L.A.'s big three it probably has the most of Thomas' strategic options left. 8. [8/92]

***The Meadow Club,*** *Fairfax. Alister MacKenzie and Robert Hunter, 1927, with alterations by Robert Muir Graves.*

North of the Golden Gate in the hills of Marin County, the Meadow Club is a destination only for the most fanatic of MacKenzie fans. It's a good golf course, but the bunkers are a weak imitation of the originals, and the contouring of the greens is not as bold as one would expect. You also have to go at the right time of year; in the winter it can be downright soggy, and in the summer it's toast. 5. [2/95]

***Mission Hills CC,*** *Palm Desert. Dinah Shore Course by Pete and Alice Dye (Lee Schmidt), 1988.*

I played this course in the company of the architect—Alice, that is. In fact, she had just finished giving me a motherly scolding for having written this book, and it's mostly out of respect for her that I've waited so long to take it public—although I know that Alice is really more concerned with how this book reflects on Perry and P.B. than how it reflects on me.

None of that ought to have any bearing on my opinion of this course, except that I was so much on my best behavior that I honestly don't remember the course that well. I do remember being very impressed with the landscape plantings—another level past PGA West's—and with the design in general, particularly the greens contouring. I also remember thinking it would be quite a venue for the annual LPGA event—adding enormous spectator interest and stadium-viewing capacity—except that, not unlike PGA West, the players are too scared of it to play it, and voted almost unanimously to play the "traditional" venue designed by Desmond Muirhead. I haven't seen that course, but I doubt it's anywhere near as interesting as this one. 6. [2/90]

*Monterey Peninsula C.C. is worth seeking out.*

***Monterey Peninsula CC,*** *Pebble Beach. Dunes course by Robert Hunter, Seth Raynor, and Charles Banks, 1926; Shore course by Bob Baldock and Robert Bruce Harris, 1961.*

The Dunes course, though rather a plain Jane by Peninsula standards, would be a standout virtually anywhere else in the world, with a stretch of really rich golfing terrain from the 8th through 11th holes where the course sweeps down to touch the sand dunes near the Pacific shore. There are also more deer in residence here than on any other course on the Peninsula. 6.

The Shore course has a couple of unusual holes working around rock outcroppings, but for the most part it lies across tame open ground and is neither difficult nor memorable. 4. [3/85]

***Moreno Valley Ranch GC,*** *Moreno Valley. Pete Dye (Lee Schmidt), 1988.*

A Landmark-developed 27-hole public facility, sitting up in the pass between Los Angeles and Palm Springs. The course, however, is mostly schlock: a lot of the Valley and Lake nines are reminiscent of the "green bathtub" condo backyards at La Quinta Hotel Dunes course, while the Mountain nine features a couple of holes through rock outcroppings that really do look like the work of Loyal H. Chapman. In a Santa Ana wind, the curb on the cart path is the only safety net from blowing off of the world at the par-3 7th. 4. [2/89]

***Northwood GC,*** *Guerneville. Alister MacKenzie and Robert Hunter, 1928.*

I went out of my way to check this nine-holer out, simply because of its lineage and its remote location north of San Francisco, among the redwoods. (Not giant sequoia, however.) It isn't well known for a reason: the soil is heavy clay, and the surface drainage is well below standard, which, combined with the excessive shade and this climate, means there is practically no turf. There are a couple of untouched MacKenzie greens left, albeit with too much grass on them; but there are only three sand bunkers left on the entire course, and they're not what they used to be. 3. [2/91]

***Ojai Valley CC,*** *Ojai. George Thomas and Billy Bell, Sr., 1925; front nine redone by Billy Bell, Jr., 1948; and significant renovation by Jay Morrish, 1987, which I haven't seen yet.*

Every time I go back to this course they've switched the nines, so I must begin with an explanation: there's one good nine and one bad one, so if my descriptions of the individual holes sound off, they've probably turned it around again. The good nine is, of course, the one which hasn't been tinkered with: this part of the property is peppered with hills, barrancas, and live oak, and they are a critical factor in the play of each of the nine holes. The best holes were the short par-4 11th with its green on high ground between barrancas, and the par-4 16th with its tee shot into a funnel of trees. But I lament the abandonment of the old 3rd hole, a 190-yarder that Thomas featured prominently in his book; Ben Crenshaw tells me he found its remains sitting out in a field in the corner of the property. 6. [8/80]

***Old Del Monte GC,*** *Monterey. Charles Maud, 1900, revised by Herbert Fowler, 1920.*

A tightly confined course with live oaks everywhere, including right in the landing areas of some fairways, with very little room to go around them. The routing is entirely of parallel holes too close together, and together with the obstacles this makes the course almost dangerous to play. 2. [8/76]

***The Olympic Club,*** *San Francisco. Lakeside course by Wilfrid Reid, 1917, with revisions by Sam Whiting, 1924; Ocean course by Whiting and Willie Watson, 1924, with some recent modifications due to coastal erosion; Cliffs course by Tom Weiskopf and Jay Morrish, 1994.*

I consider Lakeside to be one of the most difficult courses in the world—but not a personal favorite. Thousands of pines, cedars, and cypress trees (all planted after the course was laid out) overhang the fairways to such an extent that off some tees you

feel like you're hitting out of a tunnel, rather than just a chute. As a result there's very little strategy involved in the design: just the relentless pressure to drive the ball fairly long and archer-straight. The 3rd is a wonderful long par-3 and the 18th a good short finishing hole, as advertised, and the pair of long two-shotters at the 4th and 5th have never gotten the public credit they deserve for being the hardest back-to-back holes in all of golf. But there are too many nondescript (though testing) two-shotters in the middle of the course for it to rank as highly on my scale as it seems to on everyone else's.

The Ocean course has had a checkered history; originally it was Olympic's flagship, but a series of landslides over the years has eliminated the holes on the ocean side of Skyline Boulevard, and forced them to squeeze the course around the Lakeside. It does have an entirely different look to the plantings, bunkering, and fairway contours I really liked, and—if the rumors are true that the club now has permits to restore some of the holes down by the Ocean so they can widen out what's left—it could yet re-emerge as one of the best in northern California.

The new Cliffs course is a picturesque par-3 crammed onto the small promontory across Skyline Boulevard, which overlooks the Pacific. The picture-postcard holes are beautifully shaped, but there isn't much variety of shots—you'll hit a lot of different irons, but there's never much reason for a fade or draw or run-up, and 95% of the recoveries after you've missed a green will be from the sand. The most interesting aspect is that because nearly all the holes radiate from the center of the property, you could play "around the world" from one of the central tees, as eight of the nine greens (including the 9th, across Skyline Boulevard) are well within reach. Lakeside course: 8. Ocean course: 4. Cliffs course: 5. [2/95]

***Pac Grove Municipal GC,*** *Pacific Grove. Nine holes by H. Chandler Egan, 1932; expanded to 18 by Jack Neville, 1959.*

It's almost impossible these days for anyone to build a new course without paying lip service to "Scottish-style" character, even though not many of the architects even know what that means. If you want to see authentic British links character without flying overseas, try the back nine at Pacific Grove. The white sand and iceplant off the fairways aren't quite the same as Scotland's heather and gorse, but the layout does roll across the dunes much like the typical Scottish links, and the low-cost approach to course maintenance is in the true Scottish tradition. (The 12th and 14th are also first-rate golf holes.) The front nine is a very tight out-and-back among large trees and the small homes of Pacific Grove, and though quite short, does not lack for character. Overall, I would highly recommend a quick nine at Pacific Grove for your first evening in Monterey, as a warm-up for things to come. 4. [10/88]

*Another gem in Monterey—Pacific Grove Muni.*

***Pasatiempo GC,*** *Santa Cruz. Alister MacKenzie, 1929.*

Of all the courses he built in the United States, I think Dr. MacKenzie might be proudest today of Pasatiempo, because it provides excellent golf for the public-links golfers he held so dearly. The course includes some of MacKenzie's best holes, such as the 2nd, 10th, 11th, 14th, 15th, and 16th, and practically no weak links; but the course is shoehorned into the surrounding housing development quite tightly, and the trees and out-of-bounds make it a course on which it is hard to complete the backswing. True to MacKenzie form, it plays much longer than the 6,400 yards on the scorecard; wish I knew how he managed that. 7. [3/85]

***Pauma Valley CC,*** *Pauma Valley. Robert Trent Jones, 1960.*

Once, as a top 100 course, it was totally overrated; now, because of its ambiance, some would classify it as a "hidden gem." The course is surrounded by pretty hills and immaculate homes, and well isolated from the hustle and bustle and smog that plagues Southern California. But the golf is awfully dull. 5. [11/86]

***Pebble Beach GL,*** *Pebble Beach. Jack Neville and Douglas Grant, 1919, with significant adjustments by H. Chandler Egan, 1928, slight ones by Robert Hunter and Alister MacKenzie, and renovation by Jack Nicklaus, 1991.*

Not included in my "Gourmet's Choice" section mainly because I don't have much original to say about it, except that those mesmerized by the scenery often fail to realize that the difficulty of the course comes in large measure from some of the smallest, steeply pitched greens in the hemisphere. If pressed I would probably include it among the top ten courses in the U.S., but closer to tenth than to first: the two starting holes and those just after the turn have to detract from the overall standing of the course. (The par-3 12th is a real mutt.) Still, there are probably more holes at Pebble you'd consider for an all-world eclectic than on any other course. Aside from the usual holes (6, 7, 8, 17) I'm a particular fan of the strong par-4 9th, but I think that picking the 18th as a great finishing hole is a worn-out cliché—it may be a classic setting, but for good players it's two safe lay-up shots followed by a wedge approach. But I've been jaded by having the chance to play this course several times: your first time around, it's probably as thrilling a course to play as any in the world. 9. [2/85]

***Pelican Hill GC,*** *Newport Beach. Ocean course by Tom Fazio, 1991; Canyon course to follow.*

Another mega-layout from the Fazio organization, a resort-style Shadow Creek bankrolled by The Irvine Company, one of the few developers that could have afforded it. The setting is spectacular, with a view of the Pacific from nearly every hole, although the severe elevation changes (± 400 feet from the clubhouse to the clifftop 12th and 13th holes) force many uphill shots and mandate a carts-only layout. There are also some undeniably great holes, especially the par-3's (including the aforementioned 12th and 13th, a 200-yarder followed by a 130-yarder with small alternate greens) and the finishing run. But the balance of the course is too "resort-minded" for my tastes: the fairways are huge but there's no reason to play to one side, and the large greens have only big and obvious contours. It must have cost a pretty penny, especially considering that all the earthmoving had to be earthquake-proofed, and that they must have at least half a million dollars invested in artificial rock work. 7. [11/91]

*The Jack Nicklaus Private Course at PGA West—an exercise in penal design.*

***Peter Hay Par-3 GC,*** *Pebble Beach. Leonard Feliciano.*

A nine-hole par-3 job out behind the Lodge at Pebble Beach, which I include only for the record since I did play there in my youth. You'd have to be insane to waste any of your time on the Monterey Peninsula out here. 1. [8/74]

***PGA West Private Courses,*** *La Quinta. Arnold Palmer and Jack Nicklaus Private courses, designers unknown, 1987–88.*

The former was perhaps even below the standards of the typical PalmerCo effort: it was too dull, so Joe Walser and Ernie Vossler instructed Lee Schmidt to add about 40 bunkers to "spice it up." In the end it's fairly scenic where it bumps up against the mountains, and it has some memorable holes, but it's still a housing development as much as a golf course, and I *hate* the red rocks they've used here.

The Nicklaus Private course is a marvelous piece of landscape architecture: visually I think it's even more interesting than Pete's Stadium course, since they chose native plants and wildflowers strictly for show, not to imitate a Scottish look. The Nicklaus Private Course, with all its rockiness and the red mountains for a background, looks in places like it's on Mars. Don't give any of the credit for that to Nicklaus, though: give it to Landmark's golf construction people. Do you really think Jack spends much time in nurseries?

Jack's Private Course is the pinnacle of sharp-edged architecture—for better or worse, depending on your viewpoint. It does have a lot of different ideas on it, and not just copies of other Nicklaus holes (those are on the Nicklaus Resort Course at PGA West); and it takes an awesome photo. But the gimmick "signature" element of the course, where on at least three holes a wide approach may hit a boulder and bounce *anywhere*, is a bit much—one of these holes would have been plenty. 6. [2/89]

***PGA West Resort Courses,*** *La Quinta. Stadium course by Pete Dye (Lee Schmidt), 1985.*

The Stadium course is exactly what its developers set out to build—the hardest obstacle course in the world, and a great tourist attraction. Whether this is a virtue is a subject of great debate in the golf world these days, and I'm inclined to play devil's advocate on the subject, defending the course against its critics, but holding serious reservations of my own as to its final worth. A few random observations are below:

The appeal of the Stadium course for most amateurs is not that it's the Ultimate Test, but that they will encounter so many difficult shots within the 18 holes that they are quite likely to play one or two "career shots" which they will remember for the rest of their lives—which is all that most golfers generally remember about any famous course they've played.

The horror of the Stadium course for the pros is that it will seek out any flaw in their games (including lack of concentration on playing golf because they're busy trying to establish themselves as knowledgeable about golf architecture) and use it against them.

The course is visually striking, and artistically more viable than Grand Traverse or Grand Cypress because the contouring is wall-to-wall; but it still has no basis in nature. Of course, there was no natural terrain to work with at PGA West.

The course suffers tremendously in my eyes because its concept is not an original one: it is basically a clone of the TPC at Sawgrass, right down to the two finishing holes, which any court in the land would find as evidence of copyright infringement. It is true that PGA West members are unlikely to play much golf in Jacksonville and therefore do not care if the two courses possess similar holes, but in judging the art of golf architecture I think that originality must be a primary consideration. Until PGA West, originality was one of Pete Dye's long suits.

The four short holes are collectively, and perhaps individually as well, the worst that Pete has ever built: gimmicky, unimaginative, too dependent upon water hazards, and penal.

The 9th, 10th, and 16th holes are among Pete's best.

The red boulders which line the ponds are for the birds.

The golf course's worst offense is in catering to the modern player's notion of the game as a hole-by-hole amusement, like miniature golf, instead of a continuous round. The inclusion of so many exasperating holes and potential penalty shots encourages either (1) picking up, which undermines the rules and spirit of the game, or (2) six-hour rounds, which undermines the enjoyment of same.

All in all, part of me is proud to say that I had some modest input on the planning of the Stadium course; but the bigger part of me says that courses such as PGA West are not good for the future of golf, and I don't want to encourage the creation of any more, particularly at the hands of lesser designers than Pete Dye. 7. [11/86]

***Poppy Hills GC,*** *Pebble Beach. Robert Trent Jones, Jr., 1986.*

The much-publicized new home of the Northern California Golf Association, and one of the most crowded courses I've ever seen: you'd better call weeks in advance if you want to play it. I didn't, so I can't tell you what the course really plays like, but from walking around it I believe it's a fairly good routing over difficult terrain, turned goofy by Jones' specification of huge putting greens to spread out the traffic. These outsize targets present more four-putt opportunities than any other course in the world, and they slow down play to a crawl, since golfers take way

more time to read a putt than hit a chip. The 1st hole is one of the prettiest I've ever seen, spoiled only by the omission of a landing area for the tee shot. 4. [10/86]

***Rancho Santa Fe CC,*** *Rancho Santa Fe. Max Behr, 1927, with revisions by Harry Rainville.*

Probably the best golf course in San Diego, which isn't strong praise: this is just a good old-fashioned layout in two tight nine-hole loops, with small, contoured greens and well-placed bunkers. Pleasant, in contrast to the next course. 5. [3/88]

***Rancho Santa Fe Farms GC,*** *Rancho Santa Fe. Pete and Perry Dye, 1989.*

Knowledgeable friends tell me this course turned out beautifully—which I find hard to believe, since I started looking for work elsewhere immediately after working on the routing for it. When I last saw the property it was in the dirt, and it was in the process of being tremendously over-shaped: the fairways are shelved into the sides of a bowl-shaped parcel, with wild mounding to contain shots on the proper level. The native grasses they planted here must have turned the tide and softened the earthworks considerably. Incidentally, this was the course where Perry decided that his greens had to be flat, because the rest of the course was so severe: an interesting decision on shot values, but about ten times more costly than building dull fairways and interesting greens. [3/88]

***Riviera CC,*** *Pacific Palisades. George Thomas and Billy Bell, 1927.*

See the "Gourmet's Choice." 9. [11/86]

***San Francisco GC,*** *San Francisco. A.W. Tillinghast, 1915.*

See the "Gourmet's Choice." 9. [11/92]

***Sandpiper GC,*** *Goleta. Billy Bell, Jr., 1972.*

I'd heard a rumor that this course was "the Pebble Beach of the south," but it's more like "the Torrey Pines of the north," with a few holes atop high cliffs overlooking the Santa Cruz islands and the occasional oil platform basking in the Pacific. Only three of the holes are really memorable: the dogleg par-4 10th, which plays out along a ridge toward the ocean with steep falls to either side of its green; the 11th, a drop shot down to a large green at beach level; and the long 13th, with its alternate right-hand green requiring a long carry skirting the cliff edge. The other fifteen holes add little to the experience. The climate is magnificent, but Pebble Beach this is not. 5. [2/84]

***Saticoy CC,*** *Saticoy, near Oxnard. Billy Bell, Jr., 1962, with revisions by Robert Muir Graves.*

A good layout from an era that provided few good examples. The hilly site gave the routing character and necessitated some significant tilt to the greens, which are the making of the course: you can't get yourself on the wrong side of the hole here. They're in the process of rebuilding the bunkers, which weren't inspired. 6. [10/95]

***The Sea Ranch Club,*** *Sea Ranch, near Gualala. Robert Muir Graves, 1973.*

A fair nine-hole layout in the middle of a beautiful coastal development, renowned for its beauty and harmony with the environment. Unfortunately, those eco-developers didn't place the golf course very high on their master plan priority list, relegating it to a corner of the property with only a whiff of the ocean. So the course is wide open, and rather dull except for the ever-present winds and two better holes at the finish. 4. [11/87]

***Sharp Park GC,*** *Pacifica. Alister MacKenzie, 1931, with revisions by Jack Fleming.*

This was reputedly one of MacKenzie's masterpieces when opened, but just a couple of years later much of it was swept out to sea in a storm, and they didn't have the funds to restore it to its original design; a high sea wall now prevents any view of the ocean from the very flat golf course. Some interesting contouring still exists, but the greens have been shrunk dramatically in size so a lot of it is lost in the surrounds, and the conditioning is muni-poor: 100% *Poa annua* fairways, greens, and roughs, all mowed a bit high. 3. [9/93]

***Sherwood CC,*** *Thousand Oaks. Jack Nicklaus, 1989.*

A very big-ticket housing-development course, with memberships going for $150,000 and lots for $500,000 and up, and all the amenities priced to match. (The locker rooms, for example, are mostly mahogany.) Naturally, for such an undertaking, they wanted a "great championship course," too. The owner, David Murdoch, made a big step in the right direction by underwriting Nicklaus' effort to transplant more than 500 huge oaks into appropriate positions on the golf course. But once you get to the back nine, you're about worn out, and the ever-increasing difficulty of the course eventually gets to you. To compare it with Shadow Creek, another spare-no-expense course I played in the same week (and enjoyed infinitely more), the "big finish" 17th and 18th at Shadow Creek are a downhill par-3 over a spectacular water feature, and a short par-5 with water in play from tee to green. This would also describe two finishing holes at Sherwood, except that the par-3 is 190 yards instead of 160, and the par-5 is narrower—and more to the point, these holes at Sherwood are the 15th and 16th, which are followed by another "can't-miss" par-3 and a final, long par-4 with a narrow driving area and a forced-carry second shot uphill over another water feature. Classic Nicklaus-client overkill. 6. [2/91]

***Spyglass Hill GC,*** *Pebble Beach. Robert Trent Jones, 1966.*

One of Jones, Sr.'s, most controversial designs, Spyglass is a severely beautiful mixture of woods and open sand, sadly impaired by the sectionalization of the course between the two. The first five holes are among the most spectacular anywhere in golf, wandering among sprawls of white sand on the slope of Spyglass Hill facing the Pacific, though the 1st hole lost much of its character when a huge central pine tree toppled in a storm, and the 2nd much of its when the pampas grass between tee and fairway was removed. After the 5th, the course moves into the forest on higher ground, to holes that are no less difficult but which are a complete break in character from the first five. Perhaps it was impossible to accomplish, but the course would certainly have had more continuity if the routing could have worked in and out of the trees to the sand dunes. Still, the course is much better than its reputation on the Tour, where the players find its severity unflattering; maybe now that they compare it to Poppy Hills instead of Cypress Point, they're realizing it's not so bad after all. 7. [10/86]

***Stanford University GC,*** *Palo Alto. Billy Bell, 1930, with modifications by Robert Trent Jones, 1968, and John Harbottle, 1994.*

Certainly one of the premier university courses in the country: I prefer it to Ohio State's Scarlet course, but would rank it a notch or two below Yale for character. The property is made up of oak-studded hills, deep valleys, and the occasional ravine, more suggestive of Austin, Texas, than northern California to me. There are some excellent individual holes, including the unique par-4 12th with a huge oak directly in the way; but overall I found the short holes too much alike, and some of the two-shotters very nondescript. John Harbottle has done a good job of restoring the jagged edge to the bunkering, but the club's "safe call" on rebuilding the greens—making them slightly larger and flatter as they were rebuilt to USGA specs—has given Tiger Woods and his team a

lot more buffer between an errant shot and any real trouble. 6. [2/95]

***Stockton G & CC,*** *Stockton. Sam Whiting, with revisions by Alister MacKenzie.*

The history is rather fuzzy, but I'm convinced that Dr. MacKenzie was here to significantly modify the golf course during his California tenure. Unfortunately, whoever carried out the Doctor's plans must have been on valium, as they didn't even take advantage of the limited opportunities the flattish property offered for drama. 4. [8/95]

***Torrey Pines GC,*** *La Jolla. North and South courses by Billy Bell and Son, 1957.*

Until I saw Torrey Pines, if someone had called me and told me they wanted to build a golf course on clifftops overlooking the Pacific Ocean, I'd have thought I had it made. But it turns out that if the cliffs are of a certain height, you don't dare get too close to them, and all you can build is a fairly dull layout with a view. Torrey Pines has two such courses. The 3rd, 6th, and 7th holes of the North course are the only holes in the 36 that bring either the ocean or ascending ravines directly into play, and they take a much more exciting picture than they play. The 18th hole on the South course is also locally famous as the scene of Bruce Devlin's sixth-time-lucky recovery from the edge of the pond which fronts its green, but that is hardly one of the more important events in the history of golf. North course: 4. South course: 3. [3/85]

***Valley Club of Montecito,*** *Santa Barbara. Alister MacKenzie and Robert Hunter, 1928.*

Absolutely one of the most pleasant and low-key golfing experiences in my lifetime of travel, from the stylish clubhouse to the secluded fairways just two miles up from U.S. 101. We're now doing some consulting work using some 1931 photos in the club's archive to restore the bunkers to their original look—which is exciting because I don't think many people realize how dramatic Dr. MacKenzie's work really was, and how much has been rounded off by years of subtle change. The course has really grown on me this year: I had never thought of it as belonging in the same league as Pasatiempo, but it has three terrific short holes (the 4th, 8th, and 14th) and enough strong par-4's to keep good players honest. 7. [10/95]

***The Vintage Club,*** *Indian Wells. Tom Fazio: Mountain course, 1979, and Desert course, 1984.*

Overkill, Palm Springs style. The Vintage is an ultra-exclusive club with a modular modern-style clubhouse big enough to host a political convention, a maintenance budget on the first course of $1.2 million, thanks to the flowery landscape buffer around the condos; and some half-acre lots around the often-photographed 16th and 17th holes of the Mountain course which they planned to sell (just the lots, mind you) for a cool million apiece. Well, thanks to the S & L bailout, at least we can all vicariously pretend we held part ownership in the place.

The golf courses are lavishly furnished, but provide only the occasional thrilling hole. The Mountain course in particular vacillates too much between the spectacular and the bland-but-spectacularly-groomed. Meanwhile, the newer Desert course (which doesn't have much of a desert look to it) is one of the most inspired free-form designs I've seen, with bunkers that fly in the face of the laws of gravity,

since Fazio reasoned it only rains twice a year to wash the sand out of them. I'm not sure the Desert course is playable, and I'm sure it's not reasonably maintainable, but some of its bunkers belong in the Guggenheim Museum. Mountain course: 6. Desert course: 7. [2/84]

***Wawona GC,*** *Yosemite. Walter Fovargue, 1917.*

The precedent of golf inside a national park is an exciting one, but this course, ten miles from the actual Yosemite Valley, is little more than a meadow valley with some greens roughly mown out, and broomsticks with ribbon tied around them for flags. The deer are very friendly, though. 2. [11/92]

***The Wilshire CC,*** *Los Angeles. Norman Macbeth, 1918.*

This course is memorable for one particular hole, the long par-4 finisher, where a sinuous creek makes its presence known to the right of the tee shot landing area, and then surrounds the green from behind in the best traditions of the Barry Burn. The rest isn't Hamburger Helper, but it's not Macbeth, either. 5. [8/80]

***Wood Ranch GC,*** *Simi Valley. Ted Robinson, 1985.*

A beautiful new layout which suffers from trying to imitate the Nicklaus and Dye layouts that have been featured in the national magazines—Robinson succeeded in building one of the more difficult courses in Southern California, but artistically it just looks like he threw in every design element but the kitchen sink (severe greens, railroad tie bulkheads, rock walls around man-made lakes, waterfalls, alternate fairway landing areas, pot bunkers, clumps of pampas grass, etc.). This doesn't rule out the possibility that the members will enjoy it (unless they like to break 80), but in the bigger picture it's not worth going out of your way to see. Meanwhile, the grass concept—bent fairways in Southern California—wasn't looking too swift. 5. [11/86]

***Woodland Hills CC,*** *Woodland Hills. Billy Bell, Sr., 1925.*

A hilly, tightly packed layout which has much respect for its fast greens—some local Tour pros come here to tune up for the Masters. Though the course is a bit narrow for my tastes, there is topographic interest, and a stream across the property comes into play on several holes. Also, the scene of numerous golf TV commercials, and parts of the movie *Caddyshack*. 5. [2/93]

*—Gossip—*

I've spent an inordinate amount of time exploring the golf courses of California, and I have to say that it's probably the strongest state in the Union as far as quality courses go, although next to Florida it probably also has more mediocre courses than any other state. I don't think I've missed any of the truly outstanding courses, but in the L.A. basin I still hope to get around to Lakeside GC in North Hollywood, Oakmont CC in Glendale (said to be far and away the best course they play on the LPGA Tour), Hacienda CC, by Max Behr, and Annandale CC in Pasadena, one of these years, if I can tear myself away from San Francisco Golf Club, Monterey, and the Thomas triumvirate in Los Angeles long enough to look. Up north, I've seen an old picture of a short hole at Orinda CC which probably deserves a look. In Palm Springs, the new rage is The Quarry, a Tom Fazio $25 million mega-design that appears to be Shadow Creek with housing.

## HAWAII

***Francis H. I'i Brown GC's,*** *Mauna Lani Resort, Kohala Coast, Big Island of Hawaii. North and South Courses by Homer Flint and Ray Cain, with expansion by Robin Nelson and Rodney Wright.*

The original Mauna Lani eighteen was split into two, with nine holes tacked on to the far ends of each of the original nines. This is seldom the ideal way to expand a course, particularly if you change designers in mid-stream, but the original course was so bland except for the lava that there wasn't much style to sacrifice.

The South Course is considered by the resort to be the feature track—it was the site of the first Senior Skins game, and it has the two obligatory oceanfront par-3 holes. Unfortunately, these are about the only memorable holes. The balance of the course is fairly flat, so the lava beds, which look spectacular in the promotional photos (all aerials), get boring after a few holes.

The North Course offers a lot more visual interest: the new holes run through a different, chocolate-brown type of lava, and there was more topography to begin with. The greens complexes are a bit weird, with a lot of shape to the greens and some unnatural pin placements, but at least they're interesting. Of the two, I would rather play this course any day.

Don't let these evaluations steer you away from the resort, however; I'm ashamed to admit that I agree with Robin Leach on anything, but the Mauna Lani Bay Hotel is the best I've ever stayed in. North Course: 5. South Course: 4. [5/92]

***Hapuna GC,*** *Mauna Kea, Kohala Coast, Big Island of Hawaii. Arnold Palmer and Ed Seay, 1992.*

A desert-style layout in the lava across the road above Mauna Kea, which wasn't quite ready for play when we saw it. The design features exaggerated bunkering and a lot of uphill and downhill holes due to the development-oriented routing, but it looked extremely narrow for a resort layout, especially one high on the westward slope which will be bared to the trade winds. [5/92]

*The 11th hole at the Plantation Course at Kapalua.*

***Kapalua GC,*** *Kapalua, Maui. Plantation Course by Bill Coore and Ben Crenshaw, 1991.*

We were treated so well as guests of the resort (spoiled, actually), that everything I say about Kapalua should be taken with a grain of salt—especially since Ben Crenshaw has been so nice to me over the years, and we agree about so much of golf architecture. Yet, I must say I was still surprised by the design of the Plantation Course. It's a very unusual golf course, but it all works wonderfully.

A road separates the property from the oceanfront, but the entire golf course is built on the westward slope facing Molokai, leaving unbelievable views from virtually every hole. Still, this wasn't ideal land for a golf course—there's too much slope in one direction, and not enough little rolls—and as a result there aren't many holes I would consider for an eclectic 18. (The most spectacular hole, the par-4 17th, whose approach reminds me of the 13th at Pine Valley, is also the only hole that forces the average player to lay up short of the canyon, which makes the second shot so dramatic for the good player.)

What is so interesting about the course is the variety of shots it presents: blind tee shots over stakes at the crown of a fairway, such as the 4th and 10th; downhill, downwind, running approaches at the 7th, 11th, 12th, and 18th; and just all kinds of shots that force you to consider the wind. The bunkering is bold and flashy, and the greens huge, reflecting the scale of the place as well as the need to handle a lot of resort traffic. Overall, I think it's just about a perfect solution for the piece of ground and the multiple uses: a tournament-tough course big enough to handle resort play comfortably, and fun for both. 8. [6/92]

***Mauna Kea GC,*** *Kamuela, Kohala Coast, Big Island of Hawaii. Robert Trent Jones, 1965.*

This is one of the courses that made Trent Jones' career, and I'd been told by a couple of friends that it was his best work. It was also, at the time we visited, the only Hawaiian course rated among the top 100 in America by *Golf Digest.* So, I'm sorry to say I wasn't that thrilled by it. I was probably somewhat influenced by playing with Dianna, who was having her difficulties, but I had to agree with her that the severity and number of uphill approach shots to the greens was simply over the top, and ruined the flow of the course. There are some great individual holes: in addition to the famous par-threes, the 3rd and 11th, how about the long dogleg 14th or the tempting par-5 17th? But I thought that a few of the back tees stretched the course beyond credibility, obliterating the only short par-4's, and making for one of my pet peeves, the semi-blind downhill tee shot (to tight landing areas, no less) at the 2nd and 9th. Certainly not the best course in the state, maybe not even on the island, although the competition is modest. I wouldn't fly here to play golf, but I would to see the manta rays come up to the hotel's overlook each evening. 6. [5/92]

***Waikoloa GC,*** *Kohala Coast, Big Island of Hawaii. King's Course by Jay Morrish and Tom Weiskopf, 1990; Beach Course by Robert Trent Jones, Jr., 1981.*

It's hard to think of $25 million as a modest budget for a golf course, but after you get through crushing lava for the fairways and barging in sand from Australia for the greens and bunkers, there isn't much left over to be creative with (especially since cut-and-fill in lava is pretty expensive). At least, that's the best explanation I have come up with for the King's Course at Waikoloa, where all that money and a good design team produced a fairly blah course. The property certainly wasn't anything special, and neither is the result—a low-profile course with nice scenery in the distant background, but few memorable holes.

The Beach Course, on the other hand, has more topography and it does get down for the obliga-

tory touch of the coast (the second shot on the par-5 12th), but the greens design and bunkering scream "resort course" and lack interest. Swim with the dolphins instead. King's Course: 5. Beach Course: 3. [5/92]

### —*Gossip*—

Until about five years ago, nearly every course built on Hawaii conformed to the resort mentality of making it easy for the customers and giving them an affordable taste of the ocean (translation: one 170-yard par-3); so none of the products were much worth seeing, even though they all require some shotmaking skill when the trade winds blow. Courses which have apparently broken out of this mold are Bobby Jones' Prince Course at Princeville on Kauai (which has gotten rave reviews from almost everybody I've talked to, even though a couple of people on my *GOLF Magazine* committee spurned it for being too difficult), Nicklaus' Kiele Course, also on Kauai (still looking a bit "resorty" to me in the pictures), Jack's brand-new ocean-side course for the Manele Bay Hotel on Lanai (which a friend reports on enthusiastically), and the private Koolau GC on Oahu, a severe Dick Nugent design which may be breathtaking or way over the top—the slope rating is 152 even from the white tees. Reports on "The Experience" at Koele, on Lanai, are much less enthusiastic, though the rest of the resort has gotten great marks.

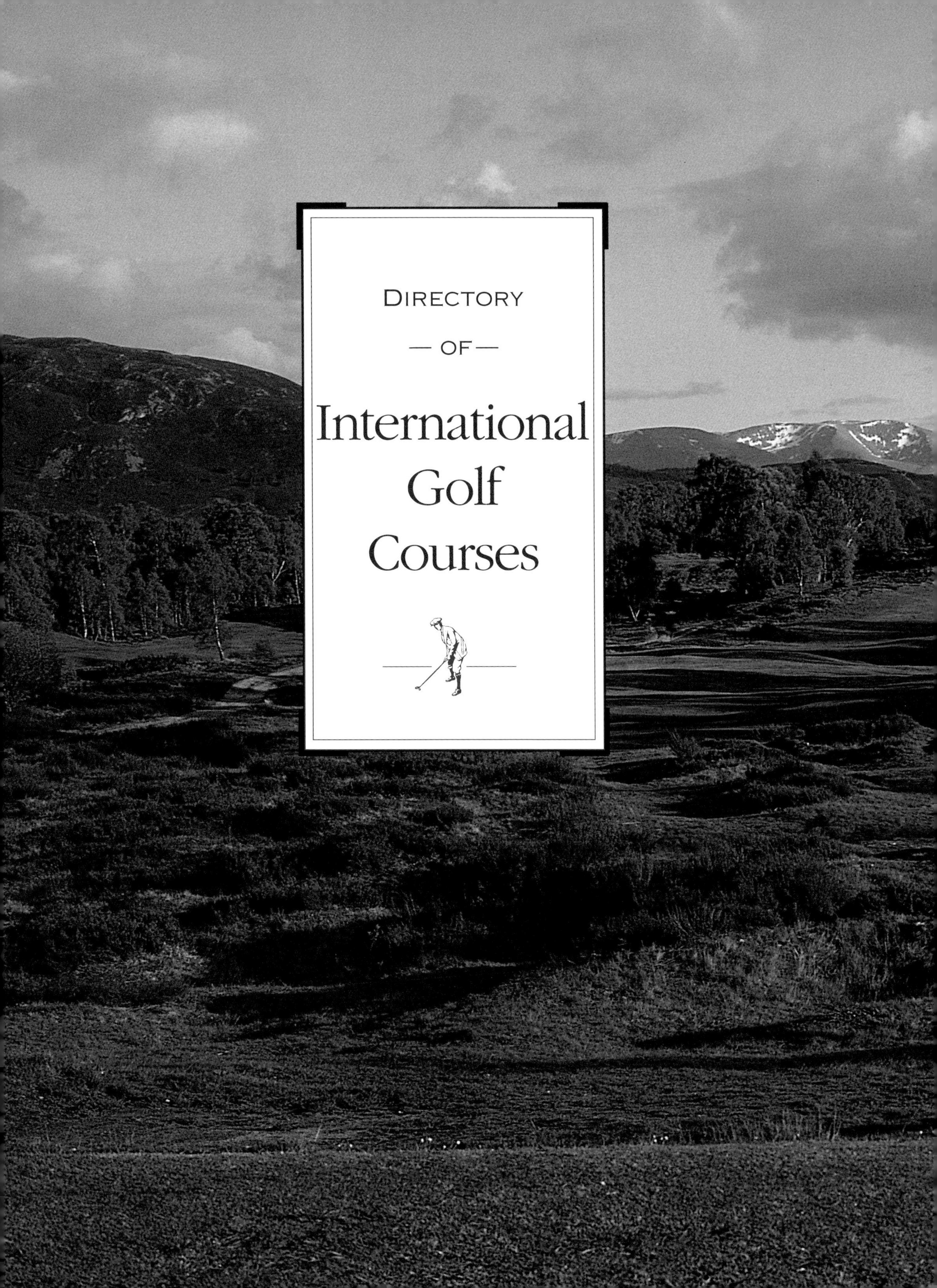
DIRECTORY
— OF —
International
Golf
Courses

## CANADA

Ninety percent of Canada's worthwhile golf courses pre-1980 are the work of one man—Canadian architect Stanley Thompson. Architect, artist, and celebrity all in one, Thompson hobnobbed with the rich and powerful to pave the way for his monumental courses from coast to coast. He picked up where Charles Blair Macdonald had left off, and led the way for his young protégé, Robert Trent Jones.

But Canada is a huge country, and so except around Toronto, where he built several top clubs, Thompson's work is so scattered about (and the Canadian golfing season is so short) that it's difficult for visitors to cover it all. What I've seen of it is terrific, from Cape Breton Highlands in the Atlantic Provinces to the parkland St. George's near Toronto to Capilano overlooking Vancouver Harbour; and I'm dying to see Banff and Jasper, which get mixed reviews from many, but which Thompson considered his masterpieces. And I haven't been able to keep up with the recent Canadian development boom, which has native architects Tom McBroom and Doug Carrick, plus American Michael Hurdzan, busy from coast to coast.

## NOVA SCOTIA

***Cape Breton Highlands Golf Links,***
*Ingonish. Stanley Thompson, 1935.*

Certainly one of the most remote of great golf courses, this course lies further to the northeast of my hometown in Connecticut than Fort Lauderdale to the southwest. I can't say it's worth a 1,200 mile-drive to see, but I was most impressed by Thompson's layout. It lies within Cape Breton Highlands National Park, and the course is a part of the park experience: the routing wanders through all aspects of the terrain, from an undulating start, then down close to the shore, back into the woods, along a river valley, and up onto high ground for a hilly finish. Where the terrain was too steep for golf, there are no holes, making for some very long green-to-tee walks: along the river from the 12th to the 13th must be 450 yards. It's a great experience, but you'd better pack a Sunday bag and a picnic lunch from the adjacent Keltic Lodge, and plenty of mosquito repellent.

The variety of golf holes is excellent. The best holes come in all lengths, from the 164-yard 5th, over an undulating bowl of fairway, to the 570-yard 7th, where I made two sevens in two attempts, and a good mixture of short and long par-4's. Unfortunately, the government-funded maintenance program is totally unreliable—a wet winter before our visit had resulted in four temporary greens, but I'm glad to hear reports from other readers that they've found it in much better form. 7. [6/89]

***Halifax G & CC ("Old Ashburn" course),*** *Halifax. Stanley Thompson, 1922.*

An interesting short-length course on very sloping ground overlooking the lovely small city of Halifax. The club also owns a newer, regulation-length course a bit further from town (I didn't try to find it), but many of the members prefer the old layout, with its par of 66 and as many as four consecutive par-3 holes around the turn. The course is very cramped, making for much visiting between members; but the variety of lengths in the par-3's and two-shotters gives ample opportunity to employ strength as well as a strong wedge game. There is one excellent hole: the par-4 16th, sharply downhill over even more sharply undulating fairway terrain, with its mid-iron second from a difficult stance over a rushing stream to a plateau green. Old Ashburn is no architectural wonder, but it looks like fun. 4. [6/89]

***The Pines GC,*** *Digby. Stanley Thompson, 1926.*

Unlike the other two Thompson layouts I saw in my Maritime swing, most of Digby is a fairly mundane parkland layout, with plenty of room to swing the club, despite the evergreen name. There is a deep ravine/stream cutting through the property, which lends itself to one excellent short hole and a couple of other fairly good ones, but there are just too many unmemorable two-shot holes here to make it a course worth recommending. The hotel is much stronger than the golf course. 4. [6/89]

## NEW BRUNSWICK

***Algonquin GC,*** *St. Andrews. Donald Ross, 1927.*

I sincerely doubt that Donald Ross ever set foot in this particular St. Andrews. The town is quaint and the hotel (operated by Canadian Pacific) magnificent, but except for five decent golf holes that overlook Passamaquoddy Bay, the golf course is pretty much a waste of time. Condition is modest to poor, and only a few of the green complexes show any flair whatsoever. Certainly not a destination for Donald Ross maniacs, but the hotel might be a good stopover on the way up to Cape Breton, just to taste the raspberry mousse. 3. [6/89]

*—Gossip—*

Up on Prince Edward Island, a new seaside course called Crowbush Cove, by Canadian designer Tom McBroom, has gotten some excellent reviews, but the pictures make it clear that it's manufactured, rather than a real links.

## QUEBEC

***Royal Ottawa GC,*** *East Aylmer. Howard Watson, 1966, with revisions by Clinton "Robbie" Robinson.*

It was in late October when I saw this course, and I didn't get that good a look; but what I saw was just your basic parkland course. 4. [10/80]

Royal Montreal is the only current World Top 100 course I haven't seen outside of Spain and Morocco; but I'm just as interested to see Willie Park's Mt. Bruno course, also in Montreal.

## ONTARIO

***Devil's Paintbrush GC,*** *Caledon Village. Mike Hurdzan and Dana Fry, 1991.*

What I saw of this course as it was under construction looked more interesting than the Pulpit—unsurprisingly, since it is a lot better piece of land. The combination of fescue fairways and the steep hills at the sides of some greens is going to make for some very interesting bounce-and-run approaches, and the greens appeared more sweeping in contour than practically anything I've seen—though I couldn't tell yet if that would be for good or bad. However, the plan they showed me had a number of gimmicks like double greens and alternate greens, which a site like this doesn't need. I'll be curious to see this one when it's done, because there's a lot more at stake here than at the Pulpit—they're playing with good land here, instead of just funny money. [5/91]

***Devil's Pulpit GC,*** *Caledon Village. Mike Hurdzan and Dana Fry, 1989.*

I probably shouldn't say anything about this course, because I really couldn't see it very well; you're supposed to aim your first drive at the CN Tower, thirty miles away in downtown Toronto, but the day I visited it was so foggy you couldn't even see *land* below the elevated tee. Maybe it's just as well I didn't. The owners are the inventors of the game *Trivial Pursuit*, so they had some spare money to throw around on building this course, and they got carried away with the whole thing, as you might guess as you're being transferred from the parking lot to the clubhouse by a chauffeur-driven Rolls-Royce.

Torontoans speak in hushed tones about the beauty of the Niagara escarpment, on which the golf course is built; but while it may be very pretty land, in terms of views or natural vegetative cover, there was so much topography here that I would hardly call it ideal land for a golf course. (The fact that they moved 1.7 million cubic yards of dirt during construction is also a fair indication that it was not very good topography for golf.) Any time you have an owner who wants to have so much input *during* construction (as opposed to before construction), you're going to be stuck with elements that do not fit in with the rest of the course, such as the railroad ties behind the 4th green or the tree in the middle of the heavily wooded 10th fairway of an otherwise open course. Suffice to say for now that any course with three 11th holes is teetering on the tightrope between artistic flair and downright overkill. [5/91]

***Don Valley GC,*** *North York. Howard Watson, 1956, with unfortunate revisions by Toronto Metropolitan Parks Authority.*

Not a bad public course, if they'd only maintain it. Certainly some of the changes brought about by the highway project through the middle of the front nine are horrible, and other holes would benefit immensely from a bit of pruning. (The par-3 7th was the most hilarious hole I saw in Toronto, with willows overhanging the right side of the tee, forcing a fade.) But even with most of that, the stretch of holes from #3 to #7 is a cut above most American public courses, even though the original Don Valley was probably two cuts above that. 2. [5/91]

***Essex G & CC,*** *Windsor. Donald Ross, 1929.*

Located just south of Windsor and within an easy drive of downtown Detroit, this course is a real throwback to the great parkland layouts from my native region of the country, with the fairways lined by tall hardwoods reminiscent of Winged Foot or Ridgewood. The course is a bit flat for my tastes, but a good set of Ross greens almost makes up for it. 6. [8/85]

***Glen Abbey GC,*** *Oakville. Jack Nicklaus, 1974.*

One of Nicklaus' first design efforts, and among his best. The holes that make the course are the 11th through 15th, which play down into and through a deep river gorge below the old Abbey, which serves as home of the Royal Canadian Golf Association. But the 17th sticks in my craw; that's the hole with the horseshoe-shaped green, but at 430 yards, it's much too common to find yourself on the wrong side of the horseshoe. Jack's elementary spectator mounding makes it an ideal site for the Canadian Open, but wouldn't it be nice to play Canada's only Tour event (and its national championship) on a Stanley Thompson design once in a while? 6. [10/81]

***Hamilton G & CC,*** *Ancaster. Harry S. Colt, 1914, with revisions by Rees Jones, 1982.*

A fine Colt layout. It's probably the hilliest piece of ground I've ever seen him work with (apart from Pine Valley), and the holes I liked best were mostly the hilly ones—especially the 10th and 18th (assuming the South nine comes second), but also the 1st, the short par-4 5th (although they've made it worse by abandoning the original tee on the left), the 7th (a strong driving hole, and a rare good uphill hole), and the par-3 13th. It's worth the drive from Toronto or Buffalo, and maybe even from Detroit. 7. [5/91]

***King Valley GC,*** *Toronto. Doug Carrick, 1991.*

It seems to me that most times an architect talks about his fondness for "classic" courses he winds up building courses that border on being dull, because the classic courses he professes to love have matured so much that what was originally very flashy is now taken for granted. I also must say that, although this was a fair piece of property, it didn't have

*Hamilton Golf & Country Club.*

nearly the topographic interest of St. George's, Uplands, Weston, or even Maple Downs or Toronto GC—so no one should really have expected the architect to produce a better course, especially when his style is not to move much dirt or get the bunkers right in your face. I do, however, feel for the young architect: in a 24-page color yardage book they never mentioned his name, even though "design consultant" Curtis Strange (who saw the course just once, midway through construction) has his picture plastered on the inside front cover. 5. [5/91]

***Ladies' GC of Toronto,*** *Thornhill. Stanley Thompson, 1924.*

I was surprised to find out that this club still existed; it is the only golf club in the world whose memberships are restricted exclusively to women. (Men can play the course as guests, but it is discouraged.)

The only real standout hole was the very pretty par-3 7th, but the course did present an interesting design example that fairness and quality rest in the eye of the individual player. A couple of the holes here make sharp doglegs, or their fairways end at about 210 yards from the tee. That's perfect for the ladies, and maybe even for a lot of 15-handicap men; but it stinks from the standpoint of a scratch player. So does that make it good or bad? 4. [5/91]

***London Hunt & CC,*** *London. Robert Trent Jones, 1959.*

A premier Canadian club which fails to live up to its potential. The property is fairly hilly, and at one point descends to parallel the course of the Thames River (yes, they have one of those in Canada, too), which ought to make for some exciting golf holes; but I thought the contouring of the greens was below Trent Jones' standard, and he screwed up the one potentially great hole along the river (the par-5 10th) by digging a small pond in front of the green. It could be a lot better. 5. [6/86]

***Maple Downs G & CC,*** *Toronto. Bill Mitchell, 1954, with revisions by Ron Garl and René Muylaert.*

A good piece of property and a pretty good course. Still, it could be a lot better: I don't think they've gotten the most out of the topography in a couple of instances (the 9th, a very good hole, could be twice as good if the tee were moved slightly), and the bunkering does not really show any artistic flair. I wasn't especially impressed with the back-side short holes, which are the members' pride and joy. Although they are undeniably challenging holes, the greens don't really fit well into their hillside settings—they probably should have moved more dirt in building the green sites, so it would look as though they had moved less. 4. [5/91]

***The National G & CC,*** *Woodbridge. George and Tom Fazio, 1976.*

The National isn't really my cup of tea. Yes, it's a hard course, and it spends more on maintenance than any course in Canada; but while all that may make the course unusual for Canada, there are a lot of courses in the States of the same standard. In fact, The National looks more like a Nicklaus course than a Tom Fazio design. The topography is hilly, but lacks the sort of shallow, sharp valleys that make so many of the smaller courses in Toronto full of character—if you get it off line at The National, you're either standing sideways or you hit it off the world (like a hook at the 7th or 14th).

I did enjoy some of the holes a lot—the stretch from the 2nd through the 5th is excellent, but they're so hard that they'd be a good finishing run on most courses. The 10th and 11th are also admirable, although they're soon forgotten because of the weird par-5 12th. Bottom line: it's easier to build a really hard golf course that will appeal to the low-handicap player than it is to build a really great course that will appeal to everyone. 6. [5/91]

***Redtail GC,*** *St. Thomas. Donald Steel and Tom Mackenzie, 1992.*

One of the most perfect golf operations I've seen, it's the brainchild of Chris Goodwin and John Drake, two partners from London who built it for themselves and share it with a select group of friends. Everything is done with taste and class, from the beautiful clubhouse with guest rooms above, to a difficult but understated golf course.

The best feature is the rolling property intersected with ravines, which suddenly appears from otherwise undistinguished farmland surroundings near the shore of Lake Erie. The ravines automatically give the course the difficult character the principals sought, though the architect had to plan carefully to limit the number of bridges, which could have blown their construction budget. Nevertheless, the provision of generally just one teeing ground per hole, combined with several difficult holes, puts it beyond the comfort zone of 18-handicappers.

My favorite aspect of the course is the greens contouring, which is among the best done in my lifetime—as at Charlotte Country Club, almost the entire green is pinnable, but there's a variety of difficult spots created by the interior slopes, and there are some tough reads without anything even bordering on excessive. But I'm not a big fan of the low mounds used in place of bunkers in a few of the green complexes; the architects swear they're similar to natural rolls found on-site, but they're the only thing on the golf course that looks created.

If I ever get to build my own course someday, it will probably look quite different than Redtail, but I couldn't hope to be a better host. 7. [5/95]

***St. George's G & CC,*** *Islington. Stanley Thompson, 1929, with revisions by Robbie Robinson, 1966.*

See the "Gourmet's Choice." 8. [5/91]

***Toronto GC,*** *Mississauga. Harry S. Colt, 1912, with revisions by Howard Watson.*

A good but subdued Colt layout, as befits its elite membership. The par-34 front side is interesting: most architects would have stretched out one of the three long two-shotters to get par to a more standard figure, but it's a more challenging course for the good player because Colt did not. I particularly liked some of the more subtle stuff, such as the approach to the 6th green (where a diagonal valley just in front of the green kicks a short ball to the trap on the right), or the way the 8th fairway falls across the ground. Most memorable stretch of holes: the 9th through 11th, three very different two-shotters. The 16th and 17th are two-thirds of a very strong finish, but then the 18th is a lay-up iron off the tee and a pitch to the green. 6. [5/91]

***Uplands G & CC,*** *Thornhill. Stanley Thompson, 1922.*

I'm glad I got to see this course before it disappears completely. Nine holes have now been abandoned to prepare for a housing scheme, but there's plenty of interest in those that remain. The par-3 8th (originally the 17th) is an arresting hole and one of the most difficult I've ever seen, a full-blooded 220 yards across a stream valley with a small green site shelved into the side of a wooded hill; I doubt I'd ever have the guts to build anything as severe, except maybe on a par-3 course. From the standpoint of what I might steal for another course someday, the green site of the 3rd (8th), the undulating fairway of the 6th (11th) and the second-shot dilemma of the 9th (18th) were all of more practical value. It's a little on the narrow side for my tastes, but it doesn't spoil the fun. 5. [5/91]

***Weston G & CC,*** *Weston. Willie Park, Jr., 1920.*

I'm not too well versed on Willie Park's style of architecture, but I enjoyed his use of the rather severe terrain here—in fact, the tee shot along the ridge at the 5th is probably the first piece of golf hole I would have found on the topo map, though I doubt most other architects would identify with it. Here, as at several other courses I saw in Toronto, the rolling property forces you to place the ball off the tee to get a good stance for your next shot (one of the principal benefits of rolling ground)—the 6th and 12th holes are both good examples. 5. [5/91]

*—Gossip—*

Lorne Rubenstein and I made a whirlwind tour of the Toronto courses—twelve in 3-1/2 days—but we still missed the old Mississauga course, and Bob Cupp's Beacon Hall to the north. When I go back to Redtail, I'll also want to check out the St. Thomas course, a hilly old Stanley Thompson design which Chris Goodwin said was great fun.

## BRITISH COLUMBIA

***Capilano G & CC,*** *West Vancouver. Stanley Thompson, 1937.*

They have every right in Vancouver to be proud of Capilano, a fine golf club on a hillside overlooking an absolutely stunning city. Stanley Thompson did a shrewd job of routing the course on its steep sloping site, so that even though the first six holes play downhill toward the Lion's Gate Bridge and the next nine tack back up the hill, there aren't any holes (other than perhaps the downhill 6th) that are just goat-hill by nature. But the site and course do lack the smaller contours that lend real character, and only a couple of the greens stand out as fascinating. Interestingly, the short holes were singled out in *The World Atlas of Golf* as noteworthy, but I found them quite tame; the long 5th and 18th, and the long par-4 13th and 17th were the best of the bunch for my tastes. 7. [5/93]

*Capilano offers great views and great golf.*

***Victoria GC,*** *Oak Bay, Victoria. Harvey Coombe, with revisions by A. Vernon Macan, 1930; Gary Panks, 1981-85; and Bill and John Robinson, 1984.*

A very short (barely 6,000 yards) and tightly packed course at the southeastern edge of the city's most fashionable suburb, with magnificent views across the Strait of Juan de Fuca to the Olympic Mountains. The flavor of golf is all there, with abundant gorse and Scotch broom in brilliant yellow bloom in the spring, occasional outcrops of rock on the holes that abut the coast, and very good small-scale contouring, especially evident in the wild 3rd and 7th greens. However, the tight property and the city street that bisects the course make it cramped and quite dangerous, in contrast to the expansive views; the routing is quirky, with two sets of back-to-back short holes; and the lack of length limits its appeal to serious low-handicap golfers. Still, it's a great place to enjoy a vacation round, as long as there's not too much crossfire. 5. [5/93]

I still haven't done the Canadian courses justice until I get to the Rockies: of late, most people in the know are recommending Jasper Park first, but I'm still more intrigued by Banff. (*Golf Digest* rates Robert Trent Jones' 36 at Kananaskis ahead of both, to show you where they're coming from.) Someday, too, I'll get to the new Chateau Whistler by RTJ, Jr., and to Wolf Creek in Ponoka, Alberta, the first solo effort by my friend Rod Whitman.

## THE ISLANDS

The development of golf in the Caribbean has little history; except for Bermuda, which was booming in the 1920s and converted most of its available real estate to golf courses during that period, there aren't any "classic" courses here to explore. Rocky terrain and the low availability of fresh water have doomed most low-budget attempts at creativity, so only the staples you've heard about — those developed by international companies like Rockresorts, Gulf & Western, and most recently Four Seasons — have had the wherewithal to build something worthwhile. The architects of choice in the first boom were Robert Trent Jones and Dick Wilson, while Robert Trent Jones, Jr., seems to have the best connections here today.

## BERMUDA

***Castle Harbour GC,*** *Tucker's Town. Charles Banks, 1932.*

The views from the first tee (literally off the porch of the Castle Harbour Hotel) and from the 18th tee playing back toward the hotel's newest wing are among the most spectacular in golf. But the hills here are among the most severe I have ever encountered on a golf course: in a couple of places they've made foot-high artificial berms across the fairway to keep drives from rolling over the brink of a hill onto a 2-to-1 downhill slope. The valley between tee and green at the short 13th must also be seen to be believed. 4. [2/88]

*The view takes your mind off golf on the 18th at Castle Harbour.*

*Mid Ocean 5th is a classic C.B. Macdonald design.*

***Mid Ocean Club,*** *Tucker's Town. Charles Blair Macdonald, 1924, with revisions by Robert Trent Jones.*

The golf course that sets the standard for Bermuda, and which none of the others live up to. Going at the right time of year is crucial: friends have commented on the crowds in the spring and the noisy road to Hamilton which cuts through the middle of the course, but on my visit the scene was serene and the golf pleasant. The layout begins by way of a sharp dogleg par-4 along a ridgetop to a green overlooking the ocean; the next two holes parallel the sea, but at the 4th the drive goes inland across the main road to Hamilton, and the next 12 holes remain inland below the pink and white cottages before returning inside the crook of the 1st at the Redan 17th. The best hole, of course, is the 433-yard "Cape" 5th, where the second shot and the contours of the green are equally as dramatic as the tee shot down across Mangrove Lake. 8. [2/88]

***Port Royal GC,*** *Southampton Parish. Robert Trent Jones, 1970.*

A government-owned, well-maintained layout overlooking the Atlantic Ocean at the western end of the island. Like the other courses in Bermuda, it is a little too hilly to really be a great layout, and the architects were a bit overzealous in tree-planting between the fairways for my tastes—sidehill and tree-lined is a bad combination. But the short 16th, at cliff's edge, is surely one of the most photogenic holes around. 5. [2/88]

## DOMINICAN REPUBLIC

***Casa de Campo Resort,*** *La Romana. Teeth of the Dog course by Pete Dye, 1971; Links course (with Lee Schmidt), 1976.*

See the "Gourmet's Choice." Teeth of the Dog: 9. Links course: 5. [11/85]

*—Gossip—*

The Caribbean is still hurting for good golf. About everything worth checking out comes from the Jones family: Trent's 72 holes at Dorado and Cerromar Beach in Puerto Rico, and Carambola Beach on St. Croix, which Brian McCallen at *GOLF* is very high on. I've also heard enthusiastic reports on the new Four Seasons course by Robert Trent Jones, Jr. on Nevis, which Dianna and I selected for our honeymoon precisely because there wasn't any golf there: the maintenance crew may well ride to work on mules, and I don't mean those Kawasaki maintenance vehicles. Jones also has a new course on Barbados—Royal Westmoreland—located partly in an old quarry that looks a lot like his Joondalup course in Perth from the photos I've seen.

## MEXICO, CENTRAL AND SOUTH AMERICA

*—Gossip—*

Mexico is one of the hottest developing areas of the world for golf, with American companies tying up coastal property all over the country. From what I've heard, Jack Nicklaus' new Cabo del Sol course at the tip of Baja might be the best he's ever done—and this isn't from the publicists of Colleton River. It's about time: Mexico's previous generations of resort development, in Acapulco and Cancun, didn't produce any noteworthy courses, although I've always been curious to see Roy Dye's very strange course at Las Hadas, where Bo Derek was a 10. Someday I also want to see Club de Golf Mexico in the capital, though I don't expect that it's really of top 100 caliber as it used to be rated.

Central America is a huge gray area: the only course I've ever heard mentioned as good is Guatemala CC.

In looking for great courses in South America we should start at the bottom and work our way up: from Los Leones in Santiago, Chile, to the Jockey Club in Buenos Aires and GC de Uruguay in Montevideo (both MacKenzie layouts; Jockey Club is dead flat, but the Uruguay course may have some significant terrain), to Gavea in Rio (spectacular but very short and tight), Lagunita in Caracas, and two courses in Colombia: Trent Jones' El Rincon in Bogota, and Joe Lee's Lagos de Caujaral in Barranquilla, which Fred Muller has always described as an interesting jungle layout.

## SCOTLAND

In the past fifteen years, golf tourism has moved past Scotland to include all the British Isles and Ireland, and I've been one of the biggest supporters of that expansion, as in my year overseas I had found the English and Irish courses tremendously underrated. Nevertheless, the Scots have been playing golf for 300 years longer than anyone else, and both the rigors of the game and its natural lack of pretensions are neat reflections of the Scottish character.

Scotland has a handful of courses which deserve their place in anyone's short list of must-sees, but it's been criticized for lacking a strong second tier of courses which hold up to international standards. That's because the Scots aren't at all interested in foreigners' standards for the game they invented, and because they can find the fun and challenge of golf in courses that have blind holes or less than eighteen holes or only a par of 68. Indeed, you'll learn more about the game by playing just any Scottish course, whether it was laid out by James Braid or Tom Morris himself, or just some local punter, than you will from most "top 100" tracks. If you don't like Scottish golf, you don't like the real thing.

## THE HIGHLANDS

***Boat of Garten GC,*** *Boat of Garten, Inverness-shire. James Braid and John R. Stutt, 1925.*

A short (5,700 yards par 68), narrow inland course among birch trees which ranks right up there among my favorites for purely fun golf. Like many of the smaller Scottish courses, it is squeezed onto a small property by excluding par-5 holes from the routing plan, but one or two driveable par-4 holes and a couple of extremely difficult long par-4's give proper due to power play, so it suffers little from a balance standpoint. The fairways are bumpy and uneven (as if tree stumps had not been removed when the course was cleared, but simply grassed over), providing problems of lie and stance more common to links courses. There are some marvelous holes, such as the dogleg 2nd and 6th, and the 433-yard 18th, and there is also the very strange "Gulley" 15th, all of which combine for a unique day's golf. With snow still glistening from the peaks of the Cairngorms in the late spring, this would be one of my first choices for a recreational game for straight hitters, but low-handicappers should leave their woods in the boot. 5. [5/85]

***Braemar GC,*** *Braemar, Aberdeenshire.*

A small course in a highland meadow not far from Balmoral, the Royal Family's summer place. The narrow, high grass banks which supplant bunkers here are unique in my travels to date, and, combined with the scenery, make for an enchanting, if not absorbing, game. 2. [8/82]

***Cruden Bay G & CC,*** *Cruden Bay, Aberdeenshire. Tom Simpson and Herbert Fowler, 1926.*

A great personal favorite of mine, which I hated to leave out of the Gourmet's Choice; but I couldn't list it as superior to Simpson's Ballybunion. Cruden Bay is more of a "cult" course, thanks to its huge sandhills, superb views, great and terrible holes, and relative anonymity; in fact, before my trip in 1982 I had only seen an old picture of the links dotted with sheep from a 1930s edition of *Golf Illustrated,* but even that small picture in black and white made it a must-see. I wasn't disappointed; the beautiful routing shows off the town, Cruden Water and the fishing village of Port Erroll at the magnificent par-3 4th, the huge coastal dunes from the 5th through 7th, the high farmland plain of the 9th, the narrow links pass of the 14th through 16th, and back below the clubhouse to finish. A couple of very weird holes toward the end keep it out of the class of the truly elite, but there aren't many holes at Cruden Bay you're likely to forget. 8. [6/85]

***Golspie GC,*** *Golspie, Sutherland. Present course laid out 1905; expanded 1967.*

Just around the Embo inlet to the north of Dornoch, Golspie is an unusual and unexpected mix of linksland and moorland holes. It's a bit on the flat side and not very well-kept even by British standards, but there are a couple of interesting holes to see. The course and town are overlooked by a large statue erected by the Duke of Sutherland on Ben Bhraggie. 3. [8/82]

***Kingussie GC,*** *Kingussie, Inverness-shire. Harry Vardon.*

Located just off the main A9 highway between Dornoch and lower Scotland, this is a mixture of parkland and moorland golf, but I cannot recommend it as competition for Boat of Garten architecturally. One interesting note: two-thirds of the club's members play the game left-handed, the consequence of another popular Highland sport. 2. [5/85]

***Moray GC,*** *Lossiemouth, Morayshire. Old course laid out by Old Tom Morris, 1889, with some revisions by Henry Cotton.*

In the old days this was known as the narrowest course in Scotland, but fortunately the gorse has been cut back some in the interim. This might be a fairly good course, but it is hard to concentrate on the architecture (or the golf) with the heat of Harrier jets on your back: an RAF fighter base adjoins the course and the landing approach towers cross it, which I found most distracting. Still, the long par-4 18th, uphill to the stone clubhouse, is one of the most picturesque and demanding finishing holes in Scotland. 3. [8/82]

***Murcar GC,*** *Bridge of Don, Aberdeenshire. Archie Simpson, 1909, with modifications by James Braid.*

Extending just to the north of the Royal Aberdeen links, this to me was slightly the better of the two courses; but my friend Bill Shean tells me I'm nuts, and he played them on my recommendation, whereas I only walked them on a blustery day. The outward half is the closer to the sea and bounded by huge sandhills, providing spectacular golfing terrain, including a couple of arresting short holes and the all-world 420-yard 7th. However, the course is lacking many stronger par-4 holes to support these, so it plays on the short side unless there is a good wind about. Shean says it's a 4, max, but I'll still give it 5. [8/82]

***Nairn GC,*** *Nairn, Nairnshire. Original layout by Archie Simpson, 1887; modifications by Old Tom Morris and James Braid.*

This is the best links along the southern edge of the Moray Firth, but I think it's been overrated by some writers to create some other reason besides Dornoch to travel to the Highlands. Most of the

*The Boat of Garten lies at the entrance to the Scottish Alps.*

course is very flat and lacking scenery unless the gorse is in bloom. (Then again, there might be some pretty views of the Highland mountains if you aren't socked in by fog, like I was.) By far the most memorable hole is the 381-yard 5th, with its drive across the edge of the beach and Braid's bunker right smack where you'd like to aim to be certain of staying dry. 6. [8/82]

***Royal Aberdeen GC,*** *Balgownie, Bridge of Don, Aberdeenshire. Golf dating back to 1589 or even before; club formed 1780. Archie Simpson, 1888, with revisions by Tom Simpson.*

Quite similar to its neighbor Murcar, with the front nine running northward among huge dunes close to the sea, and the returning holes on higher, inland terrain. The inland holes here are a bit longer and more distinguished than Murcar's, but I didn't think the holes among the dunes were as good, except for the short 8th and long 9th at the Murcar end of the links. At one point, the bunkers guarding the green at the 135-yard 8th line up three rows deep. 5. [8/82]

***Royal Dornoch GC,*** *Dornoch, Sutherland. Golf began 1616 or earlier; present layout by Old Tom Morris, 1886, with improvements by John Sutherland and Donald Ross, and five new holes (8-11,13) added by George Duncan in 1947.*

See the "Gourmet's Choice." 10. [5/85]

***Royal Tarlair GC,*** *Macduff, Banffshire.*

A clifftop course overlooking the Moray Firth, with mostly open and fairly dull holes, but there are a couple next to the water that can bring on vertigo. The short, downhill pitch at the 13th, played out onto a promontory jutting into the sea, requires nerve both in hitting the green and walking to it afterward. 3. [8/82]

***Strathpeffer Spa GC,*** *Strathpeffer, Ross-shire.*

This club introduced me to the Scottish "honesty box" method of green fee collecting when the clubhouse is unstaffed. (It works much better where

the green fee is $4.) The course is only 4,800 yards par 65, with no man-made bunkers, but the steep grades (especially at the downhill 1st and uphill 2nd) and thick rough make it an exhausting physical test. For the 2nd hole, a Sherpa would come in handy. 2. [8/82]

—*Gossip*—

I have really been somewhat negligent in my exploration of the Highlands; Royal Dornoch and Cruden Bay are such great personal favorites that I have found it hard to tear myself away and try anything else. I was already kicking myself for bypassing Tain on the shortcut to Dornoch, which comes highly recommended as a good test of golf and full of character; luckily, now Donald Steel's new ultra-posh Carnegie Course at Skibo Castle will require a return visit. And if I'm traveling with my wife instead of a bunch of 2-handicaps I may try Buckie Strathlene and Cullen (both of these short and weird) on the way from Nairn to Cruden Bay. Lastly, for pure scenery and remoteness, there are Stromness in the Outer Hebrides and Tobermory on the island of Mull, claimed by David Hamilton's *Good Golf Guide* to be among the prettiest courses in all Scotland.

## THE MIDLANDS

***Blairgowrie GC,*** *Blairgowrie, Perthshire. Wee course dates to 1889, with revisions by Braid and Stutt; Rosemount course by Alister MacKenzie, 1927, modified by Braid and Stutt, 1934; Lansdowne course added by Peter Alliss and Dave Thomas, 1980.*

Rosemount is revered as Scotland's finest inland course, but mainly because it's about the only full-length inland course they have; it's a pretty, tree-lined course, but more comparable to Pinehurst No. 1 than to No. 2. I couldn't figure out how a MacKenzie layout could have such an average set of greens, but recently I discovered that they were all rebuilt after a blight in the early 1960s.

Three holes here stand apart in my memory: the 1st and 17th of the Rosemount course, a super long par-4 and a good long one-shotter, but above all a short par-4 on the Wee nine dubbed the "Faerie Dell," with its approach between two leaning fir trees which flank the entrance to the green.

Rosemount: 5. Lansdowne: 3. Wee nine: 4. [8/82]

***Carnoustie GC,*** *Carnoustie, Angus. Golf dating to 1527; first formalized course by Allan Robertson, 1839, with revisions by Old Tom Morris, James Braid, and James Wright.*

The merits of this course must be more heavily contested than any other but the Old Course at St. Andrews. Many (especially among the older generation of players) hold Carnoustie to be the finest of all the British championship courses, while others find it bleak and totally unappealing. Personally, after careful study of its design I would have to rank it among the best of courses, yet I must admit that I have never really felt any affection for it in my heart, as I do for St. Andrews. (Then again, I haven't given the town much chance, since I've always driven up from St. Andrews to play.)

Even on a clear day there is not much scenery to be found here: the mountains are far away, the railway separates the links from the town, and there is no elevation to give one a view of the sea. The actual construction of the course is also of a Spartan, functional bent: the sod faces of the bunkers are slightly more squared off than at St. Andrews or Muirfield, and they tend to rise up from a flat base rather than shelter down into the ground as at other courses. Hole for hole, though, Carnoustie stacks up with just about any course anywhere for demanding play, and it is not as penal a course as it is made out to be—it is just depressingly efficient at exposing the weaknesses of one's game. Strategically speaking, the 2nd and 6th are among the best holes the game has to offer, and the finishing run is unquestionably the world's most demanding.

I should also address the recent waning of the course's reputation, which was partly brought on by a temporary decline in course maintenance, but mostly by the R & A's announcement that the course would no longer be considered as an Open championship venue. To an even greater degree than St. Andrews or Troon, the economy of the town of Carnoustie is tied to the influx of golfing tourism, and the consequence of the course's recent exclusion from American itineraries has been a major local depression, from both the economic and morale standpoints. I would hate to think that the reputation of one of our greatest championship layouts is going to be undermined by the lack of a posh four-star hotel with private baths. Be sure to include Carnoustie on your Scottish itinerary, on principle alone. 8. [6/85]

***Crail Golfing Society,*** *Crail, Fife. Club founded 1786 (fifth oldest in the world); present links by Old Tom Morris, 1892.*

A short (5,800 yards, par 69), basic but memorable links at the northeastern tip of Fife, not far from St. Andrews. It features some beautiful holes along a rocky beach and one of the world's best clubhouse settings, and though much of the course is rather back-and-forth, there is much fun to be had and an opportunity to post a low score if one's game is on. 4. [7/82]

***Crieff GC,*** *Crieff, Perthshire. Ferntower course opened 1980; Dornock nine the remnants from Willie Park's original layout.*

Set high up on a sidehill slope with views over the Strathearn valley, the new layout features some good holes and some fine specimen trees, but the combination of modern design and low-budget construction lacks charm. If there is one hole at Crieff that must be seen it is the 265-yard 5th on the Dornock nine, named "Highlandman's Loan," which plays over a hill to a small rectangular green at the far low side, with no real fairway at all. Ferntower course: 3. [7/82]

***Gleneagles Hotel GC's,*** *Auchterarder, Perthshire. King's and Queen's courses by James Braid with C.K. Hutchison, 1919.*

I think the King's course at Gleneagles has gotten a bad rap from some people simply because the adjoining hotel is so geared to putting on a Scottish act for the American tourists. Especially now that some new championship tees have been added, the King's course combines rare scenic trappings with some exceptionally good golf architecture, and there are several holes (the 5th, 7th, and 13th, to name three) that any course would be proud to own. It is difficult to fathom how any visitor could dismiss the course as "American" in spirit after playing the "Silver Tassie" 3rd hole.

The Queen's course is less strenuous than the King's, especially now that it has been "restored" to its original routing to make room for a condo development where it had at one time been extended. I think it includes several ordinary holes, but the scenery is still here and no one should miss the long par-4 6th or the wild 17th green. Overall, a morning's romp over the Queen's course followed by an afternoon on the King's is a hard day's golf to match.

I haven't yet had a chance to see the new Monarch's course by Jack Nicklaus, but its wall-to-wall cart paths set a horrifying precedent for Scottish golf. King's Course: 7. Queen's Course: 6. [6/82]

***Golf House Club,*** *Elie, Fife. Original layout by Old Tom Morris, 1895, with revisions by James Braid.*

A fine old links at the edge of Braid's boyhood hometown, with a brief stretch of inspiring holes along the coast yielding magnificent views across to the East Lothian coast on a clear day. The par-4 13th and par-3 3rd are the best of the holes, but most memorable of all is the opening tee shot, played blind over a ridge from beside the clubhouse only after obtaining clearance from the starter in his periscope hut. 5. [9/82]

***Lundin Links GC,*** *Lundin, Fife. Split from the Leven club and extended to 18 holes of its own, c. 1900.*

Really half a links; the first five and last four holes were part of the original Innerleven course, along with the seaside holes from Leven GC down the shore, with play commencing from either end of the links. The course extension, which lies partway up a hill facing the Firth of Forth, is of different character than the old holes. Best of the lot is the 18th, a long two-shotter up a depression in the dunes to the old clubhouse. 3. [7/82]

***Monifieth Links,*** *Monifieth, Angus. Willie Park and J. Hamilton Stutt had some input on present layout.*

Just to the south of Carnoustie, this is another fairly bleak layout next to the railway, which is out of bounds to the right of the first six holes. Strategy-wise, it is no rival to its neighbor (in fact, I hear that the neighboring course at Panmure is a more interesting layout), but at least it plays lightning fast, the way links are supposed to. 3. [9/82]

***Montrose GC,*** *Montrose, Angus. Golf dating to 1567 or earlier; Willie Park had some input on the present Medal links.*

A wide-open links laid out over flattish (but seldom level) terrain where crosswinds wreak havoc. The routing changes direction more than most links, at one point running inland altogether. Of several fairly good holes, I remember the short 3rd and 230-yard 16th as the best. 4. [8/82]

***Pitlochry GC,*** *Pitlochry, Perthshire. Willie Fernie, 1909, with modifications by C.K. Hutchison.*

One of the more charming mountain-goat courses to be found, with quite a climb for the first five holes, but some exhilarating holes as a reward. Like Boat of Garten, it excludes par-5 holes from the routing plan, but the long blind par-4 10th is a big enough hole for any course. There are also a couple of fine short holes, and the short par-4 finishing hole hurdles a swift-flowing stream just in front of the picturesque chalet clubhouse. 4. [8/82]

***St. Andrews,*** *Fife. Old course carved by nature, with some input from Allan Robertson and Old Tom Morris; New course by Old Tom in the 1880s; Eden course by H.S. Colt, 1913; and Jubilee course by Willie Auchterlonie.*

See the "Gourmet's Choice." Old course: 10. New course: 5. Eden course: 5. Jubilee course: 3. [6/85]

*Pitlochry contains many exhilarating holes as your reward for some tough walking.*

***Taymouth Castle GC,*** *Aberfeldy, Perthshire.*

A completely forgettable layout near the mouth of Loch Tay, notable only for the converted castle which serves as clubhouse. 2. [8/82]

*—Gossip—*

There is very little else in this part of Scotland which I think would rate above a 4, but one good bet is Panmure, near Carnoustie, where Hogan practiced for the 1953 Open; several friends have reported enthusiastically about it. There's also Downfield in Dundee (call for directions first: I couldn't find it); or my friend Dave Oswald's home course of Scotscraig, between St. Andrews and the Tay Bridge. David also tells me of a new course built at Letham Grange near Arbroath, a parkland course with American influences.

For the spiritual golfer, though, the #1 target is probably Auchnafree, the rudimentary six-hole course which Michael Bamberger immortalized in his book, *To The Linksland.* It lies somewhere in the glen of the River Almond, not far from Crieff; but if you want to find it, you'll have to read the book.

## THE LOTHIANS

***Dalmahoy GC,*** *Dalmahoy, Midlothian. East and West courses by James Braid, 1926.*

The East course is Dalmahoy's main attraction, and one of the few Scottish parkland courses suitable for hosting a major pro tournament. There are some fine trees and a few fairly good holes, plus good views to Edinburgh on a clear day, but it's nothing outstanding. 4. [9/82]

Dalmahoy's West course is strictly batting practice. 2. [9/82]

***Dunbar GC,*** *Dunbar, East Lothian. Present course founded 1856, although golf began much earlier.*

The easternmost of the links of Lothian, this is a shortish layout along a very narrow strip of linksland, with hazards including a lighthouse at the 9th and an ancient ruin as well. But there are no special holes that lure one back, such as North Berwick possesses in spades. 3. [9/82]

***Gullane GC,*** *Gullane, East Lothian. Three courses laid out by Willie Park.*

Gullane No. 1 has a large following, but I suspect more owing to its proximity to Muirfield than to its good (but not more) layout. From the edge of town, it climbs high up Gullane Hill and back down near the sea on its far side, with stunning views to be had on a clear day, and bared to the wind at all times. The par-5 3rd and the downhill finishing holes stand apart in my memory. 6. [9/82]

Gullane No. 2 is a shorter and less memorable test, its overall quality held back by holes such as the par-3 3rd, which is 210 yards blind up Gullane Hill. 4. [9/82]

***Honourable Company of Edinburgh Golfers,*** *Muirfield, Gullane, East Lothian. Present site from 1891, with revisions to the links by Old Tom Morris, H.S. Colt and Tom Simpson.*

Maybe the world's best championship course, Muirfield is one of just two Open venues (along with Turnberry) which low-handicap Americans are guar-

*Rigorous bunkers are Muirfield's primary challenge.*

anteed to like; its visual definition and classic route plan are what the scratch player would characterize as "fair," but it still exudes character and charm. The quality of its bunkering is unsurpassed: each one is a fearsome hazard, but the mix of old-fashioned cross-bunkers and strategically placed wing hazards encourages the player to flirt with them, instead of forcing him to drive into tight corsets. Each of the three par-5 holes is an essay on bunker placement, and as a set they're probably the best three-shotters on any course in the world. The uphill par-3 13th, to an armchair green with cruel bunkers along its flanks, is another favorite. 10. [6/85]

***Kilspindie GC,*** *Aberlady, East Lothian. Willie Park.*

This is the least known of the East Lothian links because of its secluded location, hidden from the main Musselburgh–North Berwick road by a belt of woods. It is a short and fairly primitive layout, though it can still be a challenge with the wind up. The short 8th, with its bulkheaded green near the beach, is a one-shot hole worthy of any course. 4. [9/82]

***Luffness New GC,*** *Aberlady, East Lothian. Willie Park.*

This club struck me as a junior version of Muirfield: 600 yards shorter than its famous neighbor, but featuring similar hay roughs and deep bunkers, and one of the few private clubs in Scotland where walk-ins are not welcome. However, while most of the holes are architecturally sound, none of them stand comparison with Muirfield's best, except the 8th, for its view toward Edinburgh from the tee. 5. [9/82]

***Longniddry GC,*** *Longniddry, East Lothian. H.S. Colt and Charles Alison, 1921, with modifications by Mackenzie Ross.*

One of the most surprising courses in East Lothian, with trees and seascapes reminiscent of the Monterey Peninsula over one stretch of holes. It suffers from being cramped, however: the 7th through 11th is a fine stretch of par-4's individually, but would be much improved if they weren't all in the 380-yard range. Bunkers are large, deep, and plentiful here. 5. [9/82]

***Musselburgh Old Links,*** *Musselburgh, East Lothian. Believed to be the oldest unchanged course in the world.*

This inconspicuous, rudimentary nine-hole layout belies a great history, having once been the home of the Honourable Company, Royal Musselburgh and Royal Burgess clubs, a host to the Open Championship, and a true center of the game in Scotland. But by the end of the nineteenth century, its popularity led to overcrowding of its nine holes, and the famous clubs moved away. The links became little more than the infield for the Musselburgh horse track, with the rails cutting right across holes and still interfering with play.

A few years ago the course was almost plowed under to expand the racetrack facilities, but fortunately it has been saved, and one can still play the course much as it was 150 years ago, complete with Mrs. Forman's pub, once a refreshment stop for Open contestants, just behind the 4th green. All for the outrageous sum of four pounds, a small price to pay for true history. 3. [6/83]

***North Berwick East Links,*** *North Berwick, East Lothian. Original nine by Ben Sayers, 1894, expanded to 18 by Sayers and James Braid in 1906; layout modified by Mackenzie Ross.*

A wide-open course reminiscent of Pebble Beach in its clifftop setting, but not in its design. Despite tremendous views out toward Bass Rock there is not a single hole of real inspiration, although there would be if one turned around the 14th and played down toward the 13th green near the beach from this angle. 3. [9/82]

***North Berwick West Links,*** *North Berwick, East Lothian. Natural links with modification by David Strath, Tom Dunn, and Sir Guy Campbell.*

See the "Gourmet's Choice." 8. [6/85]

***Royal Burgess GC,*** *Barnton, Edinburgh. Present course laid out by James Braid.*

This club claims to have been founded at Bruntsfield Links in 1735, which would make it the oldest golf club in the world, predating the Honourable Company by nine years. The current parkland course is no competition for Muirfield, however: it's simply uninspiring. 3. [9/82]

***Royal Musselburgh GC,*** *Prestongrange, East Lothian. James Braid, 1925, with modifications by Mungo Park.*

Parkland in character, the current home of the Royal Musselburgh club overlooks the Firth of Forth from a slight distance. There are two or three demanding holes, including the short 6th. 3. [9/82]

*—Gossip—*

In the vicinity of Edinburgh, the only course I still want to check out is the public links known as Braids Hills No. 1, a short layout high up on the rugged hills not far from the city. In the Borders region to the south, Peebles and Hawick might be fun 4's.

## WEST COAST

***Carradale GC,*** *Carradale, Argyllshire.*

A short, sporty nine holes on the leeward side of the Mull of Kintyre, with fine views toward Arran and a glimpse of the back side of Ailsa Craig. The hilltop course is grazed by sheep and dotted by outcroppings of rock, which must be carefully avoided. Altogether the course must break most of the canons of golf architecture, but it provides interesting hazards for a friendly match. 2. [6/85]

***Dunaverty GC,*** *Southend, Argyllshire.*

A small links at the tip of the Mull of Kintyre, with views across toward Northern Ireland on the clearest of days. The small square greens are surrounded by wire fencing to deter wandering sheep. Not a big course at under 5,000 yards with many short holes, but it was good enough to nurture the Scottish international standout, Belle Robertson. 2. [6/85]

***The Machrie GC,*** *Isle of Islay. Willie Campbell, 1891, with major revisions by Donald Steel.*

For an escape to golf the way it was played in the 19th century, a trip to Islay is a must. It is a quiet place (the population of the island being less than 2,000) and a peaceful, natural golf links, featuring several heroic blind approaches over its mountainous dunes, but still fewer than in the old days. The par-5 7th, with its drive over the "Scot's Maiden," is the most awesome hole, but only because the old "Mount Zion" 3rd green has been eliminated in the recent redesign. The small hotel adjoining the links has been panned by other critics, but it sure beat staying out in the wind and rain on my visit. 4. [5/83]

*The journey to Machrihanish is well rewarded.*

***Machrihanish GC,*** *Machrihanish, Argyllshire. Charles Hunter, 1876, with revisions by Old Tom Morris and Sir Guy Campbell.*

One of the first places I would go to get away from it all—the remoteness of the setting and the quality of the golf are an unbeatable combination. Those who declare these links should be an Open championship venue if they added a few back tees are going a bit overboard, but the opener, with its tee shot over a corner of the beach, is the game's best, and there are several other holes going out which would hold their own on any course. Unfortunately, the dedication of prime real estate to the front nine makes the back something of a letdown—most of the holes are sound and fairly strong, but they lack the magic of the front side. Still, the rush of the front nine is enough to make this a course to which I'll always look forward to returning, and it's probably one of the few Scottish links unchanged by the pressures of international tourism. For that alone, everyone should see it. 7. [6/85]

***Prestwick GC,*** *Prestwick, Ayrshire. Original 12-hole crossover layout by Old Tom Morris, with revisions and extension by James Braid and John R. Stutt.*

This is surely an old-fashioned course, whose design and appeal Frank Hannigan accurately summed up in one word: "kinky." Crammed into a small property which could hardly be put to other use, it is a natural course in the truest sense, with hardly any green-to-tee walks at all separating the holes: one simply plays to the first target, tees up from there and plays to another, the way golf was invented. There are several blind holes at Prestwick, and they are illustrative of the strengths and weaknesses of the type. As far as I'm concerned, a blind short hole like the "Himalayas" 5th, played blind over a ridge into open ground on the far side, is beyond the pale; if you're going to have a blind approach there ought to be a receptive target to hit to on the other end. One need look no further than the "Alps" 17th for a textbook example of what

I mean. As for other holes on the course, I admire the dogleg 4th most of all, and have grown to like the famous "Cardinal" 3rd and "Sea Heatherick" 13th with its tiny, convoluted green—an almost impossible target for a 460-yard par-4, but where is it written that "par" for a hole can't consist of a chip and a putt? The 15th, 16th, and 18th (all very short par-4's—the last two of them driveable) are fun finishing holes for match play, where anything can happen if the match is still close. All this is to say nothing of an unparalleled club history for the home of the Open Championship itself. Uptight American golfers are liable to hate this course, but I hope that none of my readers fall into that category. 8. [6/85]

***Royal Troon GC,*** *Troon, Ayrshire. Original layout by Willie Fernie, with modifications by James Braid and others.*

There are a number of holes at Troon I really admire, but for some reason it doesn't rank that highly on my list of favorites. One reason is that its straight out and straight back routing is right along the line of the prevailing wind: this makes the finishing holes among the most demanding in the world, but also makes the mundane opening stretch even less appealing. There is also one celebrated hole, the "Railway" 11th, for which I have absolutely no fondness at all. However, the 13th and 15th are two of the toughest par-4's I know, the 17th is overlooked as a terrific long par-3, and the Postage Stamp 8th lives up to its billing and more. 8. [5/83]

***Shiskine GC,*** *Blackwaterfoot, Arran*

At one time there were 18 holes here, but few of the members ever wanted to play the last six out to the back of the clubhouse, so they were abandoned. Where Carradale leaves off in breaking architectural rules, Shiskine goes one step further, with some of the oddest blind holes ever encountered, and some ingenious contraptions for players to signal the next groups that they are done. The 3rd hole of 140 yards, played blind over a rise into the face of a cliff with a precipitous drop to the left of the green, is one of the wildest I've ever seen. 2. [6/85]

***Southerness GC,*** *Southerness, Dumfries-shire. Mackenzie Ross, 1949.*

Some critics will have you believe this course, overlooking the Solway Firth in Scotland's far southwest, is another Turnberry—don't believe them. It is mostly flat and uninspired, of a character that Bernard Darwin described as "inland-super-mare," as opposed to a true seaside links. There are some marvelous views across to the English lake district on a clear afternoon, but the glories of the 12th hole are not enough to be worth a special pilgrimage. 5. [6/83]

***Troon Portland GC,*** *Troon, Ayrshire. Willie Fernie, 1895, with revisions by Alister MacKenzie.*

This relief course, lying inland from the championship links, is deceptively better than it looks, probably a result of MacKenzie's camouflage. But it was a disappointing alternative on my first trip to Scotland, when I wasn't old enough to play Royal Troon. 4. [5/83]

***Turnberry Hotel GC's,*** *Turnberry, Ayrshire. Original Ailsa and Arran courses by Willie Fernie; reconstructed after W.W. II by Mackenzie Ross (Ailsa, 1947) and James Alexander (Arran, 1954).*

The Ailsa features as good a stretch of seaside holes and scenery as there is to be found anywhere in the world of golf, but for some reason I can't help holding it against the course that it doesn't have the wild undulations of a true links. Some of its holes are overrated, particularly the 9th, which is impossible for short hitters like me from the back tee and rather bland from up front. On the other hand, holes like the 6th, 7th, 10th, and 15th get very little credit for being among the finest in Scotland.

I guess in the end analysis I wouldn't mind if you called Turnberry Scotland's answer to Pebble Beach—but if you think it's the best of the British links, you need to get to know Dornoch, Muirfield, and St. Andrews better. 8. [5/83]

***Western Gailes GC,*** *Gailes, Irvine, Ayrshire. Willie Park, 1897, with modifications by Fred Hawtree.*

A marvelously simple layout, with each hole staggered to the outside of the last in a counterclockwise loop, so that it all fits into a small stretch of linksland. There are a couple of memorable holes, in particular the short par-5 6th, but I haven't played the course and didn't develop much of a feeling for it: others, from Jim Urbina to Tom Watson, are very high on it, so I'm boosting it a notch on their word. It is one of the more private clubs in Scotland: make advance contacts to play. 7. [5/83]

—*Gossip*—

The one must-see course that wasn't there the last time I got to Scotland is Loch Lomond, the Tom Weiskopf/Jay Morrish design which suffered through a bankruptcy after it was three-fourths complete: the designers were nuts about it when they were working there, and the two reports I've heard on it post-opening have it among the top 25 in the world!

Again, in this part of the country I think I've hit all the major courses, and any sleeper you find would be a major surprise to me. Kilmarnock (a.k.a. Barassie) is supposed to be the best of the rest in the Troon area, and further to the south both New Galloway and St. Medan are small holiday courses featuring gorgeous views and one or two arresting holes.

## ENGLAND

Australia enjoys better weather, but for a long trip with the chance to enjoy fifteen or more courses, England would be my first choice as a golfing destination. The heathland courses around London are a classic setting for the game found only rarely in other places around the globe, while there is an ample variety of links terrain between the Southport area, Brancaster, Sandwich, Rye, and the southwest. And since they're all less well known than the famous Scottish links, they're less likely to be crowded in the peak season, not to mention less likely to be freezing in the off-season.

Nearly all of the top courses in the country are private golf clubs, run with an air of formality befitting the English personality. To make arrangements to play, write or fax the club secretary in advance of your trip, with a letter of introduction from your home course to establish your credentials as a non-barbarian. As long as you don't want to play on a weekend, a simple letter will open the door to 95% of the best courses in the country. You'll also need to bring a change of clothes, as a jacket and tie are *de rigeur* to have a post-round drink in clubs around the country.

Best of all, the leading continental golf course architects—Harry Colt, Herbert Fowler, Tom Simpson, J.F. Abercromby, and James Braid among them—all cut their teeth as designers on English soil. Overall, I'd guess that the average English golf course sets the standard worldwide.

## NORTHEAST

***Alnmouth Village GC,*** *Alnmouth, Northumberland. Present layout by Mungo Park, 1896.*

The second oldest club in England (founded in 1867), but it plays over no more than a pleasant nine-hole links little more interesting than a pitch-and-putt. 2. [9/82]

***Bamburgh Castle GC,*** *Bamburgh, Northumberland. Architect unknown.*

A very modest layout with some of the prettiest views in the world of golf, with the Hill District, Holy Island, and the magnificent Dunstanburgh Castle vying for the player's attention. Unfortunately, the course is not much of a test—5,400 yards all told, with some dumb goat-hill holes and an occasional good one—but for sightseeing attractions Bamburgh Castle is right at the top of my English itinerary, and it's not that far a drive from Edinburgh. 3. [9/82]

***Berwick-upon-Tweed GC,*** *Goswick, Berwick-upon-Tweed, Northumberland. Willie Park Jr., with modifications by James Braid and Fred Hawtree.*

For a course of this genealogy it has surprisingly little to recommend it: just a plain links layout with fair views down the coast toward Holy Isle. 3. [6/85]

***Brancepeth Castle GC,*** *Brancepeth, County Durham. Colt, Alison, and MacKenzie, 1924.*

Several miles to the west of the charming university town of Durham, this course is a memorable one for the several ravines which intersect it as well as the fine castle that graces its boundary. Unfortunately there are so many ravines that the routing plan resembles an obstacle course at times, which would make it a struggle for less confident golfers. But there is one monumental hole: the 200-yard 9th, playing from an elevated tee through a narrow gap in the trees across the length of a deep ravine, to a small plateau green clinging to the hillside below the castle. I came upon it at dusk so I didn't get as good a

*The 2nd green at Brancepeth Castle, located near the charming university town of Durham.*

look (or picture) as I would have liked, but it is certainly a hole that takes no prisoners, and might be one of the toughest in the world. 4. [9/82]

***Hexham GC,*** *Hexham, Northumberland. C.K. Cotton and Frank Pennink, 1956.*

A simple but pleasantly attractive parkland course in the north central part of the country, not far from Hadrian's Wall. The holes have strategic interest even though the construction is a bit basic, and there are good views down the adjoining river valley. 4. [9/82]

***Northumberland GC,*** *High Gosforth Park, Northumberland. Original layout revised by H.S. Colt and James Braid.*

One of several English courses routed through the infield of a racetrack, an early forerunner of "stadium golf." Not much can be said for the type, though, as they are of necessity mostly flat and open so as not to block sight lines for race viewing. 3. [9/82]

***Seaton Carew GC,*** *Seaton Carew, Tyneside. Revisions by Alister MacKenzie, 1925.*

This might be a reasonably good links layout, but I was too chilled by the setting to even walk the course: it occupies the fringe of an industrial wasteland between Hartlepool and Middlesborough, and the menacing cooling-tower cones of the nearby sulfuric acid plant were too reminiscent of Three Mile Island for me to concentrate on the merits of the golf. 3. [9/82]

## NORTHWEST

***Formby GC,*** *Formby, Freshfield, Liverpool. Original layout by Willie Park with revisions by H.S. Colt; new holes planned by Frank Pennink, 1978.*

A distinguished layout with an interesting variety of terrain (railside, heathland, pine tree, seaside, and true links) crammed into a small package. Unfortunately, the three holes closest to the beach (the old 8th through 10th) had to be abandoned due to coastal erosion: and while Pennink's newer holes (7-8-9) are both difficult and unusual, golfers will miss the moment of touching the shore, which added much to the links feel here. The Formby pines which line the perimeter of the course are justly famous. 7. [9/82]

***Formby Ladies' GC,*** *Freshfield, Liverpool.*

Contained within the loop of the Formby course, the relief course is run by an entirely separate ladies' club, although male visitors are welcome to play. It is of what we in America term "executive" length, but laid out over fine terrain with a couple of outstanding short holes in the mix. The big course would be proud to own the Ladies' 5th. 3. [9/82]

***Grange-over-Sands GC,*** *Grange-over-Sands, Cumbria. Alister MacKenzie, 1919.*

Even among the virtuoso architects, not every course is a gem, and this course is as low as I've seen on the MacKenzie career meter. It occupies flat ground sadly removed by a railway from some promising dunes, and I saw little to recommend it. 2. [6/85]

***Hesketh GC,*** *Southport, Merseyside. Architect unknown.*

This is the least well-known of the Southport chain of links, and rightfully so, yet the holes around the clubhouse run wild among sand dunes. The holes across the road closer to the sea, in contrast, are flat and monotonous. 4. [9/82]

***Hillside GC,*** *Southport, Merseyside. Fred Hawtree, 1962–68.*

Another big course in the dunes adjacent to Birkdale, with an even more modern aspect to its bunkers and greens. The back nine is newer and occupies much the more interesting terrain among the dunes, but I found the greens construction here especially annoying, for example the straight two-tiered cut to the par-3 16th amidst monumental undulating forms. There is one exception to my wrath: the downhill, gently twisting par-5 11th, which is the most breathtaking hole on any of the Southport courses. 5. [9/82]

***Royal Birkdale GC,*** *Southport, Merseyside. George Lowe, 1889, with substantial modifications by Fred Hawtree and J.H. Taylor, 1931, and greens revisions by Martin Hawtree, 1993.*

Among tournament players this course ranks right up alongside Muirfield as Britain's top links, but I'm not inclined to rate it so highly. Its appeal is that the design is closer in keeping with the American concept of target golf than the standard British links, with well defined fairways and greens in the valleys between impressive dunes. However, the natural problems of contour that feature so prominently on other links play little part in the course's character. You don't get odd stances, and there isn't a wide variety of holes because the dunes are constantly attacked in the same way.

Following the 1991 Open and the criticism of the greens conditioning, the club has taken the leap of rebuilding all of the greens, allowing the architect to add more contour to some in the process—the 5th and 17th are now being billed as "MacKenzie greens," but the Doctor did not specialize in the blandly two-tiered.

There are some fine holes here (though none in the world's-greatest class) and the huge dunes covered in the native willow scrub which frame the course are an impressive setting, yet I find Birkdale a place which generates little affection in my heart. 7. [4/94]

*The innocuous 8th green at Royal Liverpool (Hoylake), where Bob Jones took five to get down from the fringe on the first leg of the Grand Slam.*

***Royal Liverpool GC,*** *Hoylake, West Kirby, Wirral. Original layout by George Morris and Robert Chambers, 1869, with modifications by Braid, Colt, and Pennink.*

For those of you with a feeling for the history of English golf, Hoylake, as the home of the great champions John Ball and Harold Hilton, demands nothing less than a pilgrimage. For the rest it seems to separate the true lovers of links golf from those who only sort of understand it.

Hoylake is almost devoid of instant appeal: there are no lighthouses or railway hotels for window dressing, and the links themselves are open and flat. The challenge here is to tame the invisible enemies of wind and hard ground, and the bunkers are subtly placed to make the task harder. A simple short hole like the 13th, from a slightly raised tee to a green sheltering behind a pot bunker at front right with more bunkers guarding the left rear flank, presents a different (but never a simple) challenge with each change in the wind, favoring the cut iron approach one day and the high lofted shot the next.

Hoylake's one "signature" feature is the cops, artificial out-of-bounds hazards which come into play on several different holes, and I would hesitate to suggest they be imported to another course, but at Hoylake they must be appreciated in the context of a cheap and fearsome hazard where impressive natural hazards were few and far between. Certainly it is amusing to see just how frightened golfers can be of the deadly boundary line, as in the case of the famous "Dowie" 7th hole with a cop hard beside the left edge of the green, prompting golfers to make a flanking attack.

There are many who would contend that the cops reveal an inherent weakness in the layout of the Hoylake course, but as a study in architecture there are few courses as valuable to see, and fewer clubs more enjoyable to visit. 7. [6/83]

***Royal Lytham & St. Annes GC,*** *St. Annes-on-Sea, Lancashire. George Lowe, 1886, with revisions by Fowler, Colt, Simpson, and Pennink.*

It took a while for this course to grow on me because, like Hoylake, so many of the hazards are artificial in origin, but I've always respected the course and can now say that I have grown to really like it as well. The setting, hard against a railway line and brick row houses nearly a mile from the sea, is not awe-inspiring but can take on a certain charm in the right mood, and the clusters of small pot bunkers which direct play lend the course a look of its own, which I find very important.

The back-to-back 14th and 15th holes, at 468 yards apiece, can be absolutely brutal coming home into the wind, but I believe the last two holes constitute the perfect tournament finish—a supremely difficult 17th, where a leader might pile up a big score, followed by a birdieable 18th which places a premium on the perfect drive. On the other hand, the 206-yard opening hole is a most unusual start to a championship golf course, though for my own game at the moment a difficult long-iron shot is the perfect way to get off to a confident start. 8. [4/94]

***St. Annes Old Links GC,*** *St. Annes-on-Sea, Lancashire.*

A dullish links well removed from the sea, it nevertheless is a strategically sound layout with several good holes to recommend it, including two long par-5's to finish. The fairways are nearly dead flat, but constantly interrupted by small bunkers or cut off entirely by low hummocks. 3. [9/82]

***Silloth-on-Solway GC,*** *Silloth, Cumbria. Willie Park, Sr. and Jr., 1894.*

This is a challenging old links which produced one of the great champions of the women's game, Cecil Leitch. The course has more than its share of blind approaches over some of the many sandhills, but its natural feel and several fine holes make up for all of its sins. The excellent bunkerless par-5 13th was the best of the bunch. 5. [6/83]

***Southport & Ainsdale GC,*** *Ainsdale, Merseyside. James Braid, 1923.*

The course lies just across the railway line from Hillside, although in character the two courses are about as far apart as the drive from one clubhouse around to the other. Here the dunes are much smaller than at Birkdale, and a minefield of small pot bunkers (but not so gracefully formed as Royal Lytham's) punctuate the design. The one famous hole is the par-5 16th, with the sleepered Gumbley's cross-bunker looming ahead on the second shot, but like the rest of the course I found it a letdown. 4. [9/82]

*—Gossip—*

I never did go to Wallasey, close in to Liverpool, which in Bernard Darwin's day was the acme of blind golf holes; still, it must be worth seeing, for Darwin's comment that he didn't think he had "ever seen a course on which the contour of the hills and valleys was so infinitely picturesque." As a test of links golf, though, I'm told I shouldn't have missed West Lancashire GC, a difficult layout despite its flattish terrain and a nearby power plant for background. The links course at Castletown on the Isle of Man may also be worth the trip—it sits out on a rocky headland, and comes with its own first-class hotel.

## YORKSHIRE

***Alwoodley GC,*** *Alwoodley, Leeds. H.S. Colt and Alister MacKenzie, 1907.*

A fine heathland-type course (though there is less heather to be found here than on the Surrey courses) which was MacKenzie's first architectural collaboration, and thus worthy of a pilgrimage. The greens are big and moderately undulating and the rangy bunkers are offered in abundance, in fact becoming carried away at times. There are many fine holes, including the par-5 3rd with its green in a hollow, the two-shot 5th and 6th, the Redan 11th, and the very tight dogleg 15th. The club has a reputation for stuffiness—it has been said that no common man has ever trod its fairways—but I've got to wonder, since they let me on. 7. [9/82]

***Bingley (St. Ives) GC,*** *Bingley, Bradford. Alister MacKenzie, 1931.*

A municipally run layout adjacent to the famous Turf Research Institute, the course features an unusual combination of parkland holes set on the side of a hill opening out to four moorland holes at the summit. After the initial climb the holes are fairly interesting, though there is a notable lack of teeing space. The moorland holes are scenically memorable and good holes strategically, but they are also a messy shooting gallery of adjacent fairways, which is a disaster on such a busy course. 4. [9/82]

***Fulford GC,*** *York. Alister MacKenzie, 1920, with revisions by Donald Steel.*

Ranks right alongside Grange-over-Sands as my least impressive encounter with a MacKenzie layout: an unmemorable parkland affair. Perhaps something was lost when the course was bisected by a major highway a few years ago—the only feature Fulford shares in common with Oakmont. 3. [9/82]

***Ganton GC,*** *Ganton, Scarborough. Harry Vardon, 1899, with revisions by Braid, Colt, Fowler, Hutchison, and C.K. Cotton.*

Ganton is one of the most solid layouts I've ever played, but for some reason it's not the type of course that inspires rave reviews. Since it's not a links, it can't attract one of the British championships; it's a pleasant course, but not a scenic bombshell; and it's well removed from the major centers of British golf. What it does have is great bunkering, the making of one of the best sets of two-shot holes in the world of golf: none of them individually compelling, but complementary and collectively impressive. From the 447-yard 16th down to the 280-yard 14th with a tree placed to precision to stymie a careless tee shot, they keep you on your toes.

The club is something of a country gentlemen's affair, though after the more informal Scottish courses the standard English clubhouse dress code seems a bit out of place out here in the country. But for a course of this caliber such things are much easier to put up with. The course was also among the best conditioned I saw in Britain on my last visit, thanks to the employment of a rabbit warden. 8. [6/85]

***Harrogate GC,*** *Harrogate. Sandy Herd, 1897, with revisions by George Duncan and Alister MacKenzie.*

One of the very first inland courses in Britain, but not much of a layout. The most memorable hole is the short 3rd, with its green set just through a narrow gap in a windrow of trees. 3. [9/82]

***Ilkley GC,*** *Ilkley. Revised by Alister MacKenzie.*

A flattish parkland course laid out along the stony River Wharfe. Architecturally, the course is not a standout, but a marvelous job of landscape planting has transformed the course into one of the prettiest in the area. 3. [9/82]

***Moor Allerton Club,*** *Wike, near Leeds. Robert Trent Jones and Cabell Robinson, 1971.*

A Jewish club, and not a very well appreciated layout, as one might guess from the local joke that this is "Trent Jones' way of persecuting the Jews." On paper it probably all looked very exciting, but the 27 holes are laid out on very hilly and extremely heavy land, and it is a very difficult course to walk. 4. [9/82]

***Moortown GC,*** *Alwoodley, Leeds. Alister MacKenzie, 1909.*

Not far from Alwoodley, this is MacKenzie's first solo effort as an architect, completing the pilgrimage. The bunkering here shows greater variety and polish in construction, but I think there are fewer outstanding holes than at Alwoodley. But I don't know about the subsequent addition of two new holes, which has changed MacKenzie's pet "Gibraltar" par-3 from the 8th hole to the 10th. 6. [9/82]

***Sand Moor GC,*** *Alwoodley, Leeds. Henry Barran.*

The modern home of one of the older clubs in the area, this relatively new course features sharply cut rounded bunkers and hillier terrain than the two MacKenzie layouts. The sidehill par-3 10th is its most distinctive hole. 4. [9/82]

## MIDLANDS

***Ashridge GC,*** *Little Gaddesden, Berkhamsted, Hertfordshire. Sir Guy Campbell, S.V. Hotchkin, and C.K. Hutchison, 1932, with revisions by Tom Simpson.*

A nice parkland layout with one of my favorite holes in Britain: the short par-5 2nd. This hole is laid out along the bottom of a shallow natural valley running away toward the green, with the tee benched into the slope on the right side and a phalanx of bunkers angling in from the left just at drive's range: anything with a draw will carom inexorably off the right side of the valley and roll back up into one of the bunkers on the left, so that only a slight fade (which will reduce the chances of one's getting within range of the green in two) or a perfectly straight drive will suffice. It's a subtle design, and though the bunkering looks mild by British standards it usually requires thought. 6. [10/82]

*Don't miss your tee shot on the 13th at Notts, a 230-yard par-3.*

***The Belfry,*** *Wishaw, Staffordshire. Brabazon Course by Peter Alliss and David Thomas, 1979.*

The headquarters for the British PGA, this much-maligned layout has been Europe's Ryder Cup home since 1985, proving that a close match can make almost any course exciting. For some reason the designers have tried to bring American design concepts to British soil, but the stylized, Trent Jones–style bunkers and multiple-tiered greens, and an utterly failed attempt to imitate Pete Dye's telephone poles to line a bunker (it looks like a bunch of Lincoln logs on end in a sandbox), imitate the worst elements possible. The only exceptional hole is the short par-4 10th, with its green just beyond a small pond tempting long-hitting pros to go for broke. 4. [6/83]

***Cavendish GC,*** *Buxton, Derbyshire. Alister MacKenzie, 1923.*

A well-preserved, if modest, Alister MacKenzie design laid out for a wealthy patron among the hills south of Manchester, which, as the assistant pro informed us, features several MacKenzie-style greens. (The term is synonymous with two-tiered greens in England.) The first two holes, sidehill 340-yarders, may cause you to wonder what you're doing here, but pay attention at the 280-yard 3rd or you'll overlook a clever design with a fall-away green. The stretch of holes from the 8th through 11th, when a rushing brook comes into play, elevates the course to another class. At 5,800 yards par 68, it may not be for everyone, but Cavendish is a most pleasant setting and it's comforting to know that not every club has caved in to the pressure to standardize. 5. [4/94]

***Lindrick GC,*** *near Worksop, Nottinghamshire. Tom Dunn, 1891, with revisions by Fred W. Hawtree.*

A difficult inland layout, punctuated by gorse and trees, which until recently held the distinction of being the site for the last British Ryder Cup victory (1957). There is a good set of short holes, including, strangely, the 18th at 202 yards, but for me the best hole was the 359-yard dogleg 2nd. 5. [10/82]

***Little Aston GC,*** *Sutton Coldfield, Staffordshire. Harry Vardon, 1908, with revisions by H.S. Colt, 1925, and M.J. Lewis.*

A graceful parkland layout, perhaps the finest of that genre to be found in the British Isles (as opposed to the heathland layouts, of which there are 20 just as good). There are many fine two-shot holes, and an interesting mix of plateau and ground-level green sites, and the backcloth of silver birch and flowering rhododendrons is arresting. 6. [6/83]

***Longcliffe GC,*** *Longborough, Leicestershire. Tom Williamson, 1905.*

A modest parkland layout hemmed in by trees and ferns. The 7th, a testing par-4 along the upper course boundary, and the blind short 15th over a wooded ridge are the only two memorable holes. 3. [10/82]

***Northamptonshire County GC,*** *Church Brampton, Northamptonshire. H.S. Colt, 1911, with modifications by James Braid.*

A heathland course which is rather highly regarded by some in England, though I found it to be a rather dull affair. A profusion of gorse and some clever bunkering makes it a fairly challenging test, with some good short holes, but from my quick walk around very little stands out in memory. 5. [6/83]

***Notts Golf Club,*** *Hollinwell, Kirkby-in-Ashfield, Nottinghamshire. Willie Park Jr., 1900, with modifications by J.H. Taylor and Tom Williamson.*

A splendid and thoroughly challenging course, and one of the few in Britain which can be stretched to 7,000 yards for tournaments. There is a good variety of golf holes and of terrain, from the 2nd with its green in "Robin Hood's Chair," to the 8th with a long shot from the back tee across Hollinwell Lake, to the par-4 11th in its own mossy valley and the downhill 230-yard 13th, which is best of all. The turf is springy and fine, and the heather and ferns and birch trees enclosing the holes give the course a rich texture. 7. [10/82]

***Seacroft GC,*** *Skegness, Lincolnshire. Original layout by Tom Dunn, 1892, with revisions by Wilfrid Reid and Sir Guy Campbell.*

A good old-style links, somewhat removed from the sea by a broad marsh. Several long dune ridges are called into play in the routing, with holes running atop, transversely, and beside them. Most notable is the 13th hole, with a fine second-shot dilemma. 4. [10/82]

***Sherwood Forest GC,*** *Mansfield, Nottinghamshire. Tom Dunn, 1904, with revisions by James Braid, 1935, and Tom Williamson.*

Mediocrity, heathland style. Not really a bad course, wandering over hill and dale through the Forest (whose trees are a major disappointment, for anyone who's picturing *Robin Hood*), but there aren't any memorable holes to be found. 3. [10/82]

***Sutton Coldfield GC,*** *Sutton Coldfield, Staffordshire.*

A vastly different sort of layout than Little Aston: despite the fact that they are less than two miles apart, Sutton Coldfield is a mixture of parkland and open heath lacking the sophistication (or, I am tempted to say, breeding) of its near neighbor. 4. [6/83]

***Woburn G & CC,*** *Bow Brickhill, Milton Keynes, Buckinghamshire. Duke's course by Frank Pennink, 1970; Duchess course by Charles Lawrie and Donald Steel, 1978.*

The Duke's course is a rare shining moment in the middle ages of British golf architecture—from the reconstruction of Turnberry in 1947 until the last decade there isn't much to hold in high esteem. The routing is fairly basic, except for the short 3rd down into an amphitheater of rhododendrons, and the dogleg 4th curving uphill through a valley of tall, cathedral-like pines, but the supporting holes are set among fine trees and well-trapped to solidify the layout. 6. [11/82]

The newer Duchess course, routed by Lawrie and supervised after his death by Steel, is more heavily wooded and undulating, but somewhat shorter and more peaceful in character. It features a few tough holes, but also some tricky ones like the short 14th, with its green in an odd natural depression among the trees. 5. [11/82]

***Woodhall Spa GC,*** *Woodhall Spa, Lincolnshire. S.V. Hotchkin and C.K. Hutchison, 1926.*

See the "Gourmet's Choice." 8. [4/94]

*—Gossip—*

Up near Oxford, I always meant to get to Frilford Heath, which was the Blues' home course since Bernard Darwin's day, even if it was never a match for Mildenhall. There's also the new Rees Jones course at The Oxfordshire, which looks from pictures to be a carbon copy of The Atlantic in England. I wonder if they had to pay import duty on the design?

## EAST ANGLIA

***Aldeburgh GC,*** *Aldeburgh, Suffolk. Willie Fernie, 1894, with modifications by Willie Park and J.H. Taylor.*

Another good heathland test with a couple of unusual holes. The short 4th, with its long, narrow green bulkheaded above a bunker, is quite unexpected. 4. [6/83]

***Felixstowe Ferry GC,*** *Felixstowe, Suffolk. Rebuilt by Sir Guy Campbell, 1949, with further modifications by Henry Cotton.*

This was a pilgrimage for me, after reading of Bernard Darwin's account of the little nine-holer he played as a youth. But the layout Darwin described was seriously damaged in the war and totally abandoned upon reconstruction, leaving only the old Martello tower to stand sentinel over a dull layout. 2. [6/83]

***Hunstanton GC,*** *Hunstanton, Norfolk. George Fernie, 1892, with modifications by James Braid, 1910, and James Sherlock.*

Probably the best test of golf in East Anglia, with good length, fast greens, and the capricious winds off The Wash providing a fine natural challenge. One of the few really good courses I know without a standout hole. Also one of the friendliest clubs I've ever visited: I walked in unannounced, and within ten minutes I was a temporary honorary member. 5. [10/82]

***Royal Cromer GC,*** *Cromer, Norfolk. Old Tom Morris, 1888, with revisions by James Braid and J.R. Stutt.*

Another clifftop downland course, but with less golfing interest than Sheringham. The one noteworthy hole is the "Lighthouse" 14th, a favorite of Henry Longhurst, which lies precariously near the cliff edge. 3. [10/82]

***Royal West Norfolk GC,*** *Brancaster, Norfolk. Horace Hutchinson and Holcombe Ingleby, 1891, with revisions by C.K. Hutchison, 1928.*

Fellow architect and writer Donald Steel once told me that his ultimate golfing fantasy is to discover a gutty ball while hunting in the whins for a wayward shot. If Donald is really serious about this he is going to have to work hard at missing shots more often, but if it ever does happen it will probably be at Brancaster, for on no other links is the 19th century a more tangible prospect.

Royal West Norfolk has a lot to recommend it, but apart from the individual holes there are two particularly endearing features. The first, which you must know before you attempt a visit, is that the course is accessible only at certain times of day: the links occupy a narrow island between The Wash and a protected tidal marsh, and at high tide the approach road floods, cutting off all access for up to three hours. The links themselves are notable for the many sleepered bunkers which remain to this date, unlike at most other links, where sod faces have replaced them for stabilizing bunkers against wind erosion. At Brancaster, even some of the smallest of pot bunkers are board-faced: the place looks like it was built by a demented great-uncle of Pete Dye (who, incidentally, claims never to have seen it).

The out-and-back routing with one or two crossovers would certainly not be ideal on a crowded day, but it gets the most out of the land, though it can be most frustrating when the weather is harsh and you have to play home into a gale. But the 8th hole is in a class by itself for strategy. A short par-5 likened by Darwin to jumping from stone to stone across a marsh, challenging the bold player to make "a perilous leap from one to the other," it may tempt one into trying a difficult carry from the tee only to find, after a success, that it has only gotten him into the position of having to attempt an even more dangerous carry with his second shot in order to justify the risk of the drive. After this hole, the heroic two-shot 9th may seem trivial by comparison. 7. [4/94]

***Royal Worlington & Newmarket GC,*** *Worlington, Bury St. Edmunds, Suffolk. Tom Dunn and Captain A.M. Ross, 1892, with revisions by H.S. Colt, 1906.*

Its renown has undoubtedly been padded by the fact that as home to Cambridge University golfers, the Mildenhall nine (as it is affectionately known to Cambridge men) became familiar to such golfing luminaries as Bernard Darwin and Herbert Warren Wind at an impressionable age; but Wind saw fit to declare this "the best nine-hole course in the world," and I must simply nod in assent. Though the ground is unremarkable in contour, the course bats a perfect nine for nine, despite the interference of a public road across the 9th hole and a property so cramped that several tees are tucked into corners, requiring play across the previous green or its approach.

The genius of the course is to see how the scarce natural features of the property are employed several times each within the nine. For example, the same dip in the ground which sets off the first green continues on to become a grassy hazard behind the saucer green of the 7th and in front of the 3rd green, while a spur of this swale runs down the left side of the 3rd fairway to form the main driving hazard on that classic short par-4. Similarly, a long line of fir trees must be avoided in different ways on the approaches to the long 6th and 8th holes, and provides a stately backdrop to the vaulting-horse green of the ultra-difficult short 5th. Last but not least, the bold undulations of the greens and the fine quality of the turf are inspirational to all. Every design student should spend some time pondering how well this course works. 9. [4/94]

***Sheringham GC,*** *Sheringham, Norfolk. Original nine holes by Tom Dunn, c. 1895.*

One of the very few worthwhile downland courses I've seen in Britain: often the openness and broad undulations of "downs" terrain yield courses without sophistication, but Sheringham has some interesting greens and bunkering to it. The standout holes are the short 11th and two-shot 17th on the more inland property, but the holes along the edge of the eroding clifftop are certainly most memorable. 4. [10/82]

***Thorpeness GC,*** *Thorpeness, Suffolk. James Braid, 1923.*

A nice little heathland course with something of a Dutch atmosphere owing to its thatched-roof clubhouse and windmill behind the 18th green—which isn't illogical, considering the major trade ports to Holland lie right along this stretch of coast. Has a few interesting holes, but nothing earth-shattering. 4. [6/83]

## THE HEATHLANDS

***The Addington GC,*** *Croydon, Surrey. J.F. Abercromby, 1912.*

See the "Gourmet's Choice." 7. [6/85]

***The Berkshire GC,*** *Ascot, Berkshire. Herbert Fowler, H.S. Colt, and Tom Simpson (Red and Blue courses), 1928.*

A fine club which is the proud possessor of two appealing courses. The Red course is considered the championship layout of the two, memorable for its very unusual mix of six par-3, six par-4, and six par-5 holes: it is a makeup very conducive to birdie-making. The most outstanding individual holes are the demanding short 10th and 16th. 6. [6/85]

The Blue course is supposedly the Red's "poorer cousin," but your first look at the 217-yard 1st from the opening tee ought to convince you that things aren't going to be all that easy: this opening hole, by the way, is a forbidding stroke play opener but ideal for match play, laid out as sort of a par-3-1/2 so as to allow the confident player a go at the green with a 2-iron, but give the fainthearted or unlimber a safe way around with a 5-iron shot out to the left. The rest of the Blue course is not quite so daunting but probably a tougher course to return a low score than the Red, and certainly its fine two-shot finishing hole is an improvement over the Red's weak par-3 18th. 6. [11/82]

***Camberley Heath GC,*** *Camberley, Surrey. H.S. Colt, 1913, with modifications by Donald Steel.*

This is not a big course like most of the others around London, and it is somewhat crowded into a long, narrow property, yet it is a charming layout which provides plenty of golf for all but the champions. Its standout holes include the parallel three-shot 3rd and 13th, the short 8th, and two good two-shotters to finish. Comparable to a small, beautifully landscaped white house stuck on Millionaire's Row in Newport. 5. [6/83]

***Coombe Hill GC,*** *Kingston Hill, Surrey. J.F. Abercromby, 1909.*

Just another (yawn) excellent little heathland layout, although there isn't quite as wide a carpet of heather as a buffer between fairways and the trees, as at Sunningdale or some other courses. The short holes are a superb set. As a fairly exclusive club, you'd better make advance arrangements if you wish to try it. 6. [11/82]

***Crowborough Beacon GC,*** *Crowborough, East Sussex. Architect unknown.*

This really is not a bad course at all, with two thrilling holes in the downhill par-4 2nd beside a deep ravine, and the par-3 6th angling across the same hazard. But overall the course is just not up to the competition listed. An additional thrill for me was catching up with an elderly lady member, Miss Enid Wilson, who won the British Ladies' Championship in 1931-32-33 before retiring from competition. 4. [10/82]

***Foxhills GC,*** *Ottershaw, Surrey. Longcross and Chertsey courses by Fred Hawtree, 1974.*

A fairly new golf and leisure complex, with two semi-heath layouts modeled on American design principles. They aren't bad tracks, but in the midst of all these classic heathland courses, why would anybody want to play an American-type course? It's no wonder the development is suffering. 4. [11/82]

***Hankley Common GC,*** *Frensham, Surrey. James Braid, 1922.*

My friend Ken Macpherson thinks this is one of the best of the heath courses, but I wasn't that impressed by my one walk around, especially considering the competition. It's a bit less tree-lined and more open to the wind than the norm, but the only really memorable hole I saw was the short 7th. 4. [6/85]

***Hindhead GC,*** *Hindhead, Surrey. Architect unknown.*

By no means one of the best courses in the area, Hindhead must still be considered an attraction for the novelty of several holes on the front nine which are laid out through the deepest, narrowest valleys I've encountered. There are some very good holes, including the long 4th and 5th, but most memorable of all is the short par-5 2nd, where it is difficult to convince a golfer standing on its elevated back tee for the first time that there actually is a golf hole down there to play. 4. [10/82]

***Liphook GC,*** *Liphook, Hampshire. Arthur C. Croome, 1920, with modifications by Tom Simpson and J.S.F. Morrison.*

This is Croome's only solo effort as a designer, and a course of some sophistication, although I would not go as far as Simpson, who pronounced it in his opinion "the best inland course in Britain"; in fact, I must admit I was just a bit disappointed on my most recent visit. The course is quite short and the bunker placement most unusual, and though a couple of the greens require cunning approaches, they are not as dramatic to the eye as one would gather from the drawings in Simpson's book. It's a course worth study, but for American golfers on tour I must say there are many other courses which supersede it. 5. [4/94]

***London Kosaido G & CC*** *(formerly Old Thorns G & CC), Liphook, Hampshire. Peter Alliss and David Thomas, 1982.*

The most lavish design project of the Alliss/Thomas partnership, featuring both the best and the worst of their work all in one place. The terrain is more hilly parkland than heathland and the soil is heavy, which never helps, but there are a few holes, such as the long par-4 3rd and 18th, which show great potential. Others, such as the par-5 17th and the dogleg 1st with its huge guardian oak, have character but questionable strategic value; and still others, like the short par-4 15th, must be among the worst holes on the planet. To be sympathetic, it was a difficult site to work with and the architects got a decent amount out of it, but with Liphook just down the road they were doomed by comparison from the start. 4. [11/82]

***New Zealand GC,*** *West Byfleet, Surrey. Tom Simpson, 1931.*

A small course of only 6,012 yards, with only three two-shot holes of more than 420 yards, but a fine test for shorter hitters. The sunken bunkers fringed with heather have a rudimentary but unique look to them, and a couple of the shorter holes (particularly the 317-yard 8th) are worthy of Woking when the course is playing fast. 5. [12/82]

***North Hants GC,*** *Fleet, Hampshire. James Braid, 1904.*

Forget the date: this is one of the more modern-looking of the heath courses. It's fairly long and difficult and possesses several memorable holes, especially the short 8th. The long par-4 17th is a less fearsome version of the Road hole at St. Andrews. 5. [12/82]

***Piltdown GC,*** *Uckfield, East Sussex. G.M. Dodd.*

Another common-land course without a bunker, but this one does not benefit from the spectacular terrain of Ashdown Forest, and so the holes aren't as impressive either. Would be a worthwhile experience if you couldn't just go up the road to Forest Row. But wouldn't you love to live in a town named Uckfield? 3. [10/82]

***Reigate Heath GC,*** *Reigate, Surrey. Architect unknown.*

A heathland nine-holer which places very highly among all the courses I've seen of that length. The first five holes hold up to the starting five of any of the other Surrey courses listed here, but from the 6th through 8th the course really peters out badly. The short 9th back up to the small clubhouse makes for a pretty if not overly demanding finish. 5. [6/85]

***Royal Ashdown Forest GC,*** *Forest Row, East Sussex. Old course, A.T. Scott, 1891.*

This must be one of the most natural courses in the world, by law: it lies entirely within a Royal forest, and the club leases the land for golf only on the promise not to make any artificial construction on the ground, including sand bunkers. All that has been done is to level off tee and green sites, establish fairways (many of them starting only after a heroic carry over wilderness from the back tees), and let fly. Needless to say, not every hole is a wonder, but most modern golf architects (who almost universally move too much dirt) could benefit from careful study of such holes as the 5th, 6th, 7th, 12th, and 17th, which are worth consideration for any list of great holes with no help from the bulldozers. Only an ogre would allow the occasional awkward hole to spoil the beauties of a game at Ashdown Forest. 7. [4/94]

***Royal Wimbledon GC,*** *Wimbledon. H.S. Colt, 1908, with modifications by Charles Lawrie.*

One of the few clubs left (along with Wimbledon Common and Royal Blackheath) where the golfer is required to wear red while playing, part of the ancient tradition. The course is not pure heathland in character (parts could be described as—gasp!—parkland), but is memorable for a couple of good short holes, as well as the ancient Roman camp which one plays over from the 6th tee. 4. [11/82]

***St. George's Hill GC,*** *Weybridge, Surrey. Harry S. Colt, 1913.*

See the "Gourmet's Choice." 8. [4/94]

***Stoke Poges GC,*** *Slough, Buckinghamshire. Harry S. Colt, 1908, with revisions by J. Hamilton Stutt.*

I must begin with the clarification that this is not, in truth, a heathland course—like most of those in the northwest quadrant of London it is parkland in nature, but since it's the only one of those I have inspected, I squeezed it in here instead of giving it its own separate category. The course is graceful but not, in truth, all that special; even the short 7th, cut out of a woodland to an angled green just across a stream, is a bit more subdued than its advance billing. But the magnificent clubhouse, "a dazzling vision of white stone" (in Darwin's words) built for the Penn family in 1775, is in a class by itself, and the towering monument to Sir Edward Coke, the first Lord Chief Justice of England and former owner of the estate, makes a most interesting target at the far end of the practice range. 5. [4/94]

***Sunningdale GC,*** *Sunningdale, Berkshire. Old course by Willie Park, 1901, with revisions by H.S. Colt; New course by Colt, 1922.*

The debate rages on at Sunningdale over which of its two courses is the premier. History has been on the side of the Old course since 1926, when Bob Jones returned a "perfect" 66 (with about seven missed putts inside eight feet) in Open qualifying. It's certainly the more charming of the two sisters, and possesses the most outstanding individual holes on the property, with a great stretch of two-shotters from the 5th through 7th, and another at the 10th through 12th; but it also possesses the two or three poorest holes in the 36. Meanwhile, the New course is slightly longer and stronger, with fewer memorable individual holes but no weak links. Add in the posh clubhouse facilities, and the sum total of Sunningdale is one of the finest days' worth of golf you could arrange. Old course: 8. New course: 7. [4/94]

*Sunningdale, Old and New, is heathland golf at its best. This is the par-5 6th hole of the New course.*

**Swinley Forest GC,** *Ascot, Berkshire. H.S. Colt, 1910.*

Its creator once described Swinley Forest as "the least bad course" he had ever built, proving Colt was no Muhammad Ali when it came to self-promotion; most architects would kill to be able to claim this course for their own. At 6,001 yards from the back tees, it will never win a match of cards, but it is hardly a pushover: in place of par-5 holes Colt built six two-shotters of over 430 yards, a few shorter par fours to replace the birdie opportunities lost in the absence of par-5's, and five short holes which any course would be proud to own.

Add to this the quiet ambiance of the heathland setting—Swinley is possibly the most exclusive golf club in Britain, frequented by the diplomatic corps—and you've discovered one of the hidden treasures of English golf, if you can wangle your way to see it for yourself. 8. [6/85]

**Walton Heath GC,** *Tadworth, Surrey. Old course by Herbert Fowler, 1908; New course extended to 18 holes from Fowler's third nine by James Braid.*

I must confess that I always used to hedge my rating of the Old course at Walton Heath out of respect for Ken Macpherson, the longtime professional who was such a help to me in my year overseas. But I never was actually fond of the course until I revisited it this past year and saw it at peak form, with a strong breeze in our faces on the outgoing holes, for which I now carry an eternal respect. The 1st and 3rd holes are a bit dull, but everything else on the outward half is truly outstanding—best of all the dogleg 5th with a stunningly contoured green. The inward half also commands respect, in particular the short 11th and the par-5 14th and 16th. The heather here is the thickest on any of the London area courses, so the setting can be beautiful or bleak depending on how you're hitting it, but never again will I underestimate Mr. Fowler's masterpiece. 8. [4/94]

The New course is quite similar to the Old, but the bunkering is not quite as deep or as critically

placed in most cases. There are a couple of very good long holes at the 5th and 14th, though, and the cross-bunkered 18th is used as the finishing hole for the Old course in major events. 6. [4/83]

***Wentworth Club,*** *Virginia Water, Surrey. East and West courses by Colt, Alison, and Morrison, 1924.*

The posh home of the World Matchplay Championship, Wentworth has a great following among tournament players and TV spectators, but is not nearly my favorite of the heathland clubs. The championship West course, dubbed the "Burma Road" by returning W.W. II vets, is Britain's longest and most unrelenting inland course, with some very good holes to its credit (such as the 2nd, 8th, and 12th), but overall I think it has become vastly overrated from overexposure. For example, the long par-5 17th is a dull, curving dogleg hole with a semi-blind approach and out-of-bounds as its only significant hazard, but the exploits of Palmer and Sandy Lyle have turned it into one of Britain's most famous holes (much like the 16th at Firestone, only this hole has even less to recommend it). The Burma Road is comparable to Medinah No. 3 and Butler National as a tough course that would benefit from finishing school. 6. [4/94]

Wentworth's East course, which hardly anyone ever looks at anymore, is by contrast a much more charming and less brutal course on which mortals can enjoy the game again. There are few world-class holes, but this is a fine overall test. 6. [10/82]

***West Hill GC,*** *Brookwood, Surrey. Tom Simpson, I think.*

At one particular four-corners intersection near Woking, three of the four corners belong to this, Woking and Worplesdon—all excellent layouts. Of the three, West Hill is not my favorite but it's probably the most challenging, thanks especially to the 210-yard 15th and a complement of difficult short holes. 5. [11/82]

***West Sussex GC,*** *Pulborough, West Sussex. C.K. Hutchison, Sir Guy Campbell and S.V. Hotchkin, 1930.*

My "Gourmet's Choice" selections must be pretty strong in order to have left this course out: in many respects, I think it is the most idyllic of all the heathlands' magnificent courses. With only one long hole (the 1st) and five par-3's it hasn't got the makeup of the standard championship course, but there are as many good holes here as on any course you could name, and the setting is all one could ask for: somehow, the grass seems greener, the sand whiter, and the heather a deeper purple than at Wentworth or Sunningdale. (But that must be an illusion, since Wentworth buys the sand for its bunkers from Pulborough.) Don't miss this course. 7. [11/82]

***Woking GC,*** *Hook Heath, Woking, Surrey. Original layout by Tom Dunn, 1893, with major alterations by Stuart Paton and John Low, 1901–1915.*

I wish I had room for this course in the "Gourmet's Choice," but the cunning layout plays extremely short nowadays and I'm not sure all of you would appreciate it.

A small, quiet club these days, you might never guess that Woking was the most fashionable of the heathland clubs at the turn of the century, a bit on the order of Swinley Forest today, complete with the iconoclastic rules about not having a par or a course rating. Most of the members traveled to their Scottish estates to escape the heat of the summers, and this allowed two club members, John Low and Stuart Paton, to turn the Woking course into a sort of "proving grounds" of golf architecture. (For a full, entertaining account of the goings-on, read Darwin's *Golf Courses of the British Isles,* c. 1910.]

Every summer, Low and Paton chose one or two of the least inspiring of Tom Dunn's holes and set about to make it interesting, adding bunkers and recontouring the greens until the hole required thoughtful position play. Their first project was the short par-4 4th; with a central fairway hazard and a slight tilting of the green they produced a hole similar to the 16th on the Old Course at St. Andrews, much to the consternation of the members. (Darwin's account of this was my own inspiration for the 10th at Piping Rock.) A couple of Low and Paton's holes were eventually deemed unsatisfactory and modified, but greens such as the 2nd, 5th, 12th, 13th, and 15th are fine examples of their genius, and the dogleg 3rd hole features one of the trickiest approaches I've ever seen.

Today, at 6,400 yards, Woking is definitely too short for top-flight play, especially since the design expresses itself best when the course is playing its fastest, and all the slopes have more influence. But I feel sorry for those of you who are "too good" to enjoy it, because for the members Woking remains a tricky, fun golf course which calls for the soul of an architect to master its difficulties. For anyone who really wants to be a golf architect, I heartily recommend it as one of the most rewarding courses in the world you can see. 7. [4/94]

***Worplesdon GC,*** *Worplesdon, Woking, Surrey. J.F. Abercromby, 1908, with revisions by H.S. Colt.*

This was certainly the best-conditioned and among the most pleasant courses we played on our last trip to England, though it is neither as difficult as West Hill nor as cunning as Woking. The par-4 1st out behind the pro shop is a memorable starting hole, and the four holes across the A322 road are outstanding—especially the simple but brilliant par-5 11th, a favorite of Tom Simpson's. Unfortunately, though, the most memorable aspect of the course was having to cross the A322 amid heavy traffic—it's the most dangerous road crossing I've had to make in golf shoes. 6. [4/94]

*—Gossip—*

I don't think there are many more vintage layouts in Surrey and Berkshire which I haven't seen by now, with the important exception of Royal Mid-Surrey. But I've never really gotten around to the northwest of London at all, and therefore must recommend Huntercombe, Northwood, Hadley Wood, and Moor Park (with its mansion of a clubhouse) only from second-hand information.

This area is also the center of new-course development in England, even if none of the new tracks are truly "heathland" in character. Working anticlockwise around the ring road of London there's Jack Nicklaus II's Hanbury Manor, a country-club setup on the site of an old estate; Robert Trent Jones, Jr.'s Wisley GC right near Woking; Bob Cupp's two much-heralded courses at East Sussex National (although much of the press attention there has been directed to fast American-style greens); Jack Nicklaus' two courses at The London Golf Club (mixed reviews); and Chart Hills, the first project of the new partnership of Steve Smyers and Nick Faldo, which has some dramatic (and maybe "over the top") bunkering. I have a hard time taking any of these courses seriously, though; they must look like Frank Lloyd Wright mansions set down in between Victorian houses.

## ENGLISH CHANNEL

***Hayling GC,*** *Hayling Island, Hampshire. Original layout dating to 1888, with major revisions by Tom Simpson.*

A good, largely forgotten links layout to the east of Southampton, with fine views toward the Isle of Wight. The course gets off to a slow start, but from the 7th through the 14th is a fine run of holes featuring some of Simpson's strategic genius. 4. [6/83]

***Littlestone GC,*** *Littlestone, New Romney, Kent. Original layout by W. Laidlaw Purves, with alterations by F.W. Maude, Tom Dunn, and James Braid.*

Similar in setting to Deal, Littlestone suffers from a heavier soil, which does not support the crisp turf that makes links play such a joy. However, the design includes a number of very good strategic holes, most notably the short 17th and the long 16th, which was one of Charles Blair Macdonald's British favorites. 5. [10/82]

***Prince's GC,*** *Sandwich, Kent. Present 27 holes rebuilt after W.W. II by J.S.F. Morrison and Sir Guy Campbell, 1948.*

A long and difficult 27-hole layout, replacing the classic 18, which was badly scarred by German bombs in the Battle of Britain. In contrast to its next-door neighbor, Sandwich, the links are full of low rippling undulations, but there are no large dunes to distinguish it. The course also comes a bit too close for my tastes to the nuclear power plant at Ramsgate at its far end. 5. [10/82]

***Royal Cinque Ports GC,*** *Deal, Kent. Original layout by Tom Dunn, 1895, with revisions by Sir Guy Campbell, 1939.*

A course that must be played to be properly appreciated. It lies very close to the largest dunes on the Sandwich links, yet here the undulations of the links are not so severe, with a high sea wall shadowing the holes closest to the coast and blocking water views. But there are some outstanding features to the layout, from the beautiful undulations of the 2nd and 3rd to the ancient Roman track road which must be avoided at the 12th, and finally some of the most difficult par-4's in all of golf into the wind at the finish—hardest of all the long 16th with its green perched defiantly on a steep-faced dune. 6. [4/94]

***Royal Eastbourne GC,*** *Eastbourne, East Sussex. Charles Mayhewe and Horace Hutchinson, 1886, with revisions by J. Hamilton Stutt.*

A famous downland/parkland layout with very little to recommend it today, other than history. The present 9th green with its two tiers was once one of the most famous in Britain when the approach had to come from over Paradise wood, but today the only memorable hazard is the cavernous "Chalk Pit," which will devour a dubbed drive off the 3rd tee. 2. [10/82]

***Royal St. George's GC,*** *Sandwich, Kent. Original layout by W. Laidlaw Purves, 1887, with revisions by Alister MacKenzie and Frank Pennink.*

It is hard for me to fathom the bad reputation that Sandwich got in the Opens of 1981 and 1985. Certainly it is a difficult course to know at first glance, and with the holes wandering among huge sand dunes on an apparently endless acreage, it must be a lonely place when it's gray and windy and one is struggling to keep pace in a championship. But in any other circumstance, the scenery and scale of the course are inspiring, and I'm much more inclined to agree with Bernard Darwin's passionate declaration that Sandwich is "as nearly my idea of heaven as is to be attained on any earthly links."

Several of the famous blind holes which were responsible for the course's early renown, including the "Sahara" 3rd and "Maiden" 6th, have been changed in modern times, but there are still several holes where the large dunes are integral to the play, and so much the better—I vastly prefer this approach to that of Birkdale, where the holes are all confined to the valleys and the dunes are no more than

elaborately shaped backdrops. The front nine is the more dramatic, with hazards like the three-story bunker at the 4th, while the back nine is especially long and menacing, but much flatter after the precarious 10th green.

There is history, too—indeed, a "Trivial Pursuit" history of golf could almost be confined to championships at Royal St. George's, where J.H. Taylor was the first Englishman to capture the Open in 1894; Walter Travis the first Australian-born (and first American citizen) to win the Amateur in 1904; Walter Hagen the first American Open champion in 1922; Henry Cotton set the 36-hole scoring record for the Open, which is still on the books since 1934; and Bobby Locke the first South African to win the Open in 1947. Don't deny yourself the opportunity to make your own history here. 8. [4/94]

***Rye GC,*** *Camber, Rye, East Sussex. Original layout by H.S. Colt and Douglas Rolland, 1894, with revisions by Tom Simpson in 1932, Sir Guy Campbell in 1938, and Major H.C. Tippet in 1947.*

See the "Gourmet's Choice." 9. [4/94]

## SOUTHWEST

***Broadstone GC,*** *Broadstone, Poole, Dorset. Tom Dunn, 1907, with revisions by H.S. Colt, 1920, and Herbert Fowler.*

Bernard Darwin once called Broadstone "the Gleneagles of the South," and its wide fairways isolated from one another by thick heather do have a bit of the same look. Far from being a touristy American resort, however, this is a fairly stuffy club, as you might expect from the home of the Parliamentary Golfing Society. But at least they're not offensive about it like at Ferndown, and the course is worth a little trouble to play, with splendid holes like the Redan 11th and dogleg 13th, and the epic 420-yard 7th. 6. [6/83]

***Burnham & Berrow GC,*** *Burnham-on-Sea, Somerset. Original layout dating to 1891, with many revisions, most recently by Fred W. Hawtree, 1973.*

The Olympus of blind golf in the days of Darwin and J.H. Taylor, Burnham today has eliminated most of its blind approaches (and possibly some of its character) to become a more respected layout among towering sandhills. The first three holes, along with the short 5th and 17th, were my favorites, but as much as anything I will remember the course for the unusual bunker (a brick air-raid shelter) at the 10th, a reminder that the Second World War disrupted life throughout England and not just in the capital. 5. [12/82]

*One of the many vistas at Isle of Purbeck.*

***Ferndown GC,*** *Ferndown, Dorset. Original layout by Harold Hilton, with extension by J. Hamilton Stutt.*

I really didn't get a good look at this one, as the club secretary wanted to charge me a green fee just to walk around: it certainly isn't the most hospitable place I've visited. The course is heathland, and some sprawling bunkers have been employed to make up for rather modest topographical interest, but I don't really have much interest in going back to find out. 5. [6/85]

***Isle of Purbeck GC,*** *Studland, Swanage, Dorset. Club founded 1893, with modifications by H. S. Colt, 1925.*

One of the real hidden gems of England, the Isle of Purbeck's unique setting within a protected heathland wilderness area high above Bournemouth harbor is a powerful recommendation in itself, but the course also possesses several fine holes of which the dogleg 5th is most memorable. The club is owned and operated by the Robinson family, and I was greeted very warmly. 6. [6/85]

***Manor House Hotel GC,*** *Moretonhampstead, Devon. J.F. Abercromby, 1930, with modifications by James Alexander.*

A short, tricky inland layout high in the hills near Dartmoor, Moretonhampstead isn't a championship venue by any stretch of the imagination, but I would defy even the best players to successfully avoid the winding brook which comes into play on nearly every shot for the first eight holes. The course reaches higher ground at the 9th and takes a sharp turn for the worse. While I wouldn't recommend the course highly, a drive through the nearby Dartmoor is way up on my list of sightseeing attractions in England. 3. [12/82]

***Parkstone GC,*** *Poole, Dorset. Original layout by Willie Park, 1910, with major revisions by James Braid, 1927, and J. Hamilton Stutt.*

Another well-heeled club, but the course has a much more modern look to it, featuring hilly terrain and a relative paucity of bunkers: sort of an English cousin to Augusta, with less bold greens. The long 3rd and the par-3 finishing hole were quite good, but no match for the Amen corner. 5. [6/83]

*The 18th tee at Parkstone, an English cousin of Augusta.*

*Saunton's sea grasses haven't yet been overrun by visitors.*

***Royal North Devon GC,*** *Westward Ho!, Devon. Original layout by Old Tom Morris, 1864, with major changes by Herbert Fowler in 1908.*

See the "Gourmet's Choice." 6. [6/85]

***St. Enodoc GC,*** *Rock, Wadebridge, Cornwall. James Braid, 1907–36.*

See the "Gourmet's Choice." 7. [12/82]

***Saunton GC,*** *Saunton, Devon. East course originally laid out by Herbert Fowler, 1922, and rebuilt after W.W. II by Cotton and Pennink, 1952; West course by Frank Pennink, 1973.*

The sandhills of Saunton, an extension of the nationally protected Braunton Burrows, must be among the largest on any British links, but the biggest dunes are tight along the coast and unfortunately the golf courses can employ them only for backdrop. The East course enjoys considerable support as one of the best links courses in Britain, but I would not go that far in my support for it: the very unusual mix of eleven two-shot holes in the first twelve certainly does not fulfill Herbert Warren Wind's test that each hole be distinctly memorable, even though there are a number of good holes in the stretch, and the 472-yard 1st is enough to cause a heart attack for those expecting to match par without a rigorous warm-up session. The short 13th and par-4 16th are excellent holes, but the rest do not stack up as well. 6. [12/82]

The par-4 1st hole of the West course heads straight into the largest of the dunes from the clubhouse, but the course turns around and comes right back out of the promising terrain at the 2nd, and after that start it must rate a disappointment. 5. [12/82]

***West Cornwall GC,*** *Lelant, St. Ives, Cornwall. Architect unknown.*

A look at golf as the game was probably intended to be: a rugged links layout over a minimal stretch of ground, completely exposed to the mercy of the weather. Even though it is crammed together the course does offer some memorable holes, such as the two-shot 4th, where the ideal line from the tee is blasphemously close to an old church and not recommended for those with a vivid imagination, and never on Sunday. The views of St. Ives sands at low tide are also stunning on a bright day. In case you were wondering how close the course gets to the water, a note from the local rules on the scorecard: "When playing the 6th and 7th holes a ball lying in, or within two club lengths of a boat, may be lifted and dropped not nearer the hole without penalty." (Any time the British allow a free drop, you're dealing with a serious hazard.) 3. [12/82]

## WALES

Wales is not exactly a popular tourist destination, nor a center of development in the UK; with its coal and steel industries on the decline, its economy is comparable to that of central Pennsylvania. On the other hand, there's some dramatic scenery, and the joy that comes with uncrowded golf courses. Porthcawl and Harlech are the standard-bearing championship links for south and north, but for me the character of Welsh golf will always be in wild and woolly venues like Nefyn and Pennard.

*The natural golf terrain at Royal St. David's can't be denied.*

***Aberdovey GC,*** *Aberdovey, Gwynedd. Club founded 1893; present layout includes revisions by Braid, Colt, and Fowler.*

A pilgrimage for a dedicated reader of Bernard Darwin, who developed his love for the game over these links as a youth. It has changed considerably since Darwin's youth, and not always for the best, in the case of the famous "Cader" short hole, where a sandhill has been cut away to afford a limited view of the target. (Originally, a periscope afforded a look over the hill at the ghastly bunker which must also be cleared with the tee shot, and one can only imagine the masochistic temptation for club members of the day to peek at the hazard which they would have been better advised to put out of their minds.) But other things are well preserved: the fine short 12th with its green high in the dunes near the shore, the intriguing 288-yard 16th, which all too closely follows the curve of the railway line, and the unpretentious clubhouse, which lies just down the track from the station. 5. [4/83]

***Ashburnham GC,*** *Pembrey, Dyfed. J.H. Taylor, 1914, with revisions by Fred Hawtree and C.K. Cotton.*

By contrast with others in Wales, this is a very well-groomed links, with several interesting holes in the mix. Best of all is the par-5 14th, with its green in a slight hollow closely surrounded by small dunes to cause trouble for the long hitter who goes for the green with his second and fires wide. 5. [12/82]

***Borth & Ynyslas GC,*** *Borth. H.S. Colt.*

A modest links for a small town, neither very long nor especially alarming in appearance, but which still requires some playing in a wind. 2. [5/83]

***Caernarvonshire GC,*** *Conwy. Original links revised by Frank Pennink.*

A short drive from Llandudno across the Telford Suspension Bridge and past Conwy Castle, this more modern-looking links abounds with gorse bushes, calling for straight tee shots or heavy clothing if you wish to complete play with a single ball. You may recognize the surroundings from the Dou-

*Nefyn's cliffs are reminiscent of Pebble Beach.*

glas Adam series of prints, "The Drive," etc., which depict play at Conwy. 3. [5/83]

***Holyhead GC,*** *Holyhead, Anglessey. James Braid, 1912.*

A stunning show of green fairways amid outcrops of white granite and banks of gorse, the Holyhead course has the crisp air of a links (and better views to the sea than many courses of that variety), but a more inland character to its turf. Sadly, the holes are confined and not particularly noteworthy. 3. [5/83]

***Nefyn & District GC,*** *Morfa Nefyn. Original architect unknown; some revisions to layout by Fred Hawtree and A.H.F. Jiggens.*

This is without question one of the most memorable courses I've seen. All golf courses are supposed to challenge the player to grapple with the terrain and the elements, but at very few other courses does the challenge become so severe as to smack of survivalism.

Even though the cliffside 2nd and 3rd holes are vaguely reminiscent of Pebble Beach, for all intents and purposes Nefyn begins and ends on the narrow spit of land which comprises the last eight holes. The alarming tee shot across a deep chasm at the 13th would make it a great hole were it not for the vagaries of the rock outcroppings to either side of the green; but for all its glories, *the* hole at Nefyn must be the par-5 12th. From the back of the tee, the drive appears to head straight off into the Irish sea, so much so that I would think that even 30-year members must walk forward to reassure themselves there is a fairway ahead down below on which to light; that accomplished, the second shot must surmount a hill and avoid a monstrous sinkhole in the middle of the fairway just short of the green (from which one is allowed a free drop, but there is no chance of recovering a lost ball). Be sure to look over the cliff edge to the right of the green—there's a tiny fishing village sheltered below, including the neighborhood pub, the Ty Coch Inn, if your score is adding up too quickly. As an attraction Nefyn would rate much higher, but as a golf course: 4. [5/83]

***North Wales GC,*** *Llandudno. Architect unknown.*

A rudimentary links layout which is remembered for the clever names attributed to two short holes near the finish: the long, difficult, semi-blind 16th, "O.L.", and the much shorter and easier 17th, "L.O." 3. [5/83]

*The 18th at Pennard is a keen finish to a special day of golf.*

***Pennard GC,*** *Pennard, Mid-Glamorganshire. Architect unknown.*

One of my all-time favorites, but I hesitate to recommend it for general consumption; it's awfully quirky. The site, on a promontory of undulating ground between the sea and the "Pill" (a deep stream valley), is one of the most spectacular I've ever seen—even Jack Nicklaus would be tempted to sit down and take it all in at the 7th, where you drive over a deep valley to a tight fairway between the ruins of a castle and an ancient church, before an approach to a hidden green that plunges criminally away from the line of the shot. And there are certainly a few memorable holes, in particular the three long holes at the finish. But the conditioning is very iffy, and the terrain is probably a little too spectacular for the tastes of many. The course is home to Vicki Thomas, who played on the last four British Curtis Cup squads; next to Pennard, other courses must look tame to her. 6. [6/85]

***Pwllheli GC,*** *Pwllheli. Original layout by Old Tom Morris, 1900; extended to 18 by James Braid.*

A very simple little course with one of those Welsh names that's so easy to pronounce. Morris' original four holes along the coast (now the 7th through the 10th) are memorable, but the inland holes are rather undistinguished, with one exception: the par-4 17th. 3. [5/83]

***Pyle & Kenfig GC,*** *Pyle, Porthcawl, Glamorganshire. H.S. Colt, 1922, extended to 18 holes by Mackenzie Ross, with revisions by J. Hamilton Stutt.*

The front nine, on the inland side of the road, is completely forgettable, but the second nine gets into some rough dune country and there are some real golf holes, particularly in the stretch of the 11th through 13th. 4. [12/82]

***Royal Porthcawl GC,*** *Porthcawl, Glamorganshire. H.S. Colt, 1913, with revisions by Hawtree, Braid, Simpson, and C.K. Cotton.*

Porthcawl is unquestionably Wales' most suitable championship venue, an excellent layout on a particularly exposed piece of coastline, making it a more likely prospect for really severe weather than any of the championship links except Turnberry. One of the course's claims to fame is that it is the only championship links on which the sea is in view from every hole, although part of the reason for that is that much of the layout wanders up onto higher ground well removed from the shore—so far that the 6th through 9th holes are not on linksland at all, even though the first three holes are practically *in* the sea. I disagree with those who believe the par-5 holes to be the class of the course: I thought they were the weakest links in the chain, but mostly because I liked the rest of the holes so much. 7. [12/82]

***Royal St. David's GC,*** *Harlech. Original layout by Harold Finch-Hatton; modifications to present layout by Fred Hawtree.*

Few courses can offer as impressive a first sight as Harlech, approached from the high south road with the links stretching out on the inland side of a massive dune range far below, the imposing Harlech castle standing sentinel, and the mountainous Snowdonia region in the near distance. Unfortunately, the links can never live up to this first impression: they are mostly trapped inland from the gargantuan dunes, and only the stretch of holes from the 14th through the 17th penetrates the country we long to play over. Still, that is enough to provide two very distinctive par-4 holes in the 15th and 17th, each of which weighs in at 435 yards. 5. [4/83]

*From the 2nd at Southerndown, Porthcawl is visible on the horizon.*

***Southerndown GC,*** *Bridgend, Ewenny, Glamorganshire. Willie Fernie, 1905, with revisions by Willie Park, Herbert Fowler, and H.S. Colt.*

Far and away the best "downland" course I've seen in the British Isles—and no wonder, with the architectural credits above. The clubhouse occupies a magnificent prospect high on the downs above the Bristol Channel, with marvelous views across a long range of dunes toward Porthcawl, seven miles in the distance, and the first few holes of the course offer similar views before the course turns away to the south. The course is plenty long at 6,615 yards, if not almost too demanding, with the profusion of gorse about and a strict par of 70, but there are many outstanding individual holes to be savored, winding up with the double-decked fairway of the 18th. Definitely worth checking out if you make it as far as Porthcawl. 6. [12/82]

***Tenby GC,*** *Tenby, Mid-Glamorganshire. C.K. Cotton.*

This is an almost unmaintained links with more of a downland variety of turf (replete with clover), but some very interesting holes. The short par-4 3rd is one of Wales' most beautiful, with magnificent sprawls of sand behind the raised green; and the naturally eroded bunkers along the dunes to the left of the 4th fairway are also worth a close look. But it's definitely not for turf-nursery fans. 4. [4/83]

### —*Gossip*—

The only other course I've heard anything about is the "golf complex" at St. Pierre in Chepstow, an inland course and resort which hosted the Curtis Cup several years ago.

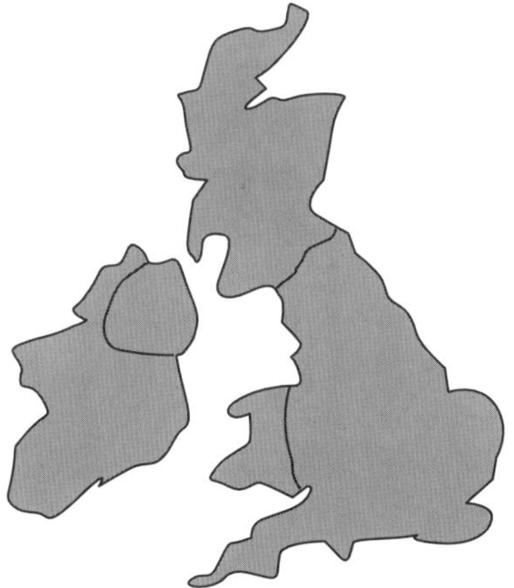

## NORTHERN IRELAND

Anyone who has watched the evening news over the past 30 years must have just a slight twinge of trepidation over the safety of traveling to Northern Ireland, despite the success so far of the recent cease-fire. Strangely, I've never traveled anywhere with more peaceful scenery, and because tourism is one of the cornerstones of the economy both here and in the south, even the IRA has a vested interest in avoiding incidents involving tourists. I don't believe the threat is worth worrying about, although that won't prevent the queasiness in your stomach when you first see a British security patrol sweep through a small town, armed with automatic weapons. And truce or no truce, I wouldn't spend any time in Belfast or Londonderry, where the violence is much less well organized.

***Castlerock GC,*** *Castlerock, County Londonderry. Ben Sayers, 1901.*

A modestly interesting links layout in a picturesque small town just the other side of Coleraine from Portrush. However, few of the holes are in the dunes, and the rail line affects more holes than they do. 4. [5/85]

***Malone GC,*** *Upper Malone, Belfast. Frank Pennink.*

A fine club occupying an old estate, with a good parkland course laid out across the hills. There are some particularly strong and interesting holes on the front side, including the par-5 3rd and the long dogleg par-4 7th; but I still don't think they're enough to justify a pit stop between Portrush and Newcastle. 5. [4/94]

***Royal County Down GC,*** *Newcastle, County Down. Original layout by Old Tom Morris, 1889, with revisions by Seymour Dunn and Harry Vardon.*

A few years ago, *GOLF Magazine* ranked these links #3 in the world, causing quite a stir. It has since moved down a few notches, and indeed the original ranking was high on careful analysis, but analytical study is not what Royal County Down is all about. Its support comes from two factors. It might well be the most beautiful of all the world's courses, with emerald green playing areas set off by

*Royal Portrush, at the very top of Ireland, must be near the top of an Irish golfing expedition.*

great banks of yellow-blooming gorse, sprawls of white sand fringed by coarse grasses, and its views of the Irish Sea, the spires of the town, and the Mountains of Mourne. It might also be the toughest golf course in the world from the back tees, with most of its fairways occupying narrow valleys in between the sandhills, which would make the course one of the most exacting tests of driving in the world even before the wind, the difficult fairway bunkering, and the considerable carries over sandhills required on five different tee shots were taken into account.

Some people discredit County Down because of the blind drives, but in fact several of those holes are undeniably among the best on the course, and in no case does one require more knowledge for the tee shot than the line over the white stone marker atop the intervening sandhill. The greens aren't as sophisticated as those of Portrush or Ballybunion, but they're more interesting than I had remembered, and they were beautifully keen on my last visit.

All in all, Royal County Down is one of the best places you could choose to test yourself if you fall into thinking you have really mastered golf, and the beauty of the course is fair consolation once you have found out the truth. No. 1 course: 9. No. 2 course: 2. [4/94]

***Royal Portrush GC,*** *Portrush, County Antrim. Dunluce and Valley courses by H.S. Colt, 1929, with some revisions by Colt & Morrison, 1946.*

The championship Dunluce links is probably the least-known of the great Irish links, and one of the very best in the British Isles. It enjoys the advantages of both a majestic duneland site and, unlike many links, first-rate architectural design: Harry Colt gave the layout great balance and variety and a great set of greens, as well as the spectacular holes, which an early-day architect might have found. The most famous hole is "Calamity Corner," the 213-yard 14th, which plays along the rim of a yawning chasm some 80 feet down to the Valley course; but for mere mortals the best hole is the dogleg 5th, played across tumbling ground to a green at the brink of the cliff, with views along the water toward Whiterocks and Dunluce Castle—even to Scotland on a clear day.

I also happen to think that Colt's Valley course is an exceptional, overlooked layout—perhaps the third best in Northern Ireland. Most of it is contained in the "War Hollow" between the Dunluce course and the high range of sandhills along the beach. There are a minimum of bunkers, but some really excellent holes, including the 227-yard 6th funneling to a narrow shelf of green, the short par-4 9th, and the long 10th, and the run in from the 15th, four good holes all under 400 yards. Don't miss it while you're here. Dunluce: 9. Valley: 6. [4/94]

## —*Gossip*—

The two big courses in Northern Ireland are world-beaters; there's not much of a second tier. Portstewart, just west of Portrush, is generally tagged as #3 in the North since an expansion several years ago, which took the opening holes into narrow valleys among the dunes: every tourist article mentions it, yet neither the pictures nor descriptions have convinced me it's in the same league as the Valley course at Portrush, much less Dunluce. Around Belfast, Belvoir Park and Royal Belfast are spoken of as interchangeable with Malone, but not clearly superior. I'm more anxious to see Ardglass, just north of Newcastle, a modest course with two spectacular short holes along the bay, or Kirkistown Castle GC on the Ards Peninsula, "an eerie exposed course" of which James Braid was particularly proud.

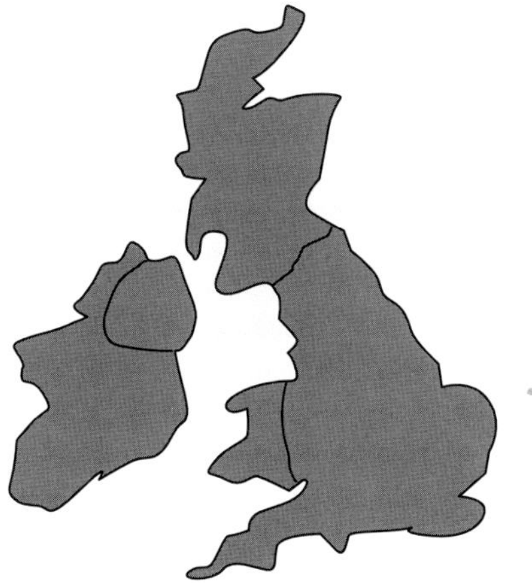

## IRELAND

From the standpoint of pure enjoyment, Irish golf is hard to challenge. The atmosphere is relaxed, the pub chat entertaining, and the Big Five—Portrush, County Down, Portmarnock, Lahinch, and Ballybunion—are as good a group of golf courses as you can find anywhere in the world, and they're all readily accessible by the golfing tourist, although the two in the West are suffering from their reputations and becoming much too crowded in the summer season.

After those five, until recently, there was a small shelf of good courses (Waterville, Rosses Point, and Baltray) before a great drop-off to the average, low-key Irish club. Despite the spectacular scenery of the Irish countryside, there has never been much money for development here to attract top golf architects, and in fact even some of the great courses like Ballybunion evolved mysteriously with little help from famous designers. That's changing in the past decade, as the Irish Tourist Board is using European Community grant money to subsidize new golf course construction as one of the country's principal sources of foreign trade.

But I have yet to see most of the new courses—despite making several recent trips to Ireland—because the word of mouth in-country is much less encouraging than the tourist brochures. American architects have gotten a particularly bad reputation in recent years, whether for wasting spectacular land (see Ballybunion New) or spectacular sums of money, as at Nicklaus' Mount Juliet, Palmer's K Club, or Jones' Adare Manor (all of which, according to the Irish, were built without due consideration of local conditions, and still suffer drainage problems as a result)—but more importantly, all of which are priced beyond the reach of all but wealthy American and European tourists, and none of which can offer the links experience Americans visit for. So the Americans still go to Dooks, and the developers of Mount Juliet set their eyes on Europeans, who may not yet have had their fill of Jack Nicklaus designs.

The failure of American designers in Ireland may bode better for new local developments, which are more understanding of the special appeals of Irish golf. Projects like the European Club, an hour south of Dublin, and the new PGA European Tour course at Portmarnock are a true links product, and there are a host of other seaside courses around the south and west coasts being designed by Irish tour professionals. We don't yet know whether any of these architects will prove themselves worthy of the terrain, but at least the chance of success is there.

## EAST

***County Louth GC,*** *Baltray, Drogheda, County Louth. Cecil Barcroft, c. 1914, with revisions by Tom Simpson, 1938.*

A fine course, but very dull by comparison with Ireland's other top layouts: the fields on the inland side of the links make it look quite tame, and Simpson's minimalist design is the height of subtlety, although the course does possess a fine set of short holes. 6. [5/83]

***The Island GC,*** *Donabate, County Dublin. Revisions to original layout by Eddie Hackett, 1985.*

Many of this club's members reside across the inlet from the course at Malahide or Swords, and until fairly recently the most common means of reaching the club was to be ferried across from Malahide in a dinghy, hence the name "Island" even though the course is firmly attached to the mainland. Now, alas, everyone takes the long way around via the road.

The original 18 was one of those very "sporty" layouts featuring several blind shots, but when I visited the club they were in the process of reorganizing the course along more modern lines. Many of the blind holes are now eliminated and, whether for good or bad, this will undoubtedly change the character of the course, but the three holes to remember will still be the leftovers from the old days, which lie at the very tip of the peninsula, straight across from Malahide. The old 5th is a superb short hole across a dip to a high plateau green set precariously close to the beach on the right; the 6th is just 275 yards and driveable, but no wider than a single-track road from tee to green (it is indeed the narrowest fairway I have ever seen, not excluding U.S. Open conditions); and finally the 7th is a three-shot hole which takes two long pokes to clear a rough ridge and obtain a good view of the green for the approach. I believe that these holes were to be the 13th through 15th in the reorganized course. 4. [5/85]

***Portmarnock GC,*** *Portmarnock, County Dublin. George Ross and W.L. Pickeman, 1894, with revisions and extension to 27 holes by Fred and Martin Hawtree.*

If one had to pair off the great courses of Scotland and Ireland in order to make comparisons of their quality, the first and easiest pairing would be between Portmarnock and Muirfield. I am not as big a fan of the former as the latter—I think Muirfield has clearly the superior collection of golf holes, and prettier scenery too—but in the nature of their challenge and the prestige of the clubs they are of a kind.

Portmarnock occupies a long tongue of linksland, with only low dunes and an occasional fir tree to offer any respite from the winds that howl across its plain. As at Muirfield, an ingenious routing plan changes the direction of play continually, requiring an adjustment on every tee, and while there is a bit more roll to the fairways and tilt to the stances at Portmarnock, there is again rarely the intrusion of a terrible bounce into trouble; however, there are a few pot bunkers at holes such as the 8th, 10th, and 14th, which one must give plenty of room on an approach. I find myself liking some of the less well-known two-shotters (the 9th, 10th, 14th, or 18th) as much or more than the 192-yard 15th, which has been immortalized by one particular swing in Arnold Palmer's career.

The course was extended to 27 holes a few years ago (there is some talk of 36), and this is one of the few courses of that length where the third nine is more than a letdown: some of its long holes are excellent, and it stops just short of being an interchangeable part with the first 18. It is an excellent nine on which to become accustomed to the wind prior to a serious round on the main course. 8. [5/85]

***Royal Dublin GC,*** *Bull Island, Dublin City. Original layout revised by H.S. Colt and Sir Guy Campbell, c. 1935.*

Dollymount, as the Royal Dublin course is familiarly known, may be closer to the center of a major city than any other championship course—just three miles from the Dublin post office, on an island of links in an otherwise industrial section of the harbor. I wish I could recommend the layout more highly, but in fact it is fairly unappealing, and the most storied hole, the par-5 18th with a short-cut approach to the green over the out-of-bounds "Garden," is one of the goofiest holes anyone has ever tried to pass off as great. There are some better two-shot holes on the way out, and even a better par-5 at the 11th, with its clever fall-away green. I suppose for the locals Dollymount has much the same appeal of Hoylake, but I find neither its history nor the layout as interesting. 4. [5/83]

*—Gossip—*

The "K Club" in Kildare has gotten some fine reviews as one of Palmer's best, but the photos are quite tame; I'm much more interested in seeing the European Club, a new links south of Dublin, with some Birkdale-caliber sand dunes on its back nine. I'm also told that the IMG-developed new links adjacent to Portmarnock is worth a stop.

## SOUTH

***Carlow GC,*** *Carlow, County Carlow. Tom Simpson and Molly Gourlay, 1937, with revisions by Eddie Hackett.*

If the lakeside Killarney does not qualify for the category, then Carlow may indeed be "the finest (older) inland course in Ireland" as the locals claim—which says very little about the quality of Ireland's inland courses, because Carlow isn't much better than Sterling Farms. The back nine is the more interesting of the two, but I don't remember much of it. 3. [5/83]

***Cork GC,*** *Little Island, County Cork. Original layout by David Brown, with major revisions by Alister MacKenzie, 1927, and Frank Pennink.*

Several miles to the southeast of Cork town, this interesting mixture of parkland and quarry holes provides an engaging test, especially if you play it in 30-mph winds, as I tried to. The parkland holes at the start and finish are forgettable, but the holes among the excavations have the stuff which lingers in the memory. The short 7th and 9th in the bowels of the quarry are both arresting one-shot holes, the 10th is a two-shotter of sharp undulations, and best of all is the par-5 11th with its last 200 yards along the upper rim of the quarry, increasing the risk of attempting to get home in two. 5. [6/93]

***Kinsale GC,*** *Kinsale, County Cork.*

One of the prettiest courses I've ever seen, with views from the clubhouse at the top of a hill down across the nine holes and out a long, narrow inlet to the sea. Unfortunately, there wasn't really enough land here for even nine holes, and the hill just plunges straight down into the water with barely any flat ground at the bottom for a golf hole along the lakeshore. So, there are a bunch of straight-up short par-4's and a bunch of driveable straight-down ones, neither of which is good golf. The club has gone to the trouble of building a couple of "jetty" tees out into the inlet, but instead of playing across the water to a green at its edge, they simply add a bit of length to uphill holes going away from the inlet. 2. [1/93]

***Macroom GC,*** *Macroom, County Cork. Original nine, 1910, with additional nine holes opened in 1993.*

The original nine is a real goat-hill sidehill layout with a couple of steep holes but little to recommend; the new nine is on better land, but the design is sort of mod/funky. The only attraction is the entrance to the present clubhouse—you go through the gates of the castle from the town square, and down a narrow lane along the river under centuries-old oaks—but sadly they are planning to build a new clubhouse at the far end of the new nine, making this entrance obsolete. 2. [6/93]

***Rosslare GC,*** *Rosslare Strand, County Wexford. Original layout revised by J. Hamilton Stutt.*

If you're taking the southern ferry route back to Wales from Rosslare this is a good way to wait for the boat, but it's not a destination in itself by any stretch of the imagination. The course is on flattish links ground with little view of the sea, and there are a few modestly interesting holes on the way out. 3. [5/83]

—*Gossip*—

The Nicklaus layout at Mount Juliet, near Kilkenny, has brought the usual range of reviews from "great" to "too severe" to "artificial"; the posh country retreat seems geared more to pampered Europeans than to Americans in country to play the classic links. I'm much more interested to see what happens at the Old Head of Kinsale, where I thought I had the contract to design a golf course. The clifftop site is spectacular and unique, but the developer wanted to put greens so close to the edges that I'd need a rock-climbing "buddy" to putt out. It should have been a mandatory stop on the Irish itinerary, but more likely it will become Ireland's answer to Wales' Nefyn & District—or an environmental disaster that never gets finished.

## WEST

***Adare Manor GC,*** *Adare. Robert Trent Jones, 1995.*

A brand-new expensive golf course to go with a spectacular old manor house hotel. Several holes play around or across the adjacent river, most notably the last, where the manor casts a beautiful background; but the round mounds and Jones' shallow, dandelion-shaped bunkers look somewhat out of place on the manor grounds. The hotel will draw crowds of well-to-do Americans and Europeans, and they'll probably enjoy a round at the Manor as a change of pace on their itinerary; but for those not staying here I don't know if the golf course will merit a stop. 5. [7/95]

***Ballybunion GC,*** *Ballybunion, County Kerry. Original layout by Patrick Murphy and M. Smyth, with revisions by Tom Simpson and Molly Gourlay, 1936. New course by Robert Trent Jones and Roger Rulewich, 1984.*

See the "Gourmet's Choice." Old course: 10. New course: 0–5. [6/93]

***Ceann Sibeal GC,*** *Ballyferriter, Dingle, County Kerry. Eddie Hackett.*

This small 18-hole links with the Gaelic name markets itself as part of the SWING group with Ballybunion, Lahinch, and Waterville, but being in the same brochure doesn't put it in the same class. The golf is short and fairly plain, although there are a few interesting green sites. The scenery of Dingle deserves a better course. 3. [1/93]

***Dooks GC,*** *Glenbeigh, County Kerry. Remodeled by Eddie Hackett.*

The biggest surprise of my recent return trip to Ireland, because I barely remembered the course for one ultra-severe green, the par-3 13th. I was startled by the terrain—some of the best medium-sized links undulations I've seen—the true stuff of golf. Some of the green sites and contouring are simply spectacular. At barely 6,000 yards, it isn't a classic, and I still

*The 13th at Lahinch is only 269 yards, but you may wind up in a 20-foot-deep hollow by trying to drive the green.*

haven't had a chance to see whether holes like the dogleg 6th and par-5 11th play as good as they look, but it'll be on my play list next trip. 4. [1/93]

***Dromoland Castle GC,*** *Newmarket on Fergus, County Clare. B.E. Wiggington, architect.*

What the Irish call a "parkland" course, usually meaning a terrain of poorly drained, uniformly thatchy green turf with virtually no definition of target areas, occupying the valley below the tourist resort/castle estate. The resort is for those who want to play Ballybunion and Lahinch, but return to five-course meals; this course is presumably for their semi-golfing spouses who aren't up for those links, but for you and me it isn't even worth a game while recovering from jet lag. 2. [1/93]

***Killarney G & Fishing Club,*** *Killarney, County Kerry. Original Mahony's Point layout by Willie Park, with substantial revisions by Sir Guy Campbell with Henry Longhurst and Lord Castlerosse, 1939. Killeen course added by Fred Hawtree, 1971.*

The appeals and drawbacks of Killarney are both substantial. The setting, at the shore of Lough Leane just across from the mountainous Killarney National Park, is perhaps the most beautiful of any in the world for inland golf, and between the two courses there are a number of fine holes. However, the village of Killarney itself is littered with tourists and has become borderline tacky, and after a rainy spell (which is most of the time in Ireland) the courses become terribly waterlogged, hardly appealing by comparison to the great links elsewhere in the region.

The Killeen course is probably the better choice of the two, with especially fine holes in the short 3rd and long par-4 13th, but the 202-yard finishing hole on the Mahony's Point course is deservedly the most famous of all. But I wouldn't say that either course is a real winner on anything but esthetic grounds. Killeen course: 5. Mahony's Point course: 4. [5/83]

***Lahinch GC,*** *Lahinch, County Clare. Original layout by Old Tom Morris, 1893, with revisions by Charles Gibson in 1910, by Alister MacKenzie in 1927, and by club member John Burke. Also a relief course.*

One of my favorite places in the world of golf—a friendly small-town seaside resort, and one of the most fun golf courses I've ever played. Several of my low-handicap friends who played here on their first trip to the UK hated it, probably because there is more than the usual element of chance to scoring here: holes like the "Dell" 6th, a blind par-3 into a small, deep amphitheater where shots are likely to carom off at least one of the guardian dunes before coming to rest on the shallow green, aren't meant for that kind of analysis. But every time I return I'm impressed by the mixture of incredibly strong holes like the par-4 4th and 10th; wild MacKenzie contributions like the 9th and the par-3 11th; freaks of nature like the famous 5th and 6th; and unheralded gems like the 13th, 14th, and 16th, which practically no one remembers. It's not a pushover for a good player, and it's something your wife could get around—in fact, it might be the best course in the world for satisfying both ends of the golfing spectrum at once. Old course: 8. No. 2 course: 2. [4/94]

***Tralee GC,*** *Barrow, Tralee, County Kerry. Arnold Palmer and Ed Seay, 1984.*

This course suffers from the same general problem as Ballybunion New—spectacular scenery at the expense of good golf—although the terrain itself isn't as dramatic or as integral to the course. The "signature" holes, the par-3 3rd and 13th and the par-4 12th and 17th, are probably the worst on the course, although there are some dull inland holes as well. Some love the course, but I think some good land was wasted here. 0-5. [1/93]

***Waterville GL,*** *Waterville, County Kerry. Eddie Hackett, 1973.*

This demanding modern links has now been taken over by a consortium of Americans, who have improved the conditioning considerably but also added a few American quirks—rough around the collars of the greens, and an awful pond in front of the par-3 7th. My second impression was that the back nine was much better and the scenery more spectacular than I remembered, but the severe total length (it was billed as "the longest course in Europe," and it's also one of the windiest), plus the heavier soil on the first few holes, keep it off the top rung. 7. [4/94]

***Spanish Point GC,*** *Spanish Point, County Clare. Architect and date unrecorded.*

Just off the route between Ballybunion and Lahinch, this is the most rudimentary nine-hole links imaginable, with tiny greens ringed by wire fence to keep the sheep off, fairways rife with clover, and mostly shortish holes crammed into a tight property. Instructive only to show the perception of golf in Ireland as a natural and inexpensive game. 1. [5/85]

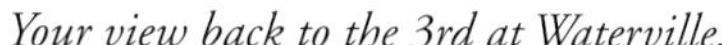

*Your view back to the 3rd at Waterville.*

## NORTHWEST

***Ballyliffin GC,*** *Ballyliffin, County Donegal. Old course architect unknown, with revisions by Eddie Hackett; New course by Pat Ruddy and Tom Craddock, under construction in 1994.*

On my last trip to Ireland, this remote links had popped up in a couple of books as "the Dornoch of Ireland." Other than the northerly location on the Inishowen Peninsula, there's little similarity; clearly a P.R. man was doing the shouting at a pub for whomever put Ballyliffin in this circle. The Old course did enjoy the splendor of a beautiful setting and a couple of good holes—particularly the par-5 12th—that is, until the club was talked into expanding to 36 holes, for the remote setting is now spoiled by construction, and some of the best parts of the old course (including the 12th) are being sacrificed at the expense of the New, which looked to be very artificial in design and construction. An unspoilt place, spoiled. Old course: 3. [4/94]

***Bundoran GC,*** *Bundoran, County Donegal. C.S. Butchart, c. 1900, with revisions by Harry Vardon.*

Bundoran is on the main route from Lahinch to Portrush, but not even worth the stop. Its character is just exactly what Bernard Darwin described as "inland-super-mare," and there are no outstanding holes. 2. [5/83]

***County Sligo GC,*** *Rosses Point, County Sligo. Colt, MacKenzie, and Alison, 1922.*

This is one of the most scenic of all the Irish links, with stunning panoramas of Sligo Bay and the west country for 360° from the high point of the course at the 2nd green; however, since the course is certainly not in the Dornoch class for architecture and at least as far removed from the beaten track, I think it's a toss-up whether it is worth including in an Irish tour or not, unless you are committed to making the long drive between Portrush and Lahinch, in which case it is a convenient stop en route. There are some very good holes, such as the downhill par-5 3rd and the double-dogleg 14th, which is on the lower, true links part of the course, and both of which are augmented by tremendously beautiful backdrops; but the absence of smaller links contours leaves it lacking in short-game interest. I think it compares favorably with Gullane No. 1, but Muirfield is not just down the street from Rosses Point. 7. [4/94]

***Enniscrone GC,*** *Enniscrone, County Sligo. Eddie Hackett.*

This newish links is divided into two distinct parts—holes on flattish ground with little real interest, and about half a dozen holes amid large sandhills which are arresting, if not always wonderful. The short par-4 10th will thrill the daredevils among us, and the short 17th from dunetop to dunetop is exciting to see, although perhaps too exacting to play. 5. [4/94]

*County Sligo—one of the most scenic of Irish Links.*

***Narin and Portnoo GC,*** *Portnoo, County Donegal. Architect unknown.*

These next three courses can all be fairly described as "remote outposts of golf," as far removed from the beaten track as you can get in the British Isles; and Portnoo is certainly the sportiest of the three. The beginning and end of the course are confined to dullish ground—on the 2nd and 17th fairways, literally a cow pasture—but the walk to the far end is worth it for the magnificent scenery and some thrilling golf holes. From the second shot to the 5th, diagonally uphill across an insidious grassy hollow, through the second shot at the short par-4 9th, which must pinpoint a tiny plateau green with the deep blue bay directly behind, and on through the roller-coaster par-4 10th and 12th, there is a series of spectacular shots to be played. But, I must say that in a dry season with wind present I'm not sure that anyone is good enough to play some of the approaches to these tiny greens; so Portnoo must ultimately be classified as a lark instead of a real find. 4. [4/94]

***Portsalon GC,*** *Portsalon, County Donegal. Architect and date unrecorded.*

I went to see this course strictly because of a short note in Bernard Darwin's *Golf Courses of the British Isles,* in which he regarded it as a "perfectly lovely spot," and I was curious to see what had come of it 70 years hence. I hardly know what to report; I'm not even entirely sure it was still there when I saw it.

What passed for the clubhouse was about the size of a snack hut at a typical American club, and there was no one on duty. The first few holes seemed to still be in use, though the fairways consisted mainly of clover, and a white ball would have been impossible to locate, and the holes themselves were marked with only the shortest pieces of plastic pipe and a makeshift flag. Even so, there were a couple of fine short holes at the 2nd and 5th, and the 7th might have been a fine two-shot hole had it not been half buried in a drift of sand. The only hole on the way home I was able to identify (other than the last two, counting backwards) was the long par-4 13th, with a strange pointed rock outcropping (with a profile like that of the Matterhorn, and the hole named to match) to be cleared on the approach, although this hole was also out of play at the moment.

I can't recommend a course which I'm not even sure is still there, but it was indeed a lovely, quiet spot, and I enjoyed the puzzle it presented immensely. 3? [5/83]

***Rosapenna GC,*** *Rosapenna, County Donegal. Original layout by Old Tom Morris, 1893, with revisions by H.S. Colt, 1916.*

Another true outpost, even though Rosapenna comes complete with its own small Golf Hotel. The links is fairly primitive, but the first ten holes along the shore and back are obvious golfing country, and for me the magnificently conceived green of the par-4 5th hole was worth the trip in itself. 4. [5/83]

—*Gossip*—

I did take advantage of my business trips to Waterville and Kinsale to check out the remote possibilities of County Donegal; I found several courses where you might take the wife and kids for fun, but certainly no Dornoch or Machrihanish. Better luck next time: Belmullet, Connemara, and Murvagh (Donegal Golf Club) are my next three prospects.

## CONTINENTAL EUROPE

It's difficult for Americans to understand how Europe can be so lacking in golf courses, while Britain is so rich in them. For starters, the European mainland is much more rocky and the climate more extreme. Then, throw in the cultural reluctance to accept anything English, and two ground wars to slow down [or wipe out] development, and you'll start to see. Until recently, what development there was, was driven by the Brits, whether the Dutch links courses just across the Channel which British architects could not resist, the vintage clubs around Paris and Brussels which were built for visiting businessmen as much as for the locals, or the courses of the Algarve and Costa del Sol, which catered mostly at their inception to English on holiday.

The growth of the PGA European Tour and the emergence of Seve Ballesteros, Bernhard Langer, Anders Forsbrand and Constantino Rocca changed all that; golf is now an "in" sport among Europeans, and they're still rushing to build courses to feed that interest. They're lucky in some countries to have the classic layouts of Tom Simpson and the partnership of H.S. Colt and John Morrison to serve as shining examples; and I've always wanted to see a bit of the work of Javier Arana, a Spanish designer of the 1950s and 1960s whose work is highly regarded. But in the new boom sizzle sells, and we'll have to wait and see whether Ballesteros, Langer et al. produce more than rubber-stamp courses under their own signatures.

## THE NETHERLANDS

***Haagsche GC,*** *Wassenar, The Hague. Colt, Alison, and Morrison, 1939, with postwar reconstruction by Sir Guy Campbell.*

An unusual links tumbling across hilly dunes just a mile from the North Sea, which is never in sight. There is much more elevation change than is to be found on the classic British links, such as at the 200-yard, drop-shot 4th hole; and the back nine includes several carries from the tee across scrub-filled ravines from which no recovery is feasible. The par-4 15th is an especially heroic hole. This may be the most private club in the Netherlands, and it is therefore less receptive to walk-in English-speaking visitors than some others in the country. 6. [6/83]

***Kennemer GC,*** *Zandvoort. J.S.F. Morrison and H.S. Colt, 1928, with a third nine added by Frank Pennink.*

Holland's most well-recognized championship links, the large rolls of Kennemer are vaguely reminiscent of Shinnecock Hills in places, and just a half hour's drive or train ride from the main Amsterdam station. The routing of the original 18 resembles Muirfield's, though the outer loop of the front nine is the anti-clockwise one; but perhaps already the championship layout has been changed to include the new nine, deleting the 4th through 12th holes of the original 18. The most sorely missed of these will be the long two-shot 9th, with its green in a basin below the thatched-roof clubhouse. 6. [6/85]

*—Gossip—*

For a country of so few courses (there were only twelve 18-hole layouts in the country as of 1984), the Netherlands can truly be said to set a very high standard for golf architecture. I've heard glowing reports of Noordwijk, a modern links along the coast between The Hague and Kennemer; and among the inland courses, Hilversum, Rosendaelsche, De Pan, and Eindhoven have all drawn comparisons with the heathland layouts of Surrey and Berkshire, the last two at least designed by the team of Colt, Alison, and Morrison, who did many of their English counterparts.

## FRANCE

***G de Chantilly,*** *Chantilly, Oise. J.F. Abercromby, 1906, with revisions by Tom Simpson, c. 1925.*

Everyone I talked to before I headed for France took it for granted that among golf courses Chantilly should be my first stop, and that it was unquestionably the best course in the country. For championship play, perhaps: but for my enjoyment the course didn't stack up to Morfontaine.

Particularly after spending a month on the links and heaths of England, the heavier soil of Chantilly is a letdown, and the course is too long for someone of my modest talents to be talked into playing the back tees. But, while I liked some of the contouring of the greens and the shaping of the bunkers from close up, overall I thought the course lacked definition and visual interest, with most of the holes either cutting through trees or out in a field. I liked the last six holes, which work around a couple of deep valleys near the clubhouse, much better than the first 12.

But don't let me talk you out of going to see the château and the stables of Chantilly, which were featured in the James Bond film, *A View To A Kill;* they are among France's most beautiful architectural treasures. I wish I liked the golf course half as much. 6. [6/85]

*Kennemer—Holland's most recognized championship links.*

***G de Hardelot,*** *Hardelot. Tom Simpson, 1927.*

A short but beautiful layout in white sandy soil and heathland trimmings, not far from the ferry port of Boulogne. The trees are closer than on the classic British heath courses, but the holes never really feel narrow unless you're swinging for the green with a brassie at one of the six three-shot holes, none of which measures more than 550 yards. Five good short holes add to the unusual makeup of the course. One is tempted to make comparisons to the Red course at the Berkshire because of the propensity of one- and three-shot holes, but personally I don't find Hardelot to be quite at that level. 5. [6/85]

*The well-protected 7th green at Hardelot, designed by Tom Simpson.*

***G de Morfontaine,*** *Senlis. Tom Simpson, 1927.*

A beautiful heathland course and club not far from Chantilly, about an hour's drive north of Paris that the German army thankfully did not harm during the Second World War. The preliminary reports I had heard of the course implied it was quite short, à la Swinley Forest, but the 474-yard par-4 first hole quickly suggested that I had been misled, and the following two holes of 225 and 485 yards confirmed my suspicions. Not all the holes are as demanding as these first three, but the course is by no means a pushover at 6,600 yards par 70. There are a number of difficult two-shotters, and some of the putting surfaces are worthy of Augusta. For some reason I have trouble placing Morfontaine in perspective with the best of London's heathland courses: one minute I'm convinced it's the equal of Sunningdale, and the next I'm rating it behind Pulborough and St. George's Hill, on the basis of a weak finish. But that's tough company; in its own neighborhood, Morfontaine est magnifique. 7. [6/85]

***GC du Touquet,*** *Le Touquet. Sea ("Mer") course by H.S. Colt, 1930, with revisions by Mackenzie Ross, 1958.*

Among English golfers the name of Le Touquet is widely known, but most of the people who will recommend it to you have never actually seen it, and I think a lot of them would be disappointed if they did. Many of the early holes (and also the last three) play across flat, scrubby property, and only the 9th through 15th are actually among the exciting sand dune country one expects. Even in the best part of the course there are as many mundane shots to be played as memorable ones, although the drive from the elevated tee at the 10th and the shots to the short 9th and 15th holes must rank very highly in the realm of golf on the Continent. It's not a bad course by any means, but I wouldn't think it's worth a hydrofoil trip across the Channel just to play Le Touquet, unless you've exhausted the possibilities on the other side, and that's pretty hard to do. 5. [6/85]

*—Gossip—*

Just recently, France has become the center of a major European golf boom, and the French are lucky to have a number of outstanding old courses to fall back on, thanks mostly to the efforts of Tom Simpson in the late twenties and early thirties. Around Paris, St. Germain, Fontainebleau, and St. Cloud come highly recommended; while in the southern part of the country is Hossegor, Colt's Chantaco, which was built for the Lacoste family, and Chiberta-Biarritz, of which designer Simpson was especially proud. Among more modern courses, I've heard better things about Bob Von Hagge's two French flagships, Les Bordes and Seignosse, than about anything he's designed in the U.S.; and I would also be curious to see Golf du Médoc in Brittany, which my friends Bill Coore and Rod Whitman recently completed; and in the category of hearsay, I will give you Sperone GC on the isle of Corsica, a clifftop Trent Jones layout which my Swiss friend Phil Herrmann raves over. The new courses around Paris include Golf National, which looks from pictures like a low-budget TPC course, and Jack Nicklaus' Paris International GC, which may be fine; but most of the boom courses are undoubtedly terrible, because anybody who knows *anything* about golf in France is trying to cash in on the boom as a course designer.

## THE REST OF THE CONTINENT

*—Gossip—*

**Scandinavia:** The one course here I would really like to see sometime is Sweden's Falsterbo, a flattish links at the tip of a peninsula at the mouth of the Baltic Sea, not far from the ferry crossing to Copenhagen. It still has considerable support for inclusion in the top 100 courses in the world, although one friend found it a bit too flat and in terrible condition. The other Swedish course of note, Halmstad (North), described by one observer as "a heathland course with the atmosphere of a links," is less than 100 miles north up the coast. Otherwise, there isn't much: I've heard good reports about Drottningholm GC and Stockholm GC, but the pictures looked rather ordinary, while Donald Steel recommends Barseback (Old), where he's done some consulting work. Rungsted GC is the most well-known course in Denmark, but my former intern James Duncan reports that Copenhagen Golf Club (by Harry Colt and John Morrison) is the class of the field there.

**Germany:** There's a big boom in new course construction in Germany right now, but the severe limits on grading (no cuts or fills of more than one meter in height) also limit the possibilities. Of the older courses, everyone's number one choice is Hamburger GC at Falkenstein, designed by Colt, Alison, and Morrison, followed by Frankfurter GC, by the same trio. One other possibility is Club Zur Vahr in Bremen, which has a glowing write-up in *The World Atlas of Golf,* but has gotten two very poor reviews from friends of mine: either it's been changed, or it's too subtle for my men to appreciate. From hearsay, the other possibilities are Beuerberg by Donald Harradine, Hubbelrath (East) in Dusseldorf, and the ancient course in the spa town of Bad Ems, still there seventy years after it was mentioned in architectural books by Robert Hunter.

**Belgium:** There are several "sleeper" possibilities here, because of the work carried out by Tom Simpson at Royal GC des Fagnes, (a.k.a. Golf de Spa), Royal Antwerp, and the Royal GC de Belgique (a.k.a. Ravenstein); they are highly unlikely to have been

tinkered with excessively, though they may be somewhat overgrown. The seaside Royal Zoute GC, by Seymour Dunn, with revisions by J.S.F. Morrison, suddenly turned up with a couple of strong supporters in my last *GOLF Magazine* poll after hosting a European Tour event. Finally, there's Royal Waterloo, with 36 holes by Fred Hawtree. If you've only got time for one, my money's on Golf de Spa.

**Spain:** Robert Trent Jones, Sr. opened a branch office in southern Spain in 1970, and assisted by Cabell Robinson, blazed the trail for a boom of resort development for snowbound northern Europeans. Jones' masterpiece was once considered to be the Old course at Sotogrande, but it has now been eclipsed by Valderrama, the former New course at Sotogrande, which was taken over by the billionaire Jaime-Ortiz Patino and further remodeled by Jones in the late 1980s. Now the home of the European Masters tournament, it draws considerable praise when the pros aren't complaining about how hard it is. Las Brisas at Nueva Andalucia is still considered Jones' other top course on the Costa del Sol, but his most recent wave of designs includes El Bosque in Valencia (maybe a good side trip from El Saler—see below). I wonder, though, if Jones' work in Spain is really that much better than the general run of his work in the USA, or whether it's just a more pleasant venue for the same thing.

I am much more intrigued to see a little of the work of Javier Arana, the Spanish golf architect of the 1950s and 1960s who built El Saler in Valencia—the highest-rated Continental course in the *GOLF Magazine* Top 100—El Prat in Barcelona, and Club de Campo near Madrid. I'm also interested in seeing a course or two designed by Spanish pro Pepe Gancedo, who's been called "the Picasso of Spanish golf architects," and whose work seems to toe the line between interesting and crazy—Torrequebrada, on the Costa del Sol, is his oldest and most famous.

**Portugal:** A course named San Lorenzo, a Joe Lee design at Quinta do Lago on the Algarve, has jumped onto our *GOLF* Top 100 list, but I'm still somewhat dubious about its architectural merits, considering Lee's track record. I'm just as curious to see Donald Steel's Vila Sol, the original Quinta do Lago course (B & C nines) by Bill Mitchell, or Trent Jones' Troia in Setubal, a sort-of links/Pine Valley combo which the late Jim Wysocki, the first man to play all of the *GOLF* Top 100 courses in the world, rated in his personal top ten. Henry Cotton's Penina also has a few avid supporters, but a lot of detractors, too. Somewhat removed from all of these is Robert Trent Jones, Jr.'s new course at Penha Longa, a beautiful resort set among ancient buildings a few miles northwest of Lisbon.

**Switzerland and Austria:** There's still not much here to see, I'm afraid. Seefeld, in Austria, has been cited as some of the most exciting golf in mountainous terrain, but I think we're talking mountain-goat steep and narrow here; Crans-sur-Sierre, high in the Swiss Alps, has absolutely no support as a great course. The only other courses I've received even fair reports about are Lausanne GC and Domaine Imperial near Geneva, which my friend Russell Talley built under Pete Dye's name.

**Italy:** Golf, here? I can't really imagine that any Italian golf course is worth distracting oneself from the antiquities of Florence or Rome. But I've heard surprisingly strong endorsements of a course called Biella in the north, and a bit more modest praise of Milano Golf Club. A couple of new courses, Castelconturbia by Trent Jones and Le Querce by Jim Fazio, also rate pretty highly in the newest European rankings, but I have no first-hand reports on either. Last but not least, there's Trent Jones' Pevero on the isle of Sardinia, built with the Aga Khan's money, which bowls over most people with its scenery but has gotten mixed reviews in terms of its golfing values—they spent a fortune grading the course through the rocky terrain, but if you're off the short grass you're still on the rocks.

**Morocco:** OK, I know it's not in Europe, but you're much more likely to fit it into a trip to Spain than to South Africa, so I'm listing it here. Trent Jones' Royal Dar-es-Salaam Red course, in Rabat, continues to hang on in the Top 100 lists; I don't know if it's in deference to King Hassan II or to its design.

## SOUTH AFRICA

Now that its government has been reformed, it's fair game to write about South Africa, and to consider going there—as if going before really would have propped up the Afrikaners. No golf book could really be complete without this country, which has given the world more than its share of golfing greats (from Bobby Locke and Gary Player to the new generation, Ernie Els), and it does possess at least one of the world's great courses, Durban Country Club.

Socially if not politically, however, South Africa is still a nation divided by race, which will take generations to change, as it has in the former Confederacy. On the one hand, it was as safe to travel there in 1993 as it was to go to New York City or Detroit; there are just certain areas you have to avoid. (It did not, however, feel nearly as safe for the tourist as Northern Ireland.) On the other hand, society, particularly at the golf course, is far from integrated. Durban Country Club is an excellent example—an international treasure of a golf course close into the city, and a social institution with more than 11,000 members, which black politicians have made overtures about condemning for low-cost housing. Yet, it's hard to feel too sorry for a club so rooted in the past that they haven't even been able to assimilate any of the city's Indian professional community into the club, to say nothing of the blacks.

Ironically, one of the few hopes for improving the country's economy is tourism, since there is universal apprehension toward investment in industry for fear it will be nationalized. If you do travel here, you'll see South Africa as the Japanese see the United States—incredibly cheaply, because of the very favorable exchange rate, and quite dangerous in terms of street violence. The only things that cost a lot are rental cars (probably for security reasons) and the game parks, which are unbelievably expensive but probably worth every penny. And, of course, there is a plentiful supply of caddies, just like Augusta in the 1930s.

Of course, it's easy for us to criticize; we prefer to color South Africa's problems by race, but it's hard to imagine what would happen if the richest 5% of Americans were asked to sacrifice their accumulated wealth for the benefit of the 95% poor. (Pat Buchanan keeps trying to tell us.) Still, I would stay very closely tuned to the international situation if I were planning another trip to South Africa.

***Beachwood GC,*** *Durban, Natal. Architect unknown.*

A tight course occupying a narrow stretch of terraced duneland north of the city, and only a stone's throw from the sea. Unfortunately, the narrowness of the parcel and the lineal nature of the topography produce few surprises. 3. [3/93]

***Dainfern CC,*** *Broederstroom, Transvaal. Gary Player Design Co., 1991.*

A very good residential development course: though the routing is obviously stretched out to maximize real estate frontage, the holes make good use of the topography and of the Jukskei River, which comes into play at five or six holes, including the spectacular par-5 17th. My only quibble is with Gary's fondness for "elephant grass" rough, which intrudes on islands in some of the bunkers, resulting in certain lost balls. I like the stuff, but you've got to keep it to tightly confined and narrow bands so players can find their balls, and so their caddies won't have to drop a replacement through the trouser leg while no one is looking. 5. [3/93]

**Durban CC,** *Durban, Natal. George Waterman and Laurie Waters, 1922, with modifications by S.V. Hotchkin, 1930, and Bob Grimsdell, 1959.*

See the "Gourmet's Choice." 8. [3/93]

**Gary Player CC,** *Sun City, Bophuthatswana. Gary Player and Ron Kirby, 1979.*

One of the most overrated courses I've seen; obviously playing for a million dollars of someone else's money has a tendency to make tournament golfers see a course through rose-colored glasses. It isn't "overdone" or gimmicky, and it's surely difficult—the 7,600-plus yards from the back tees are long even at this elevation—but I found the course lacking in creativity, imagination, and memorability. The worst feature is the convoluted cloverleaf shapes of the greens, leaving nearly all the pin positions on "petals" or wings; since most of the greens sit well above eye level, you have no clue where to aim for the "fat" part of the green. Also, the combination of those green shapes and the nature of the kikuyu grass, which encroaches right up to the collars, must yield a lot of putts that can't be aimed at the hole. The golf staff at the resort think that this course will retain its reputation as superior to the new Lost City course because it isn't as gimmicky, but they're all seriously deluded to believe it was any good to begin with. 5. [4/93]

**Glendower GC,** *Edenvale, Transvaal. Charles Alison, 1938, with recent modifications by club committee.*

For my tastes, this was the cream of the Johannesburg parkland courses, although it isn't all that different in appearance from the others. The bunkering is more prevalent, if still a bit shallow, and the greens contouring is much more pronounced. There is also a lot more water in play than I saw elsewhere in South Africa, from the narrow ponds which protect the strong 2nd, 3rd, and 10th holes, to the narrow creek across the 7th and beside the 13th, to ridiculously shallow artificial pools which have recently been dug to necessitate carrying approaches to the 6th, 8th, and 9th. Also the Sunningdale of South Africa: they like to play for high stakes. (Too bad Michael Jordan wouldn't be welcome.) 6. [4/93]

*Humewood—a true seaside links.*

***Humewood GC,*** *Port Elizabeth, Cape Province. S.V. Hotchkin, 1930, with slight modifications by Donald Steel.*

Many seaside courses around the world lay erroneous claim to the title of "links," but lo and behold!, here indeed is the real McCoy in a most unlikely place: a Spartan landscape of rock-hard fairways and greens, dominated by great native roughs and by the wind. But unlike its British antecedents it can be played in shirt-sleeves 98% of the time, and there is usually a view of the Indian Ocean. Hotchkin was probably influenced by the contemporary redesign of Muirfield in arranging the course in two loops of nine around a central clubhouse, but most of the holes run parallel on either side of the clubhouse, either into the wind or downwind instead of the progression of different angles that make Muirfield so interesting. The dominant westerly winds blowing out to the sea generally put four or five of the longer par-4's out of reach of the average player's two best, while making three of the par-5 holes reachable with mid-iron second shots as they play downhill and downwind; I'm not sure that's the ideal way to have done it, even if all those par-4's are outstanding two-shotters for the accomplished golfer. There are also a couple of excellent short par-3's playing crosswind along the back side of the property. It's a difficult test, and altogether original for South Africa as far as I have seen; but it wouldn't be one of the best links in Britain. 6. [3/93]

***Kloof GC,*** *Kloof, Natal. Architect unknown, with recent modifications by club members.*

Only 20 miles inland from Durban, the 1,500-foot elevation here provides a dramatic change in climate and character from the tropical Durban courses. Lots of impressive homes and colorful flowering trees border the course, making it expensive real estate, but a maze of public streets through the middle of the layout and Mickey-Mouse reconstruction work have added nothing to its character. 3. [3/93]

***Lost City GC,*** *Sun City, Bophuthatswana. Gary Player Design Co., 1993.*

An Arizona-style desert course connected with the fabulous Palace of the Lost City resort, the newest addition to the Sun City casino complex. By contrast with other Player courses I've seen, the shaping work of bunkers and greens is unusually good. There are several very good holes, including the 9th and 18th around a lake to the Desert Highlands–inspired "ruined" clubhouse, and all of the par-3's—even the gimmicked-up "signature" 13th, with a walled-in water hazard full of crocodiles, bunkers with sand of different colors (red, white, yellow), and a green in the shape of Africa. Elsewhere, however, the course suffers from a tendency to throw in boarded bunkers, rock faces, and everything but the kitchen sink, and I didn't like the placement of the bunkers nearly as much as the look of them. The Palace, though, is absolutely fabulous; you could spend a whole day at the water slides and wave pool. 6. [4/93]

***Mount Edgecombe GC,*** *Durban, Natal. Architect unknown, with major modifications by Dale Hayes & Co.*

An indifferent course drastically refurbished to accommodate an upscale development. The run-of-the-mill terrain makes for a modest layout, although the greens are highly contoured (if not artistically well-done) by South African standards. 3. [3/93]

***Royal Durban GC,*** *Durban, Natal. Architect unknown.*

One of the most unusual settings in the world for golf, as the entire course and clubhouse are contained within Durban Racecourse, and overlooked by the residential part of the city as well. The course is also divided in half by a major public road which tunnels under the racetrack at either end. To protect visibility for the races, there is no feature of the golf course built over one and a half meters high, but the coarse kikuyu roughs and the small greens still make this an interesting and difficult course.

Insiders footnote: at one point, this course was included among the *GOLF Magazine* Top 100 by mistake, because the former publisher mistook it for Durban Country Club. (Even so, it isn't as bad a course as Gary Player CC at Sun City, which was voted in on its own merits.) 5. [3/93]

***Royal Johannesburg GC,*** *Johannesburg, Transvaal. East course by Robert Grimsdell, 1933, with revisions by Charles Alison, 1948.*

A fine and gracious club, with the East course insulated from any surrounding developments by the shorter West course on one flank, and by the 54-hole Huddle Park public facility on the other—a total of 90 holes uninterrupted by roads or development, perhaps a world record. Despite its reputation as one of the finest courses in South Africa, I found it a tough but somewhat bland parkland layout with big, sweeping holes. The 6,000-foot elevation shortens distances considerably and the weather is always perfect, leading to what the manager at Humewood referred to as the "Transvaal handicap," but the back-to-back 500-yard par-4 10th and 11th holes are still two of the hardest holes in a row I've seen anywhere. 6. [3/93]

***Wanderers GC,*** *Johannesburg, Transvaal. Architect unknown.*

A storied sporting club on the northern outskirts of town that includes one of the largest cricket grounds in South Africa, and facilities for dozens of sports. Golf has taken something of a back seat here, and though the course is quite good, there is little to distinguish it from others in the area. 5. [4/93]

*—Gossip—*

I didn't get to Cape Town in my itinerary, to the dismay of every South African I met; but it's highly regarded as a great city more than for the golf at Mowbray and Royal Cape. I did fly over East London CC en route from Durban to Port Elizabeth, and would rate it as a potential sleeper on the basis of my peek. There's also Wild Coast, a Robert Trent Jones, Jr. layout which reportedly has a couple of spectacular holes across rocky ravines, but lacks consistency, and Royal George on the Garden Route. Finally, there are several more parkland courses around Johannesburg, particularly Houghton GC and the exclusive River Club—but all the Jo-burg courses looked fairly interchangeable to me.

*There's no denying the beauty at Lost City.*

## JAPAN

We all have an impression of golf in Japan, but what I saw there was quite different than what I had imagined from afar. Yes, there is an entire class of driving-range golfers who almost never get to see the real thing, but it did not strike me as a golf-crazy society. Real golf is prohibitively expensive—even supported by their businesses, most Japanese golfers can only afford to play once a week or once a month, so it's difficult to get down to a single-digit handicap.

While the variety of courses I found in Japan was somewhat better than I expected, it is very difficult to rate them except in the context of Japan itself. There are a few older clubs with good, even excellent courses; but virtually all of the older courses still have two greens for every hole, a throwback to the American occupation after World War II, when an Atlanta general suggested it as a solution to the extreme changes of climate. Practically speaking, it was a big help in a land where qualified golf course superintendents were few and far between, but obviously the convention severely inhibits variety of greenside bunkering and design, not that many of their early designers were innovative enough to consider these esoterica. The builders of the first boom (1950-1970) also had a fetish for 7,000-yard golf courses, even though hardly any Japanese golfer would consider playing the back tees.

Modern Japanese courses are another thing altogether. The population crunch and severe topography have forced the nation to reserve all serviceable property for agriculture or housing, so new courses must be tacked up onto the sides of mountains as a result of moving, typically, three million cubic yards of material. These projects are so prohibitively expensive that many expensive memberships must be sold, and since the average prospective member's knowledge of golf is limited, subtle design takes a back seat to sales and marketing. The successful Japanese designers, stressing tradition, copycat features of famous courses overseas—say, the stone bridge at St. Andrews—while the most successful American designers, like Perry Dye and Desmond Muirhead, have been those who spend lavishly and build for the cameras. None of these traditions has yielded the quality of golf courses you would want to travel 5,000 miles to play.

There is also the question of cost—if you're not on the *GOLF Magazine* VIP tour like I was, the green fees alone will run $200 to $300, and the taxi rides out into the boonies and back maybe $75 to $100 each way. Even at that, you couldn't do it yourself; unless you speak Japanese, you'll probably have to bring your own translator with you just to get where you're going, much less communicate. From my standpoint, there aren't many courses anywhere worth that much to play; you'll have to make your own judgment.

***Caledonian GC,*** *Yamatakegun, Chiba. Michael Poellot, 1990.*

A visually stunning new course out near the Narita airport that is difficult to classify. There are some terrific holes, mostly on the back nine—the "Cape" par-4 13th around the lake at the back of the clubhouse, the par-5 15th whose approach is vaguely reminiscent of the 13th at Augusta, and the par-5 18th with an alternate route like the 15th at Seminole. But on other holes, like the par-5 2nd or par-4 7th, the terrain is over-shaped and the strategy is over-cooked. The sprawling bunkering is the signature of the course—it's just different enough to be really original—but the greens are overdone, with moderate-sized pin placement areas separated by

sweeping transitions making for a lot of difficult lag putts. And even the magnificent club facilities cannot fully distract one from the huge high-voltage lines that run around the perimeter of the course, especially when they provide aiming points for some of the tee shots on the front nine. 6. [7/93]

***Golden Valley GC,*** *Nishiwaki, Hyogo. Robert Trent Jones Jr., 1987.*

In contrast to its sister course, Pine Lake, which is next door, Golden Valley is a much more artificial layout shelved into two valleys. There are some spectacular modern holes, but the overall impression is that the course is overdone, particularly the greens where several back pin positions are almost impossible to get at. In addition, nearly every one of the longer holes is built into a right-to-left slope, which gets monotonous after a while. (I know the idea was to keep the slicer from bounding down into water hazards, but they could have mixed it up a little.) One of the hardest courses I've ever played—don't go all the way back here unless you're playing out of your mind. 0–5. [8/93]

***Higashi Hirono GC,*** *Miki, near Kobe, Hyogo. Architect unknown, 1988.*

A classic "modern Japanese" layout with more than 4 million cubic yards of dirt moved to transform mountaintops and valleys into a golf course. The designer, in-house for the development company, favored downhill par-3's over water with lavish landscaping around the tees—there are three of them within the 18, including the island green 3rd hole. There are also a couple of the longest moving walkways I've ever encountered to transport golfers up to tees on the front nine holes. Really, it's not bad at all, considering the site. 4. [7/93]

***Hirono GC,*** *Miki, near Kobe, Hyogo. Charles Alison, 1932, with reconstruction by K. Ohashi, 1988.*

For years this has been number one on my most-wanted list, so I was thrilled to have the chance to visit in an official capacity, but though I would rate it the best course in Japan I must admit to a twinge of disappointment in finally seeing it. Though the club tried diligently to preserve Alison's concepts in its reconstruction, the greens complexes were rebuilt and the greens enlarged in 1988 to accommodate bentgrass surfaces, and the simple fact that these were not the original surfaces detracted from the enjoyment of them.

Despite this objection, Hirono is an excellent course, much longer and stronger than I had imagined. The gently rolling property, intersected by several shallow valleys and a couple of deeper ravines, is virtually perfect for laying out a golf course, in direct contrast to the current Japanese standard, and the routing makes great use of it: for example, on the celebrated par-5 15th, which was the impetus for my trip, a deep ravine provides a dramatic cross-hazard for the second shot, and a shallower valley right in front of the green is the natural setting for the greenside bunkers. (A large pine tree in the left-hand dogleg corner, just past driving distance, is the other critical factor in making an excellent three-shot par-5.) There are other excellent holes of all lengths: the short par-4 10th and 14th, strong par-4's like the 2nd, 3rd, and 18th, and a world-class set of short holes including the 5th and 7th, although the 13th has been temporarily ruined by the club president of 1988, who insisted on a "bunker" in the right front quadrant of the green, absolutely flush with the putting surface—like the grass didn't take there. Alison's spirit will continue to be troubled until the thing is removed. 8. [7/93]

***Hokkaido Classic GC,*** *Tomakomai, Hokkaido. Jack Nicklaus, 1991.*

An excellent golf course, even though Americans will find it to be "just another Nicklaus course." The land was flattish, and it wasn't over-shaped at all; but the dented greens are quite severe in spots, and the long lake which stretches through the middle of the course comes into play rather too much for the

less-than-scratch player. Greens are vintage Bear or Sycamore Hills, with severe terraces—not my favorite style, but interesting at least. 6. [7/93]

***Hokkaido GC,*** *Tomakomai, Hokkaido. Lion and Eagle courses by Shunsuke Kato, 1991.*

The Lion course, which I actually broke 80 on, is Mr. Kato's interpretation of a "mountain links," which apparently means a ridiculously over-shaped golf course. Like most layouts of its generation, the land was so severe it would have been difficult to build anything truly worthy, but I did not think the design took good advantage of its dramatic opportunities. The other drawback was the narrowness of the fairways—many landing areas were only 15-20 yards wide, and in some intermediate areas as little as 6-8 yards wide, which no one can hit consistently. The course is also prodigiously long from the back tees, including three "short holes" at 230-plus, and the 674-yard par-5 15th, one of the hardest holes in my acquaintance.

The Eagle is quite different in style, with bulkheaded water hazards and less abrupt mounding; but the greens are still large and fairly uninteresting, and the severe terrain still makes for unplayable lies outside the regraded area of the course. Lion course: 0. Eagle course: 4. [7/93]

***Kasumigaseki CC,*** *Kawagoe, Saitama. East course by Hiro Akaboshi, Kinya Fujita, and Charles Alison, 1929; West course by Seichi Inouye, with revisions by Tai Kawata, 1991–/93.*

Bordering on Tokyo Golf Club, the East Course is considered the premier 18 holes around Tokyo, based on the stature of the club, the strong layout with Alison roots, and a distinctive set of par-3 holes—the 180-yard 10th, across a landscaped pond, is the most celebrated of the threes, but the short 4th and downhill 16th are also postcard-quality. The longer holes are also strong and reasonably well-designed, but between the preponderance of straightaway holes and the numbing effect of the two-green system, they aren't as memorable as they should be for a course rated so highly by others. 7.

The West course was something of a surprise—I'd never heard a thing about it, but there were several excellent longer holes, particularly the par-5's, and only noticeably weaker than the East course because of the lack of world-class short holes. It was in a state of flux on our visit, as new 9th and 10th holes are being built to return to the clubhouse—these were a little bit modern in look. 5. [7/93]

***Kawana Hotel GC,*** *Kawana, Ito, Shizuoka. Fuji course by Charles Alison and Komei Ohtani, 1936.*

See the "Gourmet's Choice." 8. [7/93]

***Kobe GC,*** *Kobe, Hyogo. Rokko course by A.H. Groom, 1901.*

The oldest course in Japan, this 3,700-yard par-61 sits high atop Mt. Rokko, with spectacular views of Kobe and Osaka harbors when it's not fogged in. The course is still pretty rudimentary, with few bunkers and flattish greens, but the terrain is quite hilly and most of the short holes play across deep valleys, leaving little room for error. Fun, and a welcome respite from the heat and humidity in the city below. 3. [8/93]

***Musashi CC,*** *Iruma, Saitama. Toyooka course by Seichi Inouye, 1959.*

A pleasant member's course, with good balance and fairly good bunkering, but handicapped for variety by a flattish piece of property and by the two-green system, which limits options. Very good, but nothing really special about it; the best hole here wouldn't stand out at Hirono or Tokyo GC. 4. [7/93]

***Nagoya GC,*** *Aichigun, Aichi. Wago course by Komei Ohtani and Charles Alison, 1929.*

A very private club which doesn't care too much for overseas visitors; it was the only course in Japan I

had to pay to play. Nevertheless, it is an excellent layout on nice, gently rolling land—a perfect antidote after one too many modern Japanese courses. There are several very good par-4 holes, but none I would nominate among the truly elite. 6. [8/93]

***Naruo GC,*** *Hyogo. H.C. Crane, 1904, with revisions by Charles Alison, 1930.*

An excellent but uncelebrated course at a fine club in the hills between Kobe and Osaka. The terrain is very rolling without being too steep, and the routing creates many excellent par-4 holes. This is also the only remaining Alison course in Japan to retain both the original greens contouring and bunkering; most others have been changed to convert the greens to bentgrass and/or enlarge them. 7. [8/93]

***Otaru CC,*** *Otaru, Hokkaido. Old course by Iwaji Kuno, 1928; nine holes incorporated into Zenibaka New course by Koukichi Yasuda, 1970.*

Technically this is a seaside course, as it sits on the north coast of Hokkaido just northeast of Sapporo, but it is very flat and trees prevent even a whiff of the sea itself; the old nine has a bit more of a flat links feel. The New course is very well respected in Japan, presumably for the fine condition of its bentgrass greens and the mix of golf holes; but I found it rather dull, without enough design flair to relieve the sameness of the terrain. The standout hole was the short par-4 14th, a good drive (or iron) and pitch. Oddly, the course continues the old Japanese tradition of having a two-green system, even though here on Hokkaido both greens are bentgrass—a slavery to custom that defies all logic. 4. [7/93]

***Pine Lake GC,*** *Nishiwaki, Hyogo. Robert Trent Jones Jr., 1984.*

I really liked this course; the mountain scenery of the front nine and the landscaping throughout are spectacular, and the back nine has some excellent golf holes to boot. The greens are big and fairly dull, but at least they don't detract from the course, and even the steeper parts of the course were fairly well-shaped to minimize artificial appearance. Only bad hole: the dogleg-right par-4 3rd, which looks like a giant slalom run. 6. [8/93]

***Taiheiyo C,*** *Gotemba, Shizuoka. Gotemba course by Shunsuke Kato, 1977.*

The home of the Japanese Masters, this parkland layout is built at the foot of Mount Fuji on its southern flank, with some picturesque views of the mountain. The course is vaguely modeled after Augusta in that it has lots of white sand and water hazards, and wall-to-wall green grass between the pines. But the sloping site lacks variety, and the greens don't have anywhere near the intricacy of Augusta's. 5. [7/93]

*The 1st tee at Naruo, a classical Japanese golf landscape.*

***Tokyo GC,*** *Sayama, Saitama. Komei Ohtani, 1940, based on an earlier layout by Charles Alison, with a few modifications to the front nine by Desmond Muirhead, 1987.*

This course has an interesting history; the club was moved only eight years after Alison built his course, and the Japanese architect who assisted him attempted to reproduce many of Alison's most distinctive holes and features on the new layout. The bunkering, for the most part, isn't nearly as deep as what Alison has become renowned for in Japan, but even the flattest bunkers are quite interesting thanks to the unique wavy edge, which has been retained from the previous course. I also prefer the layout here to the more renowned Kasumigaseki—the par-4 and par-5 holes are more distinctive. But it's a smaller, more private club that doesn't spend nearly as much on conditioning, and it has suffered somewhat from the narrowing of several fairways out of proportion, probably a misguided response to criticism of the course as "not hard enough" for great players—the narrow fairways and the deep korai rough must make it very hard for the wayward-driving member. The Muirhead additions—mostly mounding for definition—stand out like a sore thumb, and ought to be carted away by men in white coats. 7. [7/93]

***Tomisato GC,*** *Chiba. Michael Poellot, 1992.*

I only saw a few holes of this course by van during a rainstorm, so I won't give it a grade; but I wouldn't rate it as highly as its sister, Caledonian. The property is quite a bit tighter, with many parallel holes as a result, and the related loss of variety and strategy. The par-3's are the feature holes, three of the four across water. But the real feature is the artificial rock work at the par-3 7th, a miracle of modern technology—but, at $2 million for this hole, indicative more of the need to introduce some dramatic feature to the course than of the borderline design overkill of Caledonian. [7/93]

## —*Gossip*—

Gossip is virtually impossible to find on Japanese courses, because nobody from outside can afford to go and check them out, and the Japanese have that cultural reluctance to say anything negative; their magazines won't print a Top 100 list for precisely that reason, but my friends in Japan have compiled one for my use. The near-unanimous choice for best course I missed was Nikko CC north of Tokyo; closer in, they rated Ibaragi (East), Oh-Arai GC, and Ryugasaki CC as the other best courses around Tokyo. There's also Kagogawa GC by Mr. Ohtani, who must have learned something from Mr. Alison, and Phoenix CC, the resort course way down in Kyushu which used to be in the *GOLF Magazine* Top 100, mostly because the tour players on the panel were inclined to like a course that paid such handsome appearance fees.

As for new-age designs, I believe that most or all are strongly limited by inferior property. Best bets: Maple Country Club, the first design of writer-turned-architect Tak Kaneda; Ishioka and New St. Andrews by Nicklaus; Glenmoor and Kimisarazu (the former Mariya CC, currently closed for restructuring) by Perry Dye, and Katsura and Onuma in Hokkaido by Bobby Jones. Or, try Segovia or Shinyo, two of Desmond Muirhead's most bizarre symbolic designs, and tell me if you can keep from cracking up.

## AUSTRALIA

I must admit, right off the bat, to being an unabashed fan of Australian tourism. In the winter, when the northeastern U.S. (home of 80% of our best courses) is blanketed by snow, this is the best place on earth a golfer can travel—a perfect mild climate with lots of sun, great beaches, beautiful cities that are remarkably safe by our standards, and great golf in the Sand Belt of Melbourne. It's a long way, but everyone ought to get there at least once in their lifetime.

If you're a golfer you must get to Melbourne, because no golfer should miss seeing Royal Melbourne. If I had to name just one course as being the best in the world, this might be the one, because all its holes are dramatic and yet it's perfectly wide enough and playable for the average golfer.

Put it this way. The three "musts" on the tourist itinerary are Sydney, the Great Barrier Reef, and Uluru, the aboriginal name for what we used to call Ayers Rock. (The Aussies get a chuckle out of Americans who want to see all three in a week, without understanding that each is 800 miles from the other two.) But the golf in Australia is good enough that so far I've only gotten to one of the three; I'm holding off on the others as an excuse to visit again.

## NEW SOUTH WALES

***The Australian GC,*** *Rosebury, Sydney. Jack Nicklaus and Jay Morrish, 1977.*

A difficult parkland course that was totally revamped by Nicklaus in 1977: though many of the holes follow a similar routing to Dr. MacKenzie's 1926 layout, none were preserved in any detail. The course of today is a fine, fair championship site, and home to perhaps Australia's finest club membership; but it is an unabashedly American-style Nicklaus layout, complete with long par-4's guarded by small ponds near the greens, and by Nicklaus' standard, a pretty dull layout. This wouldn't be considered a Top 100 caliber course if it weren't in Sydney; but it's not even the best course in town. 6. [3/88]

***The Lakes GC,*** *Rosebury, Sydney. Bob Von Hagge and Bruce Devlin, 1970.*

I haven't seen too many courses by this design tandem that have impressed me, but I did like a lot of The Lakes. It's an older club than this, but the course had to be replaced when the construction of the airport freeway sliced the original property in two, leaving the architects a cramped, bisected property dominated by large natural lakes to work with, and they did a good job with what they had. The course is sorely handicapped by mediocre par-3 finishing holes for both nines—the fault not necessarily of Von Hagge, but of whoever located the clubhouse—but the back nine has several spectacular holes, with the lakes a prime feature, and the bunkers are severe but small enough that the average player won't always find them. In Sydney the course has a negative reputation for difficulty and all that water in play, but the designers would have been stupid not to use it as they did—it was the only natural feature the site had in its favor, and the natural growth along the borders of the lakes is much more attractive than the small watering holes at The Australian. 5. [3/88]

***Long Reef GC,*** *Collaroy, Sydney. Architect unknown.*

A barren and windswept promontory in Sydney's northern suburbs, with a drop of more than 100 feet at the point to the ocean below, though the golf holes are removed from the cliff edge by bush and a public walk. There is some interesting bunkering and some mound/ridge hazards across certain fairways, but the course is too tightly packed, giving little definition between holes, and the topography is mostly one big sweep, with holes going up or down. Still, must be fun or hell when the wind blows. 4. [3/93]

***New South Wales GC,*** *La Perouse, Sydney. Alister MacKenzie, 1928, with postwar reconstruction by Eric Apperly, 1947.*

An open, exposed layout at the headland of Botany Bay and the Pacific Ocean, this must be one of the most violent golf courses in the world to battle in the elements, thanks also to the steep hills and profuse bottle-brush and other flora, which stiffen the test. While some critics of the layout seem to think the routing should have been confined to running along the valleys between the hills, making for a less stern test, I think the routing is excellent, featuring holes that attack the hills from all angles. On the other hand, there's not the usual MacKenzie sophistication in the contouring of the bunkers and greens, perhaps due to the military maneuvers carried out on the site during the Second World War: some greens are steeply banked but not exactly "rolling," and the bunkers are mostly small sand pits with little shape. Marvelous holes include the par-5 5th and the following short hole which touches the Cape Banks (the turning point for Captain Cook as he sailed into Botany Bay and discovered Oz), the short but exposed 11th, and the roller-coaster short par-4 14th with its heroic tee shot across a scrub-filled chasm. But on the downside, they have a difficult time growing decent golf turf in this location, and if they cut the bottle-brush back a bit the course would have a less nasty disposition toward the average player. 7. [3/88]

***Newcastle GC,*** *Fern Bay, Stockton. Original nine by Fred Popplewell and A.A. Franklin, 1915, with revisions and expansion to 18 holes by Eric Apperly, 1937.*

A fine and relatively unheralded course two or three hours north of Sydney, with holes laid out over a series of low sandy ridges, and some Aussie bushland at the sides of the fairways, especially on the front side. The unkempt bunkers are small but difficult to recover strokes from, while the tiny raised greens demand precise approaching. Nitpickers may not like several blind or half-blind shots, nor the fact that the club has struggled in recent years with course conditioning; yet blindness aside, there is not an indifferent hole in the entire course. Best holes include the difficult par-3's (two of them over 220 yards, the short 7th with no place to miss the green), and the telling stretch of holes from the 4th through 6th; but a personal favorite was the short par-4 11th, with perfect rolls in the fairway. 7. [3/93]

***PGA National GC at Riverside Oaks,*** *Cattai. Valley course, 1988.*

This course, the new HQ of the Australian PGA, is no better than the American and British counterparts at Palm Beach Gardens and The Belfry, and that's not saying very much. The course has championship length and a couple of interesting holes, but it's always a bad sign when the players are short-cutting over the trees to play down other fairways; and it's absolutely horrible as a spectator course. Overall, it looks way too much like an American housing development. 4. [3/88]

*14th & 15th at New South Wales.*

**Royal Sydney GC,** *Rose Bay, Sydney. S.R. Robbie, 1896, with modifications by Alister MacKenzie, 1926, and by Michael Wolveridge and Peter Thomson, 1981–87.*

A storied club with a parkland layout on prime real estate across the street from Sydney Harbour, and just over a hill from the city itself. Facilities include a yacht basin and a monolithic clubhouse. Recent modifications have added to the appeal of the main course, whose interest derives mostly from the scores of small bunkers which flank the straight and narrow path. While there are fine holes of all lengths, it is a major drawback of the routing that all of the longer holes come in the second nine, and that the majority of holes follow the north-south orientation of the property in general, instead of attacking the wind from all quarters. Still, I feel the course is underestimated in comparison to others in Sydney. 6. [3/88]

**St. Michael's GC,** *La Perouse, Sydney. Clement Glancey.*

From the upper reaches of the New South Wales course, this nearby layout, also amid the bottle-brush, looks potentially interesting, but it's only the holes on that end of the course that have any real value. 4. [3/88]

*—Gossip—*

Elanora Country Club, in the northern suburbs of Sydney, would be next in line to the courses I visited on the depth chart, but it's not a #1 draft pick; the only real prospect is Royal Canberra, in the Australian Capital Territory, which makes most Aussies' top ten or twenty. My reader Wally Chin, from Melbourne, also recommends the clifftop course at Narooma, about 175 miles along the coast to the south. Personally, I think you'd have to spend an entire winter in Sydney to search out these courses without having neglected the city and the beaches and the indigenous female population.

## VICTORIA

***Barwon Heads GC,*** *Barwon Heads. Victor East, 1920.*

Located a ferry trip across the mouth of Port Elizabeth Bay from The National (or a 90-minute drive around the freeway from Melbourne through Geelong), Barwon Heads is unanimously considered the best links golf course in Australia, even though a good portion of the holes are surrounded by scrubby trees and get away from the links feel. The golf course is quite short, at about 6,300 yards, and includes several two-shot holes which would benefit from a little more length, but with a wind blowing, the narrowness of these holes will be sufficient challenge. Of the holes on the classic open links ground, which include the first six and the 12th through 14th, there are enough memorable holes to set any course apart. As with all links courses (but especially so in the warmer Australian climate), it can be quite brown after a long summer, if that bothers you. It's a very nice change of pace from the similarity of the Sand Belt courses, and the clubhouse accommodations make a nice retreat, but in the realm of the great British links only a couple of the holes would get a second look. 5. [3/88]

***Commonwealth GC,*** *South Oakleigh, Melbourne. S. Bennett, 1921, with revisions by Charles Lane and Sloan Morpeth, 1926, and construction by Vern Morcom; some recent modifications by Kevin Hartley, 1991–93.*

See the "Gourmet's Choice." 8. [3/93]

***Flinders GC,*** *Flinders. Revised by Alister MacKenzie, 1926.*

There's not much MacKenzie here; Flinders is laid out on high ground, with good views of the southern coast, but few of the golf holes are anything more than basic. Still, it's pretty in spots, and I don't imagine the small greens are easy targets when the coastal winds blow. 3. [3/88]

***Huntingdale GC,*** *South Oakleigh, Melbourne. Charles Alison and Sam Berriman, 1941.*

I have yet to meet David Inglis, who invented the Australian Masters tournament and made it a fixture at this, his home club (which backs up onto Metropolitan), but he must be a promotional genius to have gotten a boring golf course like this rated among the Top 100 in the world. Alison laid out the course back and forth along a long, narrow property without ever setting foot in Australia, and Berriman's construction, while sound, shows very little sophistication. The resulting course is long, narrow (through trees), and therefore exacting, but completely uninspiring. It's the Firestone of Australia—if even that. 5. [3/88]

***Kingston Heath GC,*** *Cheltenham, Melbourne. Des Soutar, 1925, with bunkering added by Alister MacKenzie and Vern Morcom, 1928, and subsequent modifications by Peter Thomson, Michael Wolveridge, and Graeme Grant.*

Just as the grand scale of Royal Melbourne is comparable to Pine Valley, as sister courses Kingston Heath is very similar to Merion (East), as their respective continent's finest examples of architecture on a small acreage. Confined to just 125 acres on a fairly flat piece of ground, Kingston Heath nevertheless establishes itself clearly as Melbourne's second-best course, and perhaps one of the top 25 or 50 in the world. The routing plan, like Merion's, is so intricate that you suspect you'll have to play a hole twice somewhere to get out of a tight corner, yet the plantings of ti-trees and dense shrubs prevent any sudden attack of agoraphobia and double as an excellent background for the intricate bunkering that really sets this course apart. Most of the greens built by Soutar are only modestly interesting in contour, but a couple that have been remodeled by the present curator, Graeme Grant, are outstanding, and the 15th, which MacKenzie him-

self built to cap off that stupendous 155-yard short hole, is a classic in its own right. But I can't claim it as a personal favorite; with the tight corridors and the Coriolis force working clockwise, I have yet to break 90 here. 8. [3/93]

***Marysville District CC,*** *Marysville, Victoria. Architect unknown.*

A primitive little course in a pretty mountain valley out past Healesville Sanctuary, the town is home to a large cross-country ski area in winter. The 6,100-yard layout has no bunkers, but a rushing stream figures in at several holes, and some holes are so narrow that the tall trees produce a cathedral effect. 2. [3/93]

***The Metropolitan GC,*** *South Oakleigh, Melbourne. J.B. Mackenzie, 1908, with eight holes relocated by Dick Wilson, 1961.*

This is a fine club and has all the facilities to serve as a championship site, including a wonderfully maintained and difficult golf course, but to my mind it suffers in comparison to some of the other Sand Belt courses. While the golf course has the length and balance to challenge the expert player, the property lacked the rolling topography that some other Melbourne layouts have used to such great advantage. The club was forced to build several new holes in 1961 when part of the old layout was conscripted by the local council for new schools, but the holes added by Dick Wilson (consisting of most of the back nine) are not glaringly different in terms of architectural style, even though an experienced eye might be able to pick out the newer bunkers. 6. [3/88]

*National Golf & Country Club—severe, scenic & compelling.*

***The National G & CC,*** *Cape Schanck. Robert Trent Jones, Jr., 1988.*

A course that opened for play just the week before I first saw it, and which demands a lot of adjectives by way of description. The first that leaps to mind is spectacular: an overused term nowadays (perhaps even in this text), but the site of The National, 300 feet up in the hills looking down over forest, dunes, and the southern coast of the Mornington Peninsula, must rate right up there with Cypress Point for scenic splendor. Unfortunately, the architect tried to continue this mood by building spectacular features throughout the course, and while the bunkering for the most part looks very good, the sharp ridges which run through many of the greens are too spectacular for even modest putting speeds, and often look terribly contrived.

The second adjective is severe: the wilderness to the sides of many holes, steep grades, occasional forced carries, and openness to the whims of the offshore winds are elements of difficulty which tend to multiply together instead of just adding up. I'd bet the mortgage that this combination of factors renders this golf course virtually unplayable a couple of afternoons per week.

The third adjective is "nouveau riche": despite its recent birth the club is already loudly advertising its course as being "the best in the world," and the choice of name is something less than humble. (It's also stupid for a course trying to achieve world stature, since it requires clarification to distinguish it from The National Golf Links of America and National Golf Club in Toronto, which are already rated among the world's top courses.) But the name of the first course in the development, Cape Schanck, has even worse connotations for golfers.

But the fourth adjective is compelling: despite all the design decisions I disagree with, this course has a quality (much like Desert Highlands) that demands attention, and makes it a must-see attraction. Just go on a calm day, or else bring a shag bag with you. 0-6. [3/88]

***Royal Melbourne GC,*** *Black Rock, Melbourne. West course by Alister MacKenzie with Alex Russell and Vern Morcom, 1926; East course by Russell and Morcom, 1928.*

My dictum that I would only select one course per architect for the "Gourmet's Choice" was excruciating in the case of MacKenzie, for it forced me to pass over both Cypress Point and Royal Melbourne, which would probably both be in my personal top five. Royal Melbourne, I think, is the course Augusta wants to be: wide enough for anybody, but brilliantly routed to make use of the topography and bunkered to reward bold play and bold decisions.

Some people whine that the *GOLF Magazine* world rankings are unfair because we rate the Composite course at Melbourne, which is only played for tournaments; we do it because a lot of the pros have never seen the six holes on the West course that are omitted for gallery control. The six holes borrowed from the East course *are* superior to those left off the West—four of the six replacements are great holes, as opposed to only a couple of those they replace—but I'd still put the West course in my world Top 10 because of the overall scale and concept of it, and the all-world quality of holes like the 3rd, 4th, 5th, 6th, 10th, 11th, 12th, 17th, and 18th.

The East course is clearly inferior to the West; the terrain across the road is much flatter, and there is less of the superb native vegetation that makes Royal Melbourne's bunkers so spectacular. But the East does have several excellent holes—especially the 3rd, 4th, 17th, and 18th which comprise the last four holes of the Composite course, and the East 16th, maybe the best par-3 on the entire property, which they couldn't figure out how to fit into the Composite 18. When a club has holes like that "on the bench," it's obviously someplace special. West course: 10. East course: 6. [3/93]

***Sandringham GC,*** *Sandringham, Victoria. Alister MacKenzie and Alex Russell, 1929.*

A public layout directly across the street from the entrance to Royal Melbourne, the course features several beautiful greenside bunkers left over from the masters, though they are not as conspicuous to play as at Royal. The course suffers from a lack of fairway bunkering (I wonder if the decision not to have it to speed play was the original architects', or whether they took it out?) and from the lack of texture in the grasses that makes its neighbors so beautiful, but the uphill par-4 14th is still a classic hole. Not bad, but only if you can't get on elsewhere. 3. [3/93]

***Spring Valley GC,*** *Clayton South, Melbourne. Vern Morcom, 1948.*

I checked this course out because it was designed by Morcom, who built all the great-looking bunkers and greens at Royal Melbourne, Kingston Heath, and Commonwealth; and he didn't build a bad set at Spring Valley, either. Unfortunately, though, the property is very tight and low-lying in places, so he didn't have as much to work with here as far as contouring the bunkers was concerned, and it's a two-iron tee shot to the corners of several doglegs to keep from running through the fairway into trees. So, it's not a bad course for the members, but probably not worth a detour. 3. [3/88]

***Victoria GC,*** *Cheltenham, Melbourne. Alister MacKenzie, 1927, with revisions by Peter Thomson and Michael Wolveridge.*

In Australian circles this is generally (though certainly not unanimously) considered to be the third-best golf course in the Sand Belt, but I don't concur with the opinion. It is a fine club, including upstairs clubhouse guest facilities which merit consideration on a Sand Belt golfing trip, but I think too much of its reputation is derived from that summer in 1954 when both the British Amateur and Open Championship trophies were on display in the club foyer, courtesy of successes by club members Doug Bachli and Peter Thomson. Despite a gently undulating property catty-corner from Royal Melbourne, which provided a better start than some of the other Sand Belt layouts, I don't think the course provides quite the strategic interest of Commonwealth, the variety of Kingston Heath, or the charm of Yarra Yarra. The driveable par-4 opening hole sets up just the opposite as Commonwealth's old one, stressing length off the tee over accurate placement—a poor choice for a hole of this length; and while the next four holes going out are quite good, I think the routing suffers considerably from the arrangement of two long holes at the conclusion of each nine (even though the long 9th hole falls beautifully across the terrain). Also, Victoria's short holes are unusually dull in a neighborhood dominated by classic par threes. It's a very good course, though, and perhaps this negative review just underlines the strength of its close competition. 7. [3/88]

***Yarra Yarra GC,*** *Bentleigh East, Melbourne. Alister MacKenzie and Alex Russell, 1929.*

A wonderful golf club, whose course has none of the championship length of The Metropolitan or Huntingdale (though it's no pushover), but possesses all of the charm those others lack. The routing of the holes is not a particular feature—like many of the other Sand Belt courses, the holes march back and forth lined by trees for a long spell, like targets in a shooting gallery—but there are many standout holes, thanks to some intelligently designed green complexes, and the course when I saw it was in marvelous condition. The four short holes are collectively renowned in Australia (climaxed by the magnificent 11th), but among the longer holes there are also two superb tests—the long two-shot 5th and 13th—which never get their due. I did notice that the vast majority of the long holes slide ever so slightly from left to right, including the two mentioned above; I feel certain that the construction superintendent played a slight fade. 6. [3/93]

—*Gossip*—

Around Melbourne, try The Woodlands or Peninsula Country Club (South), but I doubt they're worth the nod versus another round on one of the courses listed. If you're really feeling adventurous, head for Thomson and Wolveridge's new nine at Yarrawonga, in the bush country. And, I've just seen photos of a brand-new links course called The Dunes, in the town of Rye (just below The National), which looks like the real thing.

## SOUTH AUSTRALIA

***The Grange GC,*** *Seaton, Adelaide. West course 1926, architect unknown.*

A solid, pine-tree/parkland layout somewhat reminiscent of Pinehurst, but not of No. 2. It is quite a bit more tightly treed than the other Adelaide courses, presenting interesting problems in the wind, particularly at the par-5's and par-3's, which all seem to play right into its teeth. The strongest hole is the long two-shot 17th, with "Jackson's gulch" awaiting the pulled approach. A big club, well-conditioned courses, and perennially busy. 5. [3/88]

***Kooyonga GC,*** *Lockleys, Adelaide. "Cargie" Rymill, 1923, with revisions by Thomson and Wolveridge.*

A compact layout in modest, tree-covered dunes right across from the airport, with some outstanding holes, especially the par-5 2nd and the short holes. The greens, more undulating than Royal Adelaide's, are quite good. But the course could flow much better: there are long stretches of holes that go back and forth between upwind and downwind, and the course could easily be renumbered to break up the consecutive par-3 holes at 14 and 15, which are a weakness. A pretty good course, but not worth the trip in itself. 6. [3/88]

*The magnificent 11th at Yarra Yarra.*

***Royal Adelaide GC,*** *Seaton, Adelaide. Present course founded 1904, with modifications by Des Soutar, Alister MacKenzie, and Peter Thomson and Michael Wolveridge.*

Aside from the biennial Arts Festival, this course is the only reason for a golfer to visit Adelaide. At first glance the aspect of Royal Adelaide must lead one to wonder if he's traveled all this way for a letdown: the flattish property is surrounded by public roads and chain-link fence, and split in two by a train track. One trip around the course dispels all fears. Some modest contour at the center of the property is used to advantage on several holes, in a routing which loops out and back into this country several times, and the parkland/heathland terrain has been carefully planted with pines, adding to the natural blessing of sparse grasses, mosses, and pigface (we call it iceplant) in the roughs. The mix of four long holes and three short ones makes for a par of 73, but it's the two-shotters that impress most, from the 301-yard third to the "crater" 11th and the 450-yard 14th, a classic driving hole that could be easily copied on flat ground. Too bad the run home from there is unworthy of the rest of the course. 8. [3/88]

*—Gossip—*

I don't know of any other courses in South Australia that anybody thinks are worth seeing.

## WESTERN AUSTRALIA

***Joondalup GC,*** *Perth. Robert Trent Jones, Jr., 1985.*

This is a spectacular achievement in itself, reclaiming an abandoned quarry for golf and thereby securing the rim for high-end housing, and Jones went for the spectacular in his design of three distinctly different nines. The Quarry nine (named even though there is some measure of quarry in play on each of the three) is probably the best and most memorable of the three, with several stunning holes and big contours in the greens, but nothing outlandish other than its rock-rimmed waste bunkers. The scale of it is dramatic and so unusual that it's difficult to judge where your drive might land.

Unfortunately, I don't think the other nines measure up to that high standard. The Dune nine, the second half of the original 18, is a bit of overkill—it features a lot of elevation change, and the native bush is much closer to the fairways; and the contouring of the greens gets a bit too wild. The third nine, Lake, required much more large-scale grading, and doesn't quite have the enclosed feel of the other two, though the golf holes aren't as "over the top" as the Dune. If it were all as good as the Quarry nine, it would be quite something; it's still pretty good, but it doesn't justify the 2,000 mile flight from Adelaide to Perth. 7. [3/93]

*You're the visitor at Lake Karrinyup.*

***Lake Karrinyup GC,*** *Karrinyup, Perth. Alister MacKenzie and Alex Russell, 1927, with revisions by Peter Thomson and Michael Wolveridge.*

Boy, am I glad I didn't fly all the way across the continent in 1988 to see this one. Only two holes (the par-5 3rd and long par-3 8th) play beside the lake; the rest of the course lays across broad hills, with few subtle undulations to lend it interest. The lines of the bunkers are very modernized, and the greens aren't MacKenzie originals. But the property encompasses three sides of the lake and probably 100 acres apart from the course, making a perfect habitat for kangaroos, which roam the course freely. 5. [3/93]

—*Gossip*—

The one course everyone in Western Australia tried to get me to play was The Vines, a Graham Marsh–designed resort track. Cottesloe is a seaside course with some interesting terrain, but quite narrow and somewhat short—and Royal Perth is too tight for comfort, according to a couple of my readers.

As for the rest of the continent, I've never traveled to Queensland, the Down Under answer to Florida, but my friend Tom Ramsey rates a new course called Hope Island (for which he is, undoubtedly, the director of publicity) as the best of Peter Thomson's work in Australia. Thanks to Tom's book, *Great Australian Golf Holes,* I feel I've been able to spy on the rest of the country, and the only place I'd like to go is Tasmania Golf Club in Hobart, where the scenery is ruggedly spectacular, even if the architecture may lack a bit of polish.

## NEW ZEALAND

Australia is something of a cross between Britain and America — they drive on the left and eat McDonald's — but New Zealand is truly England down under, with the formality and gentility of England's Lake District. Geographically, though, it's a mind-boggling world of its own, stretching more than 1,000 miles from the tropical Ninety Mile Beach in the north to Milford Sound, with its Canadian Rockies-style scenery, on the South Island. Right now golf courses of any kind are few and far between, but someday, when the rest of the world is overrun by progress and overpopulation, this will be the place to get away, and perhaps then there will be enough economic growth to justify a couple of courses which take advantage of its natural splendours.

## NORTH ISLAND

***Paraparaumu Beach GC,*** *Paraparaumu Beach, near Wellington. Substantially rebuilt by Douglas Whyte and Alex Russell, 1946.*

Probably the best links golf course in the southern hemisphere (if you don't count Durban Country Club as a true links), this is a course where familiarity breeds respect. It does not have the exciting terrain of some of my favorite unknown British links, removed from the seashore by a strand of expensive beachfront homes, but neither does it have any poor holes that remove it from consideration as a great course. Packed tightly into 120 acres, it features good-sized, fast greens, some excellent short holes (two of which are bunkerless), and three superior full two-shot holes (the 4th, 13th, and 17th) which demonstrate the need for strength as well as finesse. A fun course always, and during a good season for growing grass, an excellent test of golf, too. 7. [3/88]

***Rotorua GC,*** *Rotorua. Arikikapakapa course by Charles H. Redhead.*

Located just at the south end of the town noted for its geothermal activity, this short layout pays homage to its background: the smell of sulfur pervades the air, the stiffly lipped bunkers look vaguely volcanic, and there are even a couple of thermal fissures in a crater near the center of the otherwise gentle parkland property. Still, that wouldn't get the course much space in this tourist guide without the par-3 9th hole, which plays across the crater to a green setting worthy of Pine Valley, with the added worry that a flubbed tee shot means a close encounter with the wonders of the underground. A rerouting of the course has left the finish without any call for stout hitting, but the 16th and 18th holes are good short par-4's in their own right. 4. [4/88]

*At Rotorua there's plenty of trouble underfoot.*

***Wellington GC,*** *Heretaunga, Lower Hutt. Alister MacKenzie, 1926.*

There are all sorts of jokes about "wonderful, windy Wellington," all of which became clear on my visit to Heretaunga, a flattish parkland layout in a valley NASA could put to good use as a wind tunnel. On the day I walked the course, I kept one eye on the lookout for falling trees in 50-mph winds. The golf course is not the weakest MacKenzie design I've ever seen—there's always Fulford—but it certainly shows little of the sophistication for which he is renowned, and I don't know whether the added "executive" nine has anything to do with that. Anyway, Heretaunga is the site of a fine club, but my advice is to spend an extra day on the South Island instead of getting blown around here. 3. [3/88]

***Titirangi GC,*** *New Lynn, Auckland. F.G. Hood and Gilbert Martin, with revisions by Alister MacKenzie, 1926.*

A tight parkland layout over severely undulating terrain, showing certain touches of the MacKenzie genius, but less brilliant contouring than his true masterpieces. A road through the middle of the site handicaps the holes at the start and finish, but the midsection of the course utilizes a long ravine running through the center of the property to outstanding effect, particularly at the short 11th and short par-5 13th. 6. [4/88]

***Wairakei International GC,*** *Wairakei, near Taupo. Peter Thomson and Michael Wolveridge, 1975.*

A "championship length" layout developed a few years ago as part of a state-owned tourist resort, with fair success; but a bit of a slog from the back tees for us of modest strength. The valley in which the course is laid out includes good undulation and some majestic evergreen trees too big to consider removing; instead they serve as obstacles in the center of three different fairways, which is too much of a questionable thing. The most notorious hole is "The Rogue" 14th, 608 yards uphill to an elevated, boomerang-shaped green; the 475-yard 3rd, along a deep gulley on the right, is 475 times better. 5. [3/88]

—*Gossip*—

Near Auckland, the next-best courses to see are Middlemore, the parkland home of Auckland Golf Club, and Muriwai, a links along the west coast that was described to me as "a waste of great links land." But the potential hidden gem of the North Island is a links along Ninety Mile Beach called Kaitaia; I mentioned it off-handedly in the private edition of this book, offering "brownie points" to anyone who'd go check it out, and received snapshots of it in the mail from a devoted reader, Ran Morrissett. He reports it's a beautiful links layout with some fabulous holes, but the maintenance is very scruffy.

On the South Island, which is much less populated, the scenery is the main reason to go, but if you insist on golfing, try the Otago Golf Club in Dunedin; I just want to prove to my friend Fred Muller, the nearest I know to an expert on New Zealand golf, that the course really does exist.

—THE—
Doak
Gazetteer

*The clubhouse at Stoke Poges.*

*The 15th at the Valley Club.*

## Most Beautiful Clubhouses—Architecture

Desert Highlands
Stoke Poges
Indianwood
Seminole
Hokkaido Classic
Ridgewood
Chicago Golf Club
Sunningdale, England
Valley Club of Montecito
Desert Mountain

*My own best home hole, the 18th at Stonewall.*

### Most Beautiful Clubhouses— Setting

National Golf Links
Bel Air
Crystal Downs
Cypress Point
Crail
Desert Mountain
Southerndown
Mid Ocean
Shinnecock Hills
Stonewall

### Best Walks

Cypress Point
Fishers Island
Cape Breton Highlands
Royal Dornoch
Mid Ocean
Notts
Machrihanish
Stonewall
San Francisco Golf Club
Merion (East)

### Best Halfway House

Sunningdale
Mid Ocean
Pine Valley
Hapuna
Valley Club of Montecito
National Golf Links
Stonewall
Sylvan Resort (Treetops, Jones)
Kasumigaseki (East)
Capilano
Mrs. Forman's, Musselburgh

### Best Lunch

National Golf Links
Pine Valley
Muirfield
Chantilly
Sunningdale
CC of Birmingham, AL
Swinley Forest
Kapalua
Sherwood
The Golf Club

### Most Difficult to Walk

Ventana Canyon (Canyon)
Beaver Creek
Port Ludlow (Trail)
National G & CC, Australia
River Islands
Treetops (Jones)
Dunmaglas
Desert Mountain (Geronimo)
Pelican Hill
Castle Harbour

## Best Club Accommodations

Caledonian
Mid Ocean
Rolling Rock
The Honors Course
Augusta National
Redtail
Sand Hills
Riviera
Pine Valley
Royal Sydney

*Caledonian at night.*

## Best Entrance Drive

Old Head of Kinsale
Yeamans Hall
National Golf Links
Macroom
Augusta National
Royal West Norfolk
Crumpin-Fox
GC at Desert Mountain (Cochise)
Haig Point
Bel Air
The Creek Club
Aberdovey

## Best Outbuildings

National Golf Links—windmill
St. Enodoc—church
Bamburgh Castle—Dunstanburgh Castle
Harbour Town—lighthouse
Adare Manor— hotel
Cold Spring CC—Kahn Estate
Royal Cromer—lighthouse
Lost City—hotel

*Adare Manor.*

## Best Logo

Glen Abbey
Merion
Fishers Island
Sand Hills
Augusta National
Forest Highlands
Prairie Dunes
Machrihanish
Royal Worlington & Newmarket
Oak Tree

## Most Hospitable Clubs

Ballybunion
Lahinch
Hunstanton
St. Andrews
Durban CC
Barwon Heads
Kapalua
Crail
Gambel Golf Links
Pennard

## Most Engaging Memberships

The Australian Golf Club
Ballybunion
Butler National
Crooked Stick
Merion
Newcastle GC, Australia
Oak Tree Golf Club
Palmetto
Pennard
Prairie Dunes
Sunningdale, England
Whitinsville, MA
Woking, England

## Clubs Most Likely to Require a Family History Before Letting You Play

Alwoodley
Chicago Golf Club
Fishers Island
Highlands, NC
Jupiter Island
Maidstone
Misquamicut
Myopia Hunt Club
Old Town
Piping Rock
Round Hill
Royal Sydney
Shoreacres

## Courses Worth Groveling to Play

Cypress Point
Swinley Forest
San Francisco Golf Club
Muirfield
Shadow Creek
Seminole
Fishers Island
Augusta National
Chicago Golf Club
Old Town Club

## Best Low-Key Atmosphere

Lahinch
Valley Club of Montecito
Palmetto
Roaring Gap
Stonewall
Machrihanish
Mark Twain
Prairie Dunes
Fishers Island
Waterville

## Least-Played Courses

Deepdale
Shadow Creek
Redtail
Double Eagle
Sterling Bluff
Metedeconk National
Rolling Rock
Swinley Forest
Chicago Golf Club
Cape Breton Highlands
Naruo

## Best Courses to Own a House On

Pine Valley
Fishers Island
Casa de Campo
Crystal Downs
St. George's Hill
Yeamans Hall
Kapalua (Plantation)
Royal Portrush
Forest Highlands
Bel Air
Roaring Gap

## "Ten" Awards—Beauty Plus Brains

Royal County Down
Cypress Point
Shinnecock Hills
Casa de Campo
Gleneagles
Crystal Downs
St. Enodoc
Isle of Purbeck
Kapalua (Plantation)
Pelican Hill (Ocean)

*One of the best—Royal County Down.*

*MacKenzie's unforgettable Cypress Point.*

*Shinnecock Hills, site of the 1995 U.S. Open*

## "Ends of the Earth"— Best Places to Get Away From It All

Cape Breton Highlands
Sand Hills
Pennard
Kaitaia
Machrihanish
Narin & Portnoo
Royal West Norfolk
Machrie
Spring Island
Barwon Heads

*Stanley Thompson's Cape Breton Highlands, worth the journey.*

## "Dumb Blonde" Awards—Pretty But Lacking Substance

Arrowhead
North Berwick (East Links)
Bamburgh Castle
Bodega Harbour
Perry Park
Torrey Pines
Mauna Lani
Garrison
Victoria, BC
Kinsale
White Columns

*The 12th at Arrowhead.*

*Home of the Masters—Augusta National.*

## "L'Oréal" Awards—Best Conditioned Courses

Atlantic
Augusta National
Butler National
Double Eagle
Inverness
Kingston Heath
Merion (East)
Oakmont
Vintage Club (Mountain)
Winged Foot (West)
Worplesdon

## "Sleeping Beauty" Awards—More Than Meets the Eye

Royal Worlington & Newmarket
Woking
Royal Liverpool
Chicago Golf Club
St. Andrews (Eden)
Walton Heath (Old)
Rockport
Desert Forest
Belvedere
Ashridge

*Royal Worlington.*

## Most Fun to Play

Lahinch
North Berwick (West)
Cruden Bay
Harrison Hills
Whitinsville
Yale University
Machrihanish
Kapalua (Plantation)
High Pointe
Wawashkamo

*Cruden Bays 8th.*

## Hardest to Find

Naruo
The Dunes, MI
Yale
Royal West Norfolk
Pine Valley
Tokyo Golf Club
Royal Worlington & Newmarket
Macroom
Yeamans Hall
Blue Mound

## Courses I'd Most Like to Play with Dianna

St. Enodoc
Cypress Point
Lahinch
North Berwick (West)
St. Andrews (Old)
Royal Dornoch
Machrihanish
Royal County Down
National Golf Links
Royal Melbourne (West)

## Courses I Most Wish I Had Played

Oakmont
Myopia Hunt Club
Inverness
Morfontaine
Old Town Club
Peachtree
Hollywood
Brancepeth Castle
Roaring Gap
Southerndown

## Courses I'd Never Play Again

Stone Harbor
The Bear
D. Fairchild Wheeler
Pocono Manor Resort (East)
Long Bay
Michaywé (Lakes)
Sugarloaf, MI
Terradyne
Heatherridge
John F. Kennedy Municipal
Desert Mountain (Renegade)
Hokkaido (Lion)
Port Ludlow (Trail)
Peter Hay
Otaru
Carmel Valley Ranch

*The 11th tee at Nefyn.*

## Courses You Need a Guide to Play

Prestwick
Lahinch
Nefyn & District
Portsalon
Royal County Down
Royal St. George's
Royal Liverpool
St. Andrews (Old)
National Golf Links
St. Enodoc

## Windiest Courses

Wellington
Waterville
New South Wales
Sawgrass
Cyrstal Downs
Royal Cinque Ports
Humewood
Prairie Dunes
Walton Heath
Desert Dunes
Plum Creek
Long Reef

*Thousands of spectators at TPC Sawgrass.*

## Best Spectator Courses

TPC at Sawgrass (Stadium)
TPC of Connecticut
Muirfield Village
PGA West (Stadium)
TPC at Scottsdale (Tournament)
Muirfield
Royal Durban
Glen Abbey
Royal Birkdale
Royal Melbourne (Composite)

## Schizophrenic Courses

Austin CC—river bottom and ravines
Blackwolf Run (Meadow Valleys)—river and field
Bodega Harbour—hillside and marsh
Carmel Valley Ranch—hillside and flat
The Creek—parkland and Soundview
Golspie—links and moorland
High Pointe—open and treed
Hillside—older and modern
Inverness—Ross and not Ross
Manor House Hotel—river and hill
Misquamicut—hilly and flat
Ojai Valley—barrancas and flat
Pacific Grove—links and housing
Port Ludlow—gentle and steep
Spyglass Hill—dunes and trees

## Best Landscaping

Merion (East)
Oak Hill (East and West)
San Francisco Golf Club
PGA West (Jack Nicklaus Private)
Shadow Creek
The Honors Course
Garden City Golf Club
PGA West (Stadium)
Mission Hills (Dinah Shore)
Pelican Hill

## Worst Setting

Renaissance Park
Karsten GC at ASU
Seaton Carew
Royal Dublin
Rotorua—sulfur smell
Prince's
Fresh Pond—traffic noise
Tam O'Shanter—bury piles
Drummond Island
Moray—airfield
King's Crossing

## Worst Landscaping

Blue Mound
Spanish Bay
Onwentsia
Cold Spring CC
Manufacturers
Plainfield
White Bear Yacht Club
St. George's, NY
Fox Chapel
Grand Cypress (New)

*The mounding at Loxahatchee.*

## Worst-Looking Mounds

Loxahatchee
Hokkaido (Lion)
Wild Dunes (Harbor)
Caledonian
The Bear
Rancho Santa Fe Farms
Grand Cypress (Original)
Cypress Golf Club
PGA West (Jack Nicklaus Private)
Heather Glen

## Narrowest Courses

Marysville, Australia
Pine Bay
Olympic (Lakeside)
Elk Ridge
Grand Haven
Terradyne
Caernarvonshire
Boat of Garten
National GC of Australia
Heatherridge

*The 4th tee at Olympic and another narrow opening.*

## Hardest Courses

Desert Mountain (Geronimo)
Golden Valley
Medinah (No.3)
Kiawah Island (Ocean)
Pine Valley
PGA West (Stadium)
Hokkaido (Lion)
Wolf Run
Austin CC
Royal County Down
PGA West (Jack Nicklaus Private)
Wilderness Valley (Black Forest)
Bethpage (Black)

## Longest Courses

Desert Mountain (Renegade)—7515 yds
Gary Player CC, Sun City—7498 yds
Castle Pines GC—7453 yds
Desert Mountain (Geronimo)—7437 yds
Lost City—7431 yds
Kiawah Island (Ocean)—7371 yds
Medinah (No. 3)—7366 yds
Royal Johannesburg (East)—7366 yds
Glendower—7307 yds
Old Warson—7292 yds
Waterville—7184 yds plus wind

## Widest Courses

Royal Melbourne
Kapalua (Plantation)
Augusta National
The Legends (Heathland)
Pinehurst (No. 2)
National Golf Links
Pine Valley
St. Andrews (Old)
Reynolds National (Great Waters)
The Connecticut GC

## Hardest Back-to-Back Holes

Olympic (Lakeside)—4 & 5
Pebble Beach—8 & 9
Wolf Run—13 & 14
Royal Johannesburg (East)—10 & 11
Royal Lytham & St. Annes—14 & 15
Medinah (No. 3)—12 & 13
Carnoustie—15 & 16
Ballybunion (Old)—11 & 12
Mauna Kea—3 & 4
Kiawah Island (Ocean)—16 & 17
PGA West (Nicklaus Private)—16 & 17
Desert Mountain (Geronimo)—15 & 16
Carmel Valley Ranch—11 & 12
Stone Harbor—6 & 7
Hokkaido (Lion)—15 & 16
Austin CC—11 & 12
Ballybunion (New)—8 & 9
Golden Valley—2 & 3

## Crossovers

St. Andrews (Old)—7 & 11
St. Andrews (Eden)—8 & 10
TPC of Connecticut—16 & 17
Royal Worlington & Newmarket—4, 5, & 6
Royal West Norfolk—2 & 17
Royal Ashdown Forest (Old)—1 & 18
Indianwood (New)—4 & 13
Walton Heath—2 New & 17 Old
Lahinch—5 & 18
Claremont—5, 6, & 7

## Most Artistic Routing Plans

Cypress Point
St. Enodoc
Cruden Bay
Sand Hills
Bel Air
Fishers Island
Royal Dornoch
Pebble Beach
Cape Breton Highlands
St. George's

*George Thomas' intricate bunkering at Bel Air, under the "swinging bridge."*

*Swinley Forest, par 67.*

## Best Courses of Par Less Than 70

Rye
West Sussex
Swinley Forest
Wannamoisett
St. Enodoc
The Addington
Broadstone
Merion (West)
Cavendish
Ashburn (Old)

## Scorecard Oddities

Three holes over 600 yds:
Forest Highlands
Nine over 4,000 yds.:
CC at Castle Pines, front nine
Three consecutive par-5 holes:
Inwood CC, 3rd– 5th holes
Three consecutive par-5's for women:
Valley Club of Montecito, 1st–3rd
Two women's par-6 holes:
Cape Breton Highlands

## Best Use of Small Acreage

Royal Worlington & Newmarket
Merion (East)
Inverness
Kingston Heath
Wannamoisett
Whitinsville
Olympic (Cliffs Course)
Old Marsh
Royal West Norfolk
Crystal Downs—front nine

## Longest and Shortest Holes

Par 3's

| | |
|---|---|
| 77 yds | 7th Pocono Manor |
| 94 yds | 14th Engineers |
| 100 yds | 16th The Pit |
| 104 yds | 10th Inwood |
| 105 yds | 3rd Ventana Canyon (Mtn.) |
| 107 yds | 7th Pebble Beach |
| 107 yds | 7th Royal Porthcawl |
| 65 yds | (fwd. tee) 3rd River Islands |
| 264 yds | 4th Hokkaido (Lion) |

Par 4's

| | |
|---|---|
| 240 yds | 8th Merion (West) |
| 523 yds | 1st Kapalua (Plantation) |

Par 5's

| | |
|---|---|
| 421 yds | 18th Gulph Mills |
| 674 yds | 15th Hokkaido (Lion) |
| 670 yds | 5th CC at Castle Pines |
| 666 yds | 16th Pine Tree |
| 663 yds | 18th Kapalua (Plantation) |

Par 6

| | |
|---|---|
| 747 yds | 17th Black Mountain, NC |

### Best Opening Hole

Machrihanish
Long Cove
National Golf Links
St. Andrews (Old)
Merion (East)
Pinehurst (No. 2)
Peachtree
Royal County Down
Wilderness Valley (Black Forest)
The Links Golf Club, NY

### Worst Opening Hole

Terradyne
Port Ludlow (Trail)
Renaissance Park
Sylvan (Treetops Jones)
Secession
Coto de Caza
Mount Airy Lodge
Oak Tree GC
North Berwick (West)
The Addington
Prestwick, Scotland
E. Gaynor Brennan

### Best First Tee

Elie
St. Andrews (Old)
Castle Harbour
Machrihanish
Crystal Downs
Royal St. George's
Merion (East)
Shinnecock Hills
Desert Highlands
Desert Mountain (Geronimo)

### Best Putting Green

St. Andrews Ladies' Putting Green
Oakmont
Desert Highlands Putting Course
TPC at Sawgrass
Pocono Manor Lodge
Kingston Heath
Heritage Club
Willowbend

### Best Finishing Hole

Royal Lytham & St. Annes
Royal Melbourne (West)
St. Andrews (Old)
Whitinsville, MA—9th hole
The Country Club
Stonewall
St. Enodoc
Leatherstocking
Killarney (Mahony's Point)
Pete Dye Golf Club, WV
Philadelphia Cricket Club
Shadow Creek
Pebble Beach

### Best Practice Facility

GC of Oklahoma
Royal Birkdale
Shadow Creek
Black Diamond
Desert Highlands
Forest Highlands
PGA West (Resort)
Muirfield Village
Bob O'Link
Onwentsia

### Worst Finishing Hole

Polo Fields G & CC
Shiskine No. 9, Scotland
Barton Creek (Fazio)
Alton Municipal No. 9
Royal Dublin
Stone Harbor
Boyne Mountain (Monument)
Gettysvue
Machrihanish
Elk Ridge
High Pointe
Cypress Point
Heritage Club
Port Ludlow (Trail) #9

## Best Preserved Golf Courses

St. Andrews (Old Course)
Pine Valley
Royal Melbourne (West)
Prestwick—since 1910 expansion
Shinnecock Hills—since 1931 redesign
Royal West Norfolk
Chicago Golf Club—since 1925 redesign
Oakmont
Holston Hills
Woodhall Spa

## Best Restorations

Indianwood (Old)—Art Hills
Pinehurst (No. 2)—Jack Nicklaus/Ed Connor
Turnberry (Ailsa)—P. Mackenzie Ross
Wawashkamo—Larry Grow
The Country Club—Rees Jones
Crystal Downs—Geoffrey Cornish
CC of Charleston—John LaFoy
The Creek—Tom Doak
Metacomet—Ron Prichard
National Golf Links—Karl Olson

## Worst Redesigns

Prince's, England
Inverness
Scioto
Wampanoag
Oak Hill (East)
St. Andrews GC, NY
Aronimink
CC of Birmingham (West)
Dornick Hills
Crooked Stick
Macgregor Links, NY
Ballyliffin (Old)
Traverse City G & CC
Rochester G & CC
Tokyo Golf Club

## Best Courses That No Longer Exist

Lido Golf Club, NY
Addington (New), England
Blackheath, England
T. Tailer's Ocean Links, Newport, RI
Olympic (Ocean Links)
Waddesdon Manor
Bayside Links
Ithaca Country Club, NY
The Links Golf Club
Gambel Golf Links

*The Links' 8th hole—we wish it still existed.*

## Best Redesigns

Pebble Beach—H. Chandler Egan, 1928
Merion (East)—William Flynn, 1924
Shinnecock Hills—William Flynn, 1931
Oakland Hills—Robert Trent Jones, 1950
Kingston Heath—Alister MacKenzie, 1926
Seminole—Dick Wilson, 1948
Woking—George Low & Stuart Paton
Charlotte CC—Robert Trent Jones, 1960
Waterwood National—Bill Coore, 1978-83
Atlanta CC—Jack Nicklaus and Bob Cupp, 1981

## Best Evolved Golf Courses

Rye, England
Muirfield
Lahinch
Ganton
Augusta National
Royal St. George's
Royal Lytham & St. Annes
Carnoustie
Interlachen
Olympic (Lake)

## Worst Deterioration

Sharp Park Muni
Yeamans Hall
La Cumbre
Nassau Country Club
Grange Over Sands
Melrose, PA
Kernwood
Fulford
Northwood, CA
Wakonda

## Best Nine-Hole Courses

Royal Worlington & Newmarket
Whitinsville
Rolling Rock*
The Dunes
Harrison Hills*
Reigate Heath
Wawashkamo
Phoenixville
Uplands
Culver Military Academy
Millbrook
Musselburgh
*in process of adding second nine

*Whitinsville—an excellent 9-hole layout.*

## Best 27-Hole Complexes

Portmarnock
Ridgewood
The Country Club
Hamilton G & CC
Joondalup
La Paloma
Philadelphia CC
Innisbrook (Copperhead)
Kennemer
Amelia Island
St. George's Hill
Prince's

## Special Citations

| | |
|---|---|
| 10 Holes: | Hillandale |
| | Pine Valley (Short) |
| | Culver Military Academy |
| 12 Holes: | Shiskine |
| 19 Holes: | Knollwood |
| | Double Eagle |
| 20 Holes: | Haig Point |
| | Devil's Pulpit |
| 19 Holes in 18: | Turnberry (Open) |
| | The Country Club (Open) |
| 18 Holes, 36 Flags: | GC at Desert Mountain (Renegade) |

*The Portmarnock clubhouse, overlooking 27 holes.*

*The 5th at Royal Melbourne—one of 36 incredible holes.*

## Best 36-Hole Complexes

Royal Melbourne
Winged Foot
Sunningdale
Royal Portrush
Baltusrol
The Berkshire
Oak Hill
Olympia Fields
Merion
Ballybunion
Kasumigaseki
Vintage Club

## Top Multi-Course Complexes

Pinehurst
Gleneagles
St. Andrews
PGA West
Saucon Valley
La Quinta Hotel
Kiawah Island
Desert Mountain
Innisbrook
Treetops
The Homestead
Medinah
Boyne Highlands
The Legends
Bethpage
Blairgowrie

## Odd Couples—Distinctly Different Courses Sharing a Club House

Riverdale
Wilderness Valley
The Legends
Port Ludlow
Indianwood
Grand Cypress
Ballybunion
Forsgate
Wild Dunes
Olympic Club
Bethpage

*Looking down from the helicopter at Casa de Campo.*

## Best Par-3's

Casa de Campo (Teeth of the Dog)
Merion (East)
Rye
Harbour Town
Pine Valley
Crystal Downs
Yarra Yarra
Coombe Hill
Camargo
Sleepy Hollow
Prairie Dunes
St. Andrews (Eden)
Somerset Hills
Lahinch
Valley Club of Montecito
Manufacturers
Stonewall

## Best Par-5's

Muirfield
Long Cove
The Golf Club
Pebble Beach
Cypress Point
Desert Highlands
Woodhall Spa
Crystal Downs
Pine Valley
The Lakes, Sydney
Augusta National
Muirfield Village
Pennard
Harbour Town
Shoal Creek
Blackwolf Run (River)
Roaring Gap
Wilderness Valley (Black Forest)
The Honors Course

*Muirfield's 17th, one of three perfect par-5's.*

## Best Par-4's

Pine Valley
National Golf Links
Royal Melbourne (Composite)
St. Andrews (Old)
Crystal Downs
Cypress Point
Royal St. George's
Ganton
Merion (East)
Long Cove
St. George's Hill
Royal Adelaide
Royal Dornoch
Sand Hills
Ballybunion (Old)
Carnoustie
High Pointe

*The par-4 18th at Pine Valley.*

## Best Short Par-4's

Crystal Downs
Pine Valley
St. Andrews (Old)
Royal Melbourne (Composite)
Merion (East)
Cypress Point
Lancaster
Garden City Golf Club
North Berwick (West)
Woodhall Spa

*The 5th at Crystal Downs—one of many superb par-4's.*

## Best Bunkering—Courses

Vintage Club (Desert)
Muirfield
Woodhall Spa
St. Andrews (Old)
Wilderness Valley (Black Forest)
Ganton
Royal Melbourne (West and East)
Royal Lytham & St. Annes
San Francisco GC
Royal West Norfolk
Kingston Heath
Sand Hills
Royal County Down
Yale University
Bethpage (Black)
Caledonian
Kawana (Fuji)

*Tom Fazio's lavish bunkering at The Vintage Club (Desert).*

*Just a sample of the pot bunkers at Muirfield.*

*Another example of MacKenzie's fine work—the bunkers at Kingston Heath.*

*Bunkers guarding the 15th at Royal Lytham.*

*The cross-bunkered 18th green at Royal West Norfolk.*

*The 3rd green at Royal County Down.*

## Best Names for Bunkers

| | |
|---|---|
| Abandoned Well | High Pointe—7th |
| Cardinal | Prestwick—3rd |
| Chalk Pit | Royal Eastbourne—3rd |
| Coffins | St. Andrews—13th |
| Devil's Asshole | Pine Valley—10th |
| Eleanor's Teeth | Apawamis—4th |
| Hell's Half Acre | Pine Valley—7th |
| Pandemonium | Musselburgh—6th |
| Principal's Nose | St. Andrews—16th |
| Scabs | Crystal Downs—6th |
| Soup Bowl | Rye—18th |
| Spectacles | Carnoustie—14th |

*Two layers of bunkering enforce the 4th at Apawamis.*

*Hell's Half Acre on the 7th at Pine Valley.*

## Best Courses With No Sand Bunkers

Royal Ashdown Forest
Culver Military Academy
Piltdown
Pocono Manor (East)

## Best Courses Without Water

Royal Melbourne (all 36 holes!)
Muirfield
Sand Hills
San Francisco Golf Club
Kingston Heath
Desert Highlands
Woodhall Spa
Olympic (Lake)
Kapalua (Plantation)
Southerndown

*The Royal Ashdown Forest, where the charter forbids artificial bunkers.*

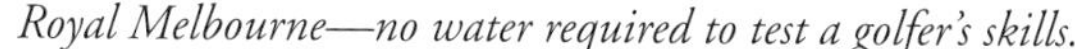

*Royal Melbourne—no water required to test a golfer's skills.*

*You had better hit this green—the 18th at Desert Mountain (Geronimo).*

## Most Ammo Required

Old Marsh
TPC at Sawgrass
Wolf Run
Golden Valley
Crumpin-Fox (leaves in the fall)
Desert Mountain (Geronimo)
Blackwolf Run (River)
Kiawah Island (Ocean)
Port Ludlow (Trail)
The Bear

## Best Front Nine

Royal County Down
Pine Valley
Crystal Downs
Royal Melbourne (West)
Rye
Royal Dornoch
Royal St. George's
National Golf Links
Pebble Beach
Machrihanish

## Best Back Nine

Ballybunion (Old)
St. Andrews (Old)
Pine Valley
Cypress Point
National Golf Links
Royal Troon
Shinnecock Hills
Carnoustie
Winged Foot (West)
Kingston Heath

## Best Starting Holes (1-2-3)

Royal County Down
Pine Valley
Long Cove
Merion (East)
Morfontaine
Royal Dornoch
Pinehurst No. 2
Machrihanish
Castle Harbour
Spyglass Hill

## Best Finishing Holes (16-17-18)

St. Andrews (Old)
Merion (East)
Pebble Beach
National Golf Links
Seminole
Carnoustie—toughest !
Shinnecock Hills
Muirfield
Royal Melbourne (West)
Pennard

## Unusual Hazards

Atlantic Ocean: 5-6-17 Ballybunion New, 7-11-17 Ballybunion (Old); 2-3-8-17 Tralee; 18 Gulf Stream; 6 Amelia Island (Oceanside); 1 Machrihanish; 2-18 Castle Harbour; 3-18 Mid Ocean; 16 Port Royal

Botany Bay: 6 New South Wales

Bunkers in Mid-Fairway: 4 Ballybunion (New); 2 Carnoustie; 18 Loxahatchee; 8 New Zealand; 15 Oakland Hills (South); 9-12-16 St. Andrews (Old); 8 National Golf Links; 14 Riverdale (Dunes); 2 High Pointe; 4 Charlotte Golf Links; 5 Nairn; 15 Boyne Mountain (Monument); 4 Woking

Caribbean Sea: 5-6-7-8-15-16-17 Casa de Campo (Teeth of the Dog)

Cattails: 13-14 The Creek; 7-9 Glenmoor; 4 Sawgrass

Caves: 18 Barton Creek; 6 Pete Dye Club

Chalk Pit: 3 Royal Eastbourne

Church: 4 West Cornwall

Cliff: 3 Shiskine; 16 Dornick Hills

Clubhouse: 18 Stonewall; 18 Royal Lytham & St. Annes; 18 Rye; 2 Philadelphia Cricket Club

Desert: The Boulders; Desert Forest; Desert Highlands; GC at Desert Mountain; Troon; Troon North; 6 La Quinta (Dunes); 5 Desert Dunes; Ventana Canyon; La Paloma; Lost City

Eroded hill: 5 Dunmaglas

Flagsticks: Secession

Great Sea Rushes: 10-11-12-13 Royal North Devon

Goats: Lahinch

Gulley: 15 Boat of Garten

Ha-Ha Wall: 4 Boyne Mountain (Monument)

*The 14th tee at The Creek.*

*The Great Sea Rushes, Westward Ho!*

*The goats at Lahinch.*

Hog Back Fairway: 5 The National; 9 Worcester; 13 Royal Troon; 14 High Pointe

Horses, Wild: Pennard

Horseshoe Greens: 17-18 Polo Fields; 7 Crystal Downs; 17 Glen Abbey; 7 Castle Pines; 15 Crooked Stick; 6 University of Michigan; Claremont

Irish Sea: 2-3-11-12-13-14-17 Nefyn; 4-5-7-9-10 Turnberry (Ailsa)

Island Greens: 17 Cherry Hills; 6 East Lake; 7 Pine Bay; 9 Ponte Vedra (Ocean); 17 TPC at Sawgrass; 6 Royal Ashdown Forest (Old); 16 Wee Burn; 16 La Quinta (Mountain); 7 Grand Cypress (third nine); 18 Boyne Mountain (Monument); 15 TPC at Scottsdale (Stadium); 17 PGA West (Stadium); 7 Stone Harbor; 17 Secession; 17 Oyster Bay; 15 Spring Island; 8 Green Bay CC

Islands in Sand: 13 Casa de Campo (Teeth of the Dog); 6 Mayacoo Lakes; 3 Kittansett; 4 The Medalist

Island Tees: 18 Leatherstocking; 9 The Honors; 8 Casa de Campo (Teeth of the Dog); 9 Treetops (Jones); 3 Camden; 9 The Medalist (on a bridge)

Jetty Tees: 5-9 Kinsale

Lava: Mauna Kea; Mauna Lani; Hapuna; Waikoloa (King's); Waikoloa (Beach)

Lighthouses: 14 Royal Cromer; 9 Turnberry (Ailsa); Pacific Grove Muni; 18 Harbour Town; Old Head at Kinsale

Tidal Marsh: 3-8-9 Royal West Norfolk; 15-16-17-18 Moss Creek (South); 18 Harbour Town; 13-14 Long Cove; 4-7 Sea Island; 8-17 Haig Point; 2-3-11 Long Point; 14 Barwon Heads; 16-17-18 Bodega Harbour; 1-2-3-4-5-6-13-14-15-16-17-18 Secession

Mound in Fairway: 17 Cruden Bay

*The boomerang 7th green at Crystal Downs.*

*Lava frames a fairway bunker on the King's Course at Waikoloa.*

*The quarry on the neat 8th at Manufacturers.*

Mound in front of green: 4 St. Andrews (Old)

North Sea: 13 Royal Tarlair; 4-5 Sheringham; 5 Nairn; 14 Cruden Bay

Out of Bounds Crossing Hole: 18 Ganton

Out of Bounds, Internal: 4 Pennard; 1-7-16 Royal Liverpool; 18 Royal Dublin; 13 Sterling Farms; 3 Pacific Grove Muni; 9 Paraparaumu Beach

Pacific Ocean: 15-16-17 Cypress Point; 18 Half Moon Bay; 4-6-7-8-9-10-18 Pebble Beach; 13 Sandpiper; 6-7 Torrey Pines (North); 17 Spanish Bay

Quarry: 8-9-11 Cork; 16-17-18 Merion (East); 17 Somerset Hills; 15 Piping Rock; 8 Pete Dye Club; 13-14-15-16-17 Black Diamond; 8-16 Manufacturers; 2-3-4-5-6 Joondalup (Quarry); 3-4 Joondalup (Dunes); 2 Joondalup (Lake); 5 Saucon Valley (Weyhill)

Racetrack: Musselburgh Old Links; Northumberland; Royal Durban; Longleaf

Railway: 16 Aberdovey; 1 Prestwick; 11 Royal Troon; 5 Castlerock; 6 Plum Creek

Ravine: Ojai Valley; Los Angeles CC (North); Kapalua; Brancepeth Castle; Sleepy Hollow; Hirono; Woodland Hills; Shadow Creek; Pasatiempo; Shoreacres; Camargo

Road: 17 St. Andrews (Old)

Rock Outcrop: 3-9 The Country Club, MA; 18 Meadow Club; 3-13 Portsalon; 7 Carradale; 8-14 Morfontaine; 4-13 Arrowhead; 17 Perry Park; 3-14 Wentworth-by-the-Sea; 17 Sugarloaf, MI; 5-9 Lookout Mountain; 2 River Islands

Ruins, Ancient: castle, 7th Pennard
round tower, 3rd Tralee
Roman road, 12th Royal Cinque Ports
building site, 10th Dunbar

Sinkhole: 12 Nefyn & District

*The quarry on the 4th at Joondalup.*

*The 16th at Aberdovey.*

*Pennard Castle.*

Split-Level Fairways: 12 Carmel Valley Ranch; 18 Southerndown; 14 Whippoorwill; 13 Winchester

Stone Walls: 3-13-16 North Berwick (West); 3-4 St. Enodoc; 7 Richland

Thermal Vent: 9 Rotorua

Tree Stumps: Port Ludlow

Trees in Line of Play: 10 The Addington; 11 Birmingham CC, MI; 18 Butler National; Old Del Monte; 14 Ganton; 3 Harrogate; 2 Blairgowrie (Wee); 14 Point O'Woods; 12 Prairie Dunes; 12 Wentworth (West); 14 Wentworth-by-the-Sea; 1-14 Wairakei; 10 Wilderness Valley (Black Forest); 6 Charlotte Golf Links; 1 American Legion; 16 Harding Park

Waterfalls: 7 Hills of Lakeway; 13 Atlanta CC; 7 CC of Birmingham (West); 2 Austin CC; 10 Pete Dye Club

Windmills: 7 Austin CC; 2-16 National Golf Links; 13 Coto de Caza; 18 Thorpeness; 9 Reigate Heath; 1 Sand Hills

*"The sinkhole" at Nefyn.*

*The 18th at Southerndown.*

*The 7th at Hills of Lakeway plays over the face of this waterfall.*

*Blairgowrie's (Wee) 2nd hole with its trees ready to defend.*

## Best Courses You Can Play— USA and Canada

| *Doak Scale* | *Course* |
|---|---|
| 10 | Pinehurst (No. 2) |
| 9 | Pebble Beach |
| | Casa de Campo (Teeth of the Dog) |
| 8 | World Woods (Pine Barrens) |
| | Yale University |
| | Harbour Town |
| | High Pointe |
| | TPC at Sawgrass (Stadium) |
| 7 | Bethpage (Black) |
| | Blackwolf Run (River) |
| | Pasatiempo |
| | Spyglass Hill |
| | Pelican Hill (Ocean) |
| | The Dunes, Myrtle Beach |
| | Cascades |
| | Wild Dunes |
| | Kiawah Island (Ocean) |
| | Spanish Bay |
| | Treetops (Fazio) |
| | PGA West (Stadium) |
| | Cape Breton Highlands |
| 6 | Crumpin-Fox |
| | Tidewater |
| | Legends (Heathland) |
| | World Woods (Rolling Oaks) |
| | Wilderness Valley (Black Forest) |
| | Golden Ocala |
| | Lawsonia (Links) |
| | Cog Hill (No. 4) |
| | Riverdale (Dunes) |
| | Troon North |
| | Linville |
| | Reynolds National (Great Waters) |
| | Sea Island |
| | Mauna Kea |
| | Grand Cypress (New) |
| | Innisbrook (Island) |
| | Innisbrook (Copperhead) |
| | Boyne Highlands (Ross) |

| *Doak Scale* | *Course* |
|---|---|
| | Boyne Highlands (Heather) |
| | Waterwood National |
| | Barton Creek (Fazio) |
| | Keystone |
| | Ojai Valley |
| | La Quinta Hotel (Mountain) |
| 5 | Kebo Valley |
| | Leatherstocking |
| | Mark Twain |
| | The Pit |
| | Oyster Bay |
| | Marsh Harbour |
| | River Islands |
| | Jones Creek |
| | Granville |
| | Elk Ridge |
| | Grand Haven |
| | Brickyard Crossing |
| | Pine Meadow |
| | Kemper Lakes |
| | Belvedere |
| | Arrowhead |
| | Pumpkin Ridge (Ghost Creek) |
| | Pacific Grove Muni |
| | La Purisima |
| | Desert Dunes |
| | Golden Horseshoe (Gold) |
| | Pine Needles |
| | Ventana Canyon (Mountain) |
| | La Paloma |
| | Waikoloa (Kings) |
| | Amelia Island |
| | Long Point |
| | Shanty Creek (Legend) |
| | Broadmoor (East) |
| | Port Royal |

## Best Golf Resort—Accommodations

Mauna Lani Bay Hotel
The Palace of the Lost City
The American Club, Kohler, WI
The Boulders
Gleneagles
Mauna Kea Beach Hotel
The Lodge at Pebble Beach
Kapalua
La Quinta Hotel
Garland
Waikoloa Beach Resort
Kawana Hotel

## Best Golf Resort—Golf

Pebble Beach
Pinehurst
Gleneagles
Turnberry
Kapalua
Kiawah Island
Blackwolf Run
Innisbrook
Treetops
The Homestead
Sea Island
Kawana

## Clubs with Locked Gates

Pine Valley
Augusta National
Shadow Creek
The Honors Course
Seminole
Loblolly Pines
The Vintage Club
Shoal Creek
Desert Highlands
Sterling Bluff

*Dishonorable Mention:*
Black Diamond
CC at Callawassie
Castle Pines
DeBordieu
Desert Mountain
GC of Georgia
GC of Oklahoma
Jupiter Hills
Long Cove
Los Angeles CC
Oak Tree GC
Old Marsh
Port Armor
Prestwick, SC
St. Andrews, NY
Seven Lakes
Sherwood
Spring Island
Wade Hampton

*Essex County's 11th hole.*

## Eclectic Eighteens

The 18 Best Holes from Courses That Aren't on Anyone's Top 100 List

| *Hole* | *Par* | *Course* | *Honorable Mention* |
|---|---|---|---|
| 1 | 4 | Machrihanish | Elie; Northland |
| 2 | 4 | St. George's | Detroit GC (North); Ashridge |
| 3 | 4 | Linville | Woking; Waterwood National; Kittansett |
| 4 | 4 | Myopia Hunt Club | Rolling Rock; Woking |
| 5 | 4 | Yarra Yarra | Royal Worlington; Mid Ocean; Old Town; Culver Military Academy |
| 6 | 4 | Olympia Fields (South) | The Creek; Stonewall; Dooks |
| 7 | 5 | Ekwanok | Murcar; Palmetto; Harbor Club; Cape Breton Highlands |
| 8 | 5 | Royal West Norfolk | St. George's Hill; Moortown; Sleepy Hollow |
| 9 | 3 | Rotorua | Royal North Devon; Whitinsville; Royal West Norfolk |
| 10 | 4 | Cavendish | West Sussex; Naruo; St. George's Hill; Highlands CC; Wilderness Valley (Black Forest) |
| 11 | 3 | Essex County | Yarra Yarra; Shoreacres; Roaring Gap; Waterville; CC of Troy; Ojai |
| 12 | 5 | Royal Ashdown Forest (Old) | Shoreacres; Pacific Grove |
| 13 | 4 | North Berwick (West) | Pelican Hill (Ocean); Tokyo Golf Club; The Addington; Mark Twain |
| 14 | 4 | County Sligo | Metacomet; Firethorn; Glen Abbey; Harrison Hills |
| 15 | 3 | North Berwick (West) | St. George's; Swinley Forest; Shoreacres |
| 16 | 5 | Dornick Hills | The Creek; Royal Cinque Ports; Halifax; Royal Melbourne (East); Harding Park |
| 17 | 4 | St. George's Hill | Prestwick |
| 18 | 4 | Stonewall | Pete Dye Club; Philadelphia Cricket Club; St. Enodoc; Killarney; Leatherstocking; Harrison Hills; Oak Hill, MA |

## The 18 Best Holes in the USA

| *Hole* | *Par* | *Course* | *Hole* | *Par* | *Course* |
|---|---|---|---|---|---|
| 1 | 4 | Long Cove | 10 | 4 | Riviera |
| 2 | 4 | Pine Valley | 11 | 4 | Augusta National |
| 3 | 4 | Linville | 12 | 3 | Somerset Hills |
| 4 | 3 | National Golf Links | 13 | 5 | Augusta National |
| 5 | 4 | Merion (East) | 14 | 4 | Metacomet |
| 6 | 4 | Crystal Downs | 15 | 5 | Harbour Town |
| 7 | 3 | San Francisco Golf Club | 16 | 3 | Cypress Point |
| 8 | 5 | Crystal Downs | 17 | 4 | National Golf Links |
| 9 | 4 | Maidstone | 18 | 4 | Stonewall |

## The 18 Best Links Holes in the British Isles

| *Hole* | *Par* | *Course* |
|---|---|---|
| 1 | 4 | Machrihanish |
| 2 | 4 | Carnoustie |
| 3 | 4 | Royal County Down |
| 4 | 4 | Rye |
| 5 | 4 | Royal Portrush (Dunluce) |
| 6 | 3 | Royal Dornoch |
| 7 | 4 | Murcar |
| 8 | 3 | Royal Troon (Old) |
| 9 | 5 | Royal North Devon |
| 10 | 4 | Turnberry (Ailsa) |
| 11 | 4 | Ballybunion (Old) |
| 12 | 3 | Royal Birkdale |
| 13 | 4 | North Berwick (West) |
| 14 | 4 | Royal Dornoch |
| 15 | 3 | North Berwick (West) |
| 16 | 4 | St. Andrews (Old) |
| 17 | 5 | Muirfield |
| 18 | 4 | Royal Lytham & St. Annes |

## The 18 Best Inland Holes in the British Isles

| *Hole* | *Par* | *Course* |
|---|---|---|
| 1 | 3 | Berkshire (Blue) |
| 2 | 5 | Ashridge |
| 3 | 4 | Woodhall Spa |
| 4 | 4 | Woking |
| 5 | 3 | Royal Worlington & Newmarket |
| 6 | 4 | Gleneagles (Queen's) |
| 7 | 4 | Broadstone |
| 8 | 3 | Moortown |
| 9 | 4 | Swinley Forest |
| 10 | 4 | West Sussex |
| 11 | 4 | Sunningdale (Old) |
| 12 | 5 | Royal Ashdown Forest (Old) |
| 13 | 3 | The Addington |
| 14 | 4 | Ganton |
| 15 | 4 | Swinley Forest |
| 16 | 5 | Walton Heath (Old) |
| 17 | 4 | St. George's Hill |
| 18 | 4 | Boat of Garten |

## The 18 Best Holes in the Rest of the World

| *Hole* | *Par* | *Course* |
|---|---|---|
| 1 | 5 | Hirono |
| 2 | 4 | St. George's |
| 3 | 5 | Durban CC |
| 4 | 4 | Royal Melbourne (West) |
| 5 | 4 | Mid Ocean |
| 6 | 3 | New South Wales |
| 7 | 3 | Newcastle |
| 8 | 5 | Durban CC |
| 9 | 3 | Rotorua |
| 10 | 4 | Naruo |
| 11 | 5 | The Lakes |
| 12 | 4 | Kasumigaseki (East) |
| 13 | 5 | Tokyo GC |
| 14 | 4 | Royal Adelaide |
| 15 | 3 | Kingston Heath |
| 16 | 3 | Casa de Campo (Teeth of the Dog) |
| 17 | 4 | Durban CC |
| 18 | 4 | Commonwealth |

## The 19 Best Holes That No Longer Exist

| *Hole* | *Par* | *Yds* | *Course* | *Architect* | *Fate* |
|---|---|---|---|---|---|
| 1 | 4 | 260 | Commonwealth, Australia | committee | redesigned |
| 2 | 4 | 425 | Waddesdon Manor, England | Simpson | course gone |
| 3 | 3 | 190 | Ojai Valley, CA | Thomas | hole eliminated |
| 4 | 5 | 466 | Lido GC, NY | Macdonald | course gone |
| 5 | 4 | 345 | St. Andrews, NY | | redesigned |
| 6 | 4 | 440 | Oak Hill (East), NY | Ross | redesigned |
| 7 | 4 | 440 | Ballybunion (Old) | Simpson | green eroded |
| 8 | 4 | 325 | Addington (New), England | Abercromby | course gone |
| 9 (tie) | 4 | 460 | Tailer's Ocean Links, RI | Raynor | course gone |
| | 5 | 505 | Olympic (Ocean Links) | Watson | hole eroded |
| 10 | 4 | 450 | Gambel Golf Links, AZ | Roy Dye | course gone |
| 11 | 5 | 550 | The Links Golf Club, NY | Macdonald | course gone |
| 12 | 3 | 200 | Garden City GC, NY | Travis | redesigned |
| 13 | 4 | 420 | Rochester G & CC, Minnesota | Tillinghast | hole eliminated |
| 14 | 3 | 175 | North Berwick (West Links) | unknown | hole eliminated |
| 15 | 4 | 435 | Lido GC, NY | Macdonald | course gone |
| 16 | 4 | 405 | La Cumbre, CA | Bryce | redesigned |
| 17 | 3 | 120 | Los Angeles CC (North) | Thomas | hole eliminated |
| 18 | 4 | 435 | Rye, England | Colt | redesigned |

*The 5th at St. Andrews, NY—terminated by Nicklaus.*

## The 18 Worst Holes

| *Hole* | *Par* | *Course* |
|---|---|---|
| 1 | 4 | Terradyne: 465 yards, narrow, green sloping away to a ditch behind. |
| 2 | 4 | Strathpeffer Spa: 300 yards straight uphill |
| 3 | 4 | Port Ludlow (Trail): Drive through a saddle cut to a precipice of fairway; second shot very steeply downhill with a forced-carry stream just in front of the green. There is a fairway to lay up, but it's so steep the ball will probably just bounce into the stream. |
| 4 | 4 | Heather Glen (New): Manufactured goofy, with the green in a hidden hollow reinforced by sleepers on three sides. |
| 5 | 5 | Golf Club of Georgia (Creekside): A short par-5 with three strategic options for the second shot after a carry over marsh off the tee. You can either: a) lay up short of another marsh crossing and be left with 175 yards to the green; b) go for the narrow green in two, though it's hemmed in by marsh in front and to the left and by trees to the right; or c) (my favorite) carry about 125 yards to a lay-up fairway on the right, only to be left with a blind shot through pine trees to the narrowest aspect of the green, which tilts away from you. |
| 6 | 5 | Pine Bay: Single-file narrow, with an overgrown wetland hiding the green. If you go for it in two, you can't tell if you've made it across. |
| 7 | 3 | Stone Harbor: Desmond Muirhead's pop-art masterpiece. If you landed in one of the island bunkers, you faced a sand shot over 30 feet of water to a sliver of green 50 feet across, with water again beyond. |
| 8 | 3 | Lakeview Par-3: A green built around a birdbath concrete pond, reeking of miniature golf. |
| 9 | 4 | Alton Municipal: The classic 110-degree dogleg left. |
| 10 | 4 | Castle Harbour: A sharp dogleg left around a steep hill, with the world falling away into brush on the right. For shorter hitters the fairway is ten yards across and split by the cart path; long hitters have to lay up at about the 200-yard mark. |
| 11 | 5 | St. Andrews, NY: The worst hole I have ever seen. The second shot is blind off the top of a hill to a small landing area shelved in between rock outcroppings, the cart path and out of bounds. In the Centennial of Golf event here in 1988, six Heroes of American Golf lost their balls here. |

| *Hole* | *Par* | *Course* |
|---|---|---|
| 12 | 4 | Carmel Valley Ranch: Slightly uphill drive to a two-decked fairway split by a broad wall, hit it down the middle and the drive will carom into the left rough. |
| 13 | 3 | CC of the South: A short hole with alternate greens divided by a narrow creek. The local rule if you wind up on the wrong green is to drop in the rough and chip across; they might as well have sloped the stone wall along the creek into a jump ramp so you could try to putt it. |
| 14 | 4 | Wentworth-by-the-Sea: a Cape hole with a long forced carry off the tee, and a spindly pine tree smack in front of the green. |
| 15 | 4 | Boat of Garten: The blind tee shot toward a marker post 125 yards on the horizon convinced me to lay back with an iron off the tee—which is the biggest mistake you can make here, because at about 175 yards the fairway drops into the gulley for which the hole is named. You can either try to carry the gulley (maybe 240 yards), hit two 7-irons, or go down into the gulley and try your luck. |
| 16 | 4 | Atlanta National: Two blind shots in 300 yards. I have seen other holes of the same description, but none other where the architect deliberately created the hills which made it a blind hole. |
| 17 | 6 | Black Mountain: 747 yards: you would think that somewhere on a hole of that length, just by random chance, they could manage to grow a patch of decent fairway turf. But you'd be wrong. |
| 18 | 4 | Polo Fields G & CC, Ann Arbor: A downhill finisher with alternate fairways split by a narrow line of trees, and a flat, horseshoe-shaped green which will ensure many three-putts. |

## The All-Scenic Eighteen

| *Hole* | *Par* | *Course* |
|---|---|---|
| 1 | 4 | Desert Highlands |
| 2 | 3 | National G & CC, Australia |
| 3 | 5 | County Sligo |
| 4 | 5 | Bamburgh Castle |
| 5 | 4 | Isle of Purbeck |
| 6 | 4 | Royal North Devon |
| 7 | 3 | Casa de Campo (Teeth of the Dog) |
| 8 | 4 | Machrihanish |
| 9 | 5 | Royal County Down |
| 10 | 4 | Arrowhead |
| 11 | 4 | Ballybunion (Old) |
| 12 | 4 | Kapalua (Plantation) |
| 13 | 4 | Paraparaumu Beach |
| 14 | 4 | Royal Cromer |
| 15 | 3 | Cypress Point |
| 16 | 3 | Sleepy Hollow |
| 17 | 4 | National Golf Links |
| 18 | 3 | Killarney (Mahony's Point) |

*Killarney's 18th.*

## The All-Blind Eighteen

| *Hole* | *Par* | *Course* |
|---|---|---|
| 1 | 4 | Elie |
| 2 | 4 | National Golf Links |
| 3 | 4 | Yale University |
| 4 | 4 | Royal Melbourne (West) |
| 5 | 4 | Long Cove |
| 6 | 3 | Lahinch |
| 7 | 5 | Ekwanok |
| 8 | 4 | Pebble Beach |
| 9 | 5 | Royal County Down |
| 10 | 4 | Shinnecock Hills |
| 11 | 4 | Sunningdale (Old) |
| 12 | 4 | St. Andrews (Old)—you can see the flag, but none of the bunkers |
| 13 | 4 | Rye |
| 14 | 5 | Carnoustie |
| 15 | 4 | Prestwick |
| 16 | 5 | Roaring Gap |
| 17 | 4 | Prestwick |
| 18 | 4 | Riviera |

*"The Dell" (6th) at Lahinch.*

## The 18 Sportiest Holes in the World

| Hole | Par | Course |
|---|---|---|
| 1 | 4 | Strathpeffer Spa |
| 2 | 5 | Hindhead |
| 3 | 3 | Ventana Canyon (Mountain) |
| 4 | 5 | Joondalup |
| 5 | 4 | Long Cove |
| 6 | 3 | Lahinch |
| 7 | 3 | Pocono Manor (East) |
| 8 | 5 | The Pit |
| 9 | 4 | Shinnecock Hills |
| 10 | 4 | Ventana Canyon (Canyon) |
| 11 | 4 | Austin CC |
| 12 | 4 | St. Andrews (Old) |
| 13 | 4 | North Berwick (West) |
| 14 | 5 | Wairakei International |
| 15 | 5 | Wakonda |
| 16 | 5 | Dornick Hills |
| 17 | 4 | Crystal Downs |
| 18 | 5 | Yale University |

*Ventana Canyon's 3rd tee.*

*The staircase 14th green at Carmel Valley Ranch.*

## The 18 Most Eccentric Putting Greens

| Hole | Course |
|---|---|
| 1 | Desert Highlands |
| 2 | St. Andrews (Old) |
| 3 | Atlanta National |
| 4 | Rolling Rock |
| 5 | Terradyne |
| 6 | National Golf Links |
| 7 | Victoria, BC |
| 8 | Engineers |
| 9 | Yale University |
| 10 | The Legends (Parkland) |
| 11 | CC of Charleston |
| 12 | Wilderness Valley (Black Forest) |
| 13 | High Pointe |
| 14 | Carmel Valley Ranch |
| 15 | Treetops North (Fazio) |
| 16 | North Berwick (West) |
| 17 | Gleneagles (Queen's) |
| 18 | Indianwood (Old) |

## The 18 Hardest Holes in the World

| *Hole* | *Par* | *Course* |
|---|---|---|
| 1 | 4 | Oak Tree GC |
| 2 | 4 | Wilderness Valley (Black Forest) |
| 3 | 3 | Golden Valley |
| 4 | 4 | Bodega Harbour |
| 5 | 4 | White Bear Yacht Club |
| 6 | 4 | The Creek |
| 7 | 4 | Glenmoor |
| 8 | 5 | Ballybunion (New) |
| 9 | 3 | Brancepeth Castle |
| 10 | 4 | St. Enodoc |
| 11 | 4 | Austin CC |
| 12 | 5 | Oakmont |
| 13 | 3 | Wolf Run |
| 14 | 4 | Oakland Hills (South) |
| 15 | 3 | Philadelphia CC (Spring Mill) |
| 16 | 4 | GC at Desert Mountain (Geronimo) |
| 17 | 4 | St. Andrews (Old) |
| 18 | 5 | Kingwood (Island) |

*Wolf Run's 240-yard, par-3 13th, Faldo hit the green, but most golfers don't.*

*The tough 3rd hole at Golden Valley.*

*Don't miss on Austin Country Club's 11th.*

## The 18 Best-Bunkered Holes

| Hole | Par | Course |
|---|---|---|
| 1 | 5 | Wilderness Valley (Black Forest) |
| 2 | 4 | Yale University |
| 3 | 5 | Prestwick, Scotland |
| 4 | 3 | Riviera |
| 5 | 5 | Cypress Point |
| 6 | 4 | St. Enodoc |
| 7 | 5 | Pine Valley |
| 8 | 3 | St. George's Hill |
| 9 | 4 | Royal West Norfolk |

| Hole | Par | Course |
|---|---|---|
| 10 | 3 | Pine Valley |
| 11 | 3 | St. Andrews (Old) |
| 12 | 4 | San Francisco Golf Club |
| 13 | 3 | Muirfield |
| 14 | 5 | St. Andrews (Old) |
| 15 | 3 | Kingston Heath |
| 16 | 3 | Royal Melbourne (East) |
| 17 | 4 | Kebo Valley |
| 18 | 4 | Sand Hills |

*Nature surely carved these bunkers at St. Enodoc.*

## The Best Holes Without a Bunker

| *Hole* | *Par* | *Course* |
|---|---|---|
| 1 | 4 | St. Andrews (Eden) |
| 2 | 4 | Crowborough Beacon |
| 3 | 4 | Piltdown |
| 4 | 4 | Rye |
| 5 | 4 | Royal Portrush (Dunluce) |
| 6 | 3 | Lahinch |
| 7 | 3 | Royal Liverpool |
| 8 | 5 | Royal Ashdown Forest (Old) |
| 9 | 3 | Brancepeth Castle |
| 10 | 4 | Royal Portrush (Valley) |
| 11 | 4 | Ballybunion (Old) |
| 12 | 5 | Royal Ashdown Forest (Old) |
| 13 | 4 | Royal Troon (Old) |
| 14 | 4 | Royal Dornoch |
| 15 | 4 | Royal St. David's |
| 16 | 4 | Aberdovey |
| 17 | 4 | Durban CC |
| 18 | 4 | North Berwick (West) |

*Getting the heartbeat up again, the 11th at Ballybunion.*

## Best 18 Holes by Donald Ross

| *Hole* | *Par* | *Course* |
|---|---|---|
| 1 | 5 | Whitinsville |
| 2 | 4 | Holston Hills |
| 3 | 4 | Linville |
| 4 | 3 | Gulph Mills |
| 5 | 4 | White Bear Yacht Club |
| 6 | 4 | Seminole |
| 7 | 4 | Inverness |
| 8 | 5 | Kahkwa |
| 9 | 4 | Whitinsville |
| 10 | 4 | Highlands |
| 11 | 4 | Oakland Hills (South) |
| 12 | 5 | Plainfield |
| 13 | 4 | Salem |
| 14 | 4 | Pinehurst (No. 2) |
| 15 | 3 | Pinehurst (No. 2) |
| 16 | 5 | Roaring Gap |
| 17 | 3 | Seminole |
| 18 | 4 | Oak Hill, MA |

## Best 18 Holes by Alister MacKenzie

| *Hole* | *Par* | *Course* |
|---|---|---|
| 1 | 4 | Crystal Downs |
| 2 | 5 | Cypress Point |
| 3 | 4 | Royal Adelaide |
| 4 | 4 | Royal Melbourne (West) |
| 5 | 4 | Yarra Yarra |
| 6 | 4 | Crystal Downs |
| 7 | 3 | Palmetto |
| 8 | 5 | Crystal Downs |
| 9 | 4 | Cypress Point |
| 10 | 4 | Cavendish |
| 11 | 4 | Royal Melbourne (West) |
| 12 | 3 | Augusta National |
| 13 | 5 | Augusta National |
| 14 | 4 | Pasatiempo |
| 15 | 3 | Kingston Heath |
| 16 | 3 | Cypress Point |
| 17 | 4 | Cypress Point |
| 18 | 4 | Royal Melbourne (West) |

## Best 18 Holes by Charles Blair Macdonald/Seth Raynor

| Hole | Par | Course |
|---|---|---|
| 1 | 4 | Mid Ocean |
| 2 | 4 | Chicago Golf Club |
| 3 | 4 | National Golf Links |
| 4 | 3 | National Golf Links |
| 5 | 4 | Mid Ocean |
| 6 | 4 | The Creek |
| 7 | 5 | The Creek |
| 8 | 4 | National Golf Links |
| 9 | 3 | Yale University |
| 10 | 4 | National Golf Links |
| 11 | 4 | Shoreacres |
| 12 | 3 | Shoreacres |
| 13 | 4 | Piping Rock |
| 14 | 4 | The Creek |
| 15 | 5 | Shoreacres |
| 16 | 4 | The Creek |
| 17 | 4 | National Golf Links |
| 18 | 5 | National Golf Links |

## Best 18 Holes by A.W. Tillinghast

| Hole | Par | Course |
|---|---|---|
| 1 | 4 | Winged Foot (West) |
| 2 | 4 | San Francisco GC |
| 3 | 3 | Somerset Hills |
| 4 | 5 | Bethpage (Black) |
| 5 | 4 | Bethpage (Black) |
| 6 | 4 | Quaker Ridge |
| 7 | 3 | San Francisco GC |
| 8 | 4 | Sleepy Hollow |
| 9 | 5 | San Francisco GC |
| 10 | 3 | Winged Foot (West) |
| 11 | 4 | Quaker Ridge |
| 12 | 5 | Ridgewood |
| 13 | 3 | Winged Foot (East) |
| 14 | 4 | Somerset Hills |
| 15 | 4 | Winged Foot (West) |
| 16 | 4 | San Francisco GC |
| 17 | 5 | Baltusrol (Lower) |
| 18 | 4 | Philadelphia Cricket Club |

## Best 18 Holes by William Flynn

| Hole | Par | Course |
|---|---|---|
| 1 | 4 | Shinnecock Hills |
| 2 | 4 | Lancaster |
| 3 | 5 | Philadelphia CC (Spring Mill) |
| 4 | 4 | Philadelphia CC (Spring Mill) |
| 5 | 4 | Lancaster |
| 6 | 3 | Manufacturers |
| 7 | 5 | Rolling Green |
| 8 | 3 | Manufacturers |
| 9 | 5 | Rolling Green |
| 10 | 4 | Huntingdon Valley |
| 11 | 3 | Shinnecock Hills |
| 12 | 4 | Shinnecock Hills |
| 13 | 4 | Rolling Green |
| 14 | 3 | Rolling Green |
| 15 | 4 | Shinnecock Hills |
| 16 | 5 | Shinnecock Hills |
| 17 | 4 | The Country Club, OH |
| 18 | 5 | Cherry Hills |

## Best 18 Holes by Pete Dye

| Hole | Par | Course |
|---|---|---|
| 1 | 4 | Long Cove |
| 2 | 4 | Pete Dye Golf Club |
| 3 | 5 | Long Cove |
| 4 | 3 | Harbour Town |
| 5 | 4 | Long Cove |
| 6 | 3 | Crooked Stick |
| 7 | 5 | The Golf Club |
| 8 | 4 | Harbour Town |
| 9 | 4 | The Honors Course |
| 10 | 4 | PGA West (Stadium) |
| 11 | 4 | Long Cove |
| 12 | 5 | Old Marsh |
| 13 | 3 | Crooked Stick |
| 14 | 4 | Oak Tree Golf Club |
| 15 | 4 | Casa de Campo (Teeth of the Dog) |
| 16 | 5 | Blackwolf Run (River) |
| 17 | 3 | Harbour Town |
| 18 | 4 | TPC at Sawgrass |

## Other Guides to Golf Courses I've Found to be "On The Mark"

Allen, Sir, Peter. *Famous Fairways.* Stanley Paul, London, 1968.

Cornish, Geoffrey, and Ron Whitten. *The Architects of Golf.* HarperCollins Publishers, Inc., New York, 1993. (for finding out-of-the-way courses by the master architects, from the listings with their biographies)

Darwin, Bernard. *The Golf Courses of the British Isles.* Original publication, 1910; reprinted by Storey Communications/ Ailsa, Inc., New York, 1988.

Davis, William H. *100 Greatest Golf Courses—And Then Some.* Golf Digest/ Tennis, Inc., Norwalk, Connecticut, 1982.

Dickinson, Patric. *A Round of Golf Courses.* Evans Brothers Limited, London, 1950; paperback edition by A & C Black (Publishers) Ltd., London, 1990.

Edmund, Nick, Editor. *Following the Fairways.* Kensington West Productions, London; published annually.

Hamilton, David. *The Good Golf Guide to Scotland.* Canongate Publishing Ltd., Edinburgh, Scotland, 1982.

Labbance, Bob, and David Cornwell. *The Maine Golf Guide.* New England Golf Specialists, Stockbridge, Vermont, 1991. (Also guides by the same authors to courses in Vermont and New Hampshire.)

Ramsey, Tom. *Great Australian Golf Holes.* Hamlyn Australia, Port Melbourne, Victoria, Australia, 1989.

Steel, Donald. *Classic Golf Links of England, Scotland, Wales, and Ireland.* Chapmans Publishers, Great Britain, 1992.

Waggoner, Glen. *The Traveling Golfer.* Bantam Doubleday Bell Publishing Group, New York, 1991.

Ward-Thomas, Pat, et al. *The World Atlas of Golf.* Mitchell Beazley Publishers Limited, London, 1976.

# — INDEX —